Acclaim for Ted Gup's

The Book of Honor

"[Gup] puts a human face on the CIA's checkered and often tragic history. . . . Is it possible for a book to have it both ways? Is it possible to criticize an agency for its conduct, its values and ethics, its very view of the world, and at the same time admire and sympathize profoundly with its agents? That seems to be what Ted Gup has accomplished in this very fine and compassionate book." —*Pittsburgh Tribune-Review*

"Ted Gup found out what the Central Intelligence Agency didn't want him to know, and now he's going to tell you." —*The Plain Dealer*

"Told against the backdrop of Cold War and superpower struggles, Gup's sleuthing is a remarkable coup, full of high-level intrigue, cover-ups and drama." —*Publishers Weekly*

"This is not a pretty story. Real espionage never is. What ace reporter Ted Gup found when he researched the CIA wasn't suave James Bonds but lively, complex, and heroic Americans lost in a web of agency coverups . . . [an] astonishing exposé." —*American Way*

Ted Gup

The Book of Honor

Ted Gup is a legendary investigative reporter who worked under Bob Woodward at *The Washington Post*, and later at *Time*. He is the recipient of numerous awards, including the George Polk Award, the Gerald Loeb Award, and the Worth Bingham Prize. Gup is a professor of journalism at Case Western Reserve University. He lives in Pepper Pike, Ohio.

by Ted Gup

ANCHOR BOOKS

A Division of Random House, Inc.　•　New York

The

Book

THE SECRET LIVES

of

AND DEATHS OF

Honor

CIA OPERATIVES

FIRST ANCHOR BOOKS EDITION, MAY 2001

Copyright © 2000, 2001 by Ted Gup

All rights reserved under International and Pan-American Copyright Conventions. Published in the United States by Anchor Books, a division of Random House, Inc., New York, and simultaneously in Canada by Random House of Canada Limited, Toronto. Originally published in hardcover in the United States by Doubleday, a division of Random House, Inc., New York, in 2000.

Anchor Books and colophon are registered trademarks of Random House, Inc.

The Library of Congress has cataloged the Doubleday edition as follows:
Gup, Ted, 1950–
   Book of honor : covert lives and classified deaths at the CIA /
by Ted Gup.
      p.   cm.
   Includes index.
   1. Spies—United States—Biography.   2. United States. Central
Intelligence Agency—Biography.   I. Title.
UB271.U5 G87 2000
327.12'092'273—dc21
[B]   99-089017

Anchor ISBN: 0-385-49541-2

Book design by Maria Carella
Author photograph © Kehres Photo Services

www.anchorbooks.com

Printed in the United States of America
10   9   8   7   6   5   4   3   2   1

To the sons and daughters of the CIA's stars,
named and unnamed alike,
and in memory of my father,
who told me the only thing a man may hope to leave behind
is his good name.

Contents

Prologue   1

TRUE BELIEVERS

1. Forgotten Man   9

2. A Pin for St. Jude   43

3. By Chance   67

4. Waiting for Godot   97

5. Faith and Betrayal   108

A TIME TO QUESTION

6. Deception   133

7. The Two Mikes   163

8. Homecoming   207

9. Honor and Humiliation   221

10. Privation and Privilege   237

CHAOS AND TERRORISM

11. Indestructible   261

12. Deadly Symmetry   289

13. Damage Control   318

14. The Last Maccabee   338

Epilogue   365

Afterword   376

Author's Note and Acknowledgments   382

Index   385

Who controls the past controls the future,
who controls the present controls the past.
GEORGE ORWELL

Secrecy, once accepted, becomes an addiction.
EDWARD TELLER, PHYSICIST

Prologue

I REMEMBER the first time I stood before the Central Intelligence Agency's Wall of Honor. It was during the Gulf War, February 1991. As a reporter for *Time* magazine, I had come to interview an Agency analyst, a specialist on Iraq. The interview was to be on deep background. I was not to reveal the analyst's name or link him to the CIA.

I arrived a few minutes early. The guards at the entrance to the vast 258-acre compound in Langley, Virginia, had been expecting me. They keyed in my Social Security number, issued me a plastic badge, and pointed me in the direction of the headquarters building. Stern-faced guards, a hedge of steel spikes in the roadway, and a landscape bristling with half-concealed monitors encouraged me to stay on course.

I remember entering the Stalinesque headquarters building, some 1.4 million square feet of marble and pillars and row upon row of recessed lights. The lobby was cavernous and cool, almost sepulchral. I had written about the CIA before, but this was my first visit to its headquarters. Set into the floor of the lobby was a huge medallion of the Agency seal featuring a vigilant eagle and a compass rose whose radiating spokes represented the CIA's worldwide reach.

Inscribed overhead, on the south wall, were words from Scripture, John 8:32: "And ye shall know the truth, and the truth shall make you free." There was no hint of irony about it, though daily, covert officers trained in deception pass through the lobby, their identities a construct of lies intended to produce some greater truth.

It was the north wall, though, that caught my eye. There, rising before me, was a field of black stars chiseled into white Vermont marble. To the left was the flag of the nation, to the right, the flag of the Agency. I drew nearer. Above the stars were engraved these words: "IN HONOR OF THOSE MEMBERS OF THE CENTRAL INTELLIGENCE AGENCY WHO GAVE THEIR LIVES IN THE SERVICE OF THE COUNTRY."

There were five rows of stars. One by one I counted them. Sixty-nine in all. Below the field of stars was a stainless-steel and glass case. It was locked. Inside was a book.

The Book of Honor, it was called, a tome as sacred to the Agency as if it held a splinter of the true cross. It was a thin volume of rough-cut pages, opened to the center, a black braid, tasseled at the end, tucked into the valley between the open pages. In neat black letters were written the years that each CIA officer died. Beside the year, in some twenty-nine cases, were inscribed the names of the fallen. I recognized two: Richard Welch, gunned down in front of his house in Athens in 1975, and William F. Buckley, the Beirut station chief tortured to death in 1985. His remains were found in a plastic sack beside the road to the airport.

But beside most of the years, there were no names, just stars. Forty nameless stars, tiny as asterisks, each representing a covert officer killed on a CIA mission.

These nameless stars spanned half a century. There was nothing to provide even a hint as to their identities—no month or day of death, no country or continent where they fell, and not a word to suggest the nature of their mission. All was veiled in secrecy.

I stood transfixed as scores of CIA employees swept past me on their way to or from the security desk, oblivious to the quiet memorial. In the minutes before my Agency escort arrived to take me to my interview, I took out a notebook and scribbled down the names and dates and stars in the Book of Honor. Who were these stars? I wondered. How and where had they died? What missions claimed their lives?

The first nameless star had died in 1950. What secret could be so sensitive that after five decades his or her identity still could not be revealed? I wondered, too, about the families these covert officers left behind, whether they were free to speak of the loss of a loved one or whether they were forced to grieve in silence. Were they told the truth of what had happened to their husbands or wives, sons or daughters? Did these stars, named and unnamed alike, represent unsung heroes, or were they, perhaps, saboteurs and assassins ensnared in their own schemes? And what, if anything, had the American people been told of these casualties? Had the U.S. government, perhaps the president himself, lied about their fates?

I had seen many such memorials before. The FBI, DEA, State Department, and even Amtrak have memorial walls to those who died in service. But all of these identify their fallen and celebrate their sacrifices. The CIA's is different, a memorial to men and women who are faceless. How, I wondered, could a memorial purport to remember those who are unknown to all but a few? And what sort of person would be willing to make the ultimate sacrifice—the loss not only of life but of identity as well?

It was that notion of anonymity even in death that moved me. When I had finished jotting down the dates and names and stars, I tore the pages out of my spiral notebook and tucked them into the pocket of my jacket.

I suspected even then that this wall, this Book of Honor, and these nameless stars would stay with me, that I would revisit them again and again until I had unraveled their secrets. But I also knew that scores of Washington reporters, all who covered the intelligence beat, had walked past this same memorial and had similar ambitions. The Book of Honor was one of Washington's most abiding mysteries. There was a reason the secret of the stars remained intact.

A moment later a hand gently tapped me on my shoulder. It was my escort, ready to take me through the security turnstile, and to my interview. As we walked down the corridor, I asked him about the nameless stars. He seemed amused and deftly fended off my question. He had had this conversation before. In my asking, I had revealed that I was a newcomer to the beat.

Later, sitting across from him in a small conference room, I raised the subject once more. "Can't be of much help," he said, and invoked the CIA's most revered words: "sources and methods." It is a catchall phrase that encompasses the myriad ways in which the CIA gathers its knowledge of the world. It goes to the very core of the Agency's mission. Identifying the nameless stars, he said, could compromise ongoing operations, expose Americans and foreign nationals to grave risk, and reveal secrets adverse to U.S. interests. In short, it would harm America's national security.

I had been put on notice. The Book of Honor and its nameless stars were not to be trifled with. Any attempt to unmask them would be viewed as a kind of larceny, a theft of the Agency's family jewels.

The inch-thick bulletproof glass and tidy lock that protected the Book of Honor were only tokens of the security that safeguarded the secrets of the nameless stars. A hundred other unseen locks and keys, oaths of secrecy, and cryptonyms stood in my way. I asked my escort about two or three of the named stars. Surely he could discuss those. Wrong.

That evening when I returned home, I slipped the pages from my pocket into a manila folder and scribbled the words "CIA Stars" on the flap. Now and again, in the months and years after, I would pick at the story in my spare time. I made little progress.

Caught up in the press of events, I left the story of the CIA's stars for some indeterminate future. It would be five years before I could devote myself to it fully. I thought that I had been drawn to the story for the sheer journalistic challenge of it. This was, after all, the ultimate secret, the forbidden. I had broken secrets before, some of them extremely sensitive and hard to ferret out.

In 1992, for example, I uncovered the existence of a top secret government installation buried beneath an exclusive West Virginia resort, the Greenbrier. It was there that Congress was to go as a kind of government-in-exile in the event of an impending nuclear war. It had been one of the nation's most closely guarded secrets since its construction during the Eisenhower and Kennedy administrations four decades earlier. My article in the *Washington Post* led to its closure and considerable embarrassment to Congress, which, but for a handful of senior members, had not been deemed trustworthy enough to have been informed of its existence.

That and other stories like it had convinced me that all too often government had used secrecy to conceal a multitude of other sins it did not want to come to light. I had seen how secrets could take on a life of their own. In time, it was not foreign enemies but domestic disclosure that the guardians of those secrets often feared most.

But my fascination with the CIA's Book of Honor went well beyond the mere challenge posed by secrecy. The nameless stars weighed upon me in ways I did not yet understand. I felt a need to restore the names to those marked only by a star. I imagined myself to be their instrument. The notion that such profound individual sacrifice could pass into oblivion disturbed me, doubtless more so than those represented by the nameless stars.

For three years I immersed myself in archival records, death certificates, casualty lists from terrorist attacks, State Department and Defense Department personnel lists, cemetery records, obituaries, and thousands of pages of personal letters and diaries, all in search of the identities of these nameless stars. I interviewed more than four hundred current and former covert CIA officers.

One by one, I learned the names of those behind the stars. But it was their lives as much as their deaths that intrigued me most. In the course of those three years I found myself looking not only into the individual faces of the nameless stars but also into the eyes of the CIA itself. In the aggregate, the stories of the stars form a kind of constellation that, once connected, reveal not only the CIA's history but something of its soul as well.

I am of that generation whose vision of the Agency is clouded by revelations of twenty, even thirty years ago. When I spoke with friends about my efforts to uncover the identities of the nameless stars, more than a few asked me if I feared for my life. They assumed my project would mark me out as a target for domestic surveillance and retaliation.

Their concerns represented a sad commentary on how the public perceives the CIA and, by extension, the tens of thousands of men and women who have worked there over the decades. No other arm of government has so sinister a public image or offers such fecund ground for conspiracy theorists. This is largely the Agency's own doing, part of a legacy that includes historic misconduct and ongoing efforts to prevent that past from surfacing.

fecund

But in the public's mind the CIA has always been seen less as an instrument of government than as a mythical creature dwelling among us. We yearn to know its secrets but wince at what they reveal about us as a people and a nation. I tried to draw a distinction between the individual and the institution, believing that what is noble in one can be put to ignoble ends by the other. Whether these stars, named and nameless, are heroes or villains, whether their courage was spent wisely or squandered in folly, is for others to decide. It is enough for me that their names be made known and their stories told.

PART ONE

True Believers

CHAPTER 1

Forgotten Man

THE ORDER to evacuate came down on July 29, 1949. It was a simply worded cable, direct from Secretary of State Dean Acheson. The Communist juggernaut had swept across China. The ascendancy of Mao Zedong was now certain. The lives of all American diplomats still in country were at risk. Embassies and consulates throughout the land were to be closed. The last remaining skeletal staffs were to torch any classified documents and beat a hasty retreat by any means available. No one was to be left behind.

No one, that is, except for one lowly vice-consul in China's hinterland. His name was Douglas Seymour Mackiernan. He had been posted to what was widely regarded as the most desolate and remote consulate on earth—Tihwa (today called Urumchi), the wind-raked capital of Xinjiang (Sinkiang) province, China's westernmost state. He and he alone was to stay behind. Mackiernan's diplomatic title was "Vice-Consul," and he had willingly done all the scutwork the State Department had asked of him. But he took his orders not from State, but from a more shadowy organization whose very name he would not utter. Even with those he trusted most, he would simply intone the words "the Company." Those who did not understand the reference had no business knowing.

Just two years earlier, on February 17, 1947, Mackiernan had applied for the position at Tihwa, going through what had appeared to be normal State Department channels. But why Tihwa, an ancient city whose heyday dated back to the time of the ancient Silk Road? With just one main street, its nomadic population was Caucasian Russians, Mongolians, and dark-skinned Chinese. Only the Soviet Union, Britain, and the United States bothered to maintain a consulate there. It was so forlorn a place that the mere mention of its name sent shudders down the spine of even the most leathery of foreign service officers. That anyone should volunteer for such a place was beyond comprehension.

Even more curious, when Mackiernan, then a thirty-five-year-old ex-GI, applied for that posting, he had been so desperate that he was willing to work there as an entry-level clerk. The pay was an abysmal $2,160 a year. The job description held little promise for advancement. The duties: keep the trucks and jeep up and running, the radio in good repair, assist in overseeing supply needs, and provide an occasional hand in code work. The State Department had been overjoyed to snag anyone willing to go to Tihwa, much less someone as worldly and talented as Mackiernan. His superior at the State Department, barely able to contain his enthusiasm, spoke of Mackiernan as "ideally qualified for . . . this wild territory."

To the few who thought they knew Mackiernan, or Mac, as he was known to many, it seemed a stunningly poor career choice. In the aftermath of World War II someone of his credentials could have had a wide array of choices. But then, Mackiernan could care less what others thought of his decision. Like a generation of covert CIA case officers to come, he would have to learn to silently endure the whispering and sympathetic looks of friends on the fast track who were ignorant of his true purpose and position. By day Mackiernan would work his humble cover job without complaint. By night he would devote himself to the real work at hand—espionage.

Mackiernan understood from the start that even if things went well he would receive no public credit. If things went "poorly"—a euphemism that needed little elaboration—he would be just another faceless functionary lost in far-off Cathay. A covert officer can ill afford ego or pride.

Besides, these were the least of his concerns. Mackiernan had a wife, Darrell, and daughter, Gail, who had seen very little of him in years. They had hoped that with the end of the war in 1945 he might at last return to them. But with each passing month of absence, the strains of separation increased.

As for Tihwa, Mackiernan was content to let others think it was the end of the earth. At that precise moment in history, cataclysmic forces were gathering. Communism had seized much of postwar Europe and now was about to swallow the most populous land on the planet. The Soviet Union was funneling matériel across its border with China, destabilizing the region, all the while feverishly working on the Kremlin's first atomic bomb. The border separating the two giants, the Soviet Union and China, would for decades obsess the U.S. intelligence community. And there, posing as a lowly clerk, Mackiernan took it all in, dutifully reporting back to Washington and, in his own quixotic way, attempting to alter the course of history.

Tihwa, far from being the remote outpost others took it to be, was a front-row seat for Scene One of the Cold War.

There was a second reason that this forbidding region was of such intense interest to the CIA. Xinjiang possessed rich deposits of uranium, gold, and petroleum. The Soviets already held 50 percent of the mineral and oil rights there. Some in Washington even suspected that the true aim of Moscow was to carve off Xinjiang and add it to its own empire.

It was into this cauldron of international intrigue that Mackiernan inserted himself. He was a quiet man, given to answering questions with a simple "yes" or "no." The compulsive talker has, at best, a short career in the clandestine service. At times, Mackiernan appeared painfully shy. He held his own counsel and respected the privacy of others as zealously as he protected his own. A lanky figure, he had boyish good looks, deep dimples, and an easy, somewhat awkward smile. His eyes telegraphed an alluring vulnerability. More than one woman saw a bit of Henry Fonda in him. Like many of his Agency colleagues, he was a wholly unlikely character for a spy, and as such, perfect for the part. Those who underestimated him made the mistake but once. He was a man of singular purpose.

Back in Washington, his personnel file was stamped "Secret." Inside was evidence of what pointed to a brilliant past and an even more prom-

Quixotic

ising future. Douglas S. Mackiernan was born in Mexico City on April 25, 1913. He was the oldest of five brothers, all of them with solid Scottish names: Duncan, Stuart, Malcolm, and Angus. His father and namesake, Douglas S. Mackiernan, had been an adventurer himself, running away from a boarding school at sixteen and signing on to become a whaler. Douglas Sr. would successively become a merchant seaman, an explorer, and a businessman of modest success. In Mexico City the young Doug Mackiernan attended a German school. By eight he had mastered English, French, Spanish, and German. As an adult he would add Russian, Chinese, and some Kazakh.

The family moved around a good bit in those early years, finally settling in Stoughton, Massachusetts. There the senior Mackiernan operated a filling station, named the Green Lantern. Mackiernan's mother was a talented commercial artist who dabbled in greeting cards. Mackiernan did not distinguish himself in the classroom—he bristled at routine and discipline. But no one doubted his intellect. He and a brother designed and built a mechanical creature that rose out of the depths of the family pond and scared the dickens out of anyone unsuspecting. He also early on demonstrated a way with radios. As an avid amateur operator, his call letters were W1HTQ. An entire room in his home was consecrated to ham radios. The yard around his house was crisscrossed with antennae.

If ever a boy was cut out to be a spy, it was Doug Mackiernan. Even as a child he would draft elaborate declarations of war under a nom de plume, then attack one of his younger siblings, all in good sport. He scoffed at his brothers' decoder rings as juvenile, preferring more sophisticated models of his own design. He knew guns and was a crack shot with his own Remington .306.

Mackiernan's boyhood home in Massachusetts featured a huge sunporch and thirty acres shaded by chestnut trees. There was even a small trout stream called Beaver Brook. The five Mackiernan boys had their run of the place.

Easily distracted in school, Mackiernan was delighted to see class end, even if it meant pumping gas at his father's filling station. His father was a stern and somewhat formal man who, even when he pumped gas, wore a felt hat and tie. In the evenings Doug Jr. would often lose himself in elaborate science experiments. In September 1932 Mackiernan, then nineteen, went off to MIT to study physics. There, too, the routine did not agree with him. One year was enough. He never did get his degree—too much bother. But his grasp of the materials was enough to impress his professors. From 1936 to 1940 he worked as a research assistant at MIT. In 1941 he served as an agent for the U.S. Weather Bureau.

That was the year Mackiernan, then twenty-eight, introduced himself to Darrell Brown. They met on a train and discovered they were both headed for a skiing trip. Later, on the slopes, they met again. Darrell had taken a spill. As Mackiernan whooshed by, he said, "You are going to have to do better than that." He then returned to help her to her feet.

They were married on July 19, 1941, in St. John's By-the-Sea Episcopal Church in Old Orchard Beach, Maine, amid sprays of ferns, white gladioli, and delphinium. On November 6 of the next year they had a daughter, Gail. But the marriage was frayed from the beginning. Shortly after the declaration of war, Mackiernan virtually vanished.

He had early on demonstrated an invaluable gift for codes and encryption, as well as an encyclopedic interest in history and foreign cultures. By 1942, not yet thirty, he was named chief of the Cryptographic Cryptoanalysis Section at Army Air Force Headquarters in Washington. But he was often away on assignment. Through most of the next year he was plotting weather maps, on temporary duty in Greenland and Alaska, in charge of the Synoptic Map Section. In November 1943 he was assigned to the 10th Weather Squadron in China. There he was to oversee communications and train personnel in the use of radios and codes. One of his primary jobs was to intercept and break encrypted Russian weather transmissions.

For the duration of the war he served in China at Station 233—Tihwa. He also monitored emerging weather patterns that would soon pass over the Pacific, providing valuable data that helped U.S. war planners target their B-29 bombing runs over Japanese-held territories.

His letters home were few and far between. His daughter, Gail, had only the vaguest recollections of him. At Christmas she would receive a gift signed "from Daddy," but she knew it was really from Mackiernan's parents—her grandparents.

It was hard for Gail to understand that her father was in a place so remote as China. Her mother would take her for drives in the black

Mercury coupe and park at Cape Elizabeth. The toddler could see Wood Island out in the bay. She imagined that the island was this far-off place called China where her father was. She wondered why she did not see more of him. She was four when she saw him last.

By war's end, Mackiernan was a thirty-three-year-old lieutenant colonel. But though he had a wife and daughter, he knew that he was not cut out for a desk job or the security of peacetime civilian life. By the spring of 1947 he was desperate to get back to Tihwa. On May 12 he set out from Nanjing for the tortuous overland journey west. The trip would take four weeks and earn him a State Department commendation.

. . .

In many ways, Mackiernan was typical of those who joined the CIA in its infancy. Nearly all had a military background and were seasoned in combat, intelligence, counterintelligence, communications, or sabotage. Like Mackiernan, many possessed other skills, not only those of warriors but those of linguists, scientists, or historians. Some were closet scholars, well read in foreign cultures. Some had served proudly with the Office of Strategic Services, the OSS, the World War II intelligence group headed by the legendary William "Wild Bill" Donovan. A successful Wall Street lawyer, Donovan had assembled a corps of operatives and analysts, many from the ranks of America's elite. From the OSS would come such formidable postwar figures as Stewart Alsop, John Birch, Julia Child, Allen Dulles, Richard Helms, Arthur Goldberg, Herbert Marcuse, Walt Rostow, and Arthur Schlesinger.

Donovan's brand of derring-do, his appeal to a sense of duty among those in positions of privilege, and, indeed, even the very structure of his OSS would continue long after to be the hallmark of the CIA. The heady victory of World War II, the sense of America's indomitability, and its newfound activist role in the world would characterize the CIA in those early days and ensure bold though often unsung triumphs. That same proud legacy would also condemn the fledgling agency in the not-too-distant future to highly publicized debacles and humiliations which would dog it forever.

No sooner had the war ended when the OSS was disbanded, many of its most talented and skilled people absorbed by private industry, Wall Street, and civilian government service. Those who stayed in the intelligence service found themselves either at the State Department or in a branch of military service. It was not until the National Security Act of 1947 under President Harry Truman that the Central Intelligence Agency came into being, reassembling many of the vital elements of the OSS.

Although the organization was profoundly weaker than its wartime predecessor, it was the constant victim of envy from the armed services branches, which maintained their own intelligence organizations. The State Department had its own research branch. Even the FBI's J. Edgar Hoover deeply resented the CIA, which wrested away from his Bureau authority over operations in Central and South America. Many in Congress, too, were suspicious of the need for an independent intelligence service in peacetime.

The CIA's uncertain status was mirrored in the tumbledown buildings to which it was relegated in the nation's capital. CIA headquarters was located in the old OSS complex at 2430 E Street. But most of the CIA worked out of what was collectively known as the Tempo Buildings. These were temporary structures left over from the war that were clustered about Washington's Reflecting Pool under the watchful gaze of Lincoln enthroned in his memorial. Each building carried a letter designation, as in "Tempo K" or "Tempo L." The buildings were dimly lit and foul-smelling, bone-chilling in winter and sweltering in summer. At lunchtime in August, Agency secretaries would roll up their skirts or pant legs to dip their feet in the Reflecting Pool to restore themselves. Offices were infested with mice and insects. Secretaries would sometimes suspend their lunches from the ceilings by a string to put them out of reach of the columns of ants.

Those same secretaries would spend their days typing and filing away the most sensitive materials in Washington, many of them related to preparations for an apocalyptic atomic confrontation with the Soviets. Some found themselves typing up top secret war plans. At day's end they would carefully account for each copy, remove their typewriter ribbons and lock them away in the vault until the next day. From the lowliest clerk to the senior-most director, there was the sense that the Agency's mission was of monumental import. Not even its grim surroundings could dull their devotion to duty. Communism menaced the world. Hitler and Mussolini and Hirohito had only recently been defeated, but now Stalin and Mao were taking their place. From the vantage point of those earliest to arrive at the CIA it was not merely a contest between ideologies but a struggle of epic, even biblical proportions, pitting the forces of light against darkness. The fate of civilization itself seemed to hang in the balance.

In what came to be called the Cold War, no action could be viewed as too extreme. It was the Agency's divine mission to blunt the thrusts of Communism worldwide and perhaps, in so doing, avoid nuclear Armageddon. If World War II had taught the nation's stunned intelligence community anything, it was that containment, not appeasement, was the only hope of staving off war. No longer was any act of barbarism deemed "unthinkable." Pearl Harbor and the ovens of Auschwitz had cured U.S. intelligence officers of that. The gentleman's code of conduct with which America's espionage community had begun World War II was the first document to pass through the shredder.

But like Mackiernan, many had joined the CIA as much out of a taste for adventure as a sense of patriotism. Following the war, it had been hard for men and women like Mackiernan, accustomed to exotic places and the rush of danger, to slip back into the routine of civilian life. Some, like Mackiernan, had discovered that they felt most alive only when they were living on the edge.

Besides, Mackiernan's life in Tihwa was hardly the stuff of hardship. Almost immediately upon arriving, the lowly clerk moved into a ten-bedroom villa he rented from a Russian. He had only enough furniture for three rooms. Soon he purchased a fine strong horse, an Arabian mixed with the breeds of the Kazakhs. On Sundays he would sling an aging English cavalry saddle over its broad back and ride out into the countryside for a day of hunting or exploration. Of course it was not all play. Sometimes he would go to where he had buried scientific equipment used to determine the mineral riches of the region.

In Tihwa Mackiernan hired a twenty-four-year-old White Russian named Vassily Zvonzov, who would be both a caretaker of his home and a stableboy for his horse. Like Mackiernan, Zvonzov had no love for the Communists. Having deserted from the Russian army in 1941, Zvonzov had joined various anti-communist resistance efforts. Zvonzov shared the house with Mackiernan but not his life. Mackiernan could be affable, even entertaining, but he did not welcome questions. He rarely spoke of family and never of his true purpose in Tihwa.

But Zvonzov soon pieced together that Mackiernan was more than he appeared to be. Not long after arriving in Tihwa, Mackiernan sought out a leader of the Kazakh anti-Communist resistance. His name was Wussman Bator. He was then in his fifties, a striking figure in his traditional Kazakh robes. The rare times Wussman consented to be photographed he posed astride a great white horse, his silken warrior's hat crested with owl feathers. "Bator" was an honorific name, and Wussman already had a reputation for valor and cunning. His band of Kazakh horsemen were nomadic and viewed by some as bandits and horse rustlers. But no one doubted Wussman's determination to resist the Communists—least of all Mackiernan.

Mackiernan would meet Wussman in the leader's yurt, a round tent-like affair with an opening at the center where light could enter and smoke exit. On his first such visit Mackiernan brought Wussman a traditional gift of fine blue cloth and a small ingot of solid gold. The relationship between the two grew closer in subsequent months as the Communist threat increased. Exactly how Mackiernan assisted Wussman—whether with tactical advice, encouragement, or outright weaponry—is not certain. What is known is that the two came to rely on one another closely, each entrusting the other with his life.

Within a month after Mackiernan's move to Tihwa, a rare American visitor arrived in town. Her name was Pegge Lyons. She was a brassy twenty-four-year-old freelance writer who wrote under the name Pegge Parker. She had long legs, shoulder-length chestnut hair, and a high-spiritedness. And, like Mackiernan, she had a taste for adventure. Already she had put in three years as a reporter in Fairbanks, Alaska. Now she was hoping that Mackiernan might direct her to some good stories on China's ragged frontier. Mackiernan was happy to oblige. Without taking her fully into his confidence, he convinced her to take photos along the Soviet border and to focus on any movement of arms or equipment, transports, trucks, men marching, or weapons. Concentrate, he said, on the faces of anyone in uniform. He handed her his Leica camera and instructed her in how to avoid attracting suspicion. But Pegge Lyons was a step ahead of him. She donned bobby socks and a skirt and by all appearance was a dipsy young American tourist. By July 1947 some of the photos she took had begun to show up in a variety of newspapers—but only after they had been closely scrutinized in Washington.

For two weeks, Pegge Lyons stayed in the consulate in Tihwa, dining on sweet melons and hot meals prepared by the Russian cook. Pegge Lyons and Doug Mackiernan's interest in each other went well beyond the professional. In Pegge's eyes Mackiernan was a dashing figure with a disarming smile. Pipe in hand and dressed in a khaki shirt with epaulets, he was the very embodiment of adventure. Fluent in Russian and Chinese, he was equally conversant in geology, meteorology, and geopolitics. He was as comfortable fixing a jeep as he was sitting astride his Arabian. That he was a man of secrets only made him that much more attractive.

Mackiernan, for his part, found in Pegge a kindred spirit, a companion who shared his taste for the exotic, for risk, and his interest in the Russian language. It had been a long time since he had allowed himself to be stirred by a woman. His marriage to Darrell had long been a marriage in name only. They had barely seen each other in years. Ten thousand miles away, in the arid and forsaken town of Tihwa, Pegge Lyons and Doug Mackiernan seemed right for each other.

. . .

Doug Mackiernan and Darrell were divorced in a brief proceeding in Reno, Nevada. Not long after, Mackiernan and Pegge Lyons were married in San Francisco. In September 1948 they took a Pan Am flight to Shanghai. That same month, Pegge Mackiernan gave birth to twins—Michael and Mary. For Douglas Mackiernan it was a second chance to be a husband and a father. This time he was determined to do it right. In a photograph a proud Papa Mackiernan, dressed in suit and tie, is cradling his newborn son, Mike. It would be the only picture taken of Mackiernan with his son.

Shortly thereafter Mackiernan returned to Tihwa—alone. The situation in China was deteriorating rapidly. On November 10, 1948, the State Department ordered all dependents of American diplomats to evacuate the country immediately. Pegge wrapped her six-week-old twins in swaddling and tucked them snugly into a straw laundry basket, then boarded a Pan Am flight for San Francisco.

. . .

What was clear to many in China was less clear to American intelligence officials in the nation's capital. At 2:30 P.M., December 17, 1948, the senior-most members of the intelligence community gathered around a long table in the Federal Works Building in downtown Washington, D.C. Chairing the meeting was Rear Admiral Roscoe Henry Hillenkoetter, director of the Central Intelligence Agency. Hillenkoetter was a tall man with close-cropped black hair, a Naval Academy graduate who carried his gold braids and ribbons well, but whose leadership qualities were suspect.

He, even more than most in that first generation of CIA directors, understood the harsh lessons of Pearl Harbor—the need for constant intelligence and vigilance. As an executive officer on the USS *West Virginia* he had been wounded when that ship was sunk at its Pearl Harbor berth on December 7, 1941. He fancied himself a student of history and took pride in being able to quote at length the writings of Marx, Lenin, and Stalin. But nothing could prepare him for the likes of Mao Zedong.

That afternoon Hillenkoetter admitted being dumbfounded by the speed and agility of the Communist onslaught. But he predicted the Communists would temper their advance, settling for a part in a coalition government—preferring to be recognized by the United Nations and wanting to court the United States in order to obtain articles of trade they coveted which their ideological brethren, the Soviets, could not provide. "They are not going to force the issue now," Hillenkoetter said. "Maybe in six months."

But neither U.N. recognition nor U.S. trade was of great interest to Mao. One month after the Washington meeting, China's Nationalist president, Chiang Kai-shek, resigned. The next day Communist forces took Beijing. On May 25 the Communists took Shanghai. Director Hillenkoetter was correct in only one regard. Six months after the meeting, there was no mistaking Mao's intentions—he had taken it all.

. . .

On the evening of February 12, 1949, Mackiernan sat down with his old Remington portable, slipped a page of white paper in the cylinder, and typed the words "My Darling baby." It was a letter to Pegge and it was one of the few letters that would reach her. The others, Mackiernan surmised, were either intercepted or censored in their entirety. Only two of her letters had reached him in Tihwa in the three months since she and the twins had been forced to evacuate China and return stateside.

In the letter Mackiernan spoke of what he called the "rather peculiar" political situation around him: the Chinese and the Soviets were growing closer, trade between the two was expanding markedly, Chinese newspapers had taken a decidedly anti-American tilt, the staff at the Soviet consulate was increasing, and Soviet influence in the region was spreading.

"To counter this," he noted, "there is the rumor that the Moslems of Sinkiang, Kansu, Chinghai and Ninghsia are joining forces to prevent the spread of Communism into the NW [Northwest] . . . My personal opinion is that the Sovs will continue strong in Sinkiang, and that the Moslems will form a sort of anti-Communist island in Kansu, Chinghai, and Ninghsia . . . In the event of a Tungkan (Moslem rebellion) life would be rather difficult."

What Mackiernan did not and could not reveal in the letter was that he was more than a passive observer of the events that he described, and that a key part of his mission was to embolden and advise the very resistance about which he had just speculated in such detached terms.

By then, Tihwa was so isolated that the only route for supplies was by water to Chungking, and then by truck to Tihwa, a three-month odyssey. And even the water route was now closed till May due to drought. None of this deterred Mackiernan from inviting his wife and twins to join him. "As far as food for the infants is concerned," he wrote, "I am convinced you can get everything you need here. Sugar, milk, oatmeal (Quaker Oats in sealed tins), vegetables are all plentiful and cheap . . ."

"So to sum it all up I am planning to try to get you all up here in March or April, provided of course that the Dept. will permit it . . ." Mackiernan asked Pegge to ready herself and the twins so that if China's airline resumed a regular flight to Tihwa they would be prepared to leave at once. But while the invitation seemed earnest enough, there was also a sense that it was Mackiernan's way of coping with the separation and of marking time. Mackiernan had already sacrificed one marriage and the pleasures of fatherhood to his work during the war. In six years of marriage he could have counted the time together in months, not years. Now again he faced the possibility of an interminable separation from the woman and the children he had only just begun to know.

Threading its way through his letter were unspoken anxieties about the deteriorating situation in China. If it became necessary to leave Tihwa, he said, the only route would be to India. That would be a tortuous journey. Mackiernan asked Pegge to send him through the diplomatic pouch two books, the " 'List of Stars for the 60 deg. Astrolabe,' by W. Arnold (the big brown book) and the 1949 and if possible the 1950 American Ephemeris and Nautical Almanac." Both tomes would be of service should he be forced to plot a route of escape using the stars as navigational reference points. Mackiernan also noted that a new jeep was slowly making its way by truck from Chungking. Within a month or so it would arrive in Tihwa, still in its crate. This could provide him with a means of escape.

"So much for business," he wrote. "How are you now and how are Mike and Mary . . . I'll bet I wouldn't recognize them now. Give them both a kiss from me and tell them they will be up here soon." Mackiernan asked for a recent picture of the twins. The only one he had was of himself cradling son Mike as a newborn.

Mackiernan could be playful, self-effacing, and romantic. "I am sporting a beautiful (to me only probably) curly black beard and as soon as I get my photo stuff set up will send a picture of me in my hirsute glory," he wrote. "Have sworn a great swear not to shave it off till you arrive, so hurry before I have to braid the thing (like a Sikh)."

"Well honey bunch," the letter went on, "I will close this down now since they are sealing the pouch. Remember that I love you my darling, and only you, and that I want you up here close to me as soon as possible. Keep writing and soon we will be together again. Give my love and kisses to Mike and Mary, and all my love for you darling sweetheart. Good night for now, darling . . . All my love—Doug."

Two months later, on April 13, 1949, Mackiernan formally asked the State Department to grant his wife and twins permission to join him in Tihwa. Two weeks later came the reply: "Regrets conditions China make impossible authorization Mackiernans family proceed Tihwa this time." A month later, undeterred, Mackiernan informed his wife of the bad news but offered up an alternative plan: "Peggy return through China out. Trying India. No mail service now. Love, Doug!"

At her end, Pegge was trying to persuade the State Department to allow her to return to China. On June 8, 1949, she wrote Walton

Butterworth, director for Far Eastern Affairs: "My husband, vice-consul at Tihwa, Sinkiang, has written me an urgent letter to make every effort to return to China, if need be through India . . . Doug and I are parents of twin infants. I would intend to take them with me . . . I realize the undertaking at first consideration seems quite complicated. Offsetting this is my own personal knowledge of Sinkiang, the Russian language, the problems presented—and the fact that my husband has just begun his tour in China. It is worth all the difficulties and hardships to keep our family together . . ."

Two weeks later, on June 21, 1949, Pegge sent a cable through the State Department's Division of Foreign Service Personnel: "Please cable my husband following: PAA [Pan American Airlines] Calcutta every Saturday planning arrival when you can meet us impossible navigate alone advise supplies love Pegge." But the State Department refused to send the cable: "I regret that it is my unpleasant duty to inform you that the Department cannot at this time approve of your proceeding to Tihwa with your twin infants."

Desperate to see her husband, Pegge turned to the influential Clare Boothe Luce, whom she had come to know during her days as a reporter. She asked if Luce might intervene on her behalf and have her husband reassigned to a less perilous environment. On July 7, 1949, Luce wrote back: "I cannot possibly *promise* to get your husband moved to a consulate a little more accessible to a mother and twins than Chinese Turkestan—but I just might be able to get him transferred to a spot as wild and woolly but a little more on the flat for an approaching caravan with cradles!"

Luce acknowledged that as a Republican during a Democratic administration, her influence was limited. "My bridges, tho' not burned, are badly bent!" she wrote. The letter closed, "With a sound buss for Mike and Maryrose [the twins], Cordially Clare Boothe Luce." But nothing more came of Luce's offer.

Two weeks after the Luce letter arrived, on July 24, 1949, the minister-counselor of embassy in China sent a telegram to Secretary of State Dean Acheson acknowledging that it was wise to close the embassies in China. But Tihwa, he suggested, should remain open. "It seems to me Tihwa, properly staffed, could be most valuable listening post and should be retained as long as possible. Withdrawal should always be possible by some route other than China."

Four days later the ambassador to China disagreed and recommended the immediate evacuation of Tihwa's personnel. The country's collapse was certain. "Tihwa even more isolated and bloody history of Sinkiang counsels that staff be removed before breakdown of law and order become imminent. Difficulty obtaining Soviet visa makes unlikely exit via USSR in event emergency, leaving only difficult mountain route to India or Afghanistan." On July 29 Secretary of State Acheson ordered the Tihwa embassy closed, its staff to leave "as rapidly as possible . . . while safe exit remains."

Bits and pieces of news were seeping out of China, all of it worrisome to Pegge Mackiernan. On August 23 she sent a telegram to the State Department: "Can you confirm NY Trib article Tihwa consulate closing and my husband coming out extremely anxious for news please telegraph collect." The next day the State Department responded that the consulate was closed but that her husband was staying behind to dispose of U.S. property.

The next morning Mackiernan sent a telegram to Acheson informing him that the consulate had been closed to the public and that all employees had been discharged. In his haste to depart, Tihwa's consul, John Hall Paxton, had left everything behind. Mackiernan told Acheson he would "destroy archives, cryptographic material and motion picture films." The only thing he would spare was a radio and enough OTPs, "one-time pads," to communicate with Washington.

The one-time pads were notebooks that provided a system of encryption that could be used only one time for each message. The code was known only to the recipient of the message who possessed the corresponding pad and code. OTPs were standard issue in the diplomatic corps as well as in the ranks of the CIA's clandestine service.

The situation deteriorated rapidly. On the morning of August 31, 1949, Mackiernan sent a telegram to Acheson reporting that many of the potential overland escape routes from Tihwa were now closed due to banditry. Corridor cities, he reported, were crowded with refugees. Food was scarce. White Russians and Chinese officials were fleeing. One hour later Mackiernan sent a second telegram: "Situation Sinkiang very grave."

Resistance to the Communist troops, he predicted, would crumble. There would be no meaningful opposition.

While Mackiernan worked feverishly to destroy sensitive documents and to plan his own escape from Tihwa, Washington's eyes were focused elsewhere—on the Soviet Union. At 10:36 A.M. on September 23, 1949, White House reporters were summoned by Truman's press secretary and handed a brief statement from the president: "We have evidence," it said, "that within recent weeks an atomic explosion occurred in the USSR." American B-29s taking high-altitude air samples had confirmed that the Soviets had detonated a nuclear device at its Semipalatinsk testing facility. So began the arms race, as a generation of American and Soviet war planners dedicated their lives to preparing for what each government unconvincingly called "the unthinkable."

For the CIA, the Soviet bomb was a stinging rebuke to its intelligence apparatus. Just three days before Truman's chilling announcement, the Agency had provided a top secret memorandum in which it estimated that the Soviets would be in no position to detonate such a device before mid-1950. Agency experts had predicted "the most probable date is mid-1953." President Truman's confidence in CIA estimates had to have been rattled.

Two days after Truman's announcement, on the morning of September 25, Mackiernan sent a telegram notifying the State Department that the provincial government of Xinjiang had accepted the authority of the Chinese Communist government in Beijing. It was to be Mackiernan's last official telegram from Tihwa.

Two days later, on September 27, Communist soldiers seized Tihwa and posted sentries at each of its four gates, watching all who attempted to enter or leave. Schoolchildren chanted "Long live Mao Zedong!"

That evening Mackiernan prepared to flee. It was a perfect night—dark and moonless. At his house he and Vassily gathered classified papers and carried them to the small detached summer kitchen, tossing them by the armful into the fireplace. Vassily put a match to them. Then came the packing: ammunition, a radio to communicate with Washington, stacks of one-time pads, his Leica camera, army air force maps of the region, a compass, an aneroid barometer, and a sheath of personal documents containing, among other papers, his divorce decree and photos of the twins.

He also packed several kilos of gold bullion with which to barter for whatever might be needed along the way. Then, as now, gold was sometimes provided to CIA officers facing unknown perils in the field.

Mackiernan also packed two machine guns, several army sleeping bags, and a large tent. From his bedroom he removed a radio with keys for transmitting and receiving encrypted messages sent in Morse code.

Virtually everything in Mackiernan's sparsely furnished residence pertained to his tradecraft as a spy. In addition to his Leica camera he had a Minox miniature camera, chemicals needed to develop and print film, binoculars, a portable Geiger counter, a shortwave radio, and a cowhide briefcase with a lock. His bookshelves were lined with dozens of specialized books, many of them purchased in the famous Vetch Book Shop in Beijing. Among the titles: *Old Routes of W. Iran, The Thousand Buddhas, Innermost Asia* (four volumes with maps), *Peking to Lhasa,* and *Peaks and Plains of Central Asia.*

Mackiernan had gone over the escape plan with his tiny band of men. There was Frank Bessac, a twenty-eight-year-old Fulbright scholar and former paratrooper who had wandered into Tihwa only weeks earlier. A prodigious reader, Bessac was nearly blind without his glasses. And there were the three White Russians who had worked with the U.S. consulate: in addition to Vassily Zvonzov were Stephani Yanuishkin, thirty, and Leonid Shutov, twenty. From Wussman Bator, the Kazakh leader and resistance fighter, Mackiernan had purchased twenty-two horses and provisions to last several months. One of Wussman's men was to meet Mackiernan east of Tihwa and lead them overland to a place where they might be safe before beginning the arduous—some would say impossible—trek to India over the Himalayas.

Mackiernan had his .30-caliber revolver in a holster on his belt. Over his shoulder he slung a carbine. Shortly before midnight, he and Bessac drove through the main gate in a battered jeep. Exiting the city was not the problem—exiting the country was. Meanwhile, Zvonzov and his two companions, who knew that they would be executed for their anti-Communist activities if they were caught, scaled the city walls under cover of night and lowered themselves by rope to the other side. Three hundred kilometers away they rendezvoused with Mackiernan, Wussman Bator, and Wussman's "Kazakh Hordes," as Mackiernan would write in his log that would carry a stamp of "Top Secret." So began a two-week trek eastward to Lake Barkol, closer to the Mongolian border.

Fifteen miles east of Tihwa, Mackiernan stopped the caravan just long enough to bury two of the embassy's radios, rather than risk having them fall into Communist hands. Three days after Mackiernan set out from Tihwa, on October 1, Mao Zedong stood triumphantly above the gate to the Forbidden City in Beijing and proclaimed the People's Republic of China.

But that was half a continent away. For two weeks Mackiernan and his men—Bessac, the White Russians, and the Kazakh guides—encamped in yurts on the southwest shore of Lake Barkol. Who could blame Mackiernan for being reluctant to leave the relative safety and comfort of the lake? The journey that lay ahead of him, even under the best of circumstances, was grim. Between Lake Barkol and the Chinese-Tibetan border lay a no-man's-land, more than one thousand hostile miles of the Taklimakan desert, known as White Death.

On October 15 they soberly set out "marching at night to avoid being seen," Mackiernan penned in his log. All along the way he would record landmarks, latitudinal and longitudinal readings, and the availability of game and water. It was a carefully detailed escape route for those who might come later. As a check against his compass, Mackiernan converted a camera, long since ruined by sand and grit, into an octant.

Seldom were there roads. Mostly they crossed open desert, their feet crunching through the salty crust of its surface, sinking six inches or more into the powder-fine sands. It was an exhausting routine that repeated itself day after day. The monotony was broken only by the occasional sighting of a gazelle or lone wolf eyeing their tedious progress. Their course was set for south-southwest. With each passing day the elevation increased. Among themselves Mackiernan and his men spoke an odd mix of languages—Russian, Chinese, and Kazakh—but little English.

In the midst of the desert Mackiernan and his men and horses went three days without even a swallow of water. Then they came upon a brackish well and fell upon their bellies unable to resist. Like wild animals, they gulped down the warm waters. For hours afterward they and the horses were racked with diarrhea and abdominal cramps.

The one constant of their odyssey was Mackiernan's insistence on stopping to radio his position to Washington. Each time, Zvonzov would set up the radio antennae while Mackiernan sent or received encrypted messages. No sooner completed, the message would be burned on the spot. Zvonzov never asked and was never told the content of those messages.

The rigor of the trek occasionally yielded to unexpected comforts. Mackiernan's log records that on November 14, at an elevation of 9,850 feet, they put in with desert nomads and feasted on mutton. Mackiernan traded gold for additional horses and camels, observing that the traders would likely spend it buying opium from the Kazakhs at one ounce of bullion per six ounces of opium.

But the journey was already taking its toll. Increasingly Mackiernan was being felled by gastrointestinal pains and diarrhea. At each stop along the way they would put in with Kazakhs who shared their yurt with them and fed them biscuits called *bursak*—a favorite of Mackiernan's—and thick fried steaks of bighorn sheep. Most of these nomadic peoples had never before seen a foreigner.

By late November, as the temperature began to drop, the terrain had become even more hostile. "Cold as hell—no water, no grass, no fuel," wrote Mackiernan in his log. "Country absolutely barren. Many skeletons of men, horses, and camels." It was not until the morning of November 29 that Mackiernan reached a place known to him as Goose Lake, where he and his men received "a royal welcome." His Kazakh hosts had prepared for Mackiernan and his men the largest yurt they had ever seen, and set aside a dozen sheep for them to consume. And there Mackiernan would spend the long winter, waiting for the mountain passes to clear.

Meanwhile, on November 25, 1949, Pegge Mackiernan received a cable from Fulton Freeman, the State Department's acting deputy director, Office of Chinese Affairs. "I am happy to inform you," Freeman began, "that word has been passed to us from the British Consul in Tihwa that Mr. Mackiernan is proceeding to India via Tibet and that he is expected to reach early in December."

For Douglas Mackiernan the next four months were filled with tedium. Winter had set in and a part of each day he gathered brush and yak droppings to burn for warmth. He spent many hours reading and rereading the few books he had brought with him, among them Tolstoy's *War and Peace*. When he could stand them no longer, they were sacrificed for toilet paper.

One afternoon, with the wind howling fifty miles an hour and the temperature twenty degrees below zero, the White Russians invited Mackiernan to join them for an outside shower. Mackiernan declined but watched in fascination. Undaunted, Zvonzov went first. He heated a cauldron of water, then cowered behind a tent flap as countrymen Leonid and Stephani hurriedly ladled warm water over him. Partly it was to stay clean, partly an effort to break the monotony.

. . .

During these long and dark winter days Mackiernan spent many hours in quiet contemplation. The grandeur and the cruelty of the icescape that surrounded him felt strangely familiar, at once threatening and comforting. In the dark of the yurt, with the winds howling outside, it was impossible not to think back on his father's own saga of survival in a frozen wilderness. From earliest childhood, Mackiernan had heard the tale again and again, until it had become the defining parable of his youth.

Douglas S. Mackiernan, Sr., had run off at age sixteen to become a whaler out of New Bedford, Massachusetts. He spent years at sea. Then in July 1903 he responded to a solicitation from a wealthy patron of exploration, William Ziegler, who dreamed of financing an expedition that would be the first to plant the American flag on the North Pole. A year earlier Ziegler had financed an aborted expedition to the pole. Now, with the blessing of the National Geographic Society, he was organizing yet another effort. His ship, the *America*, was a steam yacht, its flanks strengthened to resist ice floes.

The senior Mackiernan had signed on as a common seaman. Even if all had gone well, Ziegler's plan was a bold one. The *America* was to go north as far as the ice would permit, then anchor and put its thirty-seven men ashore. A year later, in 1904, a resupply vessel was to arrive, replenishing the stores. Instead, the *America* was crushed in the ice of Teplitz Bay early in the winter of 1903. Its vital provisions and equipment were lost and the ship was reduced to kindling. A full year later the ice was so thick that no resupply vessel could reach them. Seaman Mackiernan and the others were stranded.

Huddling there in a yurt forty-six years later, Doug Mackiernan could remember his father telling him of the endless nights of an arctic winter, of fifty-mile-per-hour winds that burned his face, and especially of the night of January 5, 1905, when the temperature sank to sixty degrees below zero. Inside their tents of pongee silk, the lanterns and stoves created vapors that condensed on the interior. They formed icicles that would later melt into tiny rivulets and find their way into the sleeping bags and then freeze again. A half hour's sleep constituted a full night's slumber. For cooking and warmth, the senior Mackiernan and the others had mined twenty tons of coal from frozen clay and carried it on their backs down a steep and slippery slope.

Mackiernan's father and the others stayed alive by eating polar bears—120 in all—as well as walruses and seals. Decades later Mackiernan would tell his wide-eyed son and namesake that he could still taste the leathery walrus meat. So tough was it that it reminded the expedition's captain, Fiala, of chewing automobile tires. Desperate for variety in their diet, the men risked their lives to scale icy cliffs and stole the eggs of gulls and loons. The cold seeped through Mackiernan's mittens as he tended the dog teams. It cut through his boots, searing his toes with a numbness that turned to frostbite. For weeks he was hobbled, unable to walk.

By day, one or another of the crew would stand as a lookout on a spit of frozen ice searching with binoculars for the promised rescue ship. Nearly every week a shout would go out that the resupply ship was in sight, but it would invariably be just another iceberg mistaken for a sail.

None of them would ever reach the North Pole, or even come close. A fireman, Sigurd Myhre, had died of disease and was buried on the summit of a bleak plateau, "the most northern tomb in the world," Fiala would later reflect. These were the memories that Mackiernan's father passed down to his son and which now came back to him here in the midst of his own frozen wasteland.

For the entire winter of 1904–5, Mackiernan and another man were alone in a remote camp, left with a team of five dogs, a rifle, a shotgun, and limited supplies. They passed that winter playing a marathon game of poker.

But in July 1905, when the men of the Ziegler expedition had come to believe that they might never again see their homes, a ship appeared against the frozen horizon. It was the *Terra Nova*, a rescue vessel whose mission was literally the dying wish of the expedition's financier, Ziegler. The two-year ordeal was over in an instant.

On board, Mackiernan's father rejoiced in a hot bath, read through two years of mail, and slept in a dry warm berth. In minutes he and the others were caught up on two years' worth of world events that had passed them by—the war between Japan and Russia, the results of the international yacht race of 1903, and the usual litany of catastrophes that afflict the world. But the sweetest memory of all, his father recalled, was breaking free of the ice and feeling the rise and fall of the open sea once more, and with it the knowledge that home was not far off. That was forty-five years earlier.

But from such memories, the younger Mackiernan could draw comfort that his ordeal, too, would have a miraculous end, that he would have his own stack of mail awaiting him and feel again the embrace of his wife, Pegge, and the twins. His father had been at the mercy of others for salvation. Mackiernan was in control of his own fate. With each step toward the Tibetan border he was that much closer to being saved.

. . .

At CIA headquarters the anti-Communist hysteria that gripped the nation also defined the Agency's agenda. On January 21, 1950, State Department employee Alger Hiss was convicted of perjury for denying that he had engaged in espionage for the Communists. Ten days later President Truman announced that he was proceeding with development of the hydrogen bomb. As the United States prepared for possible war with the Soviets, the CIA was expanding an already vigorous covert assault on Communism. This would include an ill-fated two-year attempt to overthrow the leftist government of Albania, as well as the creation of Radio Free Europe, a nettlesome embarrassment to Communist regimes. On February 9 Senator Joseph McCarthy announced his infamous list of

205 supposed Communists within the State Department, further putting pressure on the CIA in its counterintelligence role.

On the farthest edge of this ideological struggle stood Douglas Mackiernan. On January 30, 1950, Agency headquarters received a faint radio message from him. When conditions permitted, he said, he would be making his way across the Himalayas.

. . .

For Mackiernan two more months would pass at the frozen campsite. Finally, on March 20, 1950, he and his band said good-bye to the Kazakhs and commenced the final and most grueling leg of their journey, over the Himalayas, into Tibet, and eventually to India. From here on, Mackiernan and his men would be ever more exposed to the elements. At night Mackiernan would lie down in his sleeping bag, huddled against the back of a camel to shield him from the wind. At morning he and Bessac, the two Americans, could no longer assist in saddling the camels. Their fingers were too numb.

Mackiernan and his party would take turns riding the camels and then walking. Too much riding and they could freeze to death. Too much walking and they would collapse from exhaustion. Their diet, too, required a delicate balance. From the White Russians, more seasoned in the ways of survival, Mackiernan learned what to eat and what not to eat. Too much meat at such an altitude and he could find himself wooed into a nap from which he would not awake. Instead, he nibbled on bits of sugar, rice, raisins, a few bites of meat, and the ever-present biscuits he kept in his pants pocket.

It was all a matter of balance upon which his survival depended. At elevations of sixteen thousand feet or more, the air was so thin that the already taciturn Mackiernan rarely spoke at all, trying to conserve his breath. All conversation ended. In its place were hand signals and one- or two-word directives: "brush" or "dung" for fires, "snow" to be melted for water. By now, the ordeal of marching had become a mindless and silent routine, one foot in front of the other. Some days Mackiernan would lose sight in one eye or the other, the result of transient snow blindness.

Many of the horses had died from starvation. Others were useless, their hooves worn out. Knowing that the rest of the way there would be little grass to eat, Mackiernan had long before bartered for camels—not just any camels, but those that ate raw meat. Before making the purchase he tied up his prospective purchases and waited a day to see which camels consumed meat and which were dependent upon a diet of grass. Those camels that resisted meat Mackiernan promptly returned. Where he was bound, there would be no easy forage.

Though there was an abundance of game—wild horses, sheep, and yak—the elevation presented its own unique problems of consumption. At sixteen thousand feet Mackiernan found that water boiled at a decidedly lesser temperature. He could thrust his hand up to the elbow in furiously boiling water and remove it without a hint of scalding. One day Mackiernan shot a yak. The men salivated over the prospect of yak steaks. But after four hours in the boiling cauldron, the meat was still raw.

There were other problems too. A wild horse was spotted on a distant ridge and was brought down with a single shot. But almost instantly, vultures appeared overhead. By the time the men reached the animal, its carcass was nearly picked clean, its ribs rising out of the snow. After that, Mackiernan and his men shot only what they could reach quickly, then concealed their kill beneath a mound of grasses and stones until they had taken what they needed.

From morning to night the wind howled at fifty, even sixty miles an hour. It was a constant screaming sound, rising at times to a shrill whistle. In such cold, even the simplest manual tasks required superhuman resolve.

Mackiernan's clothes had long since become tatters, which he, like the other men, repaired as best he could. But a bigger concern was how to protect their feet in the deep and frigid snowdrifts. After so many miles, the men had virtually walked out of the soles of their shoes. One day Mackiernan and Zvonzov spotted two yaks. Both men were thinking shoes and meat. Mackiernan let Zvonzov, the better shot of the two, have the honors.

From three hundred yards Zvonzov brought the beast down. Right through the heart. They scurried through the snow to the animal as it lay on its side. They swiftly cut away its hide for soles and began removing steaks. But having cleared one flank, they were unable to flip the creature over, and were forced to abandon it, only half consumed.

As March, then April wore on, Mackiernan and his men plotted a course for the Tibetan border. At each new campsite Mackiernan took out his radio and wired headquarters of his progress. He requested that Washington contact the Tibetan government and ask the then sixteen-year-old Dalai Lama to arrange that he and his men be granted safe passage across the border and that they be given an escort once they exited China. Washington sent back a confirmation. Couriers from the Dalai Lama would alert the border guards at all crossing points so that Mackiernan and his band would be welcomed.

By now, Mackiernan set a course by ancient cairns and stone outcroppings. Nomads had pointed the way through the major passes, bidding them to be on the lookout for piles of rocks that rose like pyramids. Beneath each mound were the remains of others who had died in this harsh land. The ground was frozen too solid to yield to a grave, and so the bodies were simply covered with rocks. In so bleak a land, devoid of roads or signs, each such grave became a reference point, named for the person who had died there. Mackiernan passed by the grave of Kalibet and later Kasbek, fascinated at the small measure of immortality granted them. Each death was both a confirmation that Mackiernan was headed in the right direction and a reminder of the risks inherent in such a landscape.

Thousands of miles away, in Washington, the landscape of the Cold War was taking shape. On April 25, 1950, President Truman signed one of the seminal documents of the decade, National Security Council Directive 68. The blueprint for the Cold War strategy, it called on the United States to step up its opposition to Communist expansion, to rearm itself, and to make covert operations an integral part of that opposition. The policy of containment was now the undisputed security objective of the era. The CIA had its marching orders.

But for Mackiernan it was not grand geopolitical issues that concerned him, but the ferocity of mountain winds and biting cold. The border had proved more elusive than he had imagined. Finally, at 11:00 A.M. on April 29, 1950, as he scanned the horizon to the southeast with his binoculars, he caught sight of a tiny Tibetan encampment and knew that he had at long last reached the border. It had taken seven months to cross twelve hundred miles of desert and mountain. A moment earlier he had been weary beyond words, his thirty-seven-year-old frame stooped with exhaustion. Now, suddenly, he felt renewed and exuberant.

Mackiernan and Bessac went ahead, leaving the others to tend the camels. In the harsh terrain it was an hour before the Tibetans caught sight of Mackiernan, who was now a quarter of a mile ahead of Bessac. He was waving a white flag. The Tibetans dispatched a girl to meet him. They grinned at each other, unable to find any words in common. The girl stuck out her tongue at Mackiernan, a friendly greeting in Tibet, then withdrew to a hilltop where she was met by a Tibetan who unlimbered a gun. Then the two Tibetans disappeared over the hillside. Mackiernan followed and observed a small group apparently reinforcing a makeshift fortification of rocks. Their guns appeared to be at the ready.

Mackiernan decided that it would be best to strike camp here, on the east side of a stream that meandered through the valley. He chose a place in sight of the Tibetans. There he built a small fire to show his peaceful intentions. He suspected that the Tibetans might be wary of his straggling caravan, fearing them to be Communists or bandits bent on rustling sheep. As Mackiernan, Zvonzov, and the other two Russians drove tent stakes into the hard ground, six more Tibetans on horseback appeared, approaching from the northwest.

Moments later shots rang out. Mackiernan and his men dropped to the ground for cover. Bullets were whizzing overhead. Zvonzov reached for the flap of the tent and ripped it free. He tied it to the end of his rifle as a white flag and waved it aloft. The gunfire stopped. No one had been hit. Mackiernan directed Bessac to approach the first group of Tibetans and offer them gifts of raisins, tobacco, and cloth. As Bessac approached, he held a white flag and was taken in by the Tibetans.

Mackiernan, meanwhile, was convinced he could persuade those who had fired on him that his party was not a threat. His plan was a simple one. He and the others would rise to their feet, hands held high above their heads. Slowly they would approach the Tibetans as a group. Zvonzov argued against the plan. He feared the Tibetans would simply open fire when they were most vulnerable. Mackiernan prevailed.

Slowly he and the three White Russians stood up, hands aloft. They walked in measured steps, closing the distance between their tent site and the Tibetans. As they walked, Zvonzov eyed a boulder to the right and resolved that if there was trouble he would dive for cover behind it.

Mackiernan was in the lead, gaining confidence as the Tibetans held their fire. His arms were raised. Behind him walked the two White Russians, Stephani and Leonid. Fewer than fifty yards now separated them from the Tibetan border guards. Just then two shots were fired. Mackiernan cried out, "Don't shoot!" A third shot echoed across the valley. Mackiernan, Stephani, and Leonid lay in the snow. Vassily ran for the boulder. The air was thin and he ripped his shirt open as if it might give his lungs more air. A bullet smashed into his left knee. He tumbled into the snow and crawled toward the tent, his mind fixed on the machine gun and ammo that were there.

Moments later Bessac appeared, his hands tied behind his back, a prisoner of the Tibetans. Vassily, too, was taken prisoner. The six guards looted the campsite, encircled Vassily, and forced him to the ground. They demanded that he kowtow to them. Vassily pleaded for his life. Not long after, Bessac and Vassily, now hobbling and putting his weight on a stick, approached the place where Mackiernan, Stephani, and Leonid had fallen.

The wind was whipping at sixty miles an hour, the snow a blinding swirl. A half hour had passed since the shooting. Mackiernan was lying on his back, his legs crossed. Vassily looked at Mackiernan and thought to himself how peaceful he looked. Mackiernan even appeared to be smiling. It was a slightly ironic smile. Vassily was overcome with the strangest sense of envy.

Just then one of the border guards began to rifle through Mackiernan's pockets. He withdrew a *bursak*, one of those biscuits Mackiernan was never without. He offered Vassily a piece. Vassily turned away in revulsion. Then the guard pressed the biscuit to Mackiernan's teeth. The mouth fell wide open. Vassily was overcome with nausea. He turned and walked away. Mackiernan's body was already stiffening. But there would be one more indignity Mackiernan and the others would endure. The guards decapitated Mackiernan, Stephani, and Leonid, and even one of the camels that had been felled by their volley.

Shortly thereafter, the guards realized that they had made a terrible mistake, that these men were neither Communists nor bandits. They unbound Bessac's hands and attempted to put him at ease. Then Bessac and Vassily, in the company of the guards, began what was to be the last tedious march, to Lhasa and to freedom.

Five days after Mackiernan was killed, the two surviving members of his party encountered the Dalai Lama's couriers who were to have delivered the message of safe conduct and who were to have been part of Mackiernan's welcoming party. The couriers gave no explanation or excuse for their tardiness. It was small comfort that they offered Bessac the opportunity to execute the leader of the offending border guards. It was an offer he declined.

Three days later Tibetan soldiers made the arduous trip back to the border to retrieve that which had been looted—including the remaining gold—and to return the heads of Mackiernan, Leonid, and Stephani, that they might be buried with their bodies. The camel head was taken on to Lhasa. While convalescing, Vassily carved three simple wooden crosses to stand above the graves on the Tibetan frontier.

Mackiernan and the others were buried where they fell. The place was called Shigarhung Lung. There was no funeral for Mackiernan, then or ever. His grave was marked by Vassily's cross. It read simply "Douglas Mackiernan." He was buried beneath a pile of rocks, not unlike those many simple graves that he had paused to admire along the way and by which he had plotted his own course. Eleven days after the killing, the border guards who had killed him received forty to sixty lashes across the buttocks.

On June 11, 1950, Vassily and Bessac finally reached the outskirts of Lhasa. In the final entry in the log, Bessac wrote, "Good to be here—Oh God."

In Washington, State Department and CIA officials fretted over how they might keep Mackiernan's death a secret. They wondered whether, in the glare of public attention, his cover would be compromised. Such worries were overtaken by more pressing events. At 2:00 P.M. Washington time, June 24, 1950, thirteen days after Bessac and Zvonzov reached Lhasa, North Korean troops poured across the 38th parallel. The Korean War had begun.

. . .

Far from Washington, along the quiet coast of southern Maine, Mackiernan's first wife, Darrell, had just been told of Mackiernan's death. Now she would have to tell their daughter, Gail, not yet eight. It was a warm June day. She knew that there would be no keeping the news from her daughter, that sooner or later it would seep out in the press. Besides, it had been years since her daughter had seen her father. Already Gail's memories of him were faint. Still the little girl carried inside of her a gnawing pain that she had not heard from him in so long.

She missed him terribly, and though she understood that her parents were divorced, in the way that any seven-year-old may be said to understand, she could not grasp why he had not come back to visit.

Darrell decided that she would take Gail to their special place, that it was there she should tell her of her father's death. From their home at 47 Fifteenth Street in Old Orchard Beach, mother and daughter drove to Kettle Cove near Cape Elizabeth. She parked in a lot where Gail could look out on Wood Island, the tiny island that as a toddler she had long imagined was China, where her father was working.

The windows were down. The car filled with the sweet sea air. Now Gail's eyes were again fixed on the island as her mother told her that her father would not be coming back. He had been killed far, far away. The little girl's eyes filled with tears, her stare still fixed on Wood Island, as if it were there that her father had died.

. . .

It was an equally sunny afternoon in Fairfax, California, as Mackiernan's twins were taking their afternoon nap in the cribs and Pegge Mackiernan was finishing defrosting the refrigerator. There was a knock at the door. It was a gentleman from Washington, a Mr. Freeman. Pegge was embarrassed at the clutter in her living room but showed him in anyway.

He waited until she had taken a seat on the sofa. He was brief and to the point. Doug, he said, had been killed trying to cross into Tibet. Her husband, he said, had already been buried. Freeman was a man with broad shoulders, and from the moment he had entered the room, he seemed to fill it. Now he expressed condolences on behalf of all those in Washington. Before he left, he advised Pegge: "Say nothing to the newspapers. Keep your own counsel. Be so grief-stricken that you can't speak to anyone, and if you have a problem, let me know."

Pegge Mackiernan was now a widow with twins. Between changing diapers and caring for Mary and Mike, she barely had time to grieve. A few days later, on June 12, 1950, she made a humble request of the State

Department: that her husband's remains be cremated in Lhasa and then returned to the United States. At least then, she and the twins would have a place to stand in remembrance.

But the U.S government did not convey her request. It concluded that it could not ask this of the Tibetan government, given that the grave was some four weeks' travel from Lhasa and that the country was already absorbed in a struggle for its own survival against Communist China.

. . .

Even after Mackiernan's death, the CIA and State Department considered the incident extremely sensitive. A memo stamped "Top Secret," dated July 13, 1950, notes that "survivors of the Mackiernan party as long as they are in Tibet are in danger of assassination by Communist agents if latter have opportunity." But word of Mackiernan's death reached the world in a July 29, 1950, front-page article in the *New York Times*, datelined Calcutta. The story reported that Mackiernan, the vice-consul of Tihwa, had been shot at the border.

That same day, the State Department issued a press release announcing Mackiernan's death. Immediately after, the killing of Vice-Consul Mackiernan was carried in newspapers across the country. But there would be no reference to the Central Intelligence Agency, or to the true nature of his mission.

Even as the CIA and State Department prepared to sort out the death benefits due Mackiernan's widow and children, there was a growing concern that Tibet itself would soon be lost to the Communists. On August 7, 1950, the U.S. embassy in New Delhi cabled Washington, warning that Tibetan officials were extremely anxious about their fate and were unsure whether to negotiate with the Chinese Communists or to resist invasion. The cable noted that a Tibetan oracle had advised that they should resist, and Tibetan forces were experiencing some success in border clashes, emboldening them.

New Delhi referred to "wild rumors" circulating that the Chinese were massing along the border ready to invade. Tibetan nobles had fled. Food and fuel in the capital were already scarce. The Tibetans were feeling abandoned and ignored by both India and the United States.

It was this moment that news of Mackiernan's murder swept through the capital of Lhasa. There the Mackiernan incident was interpreted not merely as a tragedy or border mishap but as a grim omen. "They seem to be extremely sad at the turn of events and are now attributing the incident to the destiny of Tibet," the report from New Delhi observed.

Tibetan officials seized upon the arrival of Bessac as an opportunity to send a message of desperation to Washington. No sooner had he arrived than Bessac became a kind of diplomatic courier carrying a plea for military support to hold off the impending Chinese invasion. On August 30, 1950, Bessac arrived in New Delhi. With him he carried a letter from the Tibetan government addressed to Secretary of State Acheson and stamped "Top Secret." The letter was an urgent request for howitzers, cannons, machine guns, and bazookas. It implored Acheson to approach President Truman on Tibet's behalf.

And in a bid to mollify the United States, the Tibetan government dispatched a photographer to take a picture of Mackiernan's grave. It was sent along with a letter of condolence to the State Department to be forwarded to his widow, Pegge. But the letter and photo were never forwarded. Instead, they ended up in a dusty box at the U.S. Archives.

In late September Mackiernan's personal possessions were removed from a government safe and returned to his widow. Among the few items were twenty-seven war savings bonds, a Mongolian dictionary, his divorce decree from Darrell, a bill of sale for a 1941 Mercury coupe, and a photo of the twins. There were still many loose ends. Mackiernan had died without a will.

But he was not forgotten. On October 18, 1950, Secretary of State Acheson honored some fifteen diplomats during an hour-long ceremony in the department's auditorium. A single posthumous medal of service was presented to Douglas Mackiernan, Vice-Consul, Tihwa. On the west wall of the State Department's lobby, his name was inscribed among the columns of diplomats killed in the line of service. In death as in life, he would be remembered only by his cover story. His name would be the first CIA officer remembered on the State Department tablets, but it would hardly be the last.

Two days after the ceremony, L. T. Merchant, a State Department official from the Far East Division, met with Pegge Mackiernan. Later he expressed the department's "deep regret over the tragic death of her husband but told her that she and her children should take comfort from the fact that he had truly died a hero's death for his country."

Merchant asked if there was anything he could do for her. Pegge said she would need a job. As a former newspaperwoman, she wondered if she might work for the State Department as an information officer. And she wanted to return to that part of the world she and Doug knew best—Asia. In particular, she hoped to be close to where her husband had fallen.

The department was eager to help the thirty-one-year-old widow and her two-year-old twins. On March 15, 1951, the State Department could claim another "Vice-Consul Mackiernan," as Pegge Mackiernan was assigned to Lahore in northern Pakistan. It was the State Department's closest posting to where her husband had been killed. The twins would, for the time being, stay with Mackiernan's parents.

Not long after, Pegge Mackiernan traveled to Bombay, India, and sought out Angus Thurmer, the CIA's chief of base there. She entered his embassy office and closed the door behind her. "I have reason to believe my late husband, Doug Mackiernan, was not only a State Department officer but had other allegiances," she said quietly. "Among his effects I found this and I thought you could send it to the proper place."

With that, she unwrapped a hand towel and produced the largest revolver Thurmer had ever seen. The long barrel reminded him of one of those old six-shooters from the Wild West. Thurmer disassembled the gun, placed it inside an Agency sack, and put the package inside the diplomatic pouch to be returned to CIA headquarters. He also sent a cable giving the Agency a heads-up that the revolver was on its way. He had never met Mackiernan. He had only heard rumors that one of their own had been killed on the Tibetan border.

Little more than a year later, on October 20, 1952, Pegge Mackiernan remarried in a Jesuit cathedral in Bombay. The groom was John Hlavacek, a journalist for United Press.

Among the thousands of pages of State Department records today in the U.S. Archives relating to Mackiernan, there is but one incidental reference to the CIA. Following Mackiernan's death, the CIA's first general counsel, Lawrence Houston, formerly assistant general counsel of the

OSS, requested that Undersecretary of State Carlisle Humelsine settle up the Mackiernan estate. That meant drafting a check for $658.90 for Mackiernan's father. Ironically it was Houston that in September 1947 had advised CIA Director Hillenkoetter that the Agency had no legislative authority to conduct covert operations—at the very time that Mackiernan was doing just that.

In late November 1951 the State Department decided to ask the Tibetan government to compensate the Mackiernan family for his wrongful death. The amount sought: $50,000. But the U.S. Embassy in New Delhi argued that Tibet was already in crisis because of the Chinese Communists, and that any such request for money might suggest the United States was hostile to them or deserting them in their hour of need. Concluding the matter was "politically inadvisable," the State Department dropped the request for compensation.

As for those who resisted the Communists and whom Mackiernan had aided, they fared no better. In February 1951 the guerrilla leader Wussman Bator and one hundred of his followers were arrested in China. Another five thousand "bandits" had been killed, wounded, or captured, according to Beijing. The Chinese government publicly charged that Mackiernan had been "an American imperialist agent," a spy, who had orchestrated the resistance against the Communists. The State Department dismissed the allegation as "the usual tripe."

A year to the day after Mackiernan was murdered, Wussman was executed, according to the Chinese, in front of ten thousand cheering citizens. Beijing boasted that when its troops searched Mackiernan's house, they found an entire arsenal—153 charges of high explosives, radio equipment, and 1,835 rounds of ammunition. According to testimony during the public trial of Wussman, Mackiernan had set up a kind of "Revolutionary Committee" with Wussman. Its purpose was to recruit battalions of Kazakhs who would lead a campaign of harassment against the Communists.

Mackiernan's first wife, Darrell, meanwhile was occupied trying to ensure the financial well-being of her daughter, Gail. She persuaded a U.S. senator from Maine, Margaret Chase Smith, to introduce a bill into Congress that would provide $15,000 "as a gratuity to compensate . . . Gail Mackiernan for the loss of her father." The measure failed to win passage. Instead, the government awarded a portion of Mackiernan's death benefits—$47.15 per month—to Darrell and her daughter.

Mackiernan's body was never returned to the States. The exact location of his grave, somewhere near Shigarhung Lung along the Tibetan border, has long since been lost. Over the course of succeeding decades the few at the Central Intelligence Agency who knew Mackiernan or of his CIA employment either passed away or retired. His name, his mission, and his ordeal were, in time, utterly forgotten, erased as thoroughly as if he had never existed.

He was destined to be the CIA's first nameless star. But there was something Douglas Mackiernan had feared even more than death—imprisonment at the hands of the Chinese Communists. That fate was reserved for another covert operative not long after him.

CHAPTER 2

A Pin for St. Jude

IN A MODEST working-class neighborhood of Yonkers, New York, Bill McInenly dutifully retrieved from the basement a mahogany box containing what little was left from his Uncle Hughie's life. He placed the small treasure chest squarely on the dining room table and reverently lifted back the lid. Inside, neatly arrayed in a wooden drawer resting on slats, were all the objects Ruth Redmond could salvage of her son's life. A medal from the Boy Scouts. Honors for winning the broad jump and high jump at Roosevelt High. A silver cigarette lighter with the initials "HR" for "Hugh Redmond." He so loved his smokes.

Here was his weathered Selective Service card. It showed he did not wait for the outbreak of war to be summoned to service, but enlisted on July 1, 1941. He had blue eyes, it said, blond hair, and a fair complexion. He stood but five feet four inches and weighed 155 pounds. Actually his eyes were a pale and gentle blue, his hair thick and wavy, his complexion white as flour. And there was nothing diminutive about him. His frame was broad and taut.

Beside the Selective Service card was a small box holding a collection of military patches, among them the Screaming Eagle from the 101st Airborne. There were also a lieutenant's bars and a sharpshooter's medal.

From the contents of the box it might appear Redmond was among the lucky ones. On June 6, 1944—D-Day—he landed near the Douve River in Normandy. Of the twenty paratroopers in his group, he alone was neither wounded nor killed. Here, in an old box of matches, was a twisted and dark fragment of metal. With it was a note held by yellowing tape. It reads, "Shrapnel dug out of hip in hospital in Brussels, 1944." This was a personal souvenir of his fight in the Market-Garden campaign in Holland. The date was September 22, 1944. Again he had been lucky.

But Redmond's luck faltered at the Battle of the Bulge. His wounds required a year in a hospital bed. Set into a blue leather box was his Purple Heart "for Military Merit." A Silver Star. A Bronze Star with Oak Leaf Clusters. Beside it was a certificate of discharge from the military dated October 18, 1945. After that, judging from the contents of this drawer, he simply ceased to exist.

Mixed in with the possessions of Hugh Francis Redmond were a few things of his mother's, Ruth's. A small religious pin of St. Jude, her patron saint. On the back is inscribed "Apostle of Hopeless Cases." No other saint could have understood so well Ruth Redmond's prayers or vigil.

Beneath the drawer was a chest full of old newspapers, a passport, a birthday card to Hugh that was returned. Here and there was a scattering of old Chinese coins.

A box of clues. A life reduced to mystery.

Moments later Bill McInenly went back to the basement and returned with a second, less decorous box. This one was more of a rubber tub, blue and covered with a snap-on lid. It was the kind of container in which one might find beers on ice at a tailgate party. But inside, carefully folded to a perfect triangle, was a musty American flag.

. . .

Any telling of Hugh Francis Redmond's life must begin where the contents of his nephew's box ends. It is Shanghai, China, on April 26, 1951—just three days shy of a year after Douglas Mackiernan was gunned down on the Tibetan border. Thirty-two-year-old Hugh Redmond was now living the good life overseas. But that good life appeared threatened as the Communists tightened their stranglehold on activities in Shanghai. All foreigners were under suspicion.

A short time earlier, Redmond had secretly married. His bride was named Lydia, though he affectionately called her Lily. She was a White Russian and a piano teacher, a dark-haired and shapely woman who some would say was a femme fatale. With Redmond's help she had managed to leave China. Now it was his turn. He prepared to board a ship, the USS *Gordon*. But Redmond's voyage was abruptly ended even before it began.

Police from China's dreaded Public Security Bureau boarded the ship, escorted Redmond off, and led him away without explanation. Almost immediately rumors began to circulate around Shanghai and Washington that he had been executed.

The Chinese Communist regime under Mao Zedong had rounded up many foreigners, even missionaries attempting to spread the gospel. But Redmond was a case apart. As a commercial representative of Henningsen and Company, a British concern that specialized in the import and export of foods, Redmond appeared to be little more than a salesman—hardly a threat to Mao's regime. Never one to raise his voice, Redmond seemed so ordinary a fellow that even at the smallest of gatherings he was all but invisible. It was no wonder, then, that when the police pinched him off the ship, he literally vanished.

His parents had grown accustomed to long periods without a letter from him. But even they, in time, began to worry when they didn't hear from him, especially his mother. She was a cafeteria worker in a Yonkers public school. But it was not his personal life or business that kept her awake at nights. No, there were things that she knew about him, things that she had sworn not to discuss with anyone, that gave her ample cause for concern. His very life might depend on her discretion.

Ruth Redmond knew only that her son had joined a shadowy element of the War Department called the Strategic Services Unit, or SSU, and had gone to China on some sort of secret mission. In late August Hugh Redmond had arrived in Shanghai. His work as an import-export trader with Henningsen and Company was merely a cover, providing him the perfect pretext for travel and contact with the Chinese.

Even in the midst of China's tumultuous revolution, he appeared to prosper. On August 22, 1946, he wrote his parents: "I am living in the French section of Shanghai on the Rue De Ratard—a very nice section of town. The house has large grounds and gardens, two tennis courts, a big patio, a bar in the dining room and plenty of recreational equipment—pool tables, etc. Countless Chinese servants are running around to do anything you want." Unfortunately, wrote Redmond, he would soon have to vacate these opulent surroundings.

"Nothing much to say, everything quiet here except the Communists," he wrote. In a postscript he added, "May not write for quite a while."

"A while" stretched on month after month. A worried Ruth Redmond wrote the State Department in September 1949—long before her son's arrest—to see if the government could provide any clue as to his whereabouts. A State Department employee, unaware of Redmond's covert status, cabled Hong Kong and made inquiries of him with his employer, Henningsen and Company. A spokesman for the firm said they had no record of a Hugh Redmond working for them. The State Department concluded Ruth Redmond was confused.

But the response alarmed Ruth Redmond even more. She saw it for what it was, a slipup in the cover story. At her request the State Department made a second inquiry with the British consulate in Shanghai. They confirmed that Redmond did indeed work for Henningsen and that he was just fine. For the moment her concerns were eased.

But her underlying fears persisted. For two years the United States had been urging its citizens to leave mainland China. It could no longer offer them protection or assistance. Red China, as it was known, was not recognized by the United States. There was neither an American embassy in China nor any official U.S. presence there. Anyone who stayed did so at his or her own peril.

Like Mackiernan, Redmond understood that each day he stayed in China the risk increased. Finally his superiors decided it was time to pull the plug on his operation. An encrypted message was sent to his apartment. It read simply, "Enjoy the dance." But Redmond delayed his departure a brief time longer, tidying up his affairs there.

At the time of Redmond's arrest in the spring of 1951, there were an estimated 415 Americans still in mainland China. On April 30, 1951, four days after Redmond's arrest, the State Department compiled a secret list of Americans believed to be imprisoned in China. There were then thought to be twenty-three, eighteen of whom were missionaries. Beside Redmond's name was this notation: "may be executed." Four months later an embassy memo from Hong Kong to Secretary of State Acheson reported that "it was common belief among Chi [Chinese] and foreigners that Commies had proof against him and had executed him for espionage." The rumors were credible enough. Virtually any American still in China was suspected of spying.

There was no way of knowing if Redmond was still alive. Americans in Chinese prisons were held incommunicado. They had no right to a lawyer. Some were tortured. Few had been formally charged, though many had been accused of a wide range of offenses—plotting against the government, spreading rumors, illegal possession of radios, currency violations, fomenting disorder, and even murdering Chinese orphans.

The U.S. government kept silent on Redmond's fate, as it did with nearly all those believed to be imprisoned in China. Taking the issue public might make the Chinese even more resistant to the idea of eventually releasing them. It might also endanger their lives. Behind the scenes, the State Department persuaded Britain and eight other nations to inquire about the well-being of Redmond and other prisoners and to work for their release.

On October 19, 1951, the secret list of Americans held by the Chinese—which included Redmond's name—was provided by Assistant Secretary of State Dean Rusk to U.S. Senator William Knowland at the senator's request. Knowland had pledged that the list would remain confidential. But on December 8 Knowland released the names to the press and issued a blistering denunciation of the Chinese. The next day Redmond's name surfaced publicly for the first time in front pages around the nation.

And that was how Ruth Redmond first discovered that her son had been imprisoned, or even executed. Given what she knew of her son's covert employment with the government, she was horrified that no one from the intelligence service had informed her of her son's situation. She might have been even more disturbed if she had known that by then her son had been largely forgotten by those in the recently reorganized clandestine service.

On December 18, 1951, she penned a letter addressed simply

"State Department, Washington D.C." It read: "Dear Sirs, I have a son in China for the last few years. I naturally have been worried about him continually but was shocked beyond words to read in the newspapers that he has been in prison in Shanghai since April 26, 1951. This is the first news of any kind I have had of him. For obvious reasons he was listed as a businessman. After three years on the battlefield in Europe and now this—is there any hope for my only son? Is it possible to find out if he is well, if he is hungry, if he is mistreated. Can we write to him, can he receive any packages from us and is *anything being done to secure his release?* Thank you for any information you may have. I am sincerely, Mrs. Ruth Redmond. My son's name, Hugh Francis Redmond."

· · ·

There can be little doubt that Hugh Redmond understood the risks of his assignment. On July 24, 1946, just nine months after he had left the army, he joined a top secret intelligence organization within the War Department. Like many highly decorated veterans of World War II, he was eager to continue his service to country, but he had suffered grave wounds in the war. It was doubtful that he would have been eligible for active military duty. And so, like many other casualties of war, he sought out the next closest thing—the clandestine service. In those early days the corridors of the clandestine service had more than their share of men with limps, eye patches, and other tokens of war.

Redmond had joined the Strategic Services Unit, the SSU. After President Truman ordered the Office of Strategic Services (OSS) to be dismembered as of October 1, 1945, critical elements of that organization, particularly the Secret Intelligence and Counter-Espionage branches, were assigned to the SSU. The unit was initially under Colonel John Magruder, who had been Wild Bill Donovan's deputy director of intelligence at the OSS. SSU's role was to maintain networks of foreign agents, safe houses, and other vital elements of the intelligence apparatus in both Europe and the Far East. What remained from the glory years of the OSS was little more than a skeletal secret service. SSU would later be folded into the Central Intelligence Group, or CIG (created on January 22, 1946), and would finally become part of the Central Intelligence Agency when it was created in 1947.

With each change in name and function, the intelligence corps and its mission became more muddied, the bureaucracy more mired in paperwork and interservice rivalries. By the time of Redmond's arrest in April 1951, it had undergone so many transformations that Hugh Francis Redmond had been all but forgotten. His supervisors had been shuffled about from place to place, and Redmond, already out of country for four years, was at best a vague memory, a series of dusty file jackets in the bowels of a confused bureaucracy.

From the start his mission had been high-risk. Some might say foolhardy.

In January 1951, four months before Redmond was seized, the CIA drafted a secret memo for the National Security Council and the president. It laid out what it knew of Mao Zedong's China and the prospects for dislodging him. Titled "Position of the United States with Respect to Communist China," it was a sober read. "For the foreseeable future," the memo began, "the Chinese Communist regime will retain exclusive governmental control of mainland China. No basis for a successful counterrevolution is apparent. The disaffected elements within the country are weak, divided, leaderless and devoid of any constructive political program."

The only opposition remaining, the Agency concluded, was bandits, some minor peasant uprisings, and "actual guerrilla forces, made up of Nationalist remnants, Communist deserters, adventurers, and a few ideological opponents of the regime." It was a dire take on events in China. The best that CIA clandestine operatives could hope for would be to create diversions that, for the time being, might distract if not contain the Chinese military. Seen in that light, Hugh Redmond was a double casualty. He had been sent into an impossible situation and then had fallen through the bureaucratic cracks.

While Doug Mackiernan had been gathering intelligence on the far western front of China, Redmond had been busy in the east, operating out of that country's major economic center, Shanghai. Mackiernan and Redmond were both early versions of CIA case officers. Their job, in the lingo of the Agency, could be reduced to three simple terms—spotting, recruiting, and running agents. Contrary to popular literature and film, "agents" were not employees of the Agency but foreign nationals with access to information, documents, or matériel that could be of national security interest to the United States.

Most case officers were like Mackiernan. They operated under "official cover," meaning that to the rest of the world they worked for the U.S. government but in a consular or embassy position. They often melted into the ranks of lower-level diplomats. But Redmond, posing as a businessman, enjoyed no such official cover. He was, in the jargon of espionage, a NOC, an acronym for "nonofficial cover." Such cover is deemed deeper and more difficult to penetrate, but also affords less protection if the person's cover is compromised. Without the guise of diplomatic cover, a covert operative is more vulnerable to arrest and incarceration for espionage. All the more so in the case of Hugh Redmond, who did not limit himself to gathering intelligence, but actively supported those engaged in resistance efforts and sabotage.

For the CIA, still in its infancy, the disappearance of Hugh Redmond, while disturbing, was hardly of major import. The Cold War had turned decidedly hot with the advent of the Korean conflict. The Agency's inability to predict that monumental event, following so close on the heels of its failure to forewarn of a Soviet A-bomb, further eroded confidence in its skills.

Even the Agency's director, General Walter Bedell Smith, conceded that the CIA was not yet up to the tasks that faced it. Once-secret minutes from an October 27, 1952, meeting note: "The Director, mentioning that the Agency had recently experienced some difficulties in various parts of the world, remarked that these difficulties stemmed, by and large, from the use of improperly trained or inferior personnel. He stated that until CIA could build a reserve of well-trained people, it would have to hold its activities to the limited number of operations that it could do well rather than to attempt to cover a broad field with poor performance." Bolstering the ranks with highly trained officers was to be a top priority in the years ahead.

Adding to that pressure was the very real threat of atomic espionage and the witch-hunts of Senator Joseph McCarthy from which not even the Agency itself was exempt. On November 1, 1952, the United States detonated the first hydrogen bomb, over the Marshall Islands, all but vaporizing the island. It was a none-too-subtle warning to Moscow and Beijing that the United States was not to be taken lightly.

But anti-Communist hysteria was rampant. Senator McCarthy held the government hostage with his bogus list of Communist infiltrators and his choreographed hearings. The very culture of the country seemed obsessed with "the Red Scare." In 1952 the film *High Noon* was released. Billed as a cowboy movie, it was a thinly veiled allegory of the plight of liberals and leftists nationwide and of the impact of fear and suspicion on a community.

The next year the Rosenbergs, Julius and Ethel, were electrocuted for selling atomic secrets to the Soviets. That same year *Casino Royale*, by British author Ian Fleming, was published. It introduced readers to suave and swashbuckling James Bond, Agent 007, who liked his martinis "stirred not shaken." Redmond and Mackiernan, trained in maintaining invisibility, would have scoffed at such high-profile antics.

Throughout these early years the CIA was busy trying to keep up with an ever-expanding mandate. Resigned to the fact that it had little chance of actually toppling the Soviet Union or China, it contented itself with sponsoring behind-the-lines acts of sabotage designed to divert and frustrate the two Communist giants who were seen as bent on expansionism. It also resolved that it would blunt any attempt to spread Marxism beyond the Communist states' existing borders. That meant turning its attention and resources to those regimes and proxy states that tilted even remotely to the left.

But the Agency's successes would have been of little consolation to Ruth Redmond. On May 20, 1952, more than a year after her son's disappearance, she wrote U.S. Senator Herbert Lehman, "My son is one of the Americans held in prison for more than a year and so far nothing has been done to secure his release—one cannot help but ask why a country like ours for which he fought in World War Two can be so lax in behalf of her people. My one ambition is to again see my only son and beseech you to add your efforts in his and the other Americans behalf by appealing to the Dept. of State to take effective action."

Month after month Redmond's name appeared on the State Department's internal list of Chinese prisoners, always accompanied by the notation "may be executed." Even if somehow Redmond was alive, his condition was likely to be grim. In July 1952 the State Department interviewed an American attorney named Robert Bryan, who had been in Shanghai's notorious Ward Road jail—where Redmond, too, would have been held, if he was still alive. Bryan had been living in Shanghai for years and had been arrested just two months before Redmond. He was placed in "the death cell," given a leaky bucket as a latrine, and branded an "American imperialist pig" by his captors. His treatment gave the State Department a picture of what Redmond, too, might be going through.

"Your hands are stained with the blood of our comrades," the Chinese had shouted at Bryan. He was subjected to an endless barrage of indoctrination and interrogation. He was beaten with a rubber hose. He was held in solitary confinement and lost forty-six pounds. Twice, he said, he was given a spinal injection of some kind of truth serum. Finally he signed a series of confessions and on June 26 was released and placed on a train to Hong Kong and freedom.

That summer, eighteen other Americans in prison or under house arrest were also set free. In the months after, more were released, many of them missionaries who had been tortured. But those stories were largely stifled at the State Department's request. Reports of brutality, they feared, could inflame the Chinese and endanger those Americans still captive.

But Redmond's arrest had no effect on the CIA's pursuing its high-risk operations against China. Notwithstanding its own findings that the Communist regime was firmly in command and control of the country, it continued to support and equip cells of resistance on the mainland, taking enormous risks in the process. One of those gambles went badly awry.

On November 29, 1952, an unmarked C-47 Dakota based in Japan and equipped with flame suppressors to render it less visible at night was flying over Manchuria on a top secret mission. On board were two American pilots, seven Taiwanese agents set to infiltrate the mainland and set up a communications post, and two covert CIA officers overseeing the operation. One of these Agency officers was twenty-five-year-old John T. Downey, nephew of the singer Morton Downey. A classic Agency blue blood, he was the son of a Connecticut judge. He had attended Choate, where he was voted "most likely to succeed," and Yale, where he was captain of the wrestling team. Downey had been one of thirty Yale students the spring of his senior year who had been drawn to a CIA recruitment notice posted on the New Haven campus. He and the others were wooed by an Agency recruiter, a tweedy veteran of the OSS who smoked a pipe and wore a Yale tie. Immediately after graduating in June 1951, Downey enlisted. Back then, the Agency was so young that most of these natty recruits had never even heard of the CIA.

The other Agency man aboard the C-47 that night was twenty-two-year-old Richard G. Fecteau. He was a shy and withdrawn man, a twin and father of twin three-year-old daughters.

At a preset rendezvous point the plane, part of the CIA proprietary airline Civil Air Transport, was to descend and scoop up an agent in a sling, then go on to drop a team of Chinese Nationalist paratroopers into the Manchurian foothills. As the plane came in on its approach, it came under small-arms fire and crashed. The two pilots, Robert Snoddy and Norman Schwartz, died in the crash and were buried on the spot. Their graves were never found. The paratroopers were executed by the Chinese. As for CIA officers Downey and Fecteau, nothing more was heard from them. Like Redmond, they had vanished.

The United States, clinging to the Agency's cover story, said Downey and Fecteau had been employees of the Defense Department on a routine flight between Seoul and Tokyo. Out of public view the CIA silently mourned the loss of Downey and Fecteau, as did the mothers and widows they left behind.

By then, more than a year had passed since Redmond's disappearance. The presumption was that he, too, was dead.

Then, on March 29, 1953, a former German citizen who had been held in a Shanghai jail since March 1951 was released and arrived in Hong Kong. With him he brought the first word of Hugh Redmond. Between March and October 1951 the German had occupied a cell next to Redmond in the Lokawei military barracks. At the time, he reported, Redmond appeared to be receiving relatively "soft treatment" in an effort to get him to confess to espionage. Then later, between March 17 and 24, 1952, at the Ward Road prison he could hear Redmond being interrogated on the floor below.

Others released from Chinese prisons later told U.S. authorities that while they had not seen or heard anything of Redmond, those who had associated with him prior to his arrest were being rounded up and charged with espionage.

By the fall of 1953 the State Department had begun to worry even more about the well-being of Redmond and the other twenty-eight Americans still held by the Chinese. Another winter was approaching. At least five Americans had already perished in Chinese prisons, presumably from maltreatment.

. . .

In November 1953, a year after the downing of the plane carrying Agency officers John Downey and Richard Fecteau, the CIA assembled a panel of experts in a conference room in the Curie Building, one of the temporary structures beside the Potomac. They gathered to weigh all available intelligence and decide whether it was reasonable to conclude that Downey and Fecteau were dead. Present that day was a representative from the general counsel's office, an Agency physician, another from operations in the Far East Division, and someone knowledgeable about the terrain and conditions of the crash site. Also present was Ben DeFelice, soon to be named chief of the Casualty Affairs Branch.

Then, and in the decades ahead, it was DeFelice who was the liaison between the Agency and the families of those CIA employees who were imprisoned, killed in the performance of duty, or missing in action. It was a difficult job, balancing the need for continued security and secrecy with the demands of compassion and patience. DeFelice would repeatedly do battle with the bureaucracy on behalf of those who had suffered a loss. His gentle hand would assuage the grief of generations of widows and children orphaned by the not-so-cold Cold War, even as he reminded the families of the need to maintain silence.

It was DeFelice who inherited the Redmond, Downey, and Fecteau cases and who redefined how the Agency would help stricken families while shielding the Agency from unwanted exposure. He would quietly remind them that if the press should make inquiries, nothing need be said.

DeFelice would draft letters of condolence to the widows or widowers of those who suffered losses. Those letters would find their way to the desk of the Director Central Intelligence and go out under the director's name. So it was with Allen Dulles, Richard Helms, George Bush, and the other Directors Central Intelligence.

Such letters would typically be hand-delivered to the wi
after the funeral. The widow would be permitted to read the l
then, in the interest of national security, she would be asked to return
it to the Agency officer who was present. The letter would then be
placed in the deceased's personnel file and the widow or widower
would be left without any potentially embarrassing evidence to link the
decedent to the CIA. As DeFelice would tell the grieving widow, he
didn't want to burden her unnecessarily. Medals, too, would often be
presented and then immediately withdrawn and secured in the personnel file at headquarters.

In November 1953 DeFelice and other Agency officers gathered for
the sober purpose of reviewing the Downey and Fecteau files. After a person had been missing for a year, the Agency was empowered, under the
Missing Persons Act, to deliberate whether it was reasonable to conclude
that he or she was dead. After a year there had been not even a hint that
the two CIA airmen had survived the shoot-down of their aircraft over
Manchuria. The terrain of the crash site was rough and it was known to
be rife with wolves. Had they been lucky enough to outlive the crash and
avoid the hail of gunfire, then the wolves would surely have devoured
them.

That was the official conclusion reached by DeFelice and the other
CIA panelists that day as they issued a formal "Presumptive Finding of
Death." With that finding in hand, DeFelice could start the process of releasing workers' compensation benefits to the families of the two men, as
well as insurance proceeds. The case was closed, a copy of the finding was
placed in the men's personnel folders, and benefits were settled. The
Agency explained to the Fecteau and Downey families that no mention
was ever to be made of their loved ones' connection to the Agency. Both
families honored that request.

. . .

Meanwhile the fate of Hugh Redmond remained clouded. It would
be some time before anyone at the CIA would take a personal interest or
even be made aware of Redmond's fate. That person was Harlan Westrell.
He had joined the Agency in 1948. By the mid-1950s he was chief of
counterintelligence in the Agency's Office of Security. His office was in

the decrepit Tempo I building. When it rained, the roof leaked. On sweltering days, and there were many, he had to peel off the classified papers that stuck to his forearms.

By all rights, the Redmond case should never have found its way to Westrell's desk. It had little if anything to do with counterintelligence. Westrell's job, among others, was to ferret out so-called penetrations, to look for moles and evidence that the Agency's security had been breached. It was not an easy job. He was often butting heads with FBI Director J. Edgar Hoover, who refused to cooperate with Agency investigations. Hoover was still steamed that the FBI had been forced to relinquish to the CIA its intelligence jurisdiction over Central and South America. Westrell was also preoccupied with fending off Joe McCarthy's accusations that the Communists had plants throughout the CIA.

Sometimes Westrell's responsibilities bordered on the absurd. In one instance, he was called upon to dispatch one of his staffers to head up a CIA team consisting of a chemist knowledgeable about poisons, a physician, and an operative. The team leader was James W. McCord, later one of the Watergate burglars. Their mission was to investigate whether someone was slowly poisoning the U.S. ambassador to Italy, Clare Boothe Luce. The team concluded that Luce was not the target of any plot, but that over time, flakes of paint containing lead had fallen into her nightly glass of wine.

Westrell was also responsible for protecting case officers under deep cover from being exposed. The name of each such operative was written on a three-by-five index card—just the name, nothing else. If someone inside or outside the Agency made an unauthorized inquiry about one of those individuals, Westrell's staff would investigate. His entire office was inside a vault. The cards containing the names of scores of deep-cover operatives like Redmond were locked in a safe within the vault each night.

Precisely how and when Redmond's name and fate came to Westrell's attention is not clear. An Agency unit called the Contact Division, which interviewed travelers returning from trips overseas, had learned from the International Rescue Committee that a recent émigré named Lydia Redmond, an attractive woman of Russian descent, was claiming that she was married to an American government employee who had been arrested in China. At the time, Lydia Redmond was living in Milwaukee.

The report piqued concern for Hugh Redmond's well-being but also raised questions about his judgment. He had not mentioned to either his family or Agency superiors that he had gotten married. Simply fraternizing with a foreign national—especially one of Russian descent—would have raised eyebrows. A marriage would not only have been subjected to close scrutiny but might even have been seen as a career-ending error in judgment.

Word of Lydia Redmond filtered down to security chief Sheffield Edwards, who asked Westrell to investigate Lydia Redmond's claim. Westrell assigned it to the CIA's Chicago field office. A preliminary inquiry suggested that she was telling the truth, though the Redmond family knew nothing of the marriage and there was nothing in the old SSU files to support the claim. But then, the files were woefully incomplete.

Westrell arranged for Lydia Redmond to move to the Washington area. He helped her get a job with the Veterans Administration and an apartment in Arlington, Virginia. At their first meeting the two dined at (appropriately enough) a Chinese restaurant, the Moon Palace, on Washington's Wisconsin Avenue. The restaurant was new and they were its first customers. Lydia spoke Chinese to the waiter.

The deeper Westrell looked into the Redmond case, the more he was convinced that in the confusion that followed the transfer of SSU's functions to CIG and then to CIA, Redmond had fallen through the cracks.

He decided to go to Yonkers to meet Redmond's mother, Ruth. She had not heard anything from her son in more than two years. In Yonkers Westrell later selected a local lawyer, Sol Friedman, to be the Agency's "front man" representing Mrs. Redmond's interests and keeping the Agency informed of her situation.

· · ·

What little was known of Hugh Redmond's situation came from interviews with those few Americans and foreign nationals who were released from Chinese prisons and later debriefed after entering Hong Kong. The one observation shared by all was that Redmond had remained steadfastly defiant of his Chinese captors.

It was ironic that, even as Redmond stood his ground, refusing to confess to espionage or to bend to relentless efforts at indoctrination, his own agency, the CIA, had become fascinated with the idea of mind control. Many were convinced that the Chinese possessed the ability to "brainwash" a man, to break his resistance and render him a willing pawn. During the Korean War the Agency watched in horror as some American servicemen held by their captors mouthed Communist propaganda. A few even opted to defect. In an effort to understand that power—and to acquire it for themselves—the CIA, under its esteemed director, Allen Dulles, began a massive research program into mind control in 1953. The idea was partly that of Richard Helms, himself destined to become one of the most powerful and controversial of CIA directors. Code-named MKULTRA, the program involved the testing of LSD and other psychoactive drugs.

On November 18, 1953, one such experiment went terribly awry as an army civilian researcher named Dr. Frank Olson was unwittingly administered a dose of LSD. In the days following, Olson became depressed and underwent changes in his personality. The CIA, alarmed at his behavior, sent him to New York for psychiatric treatment. Eight days after the LSD was administered, Olson hurled himself through the window of his tenth-floor room at the Statler Hotel, plunging to his death.

After Olson's death, the cause of which was concealed from the public for two decades, the CIA decided it was imperative to have someone from its Office of Security present each time someone was administered LSD or other psychoactive drugs. It was Harlan Westrell and his office that were called upon to provide such protective services. The MKULTRA program continued unabated until 1961. During that time the American public knew nothing of the Agency's mind-altering experiments.

When a more detailed account of Redmond's condition finally surfaced, the news was not good. On April 23, 1954, the American consulate in Hong Kong sent a cable to Secretary of State Dulles reporting on its interview with a French Catholic priest who had just been released from a Chinese prison. The priest said he had secret conversations with Redmond and shared a cell with him from September 16, 1953, until April 19, 1954. Redmond was being held in Shanghai's Rue Massenet jail under tight surveillance.

The cable noted: "He is in a cell with Chinese prisoners, forbidden talk with them and given minimum exercise, low grade food, minimum medical care to sustain life. His spirits are quite good, he resists minor tyrannies of guards and interrogators, and steadfastly refuses confess accusations of espionage and possession of arms." But the prolonged incarceration was taking its toll. His health was deteriorating. For violating minor prison rules, his hands and feet were manacled. He had been interrogated relentlessly.

On June 2, 1954, the news was conveyed to Redmond's mother. She sent the State Department a note of thanks and asked if she might send food or clothing to her son or to write to him. "We have waited so long for news," she wrote.

On June 4, 1954, another Catholic priest, Father Alberto Palacios, was released from Shanghai's Lokawei jail, a special military facility reserved for political prisoners. On August 6 the consulate in Hong Kong sent a cable to Washington summarizing what Palacios had told them. Copies of the dispatch went to the CIA. Palacios reported that Redmond was completely without private funds and that he was wearing shoes provided him by prison authorities. His clothes were now little more than rags. He was no longer being interrogated, and though he was in good spirits his health was failing. He now had beriberi, near-constant diarrhea, and an inflammation of the corneas of his eyes. The prison guards were treating him with vitamins.

Redmond's prison routine was unvarying. He and the other prisoners were awakened at 5:30 A.M. and given half an hour to wash and relieve themselves. They were allowed forty-five minutes to sit on a cold wooden floor to meditate or read. Breakfast was liquid rice gruel and occasionally turnips. There was then an hour to clean the room and go to the toilet. Lunch was served at noon and consisted of dry rice and vegetables, supplemented with meat once a month. Three times a day, for fifteen minutes each, Redmond was allowed to walk around the nine-by-eighteen-foot cell. Dinner was rice and vegetables. Most days were to be spent in meditation or reading Communist literature, both of which Redmond steadfastly refused. There were times when he was forced to stand in a corner for up to forty-eight hours.

But after four years, Chinese prison officials had still made no progress in persuading him to confess or to embrace Communism.

Instead, Redmond was increasingly hostile. When the ventilator fan was loud enough to obscure his voice, he would sing lustily. He had hectored the guards into granting him certain small privileges denied to others, including being able to go to the bathroom unaccompanied. Though the prison did not allow smoking, he had cajoled his interrogators into granting him a cigarette before he would even acknowledge their presence. And when two female interrogators attempted to interview him in Russian, he refused to speak the language, forcing them to revert to English. Slowly but surely, it was the guards who seemed to be wearing down and Redmond who appeared to be gaining control over his captors.

Conversation with Redmond had been difficult. He and Father Palacios had to wait until another inmate, a Communist informant, was out of the cell. "I was put in for spying," Redmond confided to the priest. Redmond told him that no decision had yet been made in the case against him. He spoke briefly of his wife, now in the States. In the three years of his incarceration Redmond had acquired a commanding fluency in both Chinese and Russian. Each day he read Shakespeare and studied Russian grammar. The lad from Yonkers who had dropped out of Manhattan College after only a semester was becoming a scholar.

In June 1954 the Chinese sent a signal that perhaps they were softening their position on Americans held there. At meetings in Geneva, Switzerland, the Chinese delegation announced that it would allow packages and mail to be sent through the Red Cross Society of China to American prisoners. The State Department notified Ruth Redmond, who immediately sent several letters and packages to her son.

For the first time in years, Ruth Redmond felt a buoyancy, an unspoken hope that Hugh might soon be released and his suffering brought to an end. Then came crushing news.

On September 12, 1954, the Chinese government, through its state-controlled New China News Agency, announced that Redmond had been tried and convicted of spying. The sentence was life imprisonment. Redmond was one of eight people that day convicted by the Judge Advocate General's Department of the Shanghai Military Control Committee. The regime boasted that it had smashed a major espionage ring operating out of Shanghai. It detailed Redmond's activities, from the time he was dispatched to China in August 1946 to his alleged spying in

Mukden, Beijing, and Shanghai. The Chinese court said he had been part of a covert unit called the External Survey Detachment 44.

The other seven, five men and two women, were Chinese. Two of them, Wang Ko-yi and Lo Shih-hsiang, were sentenced to death and executed immediately—in front of Redmond. Wang, the Chinese said, had worked with the OSS. Under Redmond's direction, it said, he had set up radio transmitters, expanded the spy ring, and collected sensitive military and political secrets that were sent to U.S. intelligence officers in Hong Kong. They were also said to be preparing a campaign of sabotage.

The Chinese Public Security Bureau claimed that, in rounding up the spies, it had found a cache of sophisticated espionage equipment—five radio receiving and transmitting sets, sixteen secret codebooks, six bottles of chemical developer for invisible messages, a case of machine-gun bullets, a suitcase with hidden compartments, and hundreds of pages of instructions and credentials. At the center of it all was Hugh Francis Redmond. The State Department forwarded a copy of the Chinese press release to the CIA.

In response to the espionage conviction, the State Department issued a vigorous protest. It declared that Redmond was nothing more than an American businessman who had been falsely accused. Ruth Redmond, too, though knowing full well that the charges against her son were true, publicly proclaimed her son's innocence. The image of a poor working-class mother stricken with fear and anxiety over her son moved the entire community of Yonkers and much of the region around it to rally in support of Redmond's release. In the anti-Communist hysteria of the day, the Redmond case became an emotionally explosive piece of evidence that the Reds were utterly heartless and duplicitous.

The day after Redmond's conviction, the news was stripped across the top of Yonkers's *Herald Statesman:* "Chinese Reds Jail Yonkers Man for Life." The State Department was quoted as saying that espionage was a "favorite trumped up charge of the Communists." The day's lead editorial was headlined "Yonkers Neighbor Tastes Red Barbarism." The editorial spoke of Redmond's heroic service in World War II. "We may well pray that such a fighting spirit can weather the filthy Red prison cells, the handcuffs and brain-washing or other barbarism that the Commies invent and use on him. And we can understand—from our neighbor's plight—why we must be grimmer and more determined than ever that such proved barbarians have no place in any civilized aggregation like the United Nations, if we can have anything to say about it."

Redmond had inadvertently become a cause célèbre, an instrument of U.S. propaganda—all of it predicated, of course, upon the simple fiction that he was innocent of the charges of espionage. In virtually every home in Yonkers, and far beyond, Redmond's name became synonymous with the evils of Communism.

In Yonkers, resolutions were passed and petitions signed by innumerable civic and governmental groups—the Westchester County Board of Supervisors, local chapters of the American Legion and Veterans of Foreign Wars, his alma mater, Roosevelt High, and foremost of all, the Yonkers Citizens Committee for the Release of Hugh Francis Redmond. Even New York's state Senate passed a resolution calling upon President Dwight Eisenhower to renew efforts to win Redmond's release. It cited "patently false charges of espionage." It noted that "his continued separation from his family and loved ones constitutes an affront to our sense of honor, decency and human treatment." Yonkers's High School of Commerce, where Ruth Redmond was a cafeteria worker, drafted its own resolution for Eisenhower.

In neighboring Ossining the Knights of Columbus called on "all Americans of all faiths to pray to Almighty God for the deliverance of Hugh Francis Redmond, Jr., and especially that all Catholics offer their Masses, Novenas and Prayers to implore God and His Blessed Mother to encourage and protect him." Yonkers Mayor Kris Kristensen called on Yonkers's 160,000 residents to observe a weekend of prayer in which clergy from all faiths would provide petitions to their worshipers. Every petition contained the same phrase: "false charge of espionage."

A week after Redmond's conviction, the State Department cabled instructions to its representative in Geneva, who was then meeting with a Chinese delegation. The directive was unambiguous: "You should protest charges against and sentence of Hugh F. Redmond as unwarranted and unjust, pointing out Redmond was known as legitimate trader, employed by respectable business firm, and that Chinese Communists have unfortunately been in the habit of regarding all foreigners as spies."

The U.S. delegation was to ask the Chinese to reexamine the

Redmond case. Meeting at the plush Beau-Rivage hotel in Geneva, a member of the Chinese delegation told the U.S. representative that all hope was not lost, "that if Redmond's future attitude and conduct were found satisfactory by Chinese authorities his case might then be reconsidered."

It was a none-too-subtle invitation for Redmond to confess. And indeed, as would become increasingly clear, Redmond held the keys to his own release. If he admitted to spying, the chances were excellent that he would be set free, as had others before him. But then, Redmond was nothing like the others.

Why he resisted so fervently is not clear. His spy ring had been exposed, its members executed or imprisoned. There was nothing left to compromise or protect. Even within the CIA some were whispering among themselves, marveling at his resistance, but also secretly hoping that he might confess and bring to an end his suffering and that of his family. It had been four years since his arrest. In time, many at the Agency concluded it was nothing more than Redmond's own foolish sense of honor that blocked his release, and for that they saluted him.

The ordeal of Hugh Redmond in China mirrored that of his mother, Ruth, in Yonkers. On October 8, 1954, three weeks after his life sentence was handed down, Ruth Redmond wrote a plaintive letter to the State Department. "I have had absolutely no word from my son since later 1950," she wrote. "He was in prison almost a year when I accidentally read it in the papers. Then I realized why his mail had stopped. It has been just silence since then. It is the silence and the helplessness I feel that is driving me crazy. Is there nothing our State Department can do to send our only son home where he belongs?"

. . .

The CIA was soon to get a second jolt from China. In December 1954 the Chinese announced that two other Americans were about to go on trial for spying. Their names were John Downey and Richard Fecteau—the two CIA men that two years earlier the Agency had quietly declared dead, shot down over China. Downey might well have wished he were dead. For the first ten months of his detainment he was in chains and leg irons and subjected to relentless interrogation.

As the show trial was about to begin, Fecteau was led into the courtroom past an array of cameras and lights. Downey, whom he had not seen in two years, was already in the dock. For the cameras Downey had been decked out in a brand-new black padded suit, shoes, and what resembled a beanie hat. The court officer ordered Fecteau to stand beside Downey. Fecteau could see that Downey looked discouraged. He whispered in Downey's ear, "Who's your tailor?" and a familiar smile broke across Downey's face, bewildering the Chinese guards. But the outcome of the so-called trial was never in doubt. Downey was sentenced to life. Fecteau, as his subordinate, got twenty years.

The United States reacted with predictable outrage. Henry Cabot Lodge, delegate to the United Nations, noted the incident was yet another reason why this "unspeakable gang from Peiping" did not deserve to be admitted into the ranks of that world body. The *New York Times* wrote a scathing editorial, and a U.S. senator suggested that the United States blockade the mainland. To listen to the U.S. government, Downey and Fecteau were simply innocents caught up in Beijing's vendetta.

Behind the scenes, and with a nudge from the CIA, the Labor Department agreed to waive recovery of those moneys already paid out to Fecteau's children, though certain lump sum payments were recovered. The CIA reclassified the two men as active. Henceforth they would be listed as on "Special Detail Foreign" at "Official Station Undetermined."

A year later, in 1955, DeFelice became chief of the Casualty Branch and set about to do what he could on behalf of all who were imprisoned, killed, or missing. He found himself haunted by the fate of Downey, Fecteau, and Redmond. One of his first actions as branch chief was to get permission to invest the ongoing salaries of the men, rather than have them accumulate year after year in CIA accounts. Then he worked out a complex formula that took into account the average career promotions of the men's peers at the Agency, and on that basis granted regular promotions to Downey, Fecteau, and Redmond, thereby increasing their salaries and benefits. Their cases were handled no differently than if they were still operational in the field.

DeFelice was in constant contact with the families. For hours on Sunday afternoons he would be on the phone to Downey's mother, Mary, trying to win the confidence of a woman who was profoundly distrustful of the CIA.

DeFelice also established what came to be called the Ad Hoc Committee on Prisoners, which met regularly to discuss what steps might be taken to win the freedom of those being held. It was made up principally of representatives of the operational side of the CIA. But its real purpose, as devised by DeFelice, was to set up an ongoing forum that would ensure that the men were not forgotten. That "ad hoc" group met for more than twenty years with DeFelice as the chairman.

Meanwhile the campaign by Yonkers citizens on behalf of Redmond continued to build, drawing in members of Congress. In the spring of 1955 Ruth Redmond and leaders of the Yonkers Citizens Committee for the Release of Hugh F. Redmond formally asked to see Eisenhower, both to present him with bound volumes of petitions and to call his attention to Redmond's plight. Eisenhower's staff expressed reluctance, fearing that publicity surrounding such a meeting would encourage the families of others to demand a meeting with the president. Redmond's advocates promised the meeting would remain a matter of strict confidence. The State Department drafted a memo encouraging Eisenhower to see Mrs. Redmond. But Eisenhower declined.

On Saturday, April 16, 1955, Ruth Redmond and William Gawchik, head of the citizens' committee, met with State Department officials. Eisenhower's refusal remained a sore point. A State Department memo notes that Gawchik "felt the government had displayed a deplorable indifference to the fate of Mr. Redmond." State Department officials, among them Edwin W. Martin, deputy director for Chinese Affairs, tried to reassure them that Eisenhower was aware of Redmond's situation but that the U.S. government had only limited options. "We might go to war with the Chinese Communists to satisfy national honor and pride but this would by no means assure the return of prisoners, even if we should win the war, since they might be killed in the process," the State Department official told her.

But talks in Geneva that resumed August 1, 1955, began to produce unexpected results. Within nine months, twenty-eight of forty-one Americans in Chinese prisons were released. That left only thirteen. Among these were the three CIA agents—Downey, Fecteau, and Redmond. There followed agonizing months of silence.

Then, in the fall of 1955, the postman delivered a letter to the Yonkers home of Ruth Redmond. She recognized the handwriting instantly and felt her heart racing. The letter was undated and handwritten in ink on air mail stationery. The envelope had been forwarded by the Chinese Red Cross Society in an envelope postmarked September 14, 1955.

Inside were the first words from her son in the more than five years since he had been arrested. "I am very well," he wrote, "and I hope that everyone at home feels as good as I do right now." But Mrs. Redmond already knew something of her son's failing health and that anything he wrote would have had to clear the prison censor. Even so, there was a suggestion that not all was well with him. "Where I am right now," he penned, "there is a hospital, and I am receiving adequate care." He wrote that he no longer needed medicine for his beriberi or ointment for the inflammation that afflicted his eyes. His only request: heavy woolen clothes. Winter was fast approaching.

The brief letter ended with these words: "I'm sending all my love to you and everybody back home. Keep your fingers crossed for me. Love, Hughie." That he had been allowed at long last to write she took to be evidence that the Chinese were not without feelings. It was, perhaps, the sign she had been praying for that her son's deliverance was not far off. Even those at the CIA who monitored Redmond's case felt a tinge of optimism.

But for the Redmond, Downey, and Fecteau families, a long time—seemingly an eternity—would pass before their loved ones' fates would be resolved.

CHAPTER 3

By Chance

IT WAS June 1951. Little more than a month earlier Hugh Redmond had been dragged off in shackles to a Shanghai prison. John Downey was graduating from Yale and looking forward to a long career with the CIA. Doug Mackiernan's widow, Pegge, was settling in to her new job as vice-consul in Pakistan. The Mackiernan twins, Mike and Mary, not yet two, were spending the summer with Doug Mackiernan's parents in Massachusetts, playing on the long and sloping front lawn.

In Washington, D.C., at 2430 E Street NW—once OSS and now CIA headquarters—the specter of a third world war against one or both of the Communist titans, the Soviet Union or China, appeared to be less a matter of *if* than *when*. Chinese troops were pouring across the Korean peninsula. Americans under arms numbered nearly 3 million. And the CIA, just four years old, was embarking on one of its most ambitious periods of expansion. It set its eyes upon a whole new generation of Americans, those too young to have served in World War II but who were imbued with the same unvarnished patriotism that moved their parents and older siblings to enlist. The CIA's clandestine

service, to the few who even knew of its existence, still carried the ca-
chet of an elite and gentlemanly pursuit.

The Agency had recruiters everywhere—among professors, administrators, and employers—each one strategically positioned to flag young
people possessing the requisite character and skills. A premium was
placed on those with a knowledge of foreign languages or history as well
as the sciences, in particular chemistry, engineering, and physics. But in
the late spring of 1951, as a new crop of college graduates emerged, the
Agency was the indirect beneficiary of yet another factor—the military's
draft. More than a few of those who did not relish the idea of spending a
Korean winter in a foxhole thought the CIA an attractive alternative. Not
surprisingly, not long after graduation ceremonies ended, the Agency's
ranks began to swell.

Among those to sign on in June 1951 was one William Pierce
Boteler. Known to his friends as Bill or Botz, he was but twenty-one years
old. He had joined to become a covert operative.

Only a few months earlier the girls at Bryn Mawr had thought him
a genuine Adonis. He stood just over six feet, had thick black hair, a
swarthy complexion, and incandescent eyes of hazel. The coeds melted in
his presence, though he was as yet unaware of his effect on them. He was
neither vain nor overly self-assured, but possessed a quiet confidence rare
in one so young.

He had just graduated from prestigious Haverford College on June
9, 1951. There he had immersed himself in literature, philosophy, history,
and French. Often he could be found reading poetry, much of which he
had committed to memory. His marks were, like everything else about
him, rock solid. Studies had come easily for him—so easily, it sometimes
irked his friends, who had to spend long hours in the library while Boteler
went out for a beer or burger.

On the playing field, too, Bill Boteler excelled. There was no
bravado, just unwavering determination. He played receiver on the varsity
football team and a catcher on the baseball team, of which he was co-
captain. His closest friends were his teammates. It was Boteler who
formed the nucleus around which other friendships took shape. There was
Harold "Hal" Cragin, the catcher, Bud Garrison, quarterback and short-
stop, Ed Hibberd, who played backfield, and roommate Peter Steere, a

guard. All silently admired Boteler. Among them coursed an abiding affection that promised to endure long after college.

In the classroom Boteler was serious. Around his friends he was playful. The summer before graduation he and his chums Ed Hibberd and Bud Garrison worked as "social directors" at the fashionable Hotel Dennis in Atlantic City, on Michigan Avenue and the Boardwalk. Their job was to dance with the ladies, run the bingo games and volleyball, and walk the beach making sure no one felt left out. One Saturday evening, during an intermission between dances, Boteler and his friends strutted across the hotel stage in drag. It was a faux beauty contest judged by the former director of the Miss Atlantic City pageant. Boteler, his cheeks rouged, his lips ruby red with lipstick, won the contest. He was always a formidable competitor, and on this night he had particularly good reason to want to win. The prize was a date with the real Miss Atlantic City.

Boteler neither swore nor allowed himself to lose his composure. He was a proper gentleman, maybe even a little too preppy. His close friends thought he sometimes kept his feelings too bottled up inside. But he was never cold, just reserved. He dated widely but seemed immune to the crushes that afflicted his classmates.

He was close to his father, an insurance salesman in Washington, and was distressed over his mother's spiraling illness—something he didn't talk about. He worshiped his older brother, Charles. Though seven years his senior, Charles's tenure at Haverford overlapped with Bill's. Like many on college campuses in those immediate postwar years, Charles had interrupted his college education for military service in World War II. Charles would go on to be one of Haverford's finest football players, even declining an invitation from the New York Giants.

As graduation approached, no one had to remind Boteler or his friends of the military draft that awaited them. Bud would enter the army's Counterintelligence Corps, as did Boteler's roommate, Peter Steere. Cragin had already served in the army's Military Police before college.

But Boteler, a child of Washington, D.C., was fascinated with the CIA. The first person he approached with Agency contacts was Frank Campbell, a Haverford alum, thirty years his senior and quite patrician. Campbell encouraged him and vowed to keep an eye on his Agency career. That was how it was done, how the old-boy network worked. It was less an act of recruitment than an anointing. In those early years one could be forgiven for mistaking the CIA for a kind of secret fraternity where new pledges had to be vouched for by those already accepted.

Shortly after signing up, Boteler found himself in the CIA's basic training program, then headed by the legendary Matt Baird, a Princeton man. But it fell to Harry T. Gilbert to mold the young Boteler into a first-rate case officer. Gilbert was a man of eclectic credentials. He served for a time at Los Alamos, was on General Patton's staff, and had taken part in the Normandy invasion. He would remember the fresh-faced Boteler as a standout, a sterling recruit.

Boteler was one of some thirty novitiates in that class. Under Gilbert's tutelage, he would learn to think like a case officer and acquire the essential skills of intelligence-gathering. He would also be instructed in how to keep himself and those who depended on him alive.

It was not long before Boteler got his first overseas assignment: Germany. A few weeks before departing, Boteler contacted his Haverford classmate Hal Cragin, who was then selling insurance in Philadelphia. Over lunch Boteler explained to Cragin that he needed a $5,000 life insurance policy. He never said he was with the CIA, only that his work would take him overseas and that it could involve some risk. Boteler knew he would have to pay higher premiums. There were some awkward moments as he filled out the form under his friend's watchful eye. Boteler could not reveal the nature of his work but neither could he write down anything false that might later nullify his policy on grounds of fraud. Cragin did not ask any more questions than he had to.

In the fall of 1951 Boteler packed his bags and went off to Germany. Precisely what he was doing there remains something of a mystery, though Agency colleagues say he was part of an effort to recruit Eastern European refugees there and dispatch them back behind the Iron Curtain to gather intelligence and engage in activities designed to disrupt and confuse the Communists.

In the spring of 1953 his Haverford classmate and friend Bud Garrison, then an officer with the army's Counterintelligence Corps based in Grafenwöhr, Germany, received a call. It was Boteler. He was in town and eager to get together. The two met in Regensburg in Bavaria, not far from the Czech border. They rendezvoused at the front desk of a hotel. What struck Garrison instantly was that Boteler was in uniform. Indeed, Boteler sported the silver bar of a first lieutenant, outranking Garrison, who was then a second lieutenant.

"Hey, you're not in the army!" Garrison blurted out, and feigned jealousy that his friend outranked him. Boteler laughed it off and gave some evasive answer. Within moments the question was forgotten as the two friends caught up on one another's lives. But when the evening was over, Garrison was left with the curious feeling that despite hours spent together, he knew no more about how Boteler had spent the intervening years than before they had met.

A year later Boteler caught up with another college friend, Peter Steere, his former roommate, near Stuttgart, Germany. Steere was also with the army's Counterintelligence Corps. In the course of their evening together Boteler let it be known that he was working for the government. Beyond that he gave nothing away and Steere was too respectful to ask. In those days every fit young male had a military background. The culture and climate of those times suppressed the kind of gnawing curiosity that later would require those in espionage to be constantly on their guard, even with friends.

Yet another Haverford grad stationed in Germany remembers a visit from Boteler. But though this grad was also in the CIA, Boteler told him little of his work there. Such information was "compartmented," meaning on a strict need-to-know basis only.

Boteler returned to Washington in March 1953. Within a month he was readying himself to leave again, this time for Korea. His résumé, meanwhile, was becoming increasingly a work of fiction. Between 1952 and 1953, the years he was in Germany, he had listed that he worked as a grade school teacher at the Landon School in Bethesda, Maryland. A "Statement of Personal History," dated April 1, 1953, lists three credit references, all of them located at 2430 E Street NW, CIA's paltry headquarters building. On April 2 he filled out an application to extend his active-duty service with the United States Air Force, applying to the First Air Force, Mitchell Air Force Base in New York. Yet he never spent a day of his life in the military. It was all part of an elaborate cover to conceal his identity as a covert officer of the CIA. In Germany his cover had been with the army. In Korea he would be an air force officer.

One of those who remember Boteler in Korea is Frank Laubinger. But the man Laubinger came to know in Korea called himself Butler, not Boteler. It was common practice for operatives to assume pseudonyms. The safest course was to take a name with the same initials and one not too dissimilar from their real name. It cut down on slipups and allowed operatives to continue to wear monogrammed shirts and accessories. More important, those under deep cover seemed to respond more spontaneously to names not too unlike their own.

None of this seemed strange to Laubinger. He, too, had a pseudonym in Korea. It was either Larson or Larkin, he can't recall. He'd had more than a few false names. He had joined the CIA in 1952, a year after Boteler. Both Boteler and Laubinger answered to the CIA's deputy director for plans, or simply DDP as it was known internally. "Plans" was as bland a word as the spymasters could come up with. But it was this directorate that oversaw covert operations, ran the worldwide network of case officers engaged in espionage, and directed paramilitary operatives who, in essence, did what the military could not or would not do. The Agency, in this, its first decade, relied mostly on "humint"—human intelligence—as opposed to electronic eavesdropping, overhead surveillance, and other techniques that allowed for remote rather than on-site collection.

It was an era in spying that was less dependent on circuitry and science than courage and tradecraft, as the basic skills of espionage are called. Much that was gathered was information and documentation that agents—foreign nationals—brought back to their Agency case officers. Some intelligence was the product of "black-bag jobs" in which officers stealthily entered foreign embassies, factories, and offices to photograph materials or plant listening devices. Those raw data were then collated and analyzed in Washington by those working for the deputy director of intelligence, known as the DDI. The Agency was like a giant hive deploying thousands of worker bees to gather pollen and then return to the hive where it would be processed by regional analysts and interpreted. Ultimately the most productive intelligence would end up on the president's desk, there to guide his hand.

But though both Laubinger and Boteler were under the DDP,

Laubinger reported to the Technical Services staff, or TS. He traveled extensively, in a support role, helping out officers in the field like Boteler. They could look to Laubinger and others like him for a miniature camera, a bug to be planted in a foreign consulate, and for help with myriad other technical problems that called for creative solutions.

In a James Bond film Laubinger and his colleagues in Technical Services might well be mistaken for the finicky character known as Q. One of the areas Laubinger concentrated on was SW or Secret Writing—the development of invisible inks and other hard-to-detect means of writing. A staple of espionage, SW presented a constant challenge to stay ahead of the enemy. The Chinese during that very period were swabbing outgoing letters with chemicals that made visible those secret messages written in what were to have been invisible inks. Laubinger and others devoted themselves to developing countermeasures.

During the three years Laubinger was in the Far East, he met with Boteler in Seoul three or four times. It was during those TDYs, or temporary duties, that Laubinger came to know Boteler.

He made a lasting impression on him. He remembered the stress and conflict that sometimes erupted among CIA personnel in Seoul and at the enormous Agency station there. He also remembers Boteler deftly knitting the factions together, being a healing influence. Boteler may have had the demeanor of yet another Ivy Leaguer, but he was not a prima donna. Neither was he self-important, as were some of the Agency's pampered sons.

Laubinger remembers, too, that, like many Agency people in Korea, Boteler dressed in khakis and wore the kerchief that was symbolic of the unit. Because it was a fictitious unit, the kerchiefs posed a bit of a problem. Ultimately it was decided they would be made from a green camouflage parachute material.

. . .

During the nearly two years that Boteler was in Korea, the Agency grew feverishly under the spell of Allen Welsh Dulles, its most charismatic director. In February 1953 Dulles had been named Director Central Intelligence. The son of a Presbyterian pastor, he was a Princeton Phi Beta Kappa in philosophy. His was an unambiguous vision. It was the destiny of the United States, and the CIA in particular, to bring the Communists to heel. His moral persuasion and intellectual heft, his influential Washington network—including his older brother, John Foster Dulles, then secretary of state—and his OSS experience in the field made him the most formidable of CIA directors. His personal taste for covert action earned him the moniker of "the Great White Case Officer."

His objective was to develop worldwide covert operations aimed at rolling back the Communists, blunting their aggressions, and harassing them at every turn. Spurred on by the Korean War, the election of the staunchly anti-Communist Eisenhower, and increased Soviet activity abroad, Dulles elevated the CIA's role in covert action from what had been merely a collateral servant of foreign policy to one of its principal instruments. In 1952 three-quarters of the Agency's budget went to clandestine collection of information and covert operations. By 1953 the CIA was six times larger than it had been in 1947 when it was founded. That same year, 1953, the Agency, under Operation Ajax, helped engineer the ouster of Iran's premier, Muhammad Mussadegh. A year later, in the aptly named Operation Success, it was instrumental in ridding Guatemala of its leader, Jacobo Arbenz Guzmán.

Three years into Boteler's CIA service, the Agency had shed any residual timidity. The most telling statement of its philosophy comes from a September 30, 1954, report done at the behest of Eisenhower. The author was famed World War II Lieutenant General James Doolittle. What he wrote was, in essence, the mission statement of the CIA for years to come:

"It is now clear that we are facing an implacable enemy whose avowed objective is world domination by whatever means and at whatever cost. There are no rules in such a game. Hitherto acceptable norms of human conduct do not apply. If the United States is to survive, longstanding concepts of 'fair-play' must be reconsidered. We must develop effective espionage and counterespionage services and must learn to subvert, sabotage and destroy our enemies by more clever, more sophisticated and more effective methods than those used against us. It may become necessary that the American people be made acquainted with, understand and support this fundamentally repugnant philosophy."

At the CIA, it was now no-holds-barred. If free elections and open societies could be had in the process of blocking the Communists, all the better. But already it was the unspoken consensus that it was more important to halt the spread of Communism than to promote the democratic values it threatened. If installing or propping up totalitarian regimes was the cost of stopping Soviet expansionism, so be it. If the people of those nations saved from Stalin fared no better under Washington's favor than Moscow's boot, it could be justified.

World War II had taught nothing if not that war involved casualties, and though it was called a Cold War, it was a war nonetheless. Unwittingly the CIA was mirroring its Cold War foe. Behind the high rhetoric was a realpolitik dictating that entire nations must sometimes be viewed as pawns to be sacrificed in a larger endgame strategy. U.S. self-interest was equated with what was best for the world at large. After all, from the view of the Dulles brothers and Eisenhower, Soviet hegemony threatened to extinguish the light of civilization itself.

A second hallmark of the Agency's Cold War demeanor had emerged as early as June 1948 when the National Security Council passed Directive 10/2. It stated that, with regard to covert actions, "if uncovered the US Government can plausibly disclaim any responsibility for them." Over the years, deniability would expand in an effort to shield the president from his own actions as well as the nation from its foreign policy and domestic consequences. The White House, overseer of all major covert actions, attempted to institutionally separate itself from responsibility for those operations that had gone awry or that appeared contrary to basic American principles.

"Plausible deniability" enabled the president to distance himself from the darker hand of his own foreign policy, even freeing him to chastise those who carried out covert activities that he himself had set in play. Increasingly the Agency would be forced to fall on its own sword, to suffer not only the ignominy of occasional defeats but the full moral responsibility for that defeat. In failure it was to be cast not as the instrument, but as the author. A kind of political quarantine, it created a public image of the CIA as a renegade organization, full of rogue operatives accountable to no one. This was part of the price begrudgingly accepted by those in the clandestine service.

By the mid-1950s the CIA was no longer a fledgling organization, but a mature and complex entity expected to gather, collect, and analyze intelligence and to thwart Sino-Soviet expansion with thousands of well-trained covert operatives. With such a broad mandate it could no longer rely solely on recruiting World War II veterans like Mackiernan and Redmond. Instead, it began to develop its own corps of covert case officers and paramilitary operatives from whose ranks future Agency leaders would arise. For this it turned to a former air force colonel, Matt Baird, who as the CIA's director of training was to forge the next generation of clandestine service officers. The army had West Point, the navy had Annapolis. Now the Agency, too, would have its place in which to orient, indoctrinate, and prepare its "junior-officers-in-training," or JOTs as they would come to be called. Later the word "junior" would be viewed as demeaning and the designation was changed to "career trainees," or simply CTs.

For training, the CIA transformed several thousand thickly wooded acres in southeastern Virginia near Williamsburg into the ultimate classroom for Cold War espionage. In earlier incarnations the site had been a Seabee base and even a camp for prisoners of war. Under the CIA it would have many code names, chief among them Isolation. Its name to the outside world was Camp Perry. To Agency recruits it was affectionately known as the Farm. For decades to come, there was hardly a covert operative who did not pass through its rigors and smile at the mere mention of the words "the Farm." Its existence was one of Washington's worst-kept secrets, but what went on there and who was there were matters of strictest secrecy. Even among those undergoing training, identities were sometimes tightly compartmented. Before the callow officers arrived, they would be assigned pseudonyms.

At the Farm, generations of covert officers were instructed in the basic skills of espionage—known reverently as tradecraft. The courses changed in small ways from year to year, but new recruits could count on a core curriculum. "Picks and Locks" focused on how to open doors, windows, and safes. Such skills would be useful for "black-bag jobs" such as night entries into secured foreign embassies for planting a bug or photographing sensitive documents.

"Flaps and Seals" dealt with, among other skills, how to open mail and packages and then reseal them undetected. Years later it would be revealed that those same skills were practiced not only against foreigners but against American citizens as well. Under Project SRPOINTER, the CIA's Office of Security surreptitiously intercepted, read, and sometimes photographed letters coming from or going to addresses in the Soviet Union.

The Farm also offered a course in "caching," in which recruits learned how to select a forward position, often near a border or behind enemy lines, where arms, munitions, communications gear, even gold, could be buried and later retrieved for future use. JOTs were taught to think long-term, to imagine the terrain in five, ten, even fifteen years, and to select landmarks that would endure and be recognizable—not transient objects such as trees or buildings, but immutable mountains, ravines, and boulders.

Others learned the rudiments of demolition and sabotage. Those earmarked for more specialized training would go on to even more exotic sites. Some would train at high altitude in the Rockies, others in the jungles of Panama. Most important of all were those courses that instructed case officers in the proper methods of recruiting and overseeing foreign agents.

During the 1950s Camp Perry featured what amounted to exact and elaborate reconstructions of Soviet and Eastern European border crossings. Each junior officer would be told which "border" he or she must attempt to cross. They were given three hours to penetrate undetected. The faux borders were watched by stern-faced sentinels in towers and protected by alarms, barbed wire, and toothy, though muzzled, German shepherds. Any slipup, and all hell would break loose. One savvy JOT with a way with animals prided himself in having "turned" an otherwise ferocious guard dog into a docile companion as he stealthily crossed the border.

Field trips were taken to Richmond, Virginia, forty-five minutes away. Aspiring case officers would be divided into teams of four. The cadets would be told to imagine themselves in Moscow, Budapest, or Prague. The first team would attempt to lose the second team, which was assigned to keep them under surveillance without being noticed. The first team, once it believed it had shaken the shadow team, would execute "a drop," an exchange of materials or messages. The second team would attempt to foil the exchange. It was all fun and games except that each participant knew that within months a slipup in the field could cost them their lives or those of the foreigners reporting to them.

It was that sort of rudimentary training that young Boteler had received.

. . .

In the summer of 1955 Boteler finished his tour of duty in Korea and returned to Washington. Actually it felt more like two separate Washingtons, existing side by side. Those not involved in defense or intelligence work were enjoying a halcyon summer with weekends in the Blue Ridge Mountains or on Chesapeake Bay. The economy was sound and houses were filling up with children, part of what was dubbed "the baby boom."

But at the CIA, Pentagon, and White House, war planners grimly prepared for what the rest of the nation preferred to call "the unthinkable." On the sunny Friday morning of June 17, 1955, while many in Washington were planning an early weekend getaway, Boteler's ultimate boss, Allen Dulles, was already well out of town—sequestered in a conference room buried deep inside a top secret mountain installation code-named Raven Rock.

It was but one of several relocation sites ringing the capital where the U.S. government hoped to ride out the coming nuclear war. An annual government-wide exercise, it was named Operation Alert. Dulles and his boss, Eisenhower, together with the cabinet, met in the bowels of the mountain debating the likely aftermath of a nuclear exchange. Some fifty-three cities were presumed bombed by the Soviets, the Treasury would be required to print more money to jump-start the economy, and 25 million Americans would be homeless. Top secret codes would be buried across the countryside and martial law seemed inevitable.

Boteler straddled both worlds—that of the impending apocalypse and that of a young man with some easy time on his hands. It was a good summer for him, a chance to reintegrate with an America that had changed while he had been away in Germany and Korea. He shared his father's apartment, and the two of them would go to Washington Senators baseball games and catch up with each other's life. Boteler, now a dashing and well-traveled twenty-five-year-old bachelor, found himself in a city replete with eligible women. He bought himself a little Austin-Healey sports car and zipped through Washington enjoying a lifestyle long denied to him overseas. Each time he passed another Austin-Healey he would honk his horn playfully as if greeting a relative.

But there was also work to be done and preparation for his next assignment. Until then, he had been stationed in countries of obvious importance to the Agency—Germany and Korea. Both were viewed as bulwarks against Communist aggression. They had been rife with opportunities to send agents back behind enemy lines to gather information and wreak mischief. There were innumerable Agency operatives in both countries, and Boteler had been but one member of that largely invisible corps of spies.

But when Boteler was informed of his next overseas assignment, he was rendered almost speechless. Cyprus, his superior had intoned. Boteler had only the vaguest notion of where it was, much less why the United States should care about the fate of so small and rocky an island in the Mediterranean. Comprised of a mere 3,572 square miles, it was about twice the size of Long Island and located 40 miles from Turkey and 530 miles from the Greek mainland. Worse yet, he was to be the only case officer on the entire island. There wasn't even a formal CIA station there yet. Boteler was to open a base there, bases being subordinate to stations.

But already by late 1955, Cyprus was assuming a strategic significance that dwarfed its diminutive size. The British, America's closest ally, were being pushed out of Egypt by Gamal Abdel Nasser and were now desperate to relocate their army, air, and sea bases. At stake was Britain's capacity to defend its lifeline to Mideast oil. Without it, Great Britain was lost, its industry crippled. Cyprus had been under British rule since the Crown acquired it in 1878 from Turkey, ironically in exchange for its help against the Russians. Expelled from Egypt, the Brits designated Cyprus their new Mediterranean redoubt. They set about to build formidable military bases even as their sources of oil came under increasing threats from Egypt's ultranationalistic Nasser.

But as Britain expanded its presence on the island, the domestic stability of Cyprus began to collapse. The Cypriot population was 80 percent ethnic Greeks and 20 percent Turkish Moslems. The Greek majority hungered to be unified with Greece, a movement known as *enosis*. A terrorist faction calling itself EOKA, for the National Organization of the Cypriot Fight, launched a campaign of violence against the British to drive them from the island and win unification with Greece. EOKA was headed by a shadowy figure who called himself simply Dighenis, but who was in fact a former Greek colonel, George Grivas. Adding to the volatility on the island, its ethnarch, or spiritual leader, the charismatic Archbishop Makarios, was championing *enosis* and secretly fomenting social unrest in aid of EOKA.

Meanwhile, a mere forty miles across the sea, the Turks feared that if such a union with Greece should occur, ethnic Turks would be persecuted or slaughtered. The millennia-old enmity between the Greeks and Turks was becoming more edgy with each passing month. In Turkey there were anti-Greek riots. In Greece there were anti-British riots. On Cyprus the number of Brits killed by EOKA was climbing.

The deteriorating situation in Cyprus was of far more than academic interest to the United States. The CIA and National Security Council watched in horror as three bedrock members of the NATO alliance— Britain, Greece, and Turkey—drifted further and further apart. Greece made not-so-subtle threats to abandon NATO and seek neutrality. It withdrew from some planned exercises. Turkey, a NATO member that bordered the Soviet Union, drew further away from the United States. If the situation unraveled much more, the alliance itself could crumble and the Soviets, emboldened by their closeness to Nasser and the erupting feud among NATO allies, might seek to expand their grip on the region. They might even make a play for its oil reserves.

The United States also had its own parochial interests in Cyprus. It was there that the CIA had a major communications relay station through which all cable traffic, open and encrypted, passed on its way to and from the Middle East and Washington.

As Boteler's briefings continued, he came to understand that far more was at stake than the little island of Cyprus.

In the months before being posted there, he steeped himself in the history and culture of Cyprus and the surrounding region. But because there was no U.S. military presence on the island, he could not use military cover to conceal his mission. Instead, he would have to adopt a more conventional cover—that of the diplomat. Like Doug Mackiernan before him, his cover would be vice-consul. And to pass for a diplomat he would need to develop certain skills and familiarize himself with the attendant duties of a vice-consul.

He would also, it was decided, need to learn to dance. Cyprus was, after all, a proper British protectorate and there would be formal parties and balls to attend. They couldn't have this handsome young diplomat arrive with two left feet.

One morning Boteler got into his spiffy little Austin-Healey and drove from the Agency through Washington's downtown to 1011 Connecticut Avenue, the Arthur Murray Dance Studio. He walked down the small flight of steps, entered the studio, and made his way to the reception desk, where he filled out a form, enrolling himself in a series of dance classes—at CIA expense.

The studio manager then led Boteler to a slender twenty-three-year-old dance instructor named Anne Paffenbarger. Who was this young man? she wondered as she extended her hand to him. He was simply the most beautiful of men, tall and lean and dark. It was all she could do to keep from giving herself away with a sigh. Boteler, too, was instantly taken by his own good fortune. Before him stood a heavenly woman of five feet six, her dress breaking at the knee, her hair short and dirty blond. Boteler thought of the actress Jean Simmons. Within moments his right arm was around her slender waist, his left hand in her right, as they swept across the wide floor of the ballroom, practicing a waltz and counting together: "one-two-three, one-two-three." The hour was over in an instant.

Over the course of the next several weeks Boteler learned the mambo, cha-cha, waltz, and swing, but mostly he returned to be close to Anne. She had graduated a year earlier from Columbia, majoring in Romance languages.

The man who never fell for anyone was now in something of a tailspin. But neither Boteler nor Paffenbarger would let on to the other that there was anything between them beyond a contract for dance instruction. It was, after all, forbidden for instructors to date students or see them socially. After several weeks Boteler showed up unexpectedly at one of the studio's evening sessions, an additional opportunity to practice. "I came in just to see you," he told her. That was the first time that Paffenbarger had any indication that Boteler was as drawn to her as she was to him. "Oh," was the only response she could muster. But Paffenbarger was not about to let Boteler slip away.

She quit her job at the dance studio and got a position as a clerk at Garfinkle's Department Store. Nearly every night the two went out on the town. One night he took her to see a film with Gregory Peck, one of his favorite actors. Another evening was spent in a café where a roving singer sang "Moonlight in Vermont." Paffenbarger imagined that, together, the two of them looked like moonlight itself. After that, the melody would always bring Bill Boteler to mind.

Boteler's father complained that after his son had spent so much time overseas with the government, he still had hardly any time together with him. Before long Boteler and Paffenbarger spoke of marriage. Boteler suggested that he would have a ring made especially for her. In the meantime he presented her with a pair of earrings, small and delicate silver scrolls with a cultured pearl in the center.

Finally she was introduced to Boteler's father. He asked what she had thought of his son when they first met. Paffenbarger stumbled for words that would not embarrass her. "She fainted!" quipped Bill. Later, on a country outing, Paffenbarger invited Boteler to climb Sugarloaf Mountain. Boteler feigned puzzlement. "I have been to Katmandu and Mount Everest," he said. "There aren't any mountains around here!" Still they drove to the top of Sugarloaf and had a quiet picnic.

They were well suited for each other. By nature, they were both cool and reserved. Both were sober and conservative, not given to emotional gushing. For both, this thing that had happened to them, this spontaneous romance, was as unfamiliar as it was intoxicating. Boteler once whispered to her that she was a female version of himself.

When Paffenbarger first asked what Boteler did for a living, he reverted to his old evasive ways. Finally he confided in her that he was with the CIA. But what startled her even more was his disclosure that for weeks the couple had been under CIA surveillance. The CIA's security section, he said, wanted to know whom he was seeing, how he spent his time, and where he was going. Boteler was ever conscious of being watched. Over time, said Boteler, the surveillance ended.

He would never discuss the specifics of his work, but he let it be known that he was proud of what he had accomplished and that it was thought he would have a bright future.

As the time for his next assignment drew closer, however, Boteler appeared more anxious. He confessed that his next mission had him worried. The night before his departure, Anne and he had dinner with Boteler's father. After dinner Boteler asked her not to see him off at National Airport. It was something he wanted to do alone. As he prepared to leave, Paffenbarger rushed at him, threw her arms around him, and lost herself completely. She would remember herself flying at him as if she were a missile, and of him catching her in his arms and trying to calm her down.

The next day Boteler went to the Agency to complete his checkout procedure. In Tempo Building L he bumped into his friend from Korea Frank Laubinger. The two lunched in the cafeteria. It was a brief get-together, thirty minutes at most, but Laubinger could not shake the ominous feeling—call it a premonition—that this would be the last time he would see Bill Boteler. Laubinger was not a superstitious man, far from it. But this would be the most intense feeling he would have in his twenty-eight years with the Agency. In his mind, Boteler's going to Cyprus was tantamount to his friend putting his neck in a noose. He never shared a word of his misgivings with Boteler except to wish him well and to bid him to take care of himself.

On May 7, 1956, Boteler boarded BOAC flight 510 for London. Acting Secretary of State Herbert Hoover, Jr., had arranged for Boteler to be briefed at each of the capital cities involved in the Cyprus dispute—London, Athens, and Ankara. Boteler's first two days were spent in London being briefed by the CIA's station chief and by the British. Three days later he began the second leg of his trip and wrote his first letter to Anne. "Sweetheart," the letter began, "Pardon the pencil, but I'm out of ink. At the moment, I'm 22,000 feet over Switzerland—I think—on my way from London to Rome, thence to Athens. I'm flying on one of the new Viscounts, which, unfortunately, is not much different from any other plane I've ever been on."

Boteler recounted his two days in London. Between briefings he had walked throughout London, around Piccadilly Circus, Trafalgar Square and Leicester Square, the Tower of London, Buckingham Palace, and Hyde Park. On his second night he took in Noël Coward's comedy *South Sea Bubble* with Vivien Leigh. "I found time to indulge in my favorite sport, barhopping," he jested, "and thus investigated the insides of several representative public houses." The next morning he left for Athens and a second round of briefings.

He remained focused on the situation in Cyprus. "Things are not improving on Cyprus; if anything, getting worse," he wrote Paffenbarger. "The government has refused to suspend the execution of two convicted Greek terrorists, and have announced they will be hung this week. This touched off riots in Athens yesterday, and strikes in Nicosia [Cyprus's capital]. Right or wrong, the British are sticking by their guns, and there certainly isn't likely to be any settlement for some time; the people I talked with in the Foreign Office and Colonial Office are frank to admit that."

"I miss you and am pretty lonely, despite all the new places, people I'm seeing," he wrote. "I'll be glad to get settled into a routine of work again, & to get my mind on other matters as much as possible. I'm still not quite sure how I got into this in the first place, but there's no denying that I'm in it.

"Be good and don't step on anybody's feet. Write whenever you can, and smile. My love, Bill."

In the predawn hours of May 10, the day Boteler wrote his first letter to Paffenbarger, the British hung the two convicted EOKA terrorists, Michael Karaolis and Andreas Demetriou. Both were only twenty-three years old. Their bodies were quickly buried in the corner of the prison grounds, in the hope that behind high walls topped with broken glass, their graves would not become a rallying point for terrorists. It was unhallowed ground where the Orthodox priest could not hold service. Just outside the gates, Karaolis's mother sat in a chair waiting for the news.

Retaliation was not long in coming. Twenty-four hours later EOKA's Grivas ordered two policemen shot and buried in secret.

For months the situation in Cyprus had been slipping into chaos. Even as Boteler made his way there, the State Department began to evacuate dependents. Terrorist attacks were now a daily affair. Thus far, attacks had been restricted to assaults on the British, but everyone was now wary. The Brits now had more than 22,000 troops quartered there. British soldiers had taken to covering their cars with wire screens to ward off stones from angry schoolchildren. In the twelve months before Boteler's arrival, British casualties numbered 47 dead and 125 wounded. At least as many Cypriots had fallen.

The terror campaign was stepped up following the March 9 arrest of Archbishop Makarios. He had been placed aboard a British frigate and exiled to the remote Seychelles islands, a British Crown Colony in the Indian Ocean a thousand miles east of Kenya. The new British governor of Cyprus, Field Marshal Sir John Harding, believed that with a firm enough hand he could quash the unrest. He had won a get-tough reputation fighting the Mau Mau in Kenya and now swore to crush EOKA as well.

But NATO threatened to unravel. Greece had withdrawn its ambassador from London. In Athens the street where the British Embassy stood was renamed for the two EOKA terrorists hung in Cyprus. At Athens's request, the United States canceled a planned visit of the Sixth Fleet to the Greek island of Crete. NATO's southern flank was now on the verge of disintegration. The Soviets watched with relish as their foes fell to arguing among each other over a rocky scrap of island.

On May 15 Boteler arrived in Nicosia, Cyprus, having completed briefings in Athens, Istanbul, and Ankara. The next day he wrote his father. "Living here is going to be much more of a problem than in Germany or Korea, but also much more pleasant. I have had to find and rent an apartment, furnish it, hire a maid, and in general, set up housekeeping. Fortunately, the bills will be footed by you know who . . . Things are pretty restricted here, although, by and large, you wouldn't be outwardly aware of any difficulty . . . The British are very wary, and terrorism continues. Lord knows it should be an interesting tour; however, it's a damn pretty island, and I hope things calm down somewhat, so that I can enjoy it more fully."

His second day in Nicosia he took out a fountain pen and wrote a letter to Anne. "I'm not disappointed in Cyprus," he wrote, "although it's a shame things are the way they are, as movements are severely restricted. The British are really taking it in the neck, and top British officials are guarded by hordes of soldiers." Meanwhile Boteler attended to the mundane duties of a vice-consul, his cover position, furnished his apartment, and tried to orient himself. Back in Washington, Anne had returned to Arthur Murray. In closing his letter, Boteler wrote, "Hope things aren't too grim at A.M. [Arthur Murray]; write whenever you can, & don't forget I miss you. Much love, Bill."

Boteler was fascinated with Cyprus, particularly Nicosia's old city within the walls, where most of the shops were and where, unfortunately, much of the violence was as well. Boteler had asked permission to live inside the old city but was turned down for security reasons. That first week in Nicosia was even more violent than the previous week. "The British are taking extreme repressive measures, but they don't seem to be doing much good—the entire population is solidly against them," Boteler wrote his father.

Day by day, Boteler observed the British crackdowns even as he developed an increasing fondness for the local Cypriots. "Despite the continuing violence, you seldom feel as if there's anything unusual going on," he wrote. "Americans are well thought of, and on friendly terms with the locals; still they have to stay at home at night also." Boteler had not yet met many of the nearly three hundred Americans still on Cyprus. He was now beginning to chafe against the restrictions he faced. He was young, lonely, new to the country, and unable to explore it with the vigor with which he had become accustomed in Germany and Korea.

"No one, of course, has the slightest idea how things are likely to turn out, but it seems fairly certain that the situation isn't going to be settled any time soon," he wrote his father. "All of which makes my job more enjoyable, but my social life more restricted."

Under diplomatic cover he was now representing the U.S. government. He immersed himself in the Greek language and made good headway. He marveled at the British, who showed no such interest in learning the language. It was late spring and he yearned to keep up with what was going on with baseball. He asked his father to pass along "a little inside dope on our heroes" from time to time. "Incidentally, didn't I say Mantle [Mickey Mantle of the New York Yankees] would have a great year—and didn't I also say the Phils would win a pennant? Forget the last."

By the end of May, Boteler was feeling cooped up. "We as Americans aren't at war with anybody and nobody seems to hate us, but we have to go through the same drill as everybody else in most respects," he wrote Anne on May 27, 1956. He felt confined, and instead of his beloved Austin-Healey, he had settled for a Morris Minor, a two-door sedan with what he contemptuously described as a "½ cylinder [*sic*] engine." Again he expressed his fascination with the old part of Nicosia, dangerous though it was.

LEFT: CIA case officer Douglas S. Mackiernan in his jeep in China's far west province of Xinjiang, where he was stationed undercover as a low-level State Department employee. *(Courtesy of Pegge Hlavacek)*

BELOW: Douglas S. Mackiernan and wife Pegge in New York City's Central Park the winter of 1947–1948. *(Courtesy of Pegge Hlavacek)*

Passport photo of Douglas S. Mackiernan, then working for the CIA undercover as a State Department employee. While others shunned assignment to China's remote far west, he was only too eager to set up a listening post there along the Sino-Soviet border. *(Courtesy of Pegge Hlavacek)*

Douglas S. Mackiernan cradles his newborn son, Michael, in Shanghai in the fall of 1948. It would be the only picture of Mackiernan with his son. Weeks later Pegge and the twins were evacuated. Mackiernan, still posing as a State Department employee, was left behind to gather intelligence on the encroaching Communists. *(Courtesy of Pegge Hlavacek)*

RIGHT: Douglas S. Mackiernan, shirtsleeves rolled up and standing outside the embassy in Tihwa, China. Months later he would be fleeing the Communist Chinese across an endless expanse of desert and mountains. *(Courtesy of Pegge Hlavacek)*

BELOW: Douglas Mackiernan (standing in the middle) against a snowy landscape not unlike that across which he attempted to flee the Communists. He was proud of his new beard and swore he would not take it off until he and wife Pegge were together again. *(Courtesy of Pegge Hlavacek)*

From the *San Francisco Examiner*, dated January 31, 1950. Mackiernan's widow, Pegge, with twins Mary and Michael, dismissing as "silly" the Chinese claim that her husband had been a spy. Fifty years later the CIA would still not utter his name or acknowledge that he worked for the Agency.
(Courtesy of Pegge Hlavacek and the San Francisco Examiner)

Tuesday, January 31, 1950 ★ CCCC* **San Francisco Examiner**

MISSING AIDE'S WIFE HITS REDS

Mrs. Douglas Mackiernan of 67 Rocca Drive, Fairfax, yesterday described as "silly" a charge by Chinese Communists that her husband, an American vice consul missing in Red China since September 27, is a "spy."

Mackiernan's d i s a p p e a r a n c e was disclosed yesterday by the State Department. As vice consul in Tihwa, in Sinkiang Province, he last was heard from the

day he began a hazardous journey out of China, under State Department orders.

Mackiernan was left behind to close up the Tihwa consulate last August, when Consul J. Hall Paxton and other Americans were ordered out of the city. The Paxton group reached India in October. Mackiernan radioed on September 27 that he was leaving just ahead of Communist forces.

The Communist China radio, card by the Associated Press in San Francisco, described Mackiernan as a "spy" who sought to organize bandits against the Communist advance. The State Department called the Red charges "the usual trips."

Mrs. Mackiernan, who once lived with her husband in China, said the accusation may have come from "a Communist cook we had while there." She lives in Fairfax with her year-old twins, Mary and Michael.

RIDICULES CHARGE—Mrs. Douglas Mackiernan, shewn with her twins, Mary and Michael, yesterday scoffed at charge by Chinese Communists that her husband, an American vice consul missing since September, is a spy.—Photo by San Francisco Examiner

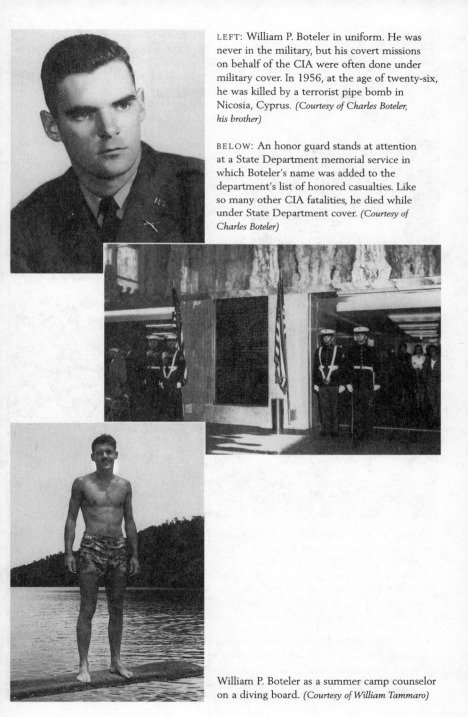

LEFT: William P. Boteler in uniform. He was never in the military, but his covert missions on behalf of the CIA were often done under military cover. In 1956, at the age of twenty-six, he was killed by a terrorist pipe bomb in Nicosia, Cyprus. (*Courtesy of Charles Boteler, his brother*)

BELOW: An honor guard stands at attention at a State Department memorial service in which Boteler's name was added to the department's list of honored casualties. Like so many other CIA fatalities, he died while under State Department cover. (*Courtesy of Charles Boteler*)

William P. Boteler as a summer camp counselor on a diving board. (*Courtesy of William Tammaro*)

A portrait of Leo Baker, one of the Alabama pilots killed in the ill-fated Bay of Pigs operation against Castro in 1961. For thirty-nine years the CIA refused to publicly acknowledge that Baker and the other Americans who died were on Agency missions. *(Courtesy of Theresa Ann Geiger, Baker's daughter)*

ABOVE: Richard Bissell, the vaunted overseer of many of the CIA's most celebrated achievements and its most devastating defeat, the Bay of Pigs, receiving the National Security Medal in March of 1961. To his right stands Allen Dulles, to his left stand President Kennedy and CIA head John McCone. *(Courtesy of the Bissell estate)*

RIGHT: Richard Bissell, in his seventies, enjoying an afternoon's sun at his Connecticut home. Writing his memoirs sapped what little strength he had left. The Bay of Pigs, even then, was a painful subject for him. *(Courtesy of the Bissell estate)*

Thomas "Pete" Ray, the Alabama pilot, in uniform. Ray was killed during the Bay of Pigs operation in April 1961 and his body became something of a trophy of war for Fidel Castro. Decades later Ray's remains were returned and buried in the Alabama soil.
(Courtesy of Thomas M. Ray, his son)

Thomas "Pete" Ray, as a young father showing off his six-month-old son, Thomas Ray.
(Courtesy of Thomas M. Ray)

Margaret Ray, the widow of Thomas "Pete" Ray, taken in 1961, the year her husband was killed in the Bay of Pigs operation. She would never recover from the loss of her husband and would feel that the watchful eye of the CIA was constantly upon her.
(Courtesy of Thomas M. Ray)

Little Tom Ray and sister Janet taken in 1961 at about the time of their father's death in the Bay of Pigs fiasco.
(Courtesy of Thomas M. Ray)

ABOVE: John G. Merriman with wife Valeria and sons Bruce and Jon on doorstep in Yakutat, Alaska, circa 1952. Merriman's daring rescues of those stranded on mountains attracted national attention. A dozen years later, as a downed CIA pilot in the Congo, he waited for someone to come to his rescue. *(Courtesy of Jon Merriman)*

A dashing young John Merriman enjoying a beer while assigned to the 82nd Airborne Division. As a pilot he was counted among the best, though his time flying for the CIA would be cut short by ground fire in the Congo. *(Courtesy of Jon Merriman)*

John Merriman's widow, Valeria Folkins, with son Jon Merriman.
(Courtesy of the author, Ted Gup)

John Merriman with a brown bear he shot in Alaska. After this kill,
he gave up hunting altogether. *(Courtesy of Jon Merriman)*

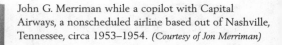
John G. Merriman while a copilot with Capital Airways, a nonscheduled airline based out of Nashville, Tennessee, circa 1953–1954. *(Courtesy of Jon Merriman)*

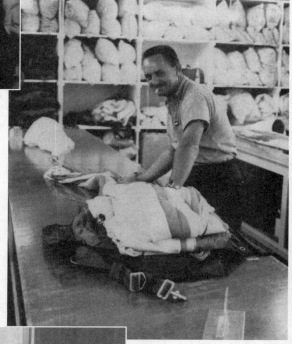

RIGHT: June 1964 at the Paraloft at Intermountain Aviation, Marana, Arizona. Although he doesn't appear to be actually packing the T-10 personnel parachute in front of him (no smoking is allowed in the rigging area), it is an excellent candid photo. This would have been the last photograph taken of him in the United States. John left for Africa in early July 1964.
(Courtesy of Jon Merriman)

Central Intelligence Headquarters, Langley, Virginia, February 15, 1965. Valeria S. Merriman receiving the Intelligence Star from Lieutenant General Marshall S. Carter, deputy director of Central Intelligence.
(Courtesy of Jon Merriman)

By June 2 Cyprus seemed to be slipping into a war. Wrote Boteler to his father: "Things are indeed progressing unsatisfactorily, at least from a personal point of view. Otherwise, they couldn't really be much worse, or at least so it seems at the moment. My arrival seems to have touched off a chain of events which has generally tended to heighten the tension here, and no doubt to attract more publicity for Cyprus elsewhere. The latest event was the bombing of an American home last night . . . generally regarded as accidental, but you never know . . . Lord knows where it will all lead." No one was hurt in the bombing, but it was a reminder of everyone's vulnerability.

Boteler marveled at the Brits' ability to tune out the violence. "Through it all," he wrote, "the British cling grimly to their social traditions; the Queen's birthday was celebrated the other night in all due pomp and splendor, in as heavily-guarded a location as you could imagine. The invitations for the affair carried a little note requesting everyone to check their personal weapons at the door."

Four days later, on June 6, 1956, Boteler wrote his brother, Charles, and Charles's wife, Deenie. "I certainly covered a lot of ground in switching from Korea to this place, although I suppose the change would be remarkable in any place after Korea. One thing is certain—I'm not likely to get bored from inactivity here. So far, as an American, I'm a man nobody hates, which can't be said by anybody else—except other Americans." Boteler wrote admiringly of the mountains. Each Sunday he would go for a swim in the Mediterranean.

But the security precautions were taking an ever greater toll on him. "All the restrictions imposed by the trouble have made living a little difficult," he wrote. "It's hard to get around at night, which cramps my style no end, and you always have to be careful where you go, and how . . . Still, with reasonably prudent behavior, the chances of getting involved in anything are almost non-existent—about the only way would be by chance."

Three days later, on June 9, he seemed to relax somewhat. In a letter to his father that began "Dear Dad," and was timed to arrive for Father's Day, he wrote, "Most every night EOKA drops a bomb on the front porch of some Englishman's home, making a big noise and not much else." His Greek lessons were going well and he was becoming accustomed to his diplomatic cover. "I diddle around with routine consular tasks, such as issuing visas, dealing with problems of assorted Americans, etc. The rest of my time is spent trying to find out what's going on here in the political field. This job will be a good deal different than the last one I held; it shouldn't prove nearly so demanding of time and nerves, but a great deal more interesting and rewarding."

. . .

The week passed. The temperature climbed to 112 degrees. Boteler was now making friends with a number of local Greeks, some of whom took him to the racetrack on Sunday. There he bet every race and lost each one. In his off-hours, when he wasn't playing bridge with the locals, he was reading. He had polished off a number of novels since arriving, among them *Fräulein* and *Islands in the Sun*.

On June 11, 1956, he wrote Anne. "Dear Sweetheart," the letter began. He described his efforts to meet as many locals as possible, part of his covert assignment to gather intelligence on the political situation on the island and to find a way to penetrate the terrorist group EOKA. Near the end of his letter he wrote, "I've finished 'Marjorie Morningstar' which I found interesting, although certainly not very weighty. It's about a girl whose true love runs off overseas because she won't go to bed with him. You never quite find out whether the author thinks she was right or wrong. In case you're wondering, that's *not* why I came to Cyprus, incidentally."

Boteler described the grand celebration for the Queen's birthday. Some fourteen hundred people were in attendance amid the strictest of security, but, lamented Boteler, "no dancing—after $400 worth of preparation for the big moment, I didn't have a chance to show off at all."

He closed, "Your letters arrive regular as clockwork—every day, almost, or so it seems. I'll have to set a schedule if I'm going to keep up with you. Be good, darling; I miss you. Love—Bill."

There followed another letter five days later. It was dated June 16, 1956. Boteler was at the consulate. It was afternoon. He had just finished reading a letter from Anne. "There are signs that the situation is improving here," he wrote. "The British appear to be having much more success in dealing with EOKA, although that's certainly not the answer by itself. I personally don't expect any radical political changes for quite some time, but then I could be wrong." His letter ended simply. "Well, back to work . . . Don't worry too much about missing me—I like it. All my love—Bill."

The next day, June 17, the British continued their massive manhunt for EOKA's leader, Grivas, who was believed to be in the forests of the Troodos Mountains. For ten days some five thousand crack troops worked to cordon off sixty-five square miles of rugged mountain terrain, closing in on their prey, as if driving a tiger out of the concealment of high grass. But even as the British believed they were closing in, the wily Grivas had already slipped through their clutches and had given orders for a renewed terrorist assault on British positions throughout the island.

The hunters became the hunted. As British troops in the mountains narrowed their search, a forest fire broke out, likely the work of EOKA. The winds changed and many soldiers were within range of exploding petrol tanks. Twenty soldiers died and sixteen were severely burned. At an abandoned campsite all that was found of the elusive Grivas was a dashing photo of the mustachioed leader wearing a beret, a cardigan, a Sam Browne belt, and a .45 automatic slung at his side.

That same evening, June 17, 1956, Boteler worked late. He was tired and needed a break. He had spotted a small café, the Little Soho, in the old walled part of the city, that he had been eager to try. By then the U.S. consul, Raymond F. Courtney, had warned American personnel not to visit the old city at night and to avoid popular restaurants. Each member of the consulate had promised to honor the restriction. Courtney considered such outings too risky.

On the way out of the consulate, Boteler bumped into Courtney and told him he was headed for the Little Soho. Courtney raised an eyebrow as if to remind him of the restrictions. He told Boteler that if he felt he had to go because it was in the line of duty—related to his collecting intelligence—then he understood. Otherwise, it was simply too dangerous. Boteler nodded and went out into the hot night air.

He reached the Little Soho shortly after 7:30 P.M. It was a small café on a narrow lane, barely wide enough for a British jeep, and just a block off Ledra Street, dubbed "Murder Mile" for all who had recently been killed there. The café's windows were covered with wire to deter any would-be terrorist from hurling a grenade into the restaurant. Ordinarily the door was locked and opened only when the owner, Mr. Tunk, recognized one of his patrons. But on this night of stifling heat, it was too hot to observe that precaution.

The door was wide open, letting in a welcomed breeze that offset the heat from the kitchen and its ovens, plainly visible through a large plate-glass window. Inside were nine or ten tables. The specialty was Hungarian fare. It was known to be especially hospitable to the British and their Royal Warwickshire Regiment. Sometimes it even served as an impromptu command post when the Brits made security sweeps through the city, raiding Cypriot homes and businesses or searching for caches of weapons and fugitive terrorists.

When Boteler arrived, many of the tables were taken. Boteler took a seat at a small table closest to the door. Just behind him was the owner's parrot, perched on a wooden swing in his cage. Boteler nodded a hello to several groups of men whom he had come to recognize as fellow Americans in the preceding week, though he did not know them by name. Despite the consulate's warnings and the pledges by U.S. personnel not to venture out unnecessarily, most of those in the restaurant were Americans, and all of these, CIA.

It was curious that Boteler, while the only employee of the CIA's Plans Division on Cyprus, was virtually surrounded by covert CIA officers posing as State Department employees. They were there to man one of the CIA's largest radio relay facilities. The age of Morse code was in its final years, and these men, tethered to headsets and keys, spent their days transmitting all the open and encrypted messages that flowed between Washington and its embassies throughout the Mideast, including Baghdad, Kabul, Ankara, Damascus, and Cairo.

Cyprus was the ideal spot for such a facility. It was free of industrial interference and centrally located. On clear days the CIA communicators could even listen in on the conversations of cabdrivers idling at hotels in Cairo and Beirut. Their division of the CIA was known by the cryptonym KU CLUB. It was the communications agency within the Agency.

On this hot night in mid-June, many of them had gathered in disregard of security restrictions that they had signed and initialed only months earlier. They had also been advised to do whatever they could to distinguish themselves from the British, who were targets of the terrorists. One long-standing CIA suggestion was to wear bow ties, something the British never did. But on this night they could not be bothered. They were just out to enjoy a cold beer and a decent meal.

Seated behind Boteler, at a table for two, were Jim Dace and Jim Coleman. Dace was thirty-one and dining on one of his favorite meals, chicken livers and rice. At a larger table in the center of the restaurant, fifteen feet from Boteler, sat Chuck Groff and Donald P. Mulvey. Mulvey was an Agency "commo" man who maintained the radio equipment. He had arrived in Cyprus six days earlier. With them was Jack Bane, who was enjoying a steak and nursing a Tom Collins. He was a CIA engineer who worked on the heating and air-conditioning units at the relay station.

At precisely 9:39 P.M. the movie let out up the street and a commotion could be heard as people exited the theater. Just then two boys, neither yet in their teens, appeared at the door of the Little Soho restaurant. Each had something in his hands, an oblong pipelike object that they tossed into the restaurant. Both objects came to rest beneath Boteler's table. The boys ran, disappearing into an alleyway.

Dace remembers the smell of punk like the Fourth of July. It was the fuse burning, the scent of cordite. Coleman, too, smelled it. Their glances met, then Dace turned away for a second, and when he looked back in Coleman's direction, he found Coleman curled up on the floor. Dace threw himself as far from the smell as he could, crouching so low he remembers it was as if he were trying to crawl into his own shoes.

He looked up just long enough to see Boteler rising from his chair, attempting to distance himself from the impending blast. But Boteler's feet became entangled in the legs of the chair.

Groff stood up and flipped the table over for protection. In the brief moment that followed, Bane and Groff dove to the floor. Mulvey remembers hearing the hiss of a fuse.

Then came the first of two deafening blasts.

The room filled with smoke. The lights went out. Shards of glass from both the front window and the rear one by the kitchen flew in all directions. Shrapnel ripped into Boteler's heart, his stomach, and his legs. And still, somehow, he stumbled forward toward the door.

When the bombs exploded, whatever came out of them skidded across the terrazzo floor. Bane, who was lying facedown, felt a hot piece of shrapnel slash at his chest, leaving what would be an oblong scar. It came to a rest in his neck, a quarter inch from his artery. His corduroy pants were tattered and bloodied. In all he suffered five wounds, the deepest one being in his right leg. Dace felt the searing of shrapnel in his buttocks and feet. His shoes and pants were full of blood. He looked down to see his left hand, between the forefinger and thumb, peeled open like a rose.

Dace gathered himself up and staggered to the door, blood squishing in his shoes. There, lying in the doorway, was Boteler, his stomach opened by the blast and his legs mangled. The blood from his left femoral artery rose like a gusher, three feet into the air. A British soldier looked on in horror. "My God," cried the soldier, "he is still alive." But an instant later the blood stopped and Boteler was still. The life had gone out of him. He was twenty-six.

The concrete walls and floor of the restaurant had been pocked by fist-sized holes from the shrapnel, but somehow the parrot that perched directly behind Boteler had survived the blast with only a few ruffled feathers.

Greek Cypriot witnesses to the explosion milled about the scene, showing no apparent concern either for the explosion or for the young man's body lying in the doorway. None of them offered assistance to the wounded, and several were observed to be grinning and chatting away as if at a social gathering.

Boteler's body was taken to the British military hospital. Bane and Dace were taken into surgery. Both recovered. Shortly after the attack, police took into custody three youths. Privately the police admitted they doubted the boys were the perpetrators.

That night, in Washington, Boteler's father, Charles, received a telegram. "Department regrets to inform you of the sudden death your son at Nicosia as result bombing cafe, and extends deepest sympathy. Advise religious preference and disposition effects and remains." Signed "Myron S. Garland, Department of State."

News of Boteler's death spread quickly. Anne Paffenbarger's mother handed her the morning paper. That was how she learned that Boteler had been killed. She ran upstairs to her bedroom and collapsed on her bed, and spent the day crying hysterically. Her father knelt down beside the bed and tried to comfort her, but it was no use. For a long time she would wake up in the depths of the night sobbing uncontrollably.

Boteler's teammates from Haverford learned one by one of Boteler's death from the morning paper or from the news on their car radios. As the first American fatality in the Cyprus conflict, his death was front-page news. But it was reported as the death of a State Department employee, a vice-consul. Never was there the suggestion that he was a covert operative of the CIA. His cover was intact.

Boteler's body was shipped to Washington's Gawler Funeral Home at 1752 Pennsylvania Avenue. His diplomatic passport—number 7758—an essential part of his cover identity, was returned to the State Department.

In Washington the State Department declared Boteler's killing "a blind and senseless" act. In Nicosia Governor Sir John Harding expressed his sorrow to the U.S. consulate and visited the two Americans still convalescing in the hospital. In Athens the Greek minister of foreign affairs, Evanghelos Averoff, expressed that government's "deepest regret" at Boteler's death but also did not miss a chance to exploit it for political advantage. "As all Greeks," he said, "I am deeply saddened by the fact that American blood was shed on the martyred island of Cyprus, which is under British Administration." In London former president Harry Truman was asked by reporters if Boteler's death might affect U.S. views of the Cyprus problem. "I sincerely hope that it will not have any terrible repercussion at home, although it is likely to do that," he said. "I shall be very happy indeed if that situation can be cleared up and settled."

There were also private expressions of sympathy to the Boteler family. Secretary of State John Foster Dulles, whose brother, Allen, headed the CIA, wrote Boteler's father the day after the killing. "He died in the line of duty, courageously advancing the high interests of the United States. In the short time he served with the Department of State he earned the friendship and admiration of all his colleagues."

The CIA, even in its official letter of condolence, did not let on that Boteler had still been working for the Agency. Deputy Director Lieutenant General Charles Pearre Cabell wrote Boteler's father: "Since we knew him better and longer than his more recent associates, I can add

e with us was marked by rapid advancement and assign-
ʒual responsibility. He had been promoted twice and a third
ʒas in process when he resigned to accept the appointment
ʒpartment of State in Cyprus, an assignment which he knew
to be naʒardous and challenging. During his employment with this
Agency, William was characterized by his superiors as 'an outstanding
young officer' with special reference to his initiative, drive, managerial
ability, high standards of accomplishment, and acceptance of responsibility. We regarded him as a young man of highest promise, whose death is
a serious loss to the public service."

Boteler's funeral was held at 2:30 P.M. on Thursday, June 21.
Family, friends, and CIA colleagues gathered at Gawler's Funeral Home,
a few blocks from the White House and just five blocks from CIA headquarters. Seven pallbearers carried the casket. Three were teammates and
friends from Boteler's days at Haverford—Hal Cragin, who had sold him
his life insurance policy five years earlier, Bud Garrison, and Ed Hibberd.
A fourth was Haverford line coach William Doherty. The other three
men had been Boteler's childhood friends or under his watch at summer
camp.

As organist Marguerite Brice played "Hark! A Voice Saith All Are
Mortal," mourners entered the room and penned their names into a book
of remembrance. Among those in attendance were Archibald Macintosh,
acting president of Haverford, Assistant Secretary of State George V.
Allen, and CIA colleague Frank Laubinger, who had lunched with
Boteler a month earlier and had tried to stifle his own ominous premo-
nitions. There, too, was Hugh J. Cunningham, a senior Agency officer
who signed the book "representing Mr. Allen W. Dulles," director of the
Central Intelligence Agency.

Following the funeral, Boteler's body was laid to rest in Arlington
Cemetery on Pershing Hill, not far from where the general himself is interred.

Six days after his death, at 10:30 Saturday morning, June 23, a memorial service was held in Boteler's honor at the Church of St. Paul in
Nicosia. The archdeacon of Cyprus, A. W. Adeney, offered a prayer that
began, "Look down, O Lord, upon our island and illuminate it with thy
celestial brightness, and from the sons of lights, vanish the deeds of dark-

ness." The U.S. flag flew beside the altar. Rarer still was the vision of a Greek monk and a Turkish religious leader there together, along with the consuls of every nation with representatives on the island. Hardly anyone in attendance had had the chance to meet Bill Boteler. He had been on Cyprus barely one month.

On July 5, 1956, eighteen days after his death, a letter arrived at the U.S. consulate in Nicosia, addressed to U.S. Consul Courtney. The three-paragraph letter was titled "Tragic Mistake." It was from EOKA's leader, Dighenis, the alias for George Grivas, whom the Agency had suspected all along was behind the killing. It confirmed what Courtney and the CIA had already concluded: that Boteler and the other Americans had not been targeted in the attack but were simply in the wrong place at the wrong time. "No Greek hates the American people, of which we are sure that the great majority with its pure liberal feeling stands on our side in our just fight," wrote Grivas. "We are deeply sorry for the loss of the American diplomat. We advise foreigners who live in Cyprus, for their safety, not to frequent British places of entertainment, as it is not always possible to distinguish them from our English enemy."

. . .

Five years later, on January 5, 1961, Secretary of State Christian A. Herter added William Pierce Boteler's name to the department's wall honoring those killed in the line of service, the same wall that featured Doug Mackiernan's name. Boteler's father attended the ceremony that day. He understood that the State Department's recognition was the only way in which Boteler, a covert officer of the CIA, could be publicly honored. Better, he reasoned, to be honored even if in the context of a cover position than not at all.

To this day Jack Bane, now seventy-nine and suffering from Parkinson's disease, carries a remembrance of that terrible evening at the Little Soho café—a piece of shrapnel lodged in his right leg. Following the attack, Jim Dace was called on the carpet by his superior, who threatened to put a black mark on his record for violating security restrictions. "Fine," shot back Dace. "You do that and I'm going to go to the inspector general and bring down your entire staff who went there every day. I paid for my visit to the Little Soho restaurant in blood and tears." Dace's superior relented and did not put anything in the personnel file. But then, neither did he speak to him again for ten years. And Dace never again could bring himself to eat chicken livers and rice, his meal that fateful night.

As for Cyprus, it remains as hotly contested a piece of property as any on earth. Turks and Greeks have drawn a line across the island, and the threat of open warfare is ever present. Nowhere is there a monument or a tablet to remember the handsome young diplomat named William Boteler who gave his life there. There is, however, a main avenue in the capital of Nicosia that is named for the man most responsible for Boteler's death, General Grivas. Today the head of EOKA is remembered by ethnic Greeks not as a terrorist, but as a freedom fighter and a hero.

Anne Paffenbarger returned to teach at Arthur Murray for another five years, then moved to Manhattan and managed a men's shirt store. But she could never bring herself to throw away Bill Boteler's letters. And never again did she speak to anyone of marriage.

CHAPTER 4

Waiting for Godot

BY 1956, the year Boteler was killed, Hugh Redmond had spent five years in a Shanghai prison. During that time, history itself had seemed to accelerate. The Korean War had come and gone, ending in a costly stalemate—55,000 American fatalities. Stalin had died. The United States had detonated the first H-bomb. The French had been humiliated at Dien Bien Phu in Vietnam, and Eisenhower had warned that the nations of Southeast Asia could fall to Communism like so many dominoes. Senator Joe McCarthy's demagoguery was but a bitter memory, except for those whose lives he'd ruined. (McCarthy himself would die a year later, at forty-eight, his liver shot from booze.) Mount Everest had been conquered, and theatergoers were scratching their heads over a play called *Waiting for Godot.*

Through all those years and changes, a defiant Redmond remained in his cell in Shanghai, cut off from the world but not forgotten. The Yonkers Citizens Committee for the Release of Hugh Francis Redmond ceaselessly campaigned to keep his name before the public. Behind the scenes, orchestrating and financing many of those efforts, was the CIA.

In June 1956, the very month Boteler died in Cyprus, Redmond's fortunes began looking up. That month Redmond and four American priests were transferred from bleak prison cells to a private house, where they were given somewhat more freedom of movement, though, to be sure, they were still prisoners. And after five years of silence, Redmond was now permitted to write monthly two-page letters to his mother, though he was not permitted to discuss the conditions of his confinement, indoctrination, or other sensitive topics.

On July 23, 1956, Redmond sat down to write his mother of his improving situation. Even the food was better. No longer would he need her to mail him tins of meat or cheese. Instead, he asked for cartons of cigarettes—Lucky Strikes—as well as powdered milk and sweets. He also asked that she send him sports columns from the *Daily News* and the baseball standings. But there was no hint that his release was on the horizon. When baseball season ends, he wrote, he wanted news of football and boxing. His only way to mark the change in seasons, besides the encroaching damp and chill of winter, was to follow from afar the rotation of sports. Each time baseball season came around again it meant another year had passed.

By December 1956 the Yonkers committee, with the blessing of the CIA, had begun a massive letter-writing campaign. Adults and schoolchildren wrote tens of thousands of letters demanding Redmond's release. All of them were addressed to Mao Zedong. To show its continuing concern, the Agency's Ben DeFelice provided Ruth Redmond with emotional support and helped her with the inevitable bureaucratic and financial issues that arose in her son's long absence. Within the Agency, DeFelice had already gained something of a reputation for compassion as he championed the interests of those widowed, orphaned, and otherwise bereaved by losses suffered in performance of Agency duties. The CIA assured Ruth Redmond that her son would not be forgotten and that the government would not rest until he was home again.

But if elements within the government were dedicated to working for Redmond's release, other parts seemed too busy to take serious notice, or too inflexible to seize opportunities. The State Department made innumerable entreaties of the Chinese in talks in Geneva, resulting in the release of forty-one U.S. citizens—but Redmond was not among them. Nor were Richard Fecteau and John Downey, the two

CIA fliers shot down in November 1952. "Utterly false," was how the State Department had dismissed charges that Downey and Fecteau were spies. They had, it was said again and again, simply been on a routine flight between Korea and Japan. And while Eisenhower had consented to see other parents whose loved ones were held in China, he refused to see Ruth Redmond, even after the State Department recommended such a visit and she had sworn to keep any such meeting a secret. This hurt her deeply and led her to believe that her son's fate was not a priority.

Finally, and most galling of all, the United States had imposed a blanket prohibition on American citizens traveling to China. On May 23, 1957, Ruth Redmond met in Washington with Secretary of State John Foster Dulles, an ambassador, and members of the department's China Affairs branch. But there was no giving-in on the issue of travel to China. It would be viewed as a violation of the Trading with the Enemy Act. Six years into Mao's regime, the United States continued to refuse to recognize the Communist government and acted as if the world's most populous nation were little more than a fiction. What tormented Ruth Redmond was that a year earlier, on January 6, 1956, Chinese authorities via Beijing Radio had extended an invitation to the families of those imprisoned to visit their loved ones. Whether it was merely a propaganda trick or a bona fide humanitarian gesture—or both—it had raised her hopes that she might at last see her son again. And now the State Department declared such a visit out of the question.

As much as Washington doubtless wanted to win the release of Redmond, Fecteau, and Downey, it was also determined, so long as they were being held, to take full political advantage of such an emotionally charged issue. The three Americans were repeatedly portrayed as innocents caught in the grasp of an inhumane and totalitarian state. The chorus demanding their release became a rallying cry against Communism, spilling over into the general tide of anti-Red hysteria. The powerful image of three young and falsely accused Americans held behind bars year after year became part of that larger collage that presented the Chinese regime as heartless and barbaric. In working-class Yonkers and beyond, the immensity of the injustice became a hallmark of the Cold War, one of those half-truths upon which all demonization is predicated.

Had the full truth come out—that the three Americans were covert CIA operatives caught in the act of espionage, that they were part of a broad and aggressive U.S. secret campaign against the Chinese government—then the American public might have been forced to reexamine the issue of their incarceration. No government goes easy on those engaged in espionage or seeking to topple it by force. And there was an even stickier problem for the United States: once Washington had so passionately denied that the three were U.S. intelligence agents, any subsequent admission would tarnish American credibility and render suspect all future protestations of innocence. No one understood this better than Redmond himself. The three were not only prisoners but pawns in the Cold War.

There was the additional complication that throughout the very years that the three were being held, the CIA was stepping up covert actions against the Chinese designed to badger the regime of Mao Zedong. Some took the form of support of remnant Nationalist groups in China, providing matériel and personnel within the mainland. Others worked on the borders.

In 1957 the Agency began an elaborate program of recruiting Tibetan refugees from India and Nepal who were flown to a top secret CIA training base in the Colorado Rockies. There they were trained in paramilitary techniques and prepared to unleash a wave of sabotage against the Chinese. Colorado had been selected because it most closely approximated the high altitude of Tibet. CIA pilots recall many of the refugees meditating or working their prayer wheels on the entire flight to the United States. All along China's extensive border—Burma, Nepal, Vietnam—for years to come, the United States would engage in covert mischief-making, a kind of deadly tit-for-tat exchange characteristic of the Cold War.

Not even the most sanguine of Agency planners imagined such pinpricks would bring down Mao's regime, but it was hoped that it might distract Chinese war planners and stretch thin military resources just enough to prevent the Communists from expanding their choke hold to the rest of the subcontinent. And there was another reason such covert operations persisted. The thorny Chiang Kai-shek, so adept at wringing massive resources out of the U.S. government during World War II, was equally successful in exploiting American fears of an unrestrained mainland. The more cynical Agency operatives came to see these covert operations against the mainland as little more than a sop to the Generalissimo, Chiang Kai-shek.

Such incessant heckling would have done little to soften Beijing's heart or convince the regime that it was time to relent and release the long-suffering Redmond, Fecteau, and Downey. Instead, it increased the toll of casualties. Some within the Agency were troubled by the continued covert assaults on the mainland. One of these was Peter Sichel. Hardly squeamish, he was a veteran of the OSS, had spent seven years in Berlin, and from 1956 until 1959 was the CIA's station chief in Hong Kong.

But the efforts to infiltrate the mainland and the risks taken by both Americans and Chinese Nationalists made little sense to him. His assessment: "It was a total waste of time and a total death mission for anyone who got involved." In 1959 he quit the Agency, disenchanted with what he saw as a "cowboy mentality" and mounting casualties. He was decorated with the prestigious DIM, the Distinguished Intelligence Medal.

Sichel, as Hong Kong station chief, had been well aware of the plight of Redmond, Downey, and Fecteau, but there was little he or anyone else in the Agency could do to effect their release. By September 1957 six years of prison had taken its toll on Redmond. He had survived his bout with beriberi, but the poor diet and lack of access to a dentist had become every bit as potent a torment as any devised by his captors. For months his teeth and gums had ached. He was only thirty-seven, but already he was nearly toothless, his gums inflamed. He was finally taken to the St. Marie Hospital, where the last of his decayed teeth were extracted, and where, in the weeks ahead, he would have repeated oral surgery. Doctors worked to fill in his jawbone. With no teeth and a mouth full of stitches it was nearly impossible to eat. He began to shed even more weight. His hair was falling out, and his right eye was afflicted with a twitch.

But there was no evidence of his surrendering to self-pity in any of his letters. "It suddenly struck me," he wrote in a September 10, 1957, letter, "when I wrote the date on the heading of this letter that today is

Ruthie's [his sister's] birthday. Please give her my regards. When a fellow has a kid sister who is 26 he doesn't feel so young anymore."

Nine days later Redmond was awakened and given five minutes to ready himself to be interviewed by a group of young Americans who had gone to China in defiance of the State Department's travel ban. Standing before them, Redmond appeared sullen and hostile. He went out of his way to deny, once again, any link to the CIA. One of those visiting Redmond described him as "100 percent American and hard as nails."

"Did you ever consider yourself to be politically conscious?" one of the young Americans asked.

"What is that—a Marxist question?" fired back Redmond. "I've been reading a lot of Marxist books and that seems familiar."

But Redmond was reading more than Marx. The bare-fisted lad who had dropped out of college after a semester and had never demonstrated any great intellectual craving, was becoming a voracious reader. Prior to prison, as a former commando and paratrooper, he had concentrated largely on developing his physical skills. Now, within the cramped confines of a cell, he showed no less energy expanding his mental horizons. It began with an interest in magazines, among them *Scientific American*, *Popular Science*, *Science Digest*, and *Harper's*. Next he set about learning other languages—first Chinese and, later, Russian, Spanish, Italian, and French. In each language he read literary classics. Oddly it was not these often provocative works that troubled the Chinese, but *Reader's Digest* they confiscated.

And still Redmond maintained an insatiable interest in sports. "The world series is all over," he lamented, "and I don't know yet who won the pennant in the National League. The Yankees looked like a cinch in the American League. Please send me some clippings on the series if you haven't already done so. Who won the Patterson-Rademacher and Robinson-Basilio fights?" A copy of *Sports Illustrated* was perennially on his request list to his mother.

Still irked by the visit from the young Americans, which he viewed as a traitorous act, he wrote his mother asking her not to make any effort to see him. It offended him that any American would challenge the travel ban, an act that implicitly recognized what he viewed as an illegitimate regime.

But on December 6, 1957, the State Department suddenly changed its mind and announced that an exception to the travel ban would be made. Ruth Redmond and close relatives of five other American prisoners still held by the Chinese would be permitted to travel to China to see their loved ones.

"I certainly am going to China even if I have to walk," declared a jubilant Ruth Redmond that very night. She had been told the cost of the trip would be about $3,000, far more than she could afford on the salary of a cafeteria worker, but local civic groups quickly offered to raise the money. The CIA also quietly made its own hefty donation. Ruth Redmond immediately cabled Chinese Premier Chou En-lai asking for an entry visa. It had been eleven and a half years since she had last seen her son. Fecteau's and Downey's mothers sent similar cablegrams to the Chinese. Just eleven days later, on December 17, the Chinese approved the request.

While Ruth Redmond readied herself for the long trip, preparations for her visit were also being made in Shanghai. At thirty-eight Redmond had almost become accustomed to life without teeth. Then, suddenly, with the prospect of his mother's visit and the attendant public attention it would bring, the Chinese took a renewed interest in Redmond's oral problems and his appearance. On Christmas Day 1957, six days before Ruth Redmond's slated departure for China, Hugh Redmond was finally fitted with a set of false teeth.

Four days later, on December 29, 1957, Redmond's wife, Lydia, paid an unexpected visit to her mother-in-law in Yonkers. Lydia, then a thirty-year-old émigré who spoke with a thick Russian accent, was struggling to make a living. She had not seen her husband in more than seven years. There had always been a rift between Redmond's mother and his wife. Redmond had written his mother that it had been more than two years since he had heard from Lydia, whom he called Lily. Now, suddenly, Lydia Redmond appeared on the eve of Ruth Redmond's departure, asking that her mother-in-law convey her love to the husband she had known for so short a time so long ago. Ruth Redmond remained deeply suspicious and resentful of her.

On January 1, 1958, three mothers—Ruth Redmond, Jessie Fecteau, and Mary V. Downey—as well as Mary Downey's son, William, gathered at New York International Airport, Idlewild, Queens. Fecteau's father decided not to go. He told the CIA's Ben DeFelice he was unsure that he could control his anger. "I would spit in the eye of the first Chinese I see," he told DeFelice.

Each of the three mothers carried a precious cargo for their sons: cigarettes, candy, socks, fruitcakes, oranges, vitamins, family photographs. They arrived in Hong Kong on January 6 and were escorted by British Red Cross representatives to the Chinese border. At the stout Lowu Bridge linking the New Territories with the mainland, the mothers were received by Chinese Red Cross officials. But when the women presented their passports, the Chinese scowled at the documents. The officials were intent upon protesting the U.S. refusal to recognize their government, and they objected to the term "Communist China." There was, after all, from their perspective, but one China. From Beijing's perspective the Republic of China, as Taiwan was known, was nothing more than another province, albeit one in rebellion.

Once across the bridge, Ruth Redmond was taken to Canton. At 6:15 the morning of January 8 she boarded a rickety two-engine plane. There was one other passenger on board, a Chinese woman carrying a large bunch of green bananas. Her name was Mrs. Ling and she would mysteriously appear in the background at nearly every stop during Ruth Redmond's three weeks in China.

From Canton it was a grueling eight-hour flight to Shanghai. Ruth Redmond shivered from the cold. There were no seat belts and she was not even offered a glass of water. Finally the plane landed in Shanghai and she was taken to the Ward Road prison.

In the hours before Ruth Redmond's arrival at the prison, the warden had carefully explained to Hugh Redmond that his mother would be arriving, that she would be asking if he was guilty of espionage, and that he should prepare a brief statement of confession so that the sound cameras could record it. Ever defiant, Redmond coolly explained that such a statement would be forbidden under prison rules, which prohibited inmates from discussing their cases before visitors.

Trying to maintain his composure, the warden offered to waive the provision in Redmond's case. Nothing doing, replied Redmond, who then noted that when Chinese prisoners received visitors there were no cameras present. If he could not see his mother in private, he threatened not to see her at all. The enraged warden was forced to accept a compromise. The cameras and reporters would be present, but they would be kept at the opposite end of the meeting room. And there was no more talk of a confession. Once again Redmond had won.

. . .

As Ruth Redmond reached the main gate of the prison, she carried under her arm a homemade sweater, woolen socks, and a carton of Lucky Strikes. She walked past the guards and was led into a large room empty of furnishings but for a single table and chairs. Ringing the room were Chinese reporters and cameramen waiting anxiously to record the event. And there stood Hugh Redmond, the son she had not seen since he had left for China in 1946. They hugged for several minutes under the watchful eyes of guards and interpreters, who monitored every word that was said. Their embrace was featured on the front page of the *New York Times*.

Redmond was dressed in a business suit, a blue shirt, a tie, and a short woolen coat. It would be the first of seven meetings with his mother. At each meeting, mother and son would hold hands and speak softly. After two hours the guards would begin to fidget and the Redmonds knew their time together was over. Then Hugh would be escorted out of the room, and some five minutes later Ruth Redmond would be led from the prison. Only once were Hugh Redmond and his mother permitted to leave the room together. That was for a momentary walk to the prison's front gate, where a Chinese official snapped a photo of the two together.

The conversation was limited to talk of family, how Redmond's ailing father was doing, and news of his own friends back in Yonkers. He could also ask of conditions and fashions in the United States. There was superficial talk of his prison routine. He was living in what had been a caretaker's house at the far end of the prison. He had a single room, furnished with a bed, a chair, a dresser, and a desk. He was permitted one bath a week. In his room he had a radio and was permitted to listen to one hour a day of classical music. Breakfast consisted of Chinese mush, tea, and bread. He said he had little to read, though he had recently read of Einstein's Theory of Relativity. Few of the books Ruth Redmond had sent had been delivered.

Redmond said he had written her a letter every month. Ruth Redmond expressed surprise. She had not heard from her son in eight months.

At their last meeting the Red Cross representatives arranged for Ruth Redmond and her son to have dinner together. A special meal was prepared at a local hotel and served in the same sparse prison room where they had been meeting.

The last time Ruth Redmond visited her son he volunteered a cryptic message that she wrote down in the log recording her visit. "He said that he hoped it would not be twelve years before we got together again and that without hope one could not live. He added that I should 'trust in the airlines' and he would be seeing me soon."

Upon her return, Ruth Redmond learned that the Yonkers Board of Education had promoted her in her absence to manager of the cafeteria at Franklin Junior High. It was not much more money, but it was good to know the community was behind her. Meanwhile, in Washington, the CIA quietly continued to accumulate paychecks in her son's account and to promote him as if he were just another promising covert employee on assignment.

Redmond for his part continued to write letters, vainly attempting to keep in touch with the realities and icons of a changing America. "Tell Billy and Tommy [nephews] to make sure they do their homework," he wrote, "and don't sit up too late watching T.V. or they'll grow up to be like Elvis. Love to all—Hughie." This from a man imprisoned so long he almost certainly had never heard a song by Elvis Presley.

At home in Yonkers, Ruth Redmond vowed to return to China one day and to see her son again. In the meantime she and her son would have to content themselves with letters. It was a cruelly superficial correspondence, censored at both ends. Ruth would write nothing that might upset her son, and he knew that his every word would pass before the prison censor. Still, it was the fact of their correspondence more than its content that sustained them for so many years.

Redmond rarely even hinted at self-pity. Instead, he ended almost every letter with the same thought—a request that his young nephews be taken out for ice cream. Over the years, the arrival of a letter from "Uncle Hughie" came to be a joyous occasion associated with a visit to the ice cream parlor. Outside the Redmond home, memories of Hugh Redmond faded. It seemed that Redmond and his Agency compatriots, Fecteau and Downey, were destined to be relegated to history, a somber footnote in the annals of the Cold War. But the ordeals of these three men were far from over.

CHAPTER 5

Faith and Betrayal

How could I have been so stupid as to let them proceed?
JOHN F. KENNEDY TO ADVISERS

AT THE AGENCY it was often the elite who made the decisions and the good old boys who paid the price. So it was with Richard Mervin Bissell, Jr., and Thomas Willard Ray. Bissell was an intellectual, the son of Yankee privilege. Born in the Mark Twain House in West Hartford, Connecticut, he grew up in tailor-made shirts and attended Groton, Yale, and the London School of Economics. Ray was from Birmingham, Alabama, the son of a construction worker and a seventeen-year-old bride. A southerner through and through, he was soft-spoken and unassuming—just "Pete," to his friends.

Bissell was cross-eyed and gangly, a poor athlete, and a man of eclectic interests. He was said to have memorized the nation's train schedules, its routes, and even the gauge of the tracks. Ray was short and stocky, a guard on the high school football team. His interests included a pet chicken—until it was stolen.

Bissell was a wunderkind who would go on to teach economics at Yale and MIT and helped forge the Marshall Plan for Europe's recovery. He joined the CIA in February 1954 with the vague title of Chief of Development Projects Staff. Soon after, he sired the U-2 spy plane, revolutionizing intelligence efforts. By July 1956 his eye-in-the-sky was flying over the Soviet Union, providing a long-denied view of that country's bomber, missile, and submarine production. Next he oversaw development of the sleek SR-71 Blackbird, a titanium spy plane that flew at two thousand miles an hour at a staggering 85,000 feet above the earth. In an hour its cameras could sweep 100,000 square miles of the planet's surface. And finally Bissell had a major hand in the Corona satellite project, which ushered in a whole new era in reconnaissance.

But in Bissell's mind his greatest achievement was the broad interpretation he gave to the doctrine of covert action. He had a major hand in the toppling of the government of Guatemala. In 1958 he was made the CIA's deputy director for plans, the vaunted chief of clandestine services worldwide and heir apparent to the fabled Allen Dulles, Director Central Intelligence.

Pete Ray had no such illustrious résumé. He had joined the Air National Guard not long after turning sixteen. He had forged his mother's signature on the enlistment papers. By 1960 he was inspecting aircraft and spending weekends as youth director of a Methodist church. Flying was all he ever wanted to do, be it behind the stick of a lumbering bomber or a gnatlike Cessna.

Bissell was formal. Even his oldest son and namesake found him emotionally inaccessible. "I'm your man-eating shark," he once said of himself. Ray was down-to-earth. "Tenderhearted," his mother, Mary, would say of him.

The two were a universe apart. Hard to imagine such divergent paths would cross, but cross they did in a crisis that forever scarred the CIA.

These two lives began to converge in 1960. It was a time of portents that would shake public faith and chip away at the nation's naiveté. A year earlier, in Birmingham, as elsewhere, Americans were shocked by congressional hearings into the TV quiz show *Twenty-One*. The audience had been had. The winning contestant had been fed the answers in advance. That same year, even the music became suspect as radio was rocked by a payola scandal. In Pete Ray's Birmingham, a listless and segregated town of coke and steel, the code of racial separation threatened to unravel.

And at the CIA it was the golden age of covert action. Emboldened by past successes in Iran and Guatemala, it increasingly saw itself as a source of action, not merely advice and analysis. It had deftly managed to embrace its triumphs and quietly slip its failures.

Notable among the failures was the case of Indonesia. In 1957 President Eisenhower had approved CIA covert actions to support rebel Indonesian army colonels in an effort to oust President Sukarno, who was seen as too cozy with the Communists. One plan involved embarrassing the Indonesian president by distributing photos of a Sukarno look-alike caught in a compromising position with someone posing as a "beautiful blond Soviet agent." The Agency even had a porno movie made featuring a man wearing a Sukarno mask. Such use of scandal as a psychological weapon dated back to the days of the OSS and remained an integral part of the CIA's kit to discredit those seen as ideological enemies. (One such ploy involved the distribution of defective condoms passed out in the name of a Philippine senator with leftist leanings.)

And as had happened before, Eisenhower would rely on the doctrine of deniability. He could remain aloof and statesmanlike while others at the Agency did his bidding in the shadows. On April 30 Eisenhower declared with reference to Indonesia: "Our policy is one of careful neutrality and proper deportment all the way through so as not to be taking sides where it is none of our business."

But the Agency's plan for Indonesia went well beyond psychological tactics. Arms were supplied to the rebels. B-26 bombers, scrubbed clean of U.S. insignia, were manned by American pilots and flew sorties in support of the rebels. In one instance a CIA aircraft mistakenly bombed a church, killing most of its congregation. On May 18, 1958, Agency pilot Allen Pope was shot down and captured. A week later he was presented at a news conference, along with documents implicating the CIA. Pope would spend four years in prison before Robert Kennedy could win his release. And Sukarno would long remain in power.

The CIA operation in Indonesia came to a close just as Bissell took charge of the division overseeing the clandestine service. Yet the failure in Indonesia was neatly contained and the Agency entered the 1960s full of self-confidence. The hard lessons of Indonesia—presidential denials, a failed ouster, disguised aircraft, downed airmen—were somehow lost on the Agency, though they would soon enough resurface with a vengeance.

In 1960 the CIA prepared to shed the decrepit temporary buildings clustered around the Reflecting Pool on the Mall left over from World War II. Soon it would withdraw across the wide Potomac to Langley, Virginia, and to a grand and gleaming edifice more befitting its new stature and ambitions. The cornerstone had already been laid. An aging President Eisenhower presided over the ceremony. The move represented the end of an epoch in Agency history. The mind-set of World War II and the OSS—that radical threats sometimes required radical solutions—continued on, but now the CIA was wholly a creature of the Cold War. Its new headquarters was a testament to its expanded authority and, as some would suggest, its hubris. No longer at the margins of foreign policy, Bissell's clandestine service was the primary arrow in the president's quiver against Communism.

Bissell's brilliance was beyond question. His projects catapulted the Agency into an entirely new era of intelligence collection. But they also carried with them their own unseen perils. The U-2, Bissell's crowning achievement, had been emblematic of American superiority and invulnerability, a spy plane assumed to be beyond the reach of the Soviets. Then, suddenly, on May 1, 1960, a Soviet SA-2 surface-to-air missile felled a U-2 at sixty thousand feet. Its pilot, thirty-year-old Francis Gary Powers, did not take the shellfish toxin given him by the CIA and contained in a hollowed-out silver dollar. Instead, he parachuted into the welcoming arms of the Kremlin. Eisenhower vehemently denied the existence of U-2 intelligence overflights, while a NASA spokesman announced it was merely a "weather research plane" gone astray. Then a gloating Premier Nikita Khrushchev paraded about his trophy, the American pilot. It was all too reminiscent of Indonesia, only two years earlier.

Another thirty-year-old pilot, Pete Ray, could not help but take note of the spectacle and watch aghast.

American credibility had taken another direct hit. The president had been caught in an outright lie, doubling the humiliation of the event. The CIA faced a barrage of unfamiliar and unwanted questions. Trust in government was shaken, and even the unflappable Bissell was momentarily at a loss. Undaunted, the CIA continued that year to expand its covert operations and to insert itself into myriad faraway places, including the Congo, Laos, and Vietnam. But it was closer to home that the Agency focused most of its attention.

. . .

Ninety miles off the Florida coast, Fidel Castro had set up a revolutionary government. Eisenhower had concluded that Castro had begun to "look like a madman," that he was a Marxist-Leninist intent upon using the island nation to export revolution throughout the hemisphere. On January 13, 1960, a year after Castro had assumed power, Eisenhower resolved that the Cuban leader must be overthrown.

It was nearly a year before that decision in Washington trickled down to Birmingham, Alabama, and to Pete Ray, then on leave from the Alabama Air National Guard to train at nearby Fort Rucker. Ray would be one of nearly one hundred Alabama guardsmen who volunteered for the top secret Cuban assignment. In the dark about the specifics of the mission, he confided what little he knew to his wife, Margaret, and an uncle, Mac Bailey. Several times he traveled to Washington for polygraph and psychological tests. Ray's mother, Mary, grew increasingly curious. "What are you going to Washington for?" she asked. He did not answer her. His next trip to the capital, she repeated the question. "I am going on a secret mission," he said. "What, for the CIA?" she joked. Ray answered with nothing but a smile.

That Ray should have responded to such a shadowy appeal from the government would have come as no surprise to those who knew him. Like many in his National Guard unit, he was no ideologue, but he had absolute faith in God and country. If the government said the Communists were atheists bent on world domination, who was he to say otherwise? "If we don't fight them on their land," he once said, "we'll be fighting them in our backyard." And the charismatic John F. Kennedy's January 20, 1961, inaugural address seemed to extend to Ray a personal invitation to service. "Ask not what your country can do for you," he had

said, "ask what you can do for your country." That sort of appeal was ir-
resistible to a man like Pete Ray.

A few days before his departure from Birmingham, allegedly to undergo training, he asked his uncle to help him "sanitize" what few belongings he intended to take with him. Together, they took out the labels
from his clothes and buffed the brands from his belts. Ray even ground
down the heels of his shoes to remove the manufacturer's name. He was
to take nothing that might link him to the United States. Soon enough
he would be assigned a pseudonym. He was said to be going to a special
training school.

Before leaving, Ray told his wife, Margaret, that when she wrote
him, she should address the envelope to Joseph Greenland. The address
was Chicago. Unbeknownst to her, the other men of the Alabama Air
National Guard were giving their wives the same instructions. Just before he left, Ray acknowledged there was an element of risk. "If I
should stump my toe, take care of the children," he told her. Should
anything happen to him, he said, he would want her to remarry. With
that, he kissed his wife, seven-year-old son Tommy, and six-year-old
daughter Janet good-bye.

A week later Margaret received the first of many letters from
him. None of them disclosed anything of his location or his mission.
"This is a very good school but it sure does take all of my time," he
wrote on February 13, 1961. "I have bought two more suits and a hat.
It has been very cold. The top coat sure has helped." These last two
sentences were deliberate misinformation. When he returned home for
a brief visit, his wife, assuming he had been in a northern clime, was
startled to see that he had a deep tan. What he had not told her
was that he was at a secret CIA base deep in Guatemala where he was
training Cuban pilots.

In that same letter he reminded his wife to file the income taxes, to
repair the brakes on the family car, and to "tell Tommy and Janet Daddy
loves them and for them to look after you."

Subsequent letters were postmarked Washington or Birmingham.
He again sent his love to his wife, his son and daughter, and even their terrier, Chase. He fretted about his son's adjustment to school after the move
from Fort Rucker back to Birmingham. "I know it is hard on Tommy to
keep up in school due to the change, so don't be too hard on my little

man," he wrote. Ray remembered that he had himself repeated a year of school as a boy, following a similar move.

Margaret sent him photos of herself, and of Tommy and Janet. He marveled at Janet's long pigtails. But, much as he wanted to keep the photos, he returned them to his wife, in keeping with the security orders given him by the CIA. They were just one more item that could tie him to the United States. Often his letters were about the most mundane of concerns. He even reminded his wife to "have the septic tank and grease trap cleaned before warm weather sets in." Other times his letters reflected deeper concerns. He opened one letter with the question "Do you have all of the insurance policies paid up?"

For the first time, he was able to save a portion of his salary. "Tell Janet it is OK if you and her bought some new things," he wrote. Again he asked about the income tax. "Please get it filed because I will not be home before the deadline." What he did not mention was that the fast-approaching tax deadline, April 15, was also just two days before the invasion of Cuba.

· · ·

In the year before Ray and the other men of the Alabama Air National Guard joined the mission, much had happened to affect its outcome. Bissell and his advisers had worked hard to devise a plan that they believed could work. The idea was to insert on the shores of Cuba a small but well-trained corps of Cuban exiles who would gradually be augmented by an anti-Castro insurgency within that country. They were to land near the town of Trinidad, selected because it was hoped that some of the twenty thousand residents might join the assault force, and also because, if things went poorly in the landing, the nearby Escambray Mountains would provide a safe haven where the men could disperse and later regroup for future guerrilla operations.

Encumbering the scheme from the beginning was a component of deception so grand and unwieldy that it would prove its undoing. At President Kennedy's insistence, the operation was to appear to the world to be solely the work of Cuban exiles. The hand of America was to be entirely invisible. This demand for so-called deniability evolved into a tortured fiction.

From the outset Bissell and his advisers agreed that success depended on domination of the skies over Cuba. Castro's meager air force had to be destroyed or the exiles' landing would be doomed. Bissell found himself walking a constant tightrope between satisfying demands of deniability and the imperatives of a successful operation. To accommodate the former, he and his planners decided they would make it appear that any air support consisted of defectors from Castro's own air force.

That meant the planes used would have to be identical to those found in Castro's air force. Bissell approved the idea of using aging B-26s, World War II planes mothballed in dizzying numbers outside Tucson, Arizona. The aircraft were painted with Cuba Air Force insignias and numbers. Most of the Cuban fliers in the CIA operation had no combat experience and were commercial or cargo pilots. They would have to be trained by men still highly proficient in flying the aging bombers. Enter the Alabama Air National Guard, the country's last unit to use B-26s. It was that thin thread of events that brought together Richard Bissell and Thomas "Pete" Ray.

But the project was dogged with grave problems early on. All CIA covert operations are compartmented, meaning only those who are deemed necessary to the planning or execution of the operation are brought into the loop. But this operation was deemed so close-held that not even the Agency's director of intelligence was consulted. Such extreme secrecy led to the anomalous situation that the very individuals planning the operation also assessed its chances for success, violating a basic tenet of intelligence. But even as the CIA took pains to ensure that the operation remained a secret, the magnitude of the undertaking guaranteed that rumors were already seeping out in Washington and Miami, where much of the recruiting and planning was taking place. Cynics would later suggest that everyone knew the invasion was coming—except perhaps those who might have contributed to its success.

In late 1960 Bissell and CIA, desperate to bring down Castro, considered a number of harebrained schemes. One idea under serious consideration involved impregnating cigars with a depilatory that would make Castro's body hair and beard fall out. There was also a more deadly version of the scheme. In February 1961 the Agency delivered to Cuba a box of Castro's favorite cigars impregnated with the botulism toxin, though the box was apparently never delivered to the Cuban leader.

Another assassination plot involved the idea of contracting with the

. Even as Bissell planned the upcoming operation, his CIA colleagues were exploring whether the mob's Joe Bonano could assassinate
Castro. Bissell was too smart to take much of a direct hand in the scheme,
though he secretly wished it well. "My philosophy . . . in the agency," he
later wrote, "was very definitely that the end justified the means, and I was
not going to be held back."

Unorthodox as the Mafia solution might have been, it would have
spared Bissell the need to plan a landing operation whose scope was without precedent in Agency history. The Joint Chiefs of Staff, while not op-
posing the plan, kept a wary distance. The State Department had grave
misgivings and seldom missed an opportunity to undermine the effort,
worried that it would create a foreign policy disaster. Kennedy, in office
less than three months, was easily persuaded by his secretary of state,
Dean Rusk, and others, who sought ever greater limitations on the operation in the name of deniability.

The plan conceived in the Eisenhower administration was repeatedly revised with an eye to ensuring that the United States would not be
implicated. With officials still smarting from the U-2 shoot-down of eight
months earlier, Kennedy was adamant that no American personnel take a
direct role in the operation. To seasoned Agency officers under Bissell it
seemed that the success of the operation was becoming less important
than the ability to immunize the United States and the administration
from embarrassment.

With each passing week the outlook was more bleak. Intelligence reports indicated there was no well-organized anti-Castro underground to
come to the aid of the exiles. The CIA's original vision of a tiny guerrilla
operation had become an unwieldy full-scale invasion. Six weeks before
D-Day, the odds against preserving the element of surprise, essential to
the operation's success, had risen to 85 to 15, according to advisers.

The original assault plan—of dubious merit itself—was now being
hastily dismantled. In response to Kennedy's misgivings, Bissell halved the
initial air assault on Castro's air force, from sixteen planes to eight. On
March 15, a month prior to the invasion, even the landing site was
changed. Kennedy deemed the proposed landing at Trinidad "too noisy."
He wanted something "less spectacular." The site selected, because of a
nearby airstrip, was Bahía de Cochinos—the Bay of Pigs.

Then came the coup de grâce. Kennedy canceled the second air strike, scheduled for April 16, the eve of the operation, intended to wipe out whatever of Castro's air force had survived the first attack. No one understood the implications of that decision better than Bissell. Yet whether out of personal ambition, presidential pressure, or the sheer force of momentum that had gathered behind him in the preceding months, Bissell never gave serious thought to aborting the mission.

From the beginning, the U.S. government had tripped over its own lies. On April 12, 1961, Kennedy pledged in a speech to the American Association of Newspaper Editors that the United States would not intervene militarily in Cuba. Then, three days later, following the first bombing raid against Cuba, pilots landed in Florida posing as fresh defectors from Castro's air force. In the United Nations an outraged representative of Cuba lashed out at the United States. The esteemed U.S. representative, Adlai Stevenson, vigorously answered the attack, assuring the international body that the United States had nothing whatsoever to do with the bombing. Inadequately briefed on the Cuban operation, Stevenson discovered to his chagrin later that same day that he had been had. American credibility at home and abroad was about to sustain a mortal wound.

But it fell to the likes of Pete Ray and the fourteen hundred Cuban exiles to move forward with the plan. Ray had not been expected to leave the Nicaraguan base from which the Cuban exile pilots were flying their sorties against Castro. But with a part of Castro's air force left intact, the men on the beach and the supply ships they counted on were now easy targets for Castro's pilots. Two vital support ships, one that carried ammunition, the other communications, were sunk. Other vessels withdrew out of range. Out of ammo and cut off from their communications, those left on the beach were subjected to a withering ground and air assault.

The Cuban pilots Ray and the other guardsmen had trained gave an able accounting of themselves. But they were forced to fly a grueling three and a half hours from the Nicaraguan base to Cuba, conduct their attack, and then return, switch planes or refuel and rearm, and take to the air yet again. Those planes that returned—and there were many that did not—were riddled with ground fire. After a full day of sorties, the pilots were bleary-eyed with exhaustion, their nerves frayed, their aircraft suspect. On the beach at Bay of Pigs, the situation was deteriorating by the second.

On April 18, at 10:00 P.M., after unsuccessfully pleading for air cover, the brigade commander sent a message. "I will not be evacuated," he said. "We will fight to the end here if we have to."

It was then that Ray and some of the other pilots of the Alabama Air National Guard were called into a tent near the runway at the Nicaragua base for a briefing. Informed of the dire position of the invasion force and of the collapse of the air wing they had trained, Ray and the others were told they could fly the B-26s in aid of the assault landing.

Ray was paired with thirty-five-year-old Leo Baker, a former flight engineer who owned two Birmingham pizza parlors. He had recently sent his wife flowers for Easter Sunday. She was expecting their second child. Ray and Baker readied one B-26, while two other Alabama guardsmen, Riley Shamburger and Wade Gray, prepared another. Before taking off, Ray gave his wallet to a fellow airman but tucked the cash into his pocket, telling him with a wink that he might be spending the night in Havana.

Shortly after midnight, Ray and Baker took off.

Earlier at the White House, Admiral Arleigh Burke had pleaded with the president to provide additional air cover and to allow navy fighters from the *Essex* to wipe out Castro's remaining air force. Kennedy refused, saying he could not permit the United States to become involved in the assault.

"Goddamn it, Mr. President," fired back an irate Burke. "We are involved, and there is no way we can hide it."

Kennedy begrudgingly authorized a single hour of air support and cover from navy jets. Ray and the others counted on that support to fend off Castro's smaller but more nimble air force. But as Ray and Baker arrived off the coast of Cuba, there were no jets to protect them. The Agency had calculated the strike on Cuban time; the navy had relied on Greenwich mean time. Now Ray and Baker would be easy prey for Castro's agile T-33s and for ground fire. Exactly what happened next is not clear, but this much is known: Ray's B-26 was hit and crashed inland, not far from a sugar mill and Castro's headquarters. Baker was killed in the crash, Ray survived. Some would report later that Ray exited the plane and put up a valiant fight against Castro's militiamen. One account, unsubstantiated, had it that he died with a gun in one hand and a knife in the other.

Ray was one of 114 men killed in the operation. The rest, 1,197, were thrown into prison, where they would remain for two years. Their release would come at a humiliating price—a ransom of more than $50 million worth of food and medicines.

In Birmingham, Alabama, as elsewhere throughout the world, news of the failed invasion was headlines. But it would be a week before the Agency would dispatch two of its own to break the news of Pete's death to the Ray family. They found Margaret and her brother Charles at the Sloan Avenue home of their mother. Charles, too, had taken part in the secret operation and had only recently returned from Guatemala. What they told Margaret Ray was that her husband had been killed in the crash of a C-46 cargo plane during a training mission and that his body was not recoverable. It was the same story told the other four Birmingham widows.

But Margaret Ray knew better. She had read the newspapers and could put two and two together. She suspected all along her husband had been a part of the Cuban operation. She told the men from the Agency that she was not about to let such a lie stand. The moment they left, her ashen-faced brother told her she should not have voiced such accusations. Nor, he said, should she disclose whatever she might know. It was dangerous. It could even get her killed.

Eventually, all that would be returned to Margaret Ray of her husband's possessions was a plastic bag containing dozens of packs of chewing gum, a small transistor radio, and some items of clothing.

She was shattered. She had to contend not only with the loss of her husband but also with the lies that surrounded his death and with the implicit threats that she was not to attempt to contradict the White House in its denials of U.S. involvement at the Bay of Pigs. Later the government would try to persuade the public that the Alabama guardsmen lost over Cuba were merely mercenaries, "soldiers of fortune" there for the money alone. Margaret Ray took that as a personal slap in the face. But she was frightened of the government and what it might do to her. She had nearly stopped eating, was put on heavy sedatives, and fell into a deep depression. It was a week before she could bring herself to tell her son and daughter, Tommy and Janet, that they had lost their father.

She waited that day until the children came home from school, then sat them down next to her in a rear bedroom on the lower bunk bed, Tommy to her right, Janet to her left. They had known something was wrong. So many strangers had come and gone and there had been so much whispering. When Margaret Ray finally told her children, Tommy sat speechless. Janet became hysterical, jumping up and down and yelling at her brother. "Our daddy's dead!" she screamed. "Why aren't you crying?"

But Tommy would not let himself cry in front of his sister and mother. Instead, he got up and walked out of the house and found the stoop of a neighbor's porch, where he sat down and let the tears stream down his cheeks. Tommy had a gift for momentarily distancing himself from events. His sister did not.

Over the course of the ensuing weeks and months, the government's version of events would change. Mysterious checks for $225 would arrive twice each month drawn on an account with the Bankers Trust Company of New York. There was no explanation of their origin, and none was needed.

. . .

The Bay of Pigs was not simply a stinging defeat for the CIA but the end of an epoch. For a time, a disgusted President Kennedy stopped reading the *Current Intelligence Bulletin* provided him by the Agency. The CIA's credibility was clouded at best, and Agency confidence in the president fared no better. Allen Dulles tendered his resignation that November. Three months later, on February 28, 1962, Bissell resigned. Days later Kennedy bestowed upon him the National Security Medal. Bissell posed for an official photograph in the Oval Office, flanked by a grim Allen Dulles, no longer with the CIA, and by Kennedy, his hands tucked into the pockets of a dark suit. In the photo an owlish-looking Bissell wears the medal pinned to his chest and clutches the citation in his hands. But as Bissell looked into the lens of the camera, standing ramrod straight, he looked like a man facing a jury, as if awaiting the judgment of history. He had changed and so, too, had the CIA. No longer could the Agency believe that moral superiority and victory inevitably went hand in hand, that it would prevail as a matter of destiny. That belief, a quaint legacy of World War II and the OSS, was now part of the detritus of history. The time for blind faith was over.

The Bay of Pigs was what historian Theodore Draper called "a perfect failure." It shattered the myth of infallibility and helped usher in a more skeptical era, not only at the Agency but in the country at large. Whatever lessons were to be gleaned from that debacle would have to be learned again and again. Cuba would not be the last time the Agency would miscalculate the willingness of indigenous insurgencies to follow its lead. Nor would it be the last time that covert operations would have to factor in deniability on a par with strategic and tactical objectives, even if it meant undertaking the impossible. Each succeeding president would be insistent that he be able to distance himself from covert actions, particularly those pursued in contravention of law or principle. Not only America's enemies were to be deceived, but Americans as well, because they might not support or tolerate such undertakings.

Ultimately the Bay of Pigs fooled no one. The price of preserving the fiction of deniability had led not only to defeat but to a wider loss of standing in the world. Such duplicity cost the United States more of its political credibility and moral authority than any outright assault on Cuba. The decision had been made by Kennedy, but it was the CIA that would bear the brunt of public rancor and suspicion. Such chicanery and deceit would prove fertile ground for those who saw CIA conspiracies behind every word and deed. As covert warriors, CIA officers were expected to fall upon their own swords in defeat, even as the architects of those disasters wagged their fingers knowingly. In the postmortems that followed the Bay of Pigs, the most unsettling finding was that men like Pete Ray had died to preserve an implausible fiction—what CIA Inspector General Lyman Kirkpatrick called "a pathetic illusion."

On September 23, 1961, a shaken CIA moved into its new headquarters building at Langley. On the wall in the marble lobby were engraved the scriptural words from John: "and the truth shall make you free." The Agency, practiced in the art of deception, had itself become the victim of deception. In places like the Congo, Laos, Vietnam, and Nicaragua, covert objectives would again run headlong into the doctrine of deniability and limits imposed by fictive political aims. If political sensitivities sometimes reduced missions to quixotic pursuits, it did not diminish the courage of those dispatched to carry them out. It did, however, make it harder for some families of the bereaved to find meaning in such sacrifice.

. . .

For the children and widows of the Birmingham pilots killed in the Bay of Pigs operation, there was neither closure nor consolation. There were no bodies and no answers forthcoming from the government—only lies. Some would go about their business, vainly attempting to put it behind them. But that was something Pete Ray's daughter, Janet, could not do. Instead, she consecrated herself to learning all she could about her father, his mission, and his fate.

In some ways she appeared to want to duplicate her father's life. She married a fighter pilot—Michael Weininger—and named their son Pete, after her father. She even named her dog Chase, after the dog she had as a child. She allied herself to the cause of freeing Cuba and spent countless hours interviewing veterans of the Bay of Pigs, searching for clues to her father's mission and death. Never was she without her small pink vinyl suitcase, the sort a child takes on a sleep-over. It held her father's dental impressions, notes, tape recordings, newspaper clips, photos, and every document she could lay her hands on related to the Bay of Pigs.

For Janet Weininger and the other family members from Birmingham, the tragedy of death was only the beginning of their suffering. Over the ensuing years, the Agency steadfastly refused to acknowledge that Pete Ray and the others had worked for the CIA, albeit on contract, or that they were anything more than mercenaries.

Worse yet, the Agency had retained a local representative, ostensibly to provide assistance and moral support to Margaret Ray. But instead of providing comfort, remembers her son, the man threatened Margaret Ray, telling her that if she tried to publicly link her husband's death with the CIA she would lose her benefits and face financial ruin and even possible criminal prosecution and psychiatric institutionalization. He informed her that he knew where she shopped, who her friends were, and what her daily routine was. He also, Margaret later told her son, made crude and unwanted sexual advances toward her.

Margaret Ray, already shattered by the loss, now believed she was under constant surveillance. She was frightened, sometimes hysterical. She never did fully recover from the trauma of loss and the pressures, both real and imagined, to keep her silent. Amid such deception, Margaret Ray could not even be certain that her husband was dead. There was, after all, neither a body nor a grave. And there was irrefutable evidence that the CIA had already lied to her about other matters. Five years after Pete Ray's death she remarried, but she was haunted by a recurring nightmare in which Pete Ray returned from his ill-fated mission, demanding to know how she could have abandoned him and remarried. For a brief time in 1969 Margaret Ray was hospitalized in a psychiatric ward. Thereafter she was placed on antidepressants.

Pete Ray's mother, Mary, was embittered and distrustful of the U.S. government. She had but one object that had belonged to her firstborn son. It was a schoolbook, a small red dog-eared volume entitled *Presidents of the United States*, which ended with Franklin Roosevelt. But for her, it was just one more bitter reminder of the government's perfidy and lies. A year and a half after Bay of Pigs, when Kennedy was assassinated, Mary was almost ashamed of her reaction. "I was sorry he was killed but I didn't cry about it," she would say. "I grieved for his children but I didn't cry for him because he was the cause of Pete's being killed."

. . .

More than twelve years after Ray's death, on November 14, 1973, William Colby, Director Central Intelligence, quietly conferred a posthumous Distinguished Intelligence Cross upon Pete Ray. The accompanying citation read: "In recognition of his exceptional heroism in April 1961 when he undertook an extremely hazardous mission of the highest national priority. Although fully aware of the dangers he faced, Mr. Ray unhesitatingly volunteered to fly the mission on which he lost his life. In doing so he demonstrated his greatest personal courage and outstanding loyalty to his country. Mr. Ray's selfless devotion to duty and dedication to the national interests of the United States uphold the finest traditions of our country and reflect the highest credit on him and the Central Intelligence Agency." It was a marked turnaround.

But for the family of Pete Ray it was too little too late. The Agency continued to refuse to release to them any information about Ray's mission or his death, and maintained for another six years that he had been killed in the crash of his plane, when they knew otherwise.

For Ray's daughter, Janet, grief had long before transformed itself into a crusade to unearth all she could about her father. In 1978 her quest took a bizarre turn when she learned that her father's body might still be recoverable. She had been told that a body, believed to be her father's, had been preserved, perhaps even frozen, by Castro, as a kind of trophy of war.

Over the course of the next two years, she worked ceaselessly to confirm that report and, if true, to win the return of her father's remains. She sent Castro telegrams and letters asking for information. Through Cuban representatives in Washington, the State Department, and sympathetic members of Congress, she learned that if she could substantiate that this body was indeed her father's, Castro would be willing to release it to her. The Cubans took fingerprints of the cadaver, which were then sent to the FBI. In September 1979 the FBI compared those prints with microfilmed prints taken at Ray's enlistment in the Alabama National Guard in 1947. The conclusion: the Havana morgue did indeed have the remains of Thomas "Pete" Ray.

Janet, pregnant with her son Pete, stood in the drizzling rain as the plane carrying the body of her father touched down at the Birmingham airport in December 1979. It was the same runway from which Ray had taken off for the mission eighteen years earlier. But before Ray's remains would be buried, she and her brother, Tom, insisted that it be autopsied. They hoped that it might yet yield some final secret of how Pete Ray died.

On the afternoon of December 6 a medical examiner at the Jefferson County Coroner's Office set about removing the five screws, sealed in red wax, that fastened the lid to the gray pine coffin. Inside, the body was in a zinc metal container with a small window over the face. It was lined with white cloth. Ray's head rested on a white pillow. As the coroner examined the body, one thing was obvious. Ray had not died in a plane crash, as the CIA had originally told the family. His body was riddled with bullets and marked by at least ten wounds—to his head, abdomen, arm, shoulder, ear, and wrist. As the procedure continued, the coroner carefully removed several fully jacketed slugs. Ray's son, Tom, then twenty-five, stood by and watched in silence.

Two days later, on Saturday, December 8, 1979, some two hundred people gathered on a Birmingham hillside to bury Ray with full military honors. Ray would have liked the view from that hill that overlooked the airport and the planes of the Alabama Air National Guard. Among those who came to remember him were family members, old friends, officers of the Cuban men he fought beside from Brigade 2506, former governor George Wallace, and even a camera-shy case worker from the CIA. As the coffin was carried to the open grave, some of those who had served with Ray in the Alabama Air National Guard saluted him. Ray's widow, Margaret, confined to a wheelchair by a recent heart attack, stared at the flag-draped casket and a black-and-white photo of her late husband. There were few words spoken.

Janet had already written a five-page letter to her father and slipped it into the uniform in which he was buried. At the funeral her remarks were brief. Said Janet, "I'm so glad my father's home."

. . .

Richard Bissell, too, had been changed by the Bay of Pigs. His name, once synonymous with brilliance and promise, was now forever welded to the Cuban debacle, like Napoleon and Waterloo. Following his CIA service, he spent two unhappy years at the Institute for Defense Analyses, a think tank, then returned to Farmington, Connecticut. There followed ten utterly unfulfilling years as marketing director of the United Aircraft Corporation. Then he retired. At his modest office his assistant, Fran Pudlo, decorated the walls with photos and keepsakes of his career.

He had mellowed and grown reflective. Pudlo and he would read to each other from passages of Greek or Roman history. One of his favorites was *The Greek Generals Talk: Memoirs of the Trojan War.* He liked to listen to the broader sweep of history, as if it might give him some perspective on his own life, if not outright absolve him. As he listened to Pudlo reading, he sipped coffee from a white china mug decorated with five gold stars and the letters "RBAF." It stood for "Richard Bissell's Air Force"—a gift from those who had worked with him on the U-2.

But at his home Bissell had almost no reminders of his CIA days. Somewhere in a drawer was a pair of titanium cuff links, a forgotten memento of the SR-71 project. He occasionally spoke of his Agency days but rarely of the Bay of Pigs. It was a reservoir of regret he would not allow himself to revisit. By the early 1990s, as he entered his eighties, he was no longer the imposing and sometimes volatile figure that loped down the long halls of Agency headquarters, already a legend. He was now frail and easily winded. He was wearing himself out trying to collect his thoughts into a memoir, a kind of footrace with his own mortality. When completed, it was unsparingly candid about his own culpability in the Bay of Pigs, but also placed much blame on Kennedy.

More and more he spent his days in the bedroom, surrounded by books and journals. In the winter of 1993 he was a sickly eighty-four-year-old man, his mind still keen, but no longer able or willing to fend off the limits of age.

It was on January 17, 1994, that Janet Weininger, daughter of Pete Ray, came to visit him in Farmington at the Bissell home, a three-hundred-year-old converted farmhouse. Bissell rarely turned down a request for an interview or a visit from a stranger. But the man Janet Weininger met that evening was a ghost of the robust Cold Warrior who had sent her father and so many others into the fray against Communism. Short of breath from pneumonia and suffering from circulation problems, he shivered in a recliner, a green plaid blanket draped over him and his feet warmed by slippers. For hours he listened as Janet spoke of her father and of the Cuban brigade. It was the least he could do, part of an endless penance.

Even Janet did not fully grasp the nature of her feelings toward this man whom she might well have hated as the architect of the fiasco that had claimed her father's life. But instead, she came to him seeking answers about her father and the mission and to pay homage to the man who had overseen the U.S. attempt to unseat Castro. With her, she brought a plaque from Brigade 2506, which she presented to him. The plaque had been made up by the Cuban veterans three years earlier as part of a thirtieth-anniversary observance. They had hoped to present it to him in person in Miami.

Bissell declined the brigade's invitation in an eloquent letter dated thirty years to the day after the invasion. "Looking back," he wrote, "one can see there were many reasons for the failure and many persons who must share responsibility for it. There were errors of planning, particularly the failure to foresee and plan for contingencies for which I accept with profound regret a share of the blame. There were equipment defects. There was a faster and more effective response by Castro than we expected. But above all there were restrictions imposed on the way the operation was designed and conducted in an attempt to maintain an unattainable secrecy about the role of the U.S. government."

But even in his later years Bissell never conceded the ultimate defeat. He closed his letter with these words: "I wish I could be with you on this occasion to drink a toast to the brave men who risked and those who lost their lives trying against all odds to overthrow a tyrant. I am confident that theirs is the wave of the future, and an increasingly isolated Communist dictatorship will collapse and that Cuba will again be free. May that day come soon." It was a remarkable exhortation considering that by then Castro had outlasted seven U.S. presidents and become the longest-serving leader in the Western Hemisphere—thanks, in no small part, to the CIA's failed attempts to oust him.

The plaque Janet carried with her that day was inscribed with the words "In Recognition and Appreciation for Gallant Services Rendered During The Bay of Pigs Military Operations. . . . . You Are One of Us." Bissell was visibly moved, though perhaps not nearly as much as Janet wished to believe. They spoke for several hours. After being subjected to years of government lies and evasion, Janet felt that at last she was getting the truth about the campaign that claimed her father's life. She would remember their meeting as a moment when a tremendous burden was lifted from her shoulders. Bissell, too, seemed to feel a sense of liberation. In coming together on a blustery winter day in Connecticut, the two had managed, at least momentarily, to exorcise some of the demons that had tormented them both for so many years.

Bissell's health continued to deteriorate, but it was his spirit more than his body that capitulated. On February 6, 1994, he was told that it might be necessary to place him in a hospital or nursing home. He did not voice any protest, but there was no concealing his disdain for his own disabilities and growing dependence on others.

That night he did not awaken from his sleep. He was found in his twin bed in a large bedroom painted red and flushed with sunlight. The newspapers said it was a heart condition, but his family knew better. At age eighty-four Richard Bissell had simply decided to let go of life.

His body was cremated, but it was not until June 26 that there was a memorial service for him. That had always been his favorite time of year. For such a public figure, once the standard-bearer of the Cold War, it was a decidedly private affair. That was how Bissell would have wanted it. It was a brilliant sunlit day. Only about thirty people were to gather to pay their remembrances, none of them from his Agency days. But among those who were in attendance was Janet Ray Weininger. A short time before the memorial service, members of Bissell's immediate family and Janet gathered in the living room, a long two-story room filled with books on politics, military history, economics, and mysteries, and even some Mark Twain. Once again, Janet had come with a gift. This time it was the blue and gold flag of Brigade 2506, which she presented to Bissell's widow. There were few words spoken.

After that, the thirty or so family members and close friends assembled on a sunlit hillside overlooking the Farmington River. Across the river was a quiltwork of cultivated fields. Bissell's ashes were placed beneath a simple granite stone that lay flush with the grass. The marker bore nothing but his name and dates of birth and death.

Neither the return of her father's body nor the hours spent with Bissell brought any lasting peace to Janet Weininger, so consumed was she by the loss of her father. But for opposition from other family members, she would have had her father's body exhumed and moved from Montgomery, Alabama, to Miami—closer to her home. And in the spring of 1997, three years after her time with Bissell, she could be found trekking through the jungles of Nicaragua in an effort to find and recover the bodies of two Cuban pilots who had crashed after taking part in the Bay of Pigs operation.

. . .

That operation had been a tragic comedy of errors, a futile quest concocted by men of great power and intellect and carried out by men of unquestioning courage. At least in part, it was the contemporaneous demand for deniability that had doomed the mission, and subsequent decades of denials and secrecy that kept public fascination with the fiasco alive. All but one of the original twenty copies of the CIA inspector general's scathing reports examining the Bay of Pigs were destroyed. The lone surviving copy was for thirty-six years securely locked in the CIA director's safe, as if it were the last of some virulent strain of pox that could once again wreak havoc on the world. Not until February 1998 did the Agency release the remaining copy, in response to a Freedom of Information Act request.

Visitors to the CIA, perusing the pages of the revered Book of Honor, would find four nameless stars beside the year 1961, one for each of the Alabama Air National Guardsmen who died in the Bay of Pigs. Long after their names had appeared in the national press and histories of the invasion, the Agency still steadfastly refused to publicly acknowledge the men or to inscribe their names in the Book of Honor. It was as if, by refusing to utter their names, the Agency did not have to look them or itself in the eye, as if accountability could be so easily sidestepped. This, too, is a fiction.

One of those four stars belongs to Thomas "Pete" Ray. His daughter, Janet, is still in pursuit of answers as if they might fill the void of her grief. In this way, she, too, has come to be counted among the casualties of the Bay of Pigs.

PART TWO

A Time to Question

CHAPTER 6

Deception

I know that I shall meet my fate
Somewhere among the clouds above;
Those that I fight I do not hate,
Those that I guard I do not love.

WILLIAM BUTLER YEATS,
"An Irish Airman Foresees His Death"

THE AFTERNOON of August 25, 1964, was hot and steamy as a tiny knot of mourners—a mother and father, a sister and a widow—gathered on a grassy Chattanooga hillside to say a last good-bye to thirty-four-year-old John Gaither Merriman. There, in grave 172, section BB, Merriman took his place in the national cemetery among many honored dead. Interred around him were more than six thousand unknown Civil War casualties who fell at Chickamauga, Missionary Ridge, and Lookout Mountain, as well as six recipients of the Congressional Medal of Honor. John Merriman would have been proud to be in the company of such men, and they in his.

All that August day, Merriman's widow, Val, had done what she could to steel herself. The night before, she had spoken with the minister, Brother Paul, and told him only that her husband had been involved in "a terrible accident." Those were the very words he used from the pulpit of the Church of Christ addressing some thirty-five mourners, among them many brawny young men with weathered faces and aviator glasses tucked into their coat pockets.

In a pew close to Val sat Dorothy "Dot" Kreinheder, a casual friend who had worked with John and now took a more than casual interest in Val's well-being. If she was there to offer Val Merriman emotional support, she was also there to ensure that the widow said nothing that might raise questions about Merriman's death or implicate the CIA. Kreinheder had made herself indispensable, even purchasing Val's mourning dress (a black affair with a low circular collar and white inset), a snug black pillbox hat, and the black fabric purse Val would clutch to her side, knowing it held a picture of her husband.

By all accounts, Merriman's was an utterly unremarkable and prosaic passing. The local newspaper reported what the family had told them: that Merriman had been in an auto accident the evening of August 20 while at Ramey Air Force Base in Puerto Rico. The precise cause of death, it was said, was a pulmonary embolism. It was all in black and white on his death certificate, his autopsy report, and his cemetery record. Merriman had had the misfortune to somehow strike "a road abutment"—the words appearing on his official death certificate. As a common traffic fatality he hardly seemed worthy of such hallowed ground.

But Val Merriman knew otherwise. She knew the death certificate had been dummied up, the newspapers duped, and the pathologist misled. She knew it was all part of one grand lie—everything, that is, except the one undeniable fact: John Merriman was dead. Still, she was determined to be a good CIA wife to the very end, to cling to the cover story and not ask questions. It was nobody's business but "the Company's." In the midst of her sorrow, she would deliver the performance of a lifetime. She was not even to tell her three young sons the truth of their father's death, at least not until years later when the boys could be trusted not to tell a soul. Jon, Bruce, and Eric were not even to be there at their father's funeral.

At least thirty-three-year-old Val Merriman might draw some

small comfort from knowing that her husband had received the best of medical attention in his final hours and that he died among people who cared about him in the Puerto Rican hospital. Syd Stembridge, a senior CIA officer and friend, had shared with Val a detailed account of Merriman's final evening. John, he told her, had known little pain. He had been resting quietly that evening and was well provided for. He even asked for a bowl of ice cream, which the nurse promptly brought him. He polished it off with boyish delight, then lapsed into a peaceful sleep from which he did not awaken. What Val Merriman could not know was that her husband was never in a Puerto Rican hospital and that the story of the ice cream was pure invention, a fiction within a fiction. No one at the Agency could bring themselves to tell her the truth. It was that gruesome.

What she did know was that her husband possessed the stuff of which heroes are made. Others knew it too. A quiet man of modest height and build, he had a glint of mischief in his eyes and a pencil-thin mustache that gave him the look of a dashing Hollywood roué. He was ruggedly individualistic, with an insatiable yen for action and a confidence in his skills that was easily mistaken as a disdain for risk.

But he also had a gentler side. In his spare time he painted with oils, especially seascapes and aircraft. He wrote short stories and poems, designed sailboats, and could turn the Sunday newspaper into a soaring box kite to the delight of his sons. A crack marksman and able gunsmith, he once brought down a monster of a Kodiak bear but was so distressed at the loss of such a majestic creature that ever after he swore off hunting.

His passion for flying dated back to earliest boyhood. At five he cajoled his parents into buying him a ticket to ride with a barnstormer who took him up for a series of stomach-churning stunts above the Chattanooga skies. After that, Merriman was intent on getting his own wings. At fourteen he soloed for the first time. At sixteen he had his pilot's license. At seventeen he dropped out of high school to join the 82nd Airborne. As a young man he once tried to put his feelings for flying into words:

The wind on the wings strong and tight
The clouds around me fleecy and white

> The cars going in and out of town
> Like ants to and from a mound.
>
> Like a high spirited steed
> With head held high
> This vision with speed
> wings across the sky . . .
>
> If I'm ever sent to heaven, and paradise I see,
> It can never be more beautiful than flying seems to me.

Long before he had thrown his lot in with the CIA, before the cloak of secrecy obscured his life, Merriman had demonstrated ample valor. For one fleeting instant he was even thrust into the public spotlight. It was July 9, 1953. Merriman was then a twenty-four-year-old pilot assigned to the Civil Air Patrol's Yakutat Squadron in Alaska. On that day another pilot flying mail and supplies to a remote climbing expedition discovered a distress signal written in the snow. The message indicated that a member of the party had come down with appendicitis and needed to be airlifted out immediately.

The pilot sent a message to Elmendorf Field, which dispatched a Grumman SA-16 Albatross in the hope that it could land safely on the glacier and retrieve the stricken climber. But the pilot found it too treacherous to land at the 7,600-foot base camp and was forced to turn back.

Merriman, then a meteorological aid, a lowly GS-5 with the U.S. Weather Bureau, heard of the situation and volunteered to make a rescue attempt. Already an experienced bush pilot, he flew a Piper Super Cruiser to the nearby Malaspina Glacier, carrying on board a set of skis to be attached to the plane for a glacial landing. The mission was perilous from the outset. Merriman's Piper aircraft was not designed for landings and takeoffs above six thousand feet. The gnatlike plane, a mere twenty-two feet in length and fueled by a one-hundred-horsepower engine, had a top speed of 114 miles per hour. As Merriman's superior would observe, "No one should have to use it" at such altitudes. When the plane landed at a midway site, the aircraft was damaged by rocks protruding through the ice. Merriman pressed on, further damaging the plane as he took off, his craft now outfitted with skis.

As Merriman flew on toward the site of the climbers' camp, the winds picked up. A driving rain pelted the windshield. By the time he reached Seward Gap, visibility was down to three miles. Only his familiarity with the wilds of the Yukon Territory allowed him to navigate. Even so, the skis of his plane twice skidded across the icy terrain at full cruising speed, violently rattling his aircraft. Merriman's commanding officer later likened it to "flying inside of a milk bottle." Finally he spied the campers' site, which had been marked off with a piece of canvas and a cargo parachute. After a week of bad weather and thawing, the snow had rotted through and barely supported the weight of the aircraft. Merriman's plane came to a slamming halt after touchdown on a glacier at the foot of Mount McArthur.

By then it was dusk. The weather was too hostile to risk taking off. Merriman grabbed a few hours' sleep while members of the trekking party swept clear a 4,300-foot runway with their snowshoes. At daybreak Merriman and his patient, Dick Long, took off, requiring every foot of the runway. Unable to put the tires back on his plane, Merriman landed on his skis in the tall grass beside the airport in Yakutat. A doctor was waiting to take Long to the lower forty-eight.

For Merriman the flight was nothing extraordinary. Four days later he was off on another mercy mission, this one to the Situck River to pick up a fisherman sick with pneumonia. But Merriman's daring rescue of Dick Long had caught the attention of his superior in Anchorage who relayed a description of Merriman's exploits on to Washington.

Six months later, on February 16, 1954, Merriman found himself standing on the stage of a cavernous auditorium in Washington, D.C., as Secretary of Commerce Sinclair Weeks presented him with a gold medallion, the esteemed Exceptional Service Award. The citation read: "For heroic action involving jeopardy of life in piloting the plane which under adverse weather and extremely hazardous operating conditions effected the rescue of a stricken mountain climber from the Malaspina Glacier."

Merriman was then just six blocks from CIA headquarters, but the thought of covert operations had yet to cross his mind. In an otherwise totally private life, this moment onstage was the one time John Merriman would come to public attention. Already, though, within the community of bush pilots and smoke jumpers, he was becoming something of a legend, as much for his guts as for his gift as an aviator. It was said of him that he could fly the box the airplane came in.

A decade later some of those same pilots who admired him most and who shared his secrets would gather inside the Church of Christ to pay their last respects to Merriman. To some it seemed a cruel irony that one who had been so willing to risk his life to rescue others should have met such an unconscionable end.

. . .

For many years John Merriman worked as a commercial pilot, but the tedium of fixed schedules and the routine of routes did not agree with him. Then in 1962 he took a job as pilot to the royal family in Saudi Arabia. But that job was cut short after less than two years when King Saud was deposed. After that, Merriman put out feelers for a job within the community of clandestine operatives.

In 1963 he was contacted by Intermountain Aviation, ostensibly a private firm, but one that, in reality, was part of the CIA's growing stable of wholly owned airlines called proprietaries. Collectively this network of seemingly private companies created a virtually invisible air force at the disposal of the CIA, permitting it to expand its clandestine paramilitary activities around the globe. Undetected, such CIA front companies as Civil Air Transport, Air America, Evergreen, and Intermountain could move vast amounts of matériel—weapons, communications gear, and provisions—and men in support of America's proxy wars against the Communists, be they in Europe, Africa, Asia, or Latin America. Such firms were always on the lookout for savvy pilots. There was none better than John Merriman.

During the year that Merriman underwent an extensive CIA background and security check, he signed on with Johnson's Flying Service in Missoula, Montana. There he ferried smoke jumpers to forest fires. In its wisdom the Agency had steered him to a job that would polish precisely those treetop turns and acrobatic flying skills needed in counterinsurgency operations. It would also allow him to gain the trust and confidence of many of the very men who were to become the backbone of the CIA's daring covert paramilitary efforts in places like the Congo, Laos, and Vietnam. Even the smoke jumpers were impressed with

Merriman's sangfroid. Before taking off, he calmly slipped a leather glove over his left hand. On it was written the word "Bandersnatch." Many of the jumpers took to calling him that as a nickname of affection and respect.

When he had finally cleared Agency scrutiny, Merriman and his family were moved to Intermountain's headquarters at a vast top secret facility a half hour northwest of Tucson, Arizona. Its name was Marana Air Base. A former World War II facility, it offered three runways intersecting in a triangle and set upon a perfectly flat stretch of barren earth. In the distance to the west, the Sawtooth Mountains broke the monotony of land and sky. For years it would be the premier CIA training ground for paramilitary air operations, offering a kind of postgraduate curriculum in air ops. Merriman was jubilant. In a letter to a friend he wrote, "I'm sure I've found my life's work if I don't get fired."

From around the country the CIA had recruited top experts in all the arcane arts needed to carry out covert operations—smoke jumpers and "riggers" adept not only in making complex jumps but in the packing of specialized parachutes, "kickers" capable of designing and delivering pallets and chutes for extraordinary supply drops, pilots willing and able to fly through torturous weather conditions, and mechanics, armaments experts, and engineers eager to convert conventional aircraft and apparatus to meet the needs of the most exotic missions. Together they formed a tightly knit community—all of them sworn to absolute secrecy. The unseen instrument of U.S. foreign policy, they were warriors in a world of undeclared wars.

More than a mere training base, Marana was a realm unto itself, withdrawn from all the world. Ordinarily there was little visible security that might call unwanted attention to the base. It was said that not even Arizona Senator Barry Goldwater was privy to its mission and that when he finally learned of it he went to the CIA's Dick Helms demanding to be briefed. When sensitive equipment was being tested, signs would go up that read, "Warning: Do Not Proceed Further; Use of Deadly Force Authorized."

Over time there evolved a distinct culture of secrecy, a society within a society in which the mores were defined by security classifications, compartmentation, and an unspoken taboo on asking too many questions.

For the families living on or around Marana it was anything but a hardship post. When the household chores were done, Val Merriman and the other wives passed the afternoons playing cards beside the Olympic-sized swimming pool or looked forward to bowling leagues, bingo nights, and turkey shoots. Even the teenagers became a part of the enterprise. Some worked as lifeguards or in the carpentry shop or on the watering crew. Others painted numbers and lines on the runways. The men would gather after hours at the base's watering hole for drinks and the chatter of good old boys reveling in doing what they loved best. In the evenings the base featured not a crude canteen, but a polished dining hall offering fine cuisine with ice sculptures and a chef who had worked on a cruise ship.

Periodically the men, especially the riggers, would disappear for weeks and months at a time. No one asked where they had gone. Most already knew. Those who didn't had no business knowing.

When the Merrimans arrived at Marana in early 1963, the Agency was still licking its wounds from the Bay of Pigs fiasco of two years earlier. By then, several of the Agency's most vaunted figures had been publicly discredited and quietly departed, men like Director Allen Dulles and Deputy Director for Plans Richard Bissell. But the Bay of Pigs had not put a damper on covert operations. Far from it. Between 1960 and 1965 the CIA expanded its operations in the Western Hemisphere Division by 40 percent, reflecting a perceived increase in Soviet activity in Peru, Bolivia, Colombia, and elsewhere.

Decolonization in Africa led to expansions in CIA activity on that continent as well. Again the aim was to stymie Soviet and Chinese efforts to extend their spheres of influence. Until such perceived threats, Africa had commanded little interest at the Agency. Indeed, African operations, before 1960, had been folded into the divisions overseeing Europe and the Mideast. Between 1959 and 1960 CIA stations in Africa increased by 55 percent. Asia, too, was demanding greater covert resources, particularly in Laos and Vietnam. Those theaters of operations would provide an entire new generation of CIA leaders and station chiefs who would take the place of the graying OSS veterans still at the helm in the late 1950s and early 1960s. Overseeing much of this expansion, after Bissell's departure, was his replacement in 1962 as deputy director of plans, Richard Helms, as experienced and hard-core an operative as any the Agency had. The clandestine service would continue to extend its reach and resources until the late 1960s when public suspicion, budgetary constraints, and concerns about exposure reduced the frenzied pace of covert operations.

The core of senior CIA officers who had overseen the Bay of Pigs operation had escaped their superior's fate and had been reconstituted as if nothing untoward had happened. Indeed, they would help usher in the new era of covert paramilitary operations.

Perhaps it was because they were below the screen of public criticism, perhaps because they possessed skills or experience too valuable to lose. Whatever the reason, the men most closely involved with the Bay of Pigs simply packed up from their ill-named "Happy Valley" operations base in Nicaragua and ended up at Marana, where they played pivotal roles in an ensuing decade of CIA adventures and misadventures. For them the Bay of Pigs was not a career-ending disaster, but merely a stepping-stone to the next assignment.

Chief among these was Gar Thorsrude, Marana's commander and undisputed top dog. It was Gar who had overseen base operations at the Bay of Pigs and briefed men like Alabama pilots Pete Ray and Leo Baker. A company man through and through, he accepted long odds and operational failures as part of the landscape. He was nothing if not a survivor. A commanding figure, he stood well over six feet, had a stony, often sullen face, a mouth full of gold teeth, a crew cut, and a volcanic temper. A former smoke jumper himself, he knew his stuff and knew it well. For this he was widely respected, but not universally beloved.

The less kindly disposed used words like "prickly" to describe him. He had played an integral role in the covert war against China by training Tibetans and providing them with weapons and provisions. He had overseen operations from which more than a few men had not returned. It was said of him by one Agency wife that when he died it would be hard to round up enough people to serve as pallbearers, to which another Agency wife added that she would volunteer—if for no other reason than to make sure he was indeed dead. No one, not even the brassiest of the flyboys, had the *cojones* to ask Thorsrude about the Bay of Pigs. As head of Marana, he was Merriman's ultimate boss.

Others at Marana were veterans of the Bay of Pigs too, among them the base's chief pilot, Connie Seigrest, the smoke-jumping brothers Miles and Shep Johnson, and the head "kicker," Jack Wall. Many had known each other for more than a decade, dating back to the early 1950s when they had been with the CIA front company called Western Enterprises based in Taiwan. There the mission had been to relentlessly heckle the Chinese. Even Gar had once been a kicker for Western Enterprises.

From Asia to the Bay of Pigs to Arizona, and from there to points around the world. Technically, few if any of them were CIA employees but merely contract workers. But they would have taken strong offense at any suggestion that they were mercenaries. They saw themselves as soldiers out of uniform, not soldiers of fortune, part of an elite cadre forged by more than a decade of covert combat. The men of Marana were the leading edge of any CIA air operation, the go-to guys of Langley. While the State Department boys politely parsed policy in the salons of Georgetown, their stubble-cheeked alter-egos at Marana were flying above treetops through blackest night rehearsing supply drops.

And as John Merriman was soon to find out, even the Cuban exile pilots themselves, those who had survived Castro's murderous fire, would find steady work for the CIA. They would provide a perfect ready-made force—already trained in flying, experienced in aerial combat, only too eager to take on the Communists, and just distant enough from the professional ranks of Langley for Washington to once again deny any knowledge of them. It was some of these very pilots that John Merriman was expected to polish and prepare for covert combat missions overseas.

One of these pilots was Gus Ponzoa, the senior Cuban pilot in the Bay of Pigs operation. It was up to Merriman to test Ponzoa and to certify that he was ready to take a T-28 into combat. The first time up together, Merriman had Ponzoa do a series of acrobatic rolls. Ponzoa had trouble controlling the aircraft, the g-force got out of hand, and Ponzoa vomited in the cockpit. Within a day Merriman had him in full control.

Even among the crack fliers of Marana, Merriman was a standout. "He was one of the best pilots I ever flew with," remembers Don Gearke. "He was a Hollywood-type pilot. I've never seen anybody so calm in my life. He'd always go to the end of the runway. When he was cleared for takeoff, he'd sit back in his seat, pull his gloves on one at a time, and like Smilin' Jack, light a cigarette and say 'Let's go.' That was pretty cool."

Sometimes Merriman's playfulness got out of hand. On one occasion he was teaching less experienced pilots how to pursue and attack a plane in flight. He noticed a small private aircraft overhead and decided to incorporate it into his gunnery lesson by dive-bombing it and hectoring it midair with his more nimble T-28. Again and again he dove on the plane. Unbeknownst to Merriman, the pilot was an air force general on his way to David Mothan Air Force Base. When the officer landed, he immediately filed a formal complaint against Merriman with the Federal Aviation Administration.

Such friskiness was a part of Marana's culture. The timid, they said, need not apply. Even the stern Gar Thorsrude was not above the occasional hotdogging. From time to time he would fly the gauntlet below the Grand Canyon's rim. One time, after a prolonged overseas assignment, he took the canyon route. He was flying below the rim and above the Colorado River, a twisting course, when suddenly, as he rounded a bend, there loomed in front of him, filling his windshield, a solid wall—the Glen Canyon Dam. "Oh shit!" yelled Don Gearke, a passenger in the backseat. In the time that Thorsrude had been overseas the dam had risen to its full 710-foot height. Thorsrude pulled back on the stick and barely cleared it.

. . .

On May 29, 1964, Merriman offered to fly Cuban pilot Gus Ponzoa from Marana to Las Vegas, where Ponzoa was to catch a plane back to Miami. It was a cloudless day, not even a hint of a breeze. As a send-off gift for his newfound friend, Merriman took the canyon route, flying below the rim, artfully zigzagging between the canyon walls at 170 knots. It was Ponzoa's most memorable flight and a celebration of his having checked out in the T-28.

In a month, Ponzoa would leave for a top secret mission to the Congo. There he was to head up a cadre of fifteen Cuban pilots, all of them Bay of Pigs veterans. Recruited by the CIA, they were to pose as mercenaries working for the Congo Air Force under orders from General Joseph Mobuto. Merriman's parting words to Ponzoa: "I would give anything to be going with you."

One month later Merriman got his wish. He was to ready himself for the Congo, where he would oversee air operations. His was to be a supervisory role. The last thing the United States needed was to expose its hand in that faraway conflict. But nothing could have prepared Merriman for the quagmire that was the Congo.

. . .

The CIA had had a secret role in the Congo that dated back to 1960 when Belgium granted its former colony independence, one of a series of colonies that won their independence in the early sixties. Against the backdrop of the Cold War and superpower struggles, each of these young nations became yet another target of opportunity caught in the tug-of-war between East and West. The United States and its handmaiden, the CIA, were intent upon preventing the Soviets or Chinese from gaining a new foothold anywhere in the world, especially in a land as rich in minerals and as strategically located as was the Congo. Just how far the CIA was willing to go was made plain in the fall of 1960.

It was September 19, 1960, that the CIA sent a message to Lawrence Devlin, its station chief in Léopoldville (today called Kinshasa), the Congolese capital. The message, classified "Eyes Only," was cryptic even by CIA standards. It alerted Devlin that he would soon be receiving a visit from "Joe from Paris" and that he was to take his instructions from him. Not long after, as Devlin was walking to his car near the Café de la Presse, he saw a familiar face—Dr. Sidney Gottlieb, a senior scientist on the technical side of the Agency.

Gottlieb was an odd figure by any measure. Born with a clubfoot and stricken with a severe stutter, he had been a socialist in his youth and a Buddhist as an adult. A chemist by training, he put his formidable talent in the lab to exotic use, making poison darts and handkerchiefs, and overseeing a program with LSD that tested theories of mind control. His subjects were not always privy to the fact they had been dosed. A genius by many accounts, he would have been a perfect model for Dr. Strangelove. In Léopoldville he arrived with a plan for Devlin to carry out.

Devlin took Gottlieb to a safe house, where the two men huddled over a radio whose volume was cranked up high enough to obscure their voices from any eavesdroppers or listening devices. Gottlieb said it was the CIA's directive that Gottlieb assassinate former Congolese premier Patrice Lumumba. A charismatic leftist trained in the Soviet Union, Lumumba was viewed as a threat to U.S. objectives in the region. "Jesus Christ! Isn't this unusual?" asked Devlin, demanding to know upon whose authority such an order had been given. In-house the plan had been approved by none other than Deputy Director for Plans Richard Bissell. CIA head Allen Dulles had branded Lumumba "a Castro, or worse." But the scheme also, Devlin said, had the blessings of an even higher authority—President Eisenhower.

From his bag, Gottlieb produced a small kit containing a well-known brand of toothpaste. Inside was a deadly poison. The kit also contained rubber gloves, gauze, masks, and even a syringe in the event that the toothpaste could not be slipped into Lumumba's possessions. Devlin had no intention of carrying out the directive, but in the interest of preserving his career, he decided to quietly stall for time. He slipped the kit into a drawer in the embassy safe.

Three months later Devlin's and the Agency's dilemma was resolved. On January 17, 1961, Lumumba was brutally murdered by a rival Congolese faction. Whether that killing was purely fortuitous or given an assist by the Agency has been a subject of debate. One week later, under cover of darkness, a much-relieved Devlin drove to the edge of town and tossed the poison into the rapids of the Congo River.

But neither Lumumba's death nor the intervening four years had done anything to stabilize the Congo. Eisenhower, Kennedy, and Lyndon Johnson had all secretly deployed the CIA in a desperate effort to shore up the Congolese government as the nation teetered on the brink of anarchy.

So it was when Merriman arrived in Léopoldville on July 17, 1964. A two-month-old revolt in the eastern province of Katanga once again threatened the country. But Merriman's spirits were high, the weather cooler than he expected, and the Congolese ivory and wood carvings caught his eye. "Looks as if I will be able to bring you some pretty presents from here," he wrote his wife. "Love boys for me and remember that you are the one I love most in the world."

The letter was necessarily brief. There was much to do. His assignment was to oversee the Cuban pilots, to help prevent a breakup of the Congo, and to suppress the revolt in Katanga. Merriman spent less than two weeks in Léopoldville before taking command of the CIA's air operations and the Cuban pilots who worked under cover of the Congo Air Force.

On July 20, 1964, he and three Cuban pilots, all veterans of the Bay of Pigs—Jack Varela, René García, and his friend Gus Ponzoa—ferried three T-28s to Kamina Air Base in Katanga. As Merriman approached Kamina flying the lead plane, he was dumbstruck at the enormity of the base rising up in the middle of nowhere. Composed of hundreds of barracks, depots, and hangars, it was the largest air base south of the Sahara. But for a skeletal crew of mechanics and engineers from the Belgian Air Force, and the few Cuban pilots, Kamina was deserted, a ghostly expanse of runways and empty buildings stretching as far as the eye could see.

Even more haunting was its original purpose. Built at the height of the Cold War by the Belgians, it was intended to be the relocation site for the Belgian royal family, as well perhaps as the government and elements of NATO, as they rode out what appeared to be the inevitable nuclear war. Kamina was a completely self-contained redoubt, a concrete and steel colossus created to withstand the Cold War's ultimate nightmare. Not far off was an entirely different world inhabited by zebras, antelopes, elephants, and the occasional cobra sunning itself on the road.

Merriman unpacked his gear in a barrackslike structure known as the Ops Center. He had a two-room suite complete with a private bathroom—but no running water. The base boasted an enormous mess hall, but that, too, was abandoned. Instead, Merriman and his Cuban cohorts ate mostly tins of sardines and basic rations. Merriman was embraced almost instantly by the Cubans. Devoid of pretensions and the John Wayne swagger of some of his CIA predecessors, he was immediately welcomed. For his part he soon appreciated the hazards the pilots faced in the field. The Agency had made it clear to the Cuban pilots that if anything happened to them, if they crashed or were captured, the U.S. government would disavow any knowledge of them.

Nor was there any recourse to the Geneva Convention for those who were downed. Rebel tribesmen, it was said, would eat the testicles of their foes if they thought them brave, and their hearts if wise. Cuban pilot Fausto Gómez had been found literally butchered. By such a standard, Mario Genebra was luckier. His engine failed as he was taking off from Albertville and his plane flipped over into the lake at the edge of the runway. Unable to open the cockpit, he drowned in two feet of water.

Merriman was prepared for the risks, but not the disorder. "The situation here is a real bucket of worms," he wrote his wife the day of his arrival at Kamina. "I thought it would come more clear after I arrived here but so far it hasn't."

On July 25 Merriman returned for the day to Léopoldville for a doctor's appointment. He had been having trouble with his right eye, out of which he saw only "a blank spot." In a moment of downtime, he wrote his wife another letter. "A lot of the work so far is frustrating as the organization is still disorganized," he wrote. "However the one worry I don't have is the personnel. My people are a real bunch of tigers. The pilots are all veterans of the Bay of Pigs & good at their jobs. Some of them are real friends already. Some day maybe we'll visit them in some happier place."

The next day, July 26, 1964, Merriman returned to Kamina. That afternoon he received an intelligence report from the Belgians that a convoy of rebels known as Simba, Swahili for "lion," had been spotted on the road from Kabalo. It was a vulnerable target and Merriman was eager for combat. He approached his friend Gus Ponzoa, hoping he would join Merriman in a strike on the convoy. But Ponzoa and the other pilots had already had a full morning of combat. Besides, Ponzoa's energy was sapped from a lingering case of hepatitis. He tried to discourage Merriman, arguing that it was already 4:00 P.M., that the target was a good hour away, and that it would be dark by the time they returned. René García also opposed the idea. If they crashed at dusk in enemy territory, there would be no one to rescue them and, besides, the convoy was of little importance.

But Merriman could not be dissuaded. García and Varela reluctantly agreed to join him. Merriman suited up and climbed into Ponzoa's T-38, plane number 496. The three T-28s flew wing-to-wing, at times so close they could read the names written on each other's helmet. Finally Merriman spotted the convoy, a line of four jeeps and half a dozen trucks snaking their way across the open expanse. Jeeps often indicated someone of senior rank. Merriman pointed below, then peeled off, his twin .50-caliber machine guns blazing. Varela was close behind. The convoy was riddled with bullets, but now the T-28s themselves became a target of ground fire. García saw that there was still movement below in one of the jeeps and made a third pass, watching the gunners dropping beneath a withering fire. He came out of his strafing run and began to climb but became aware that something was wrong. As he and Varela prepared to join up with Merriman, he waved them off.

"Open up!" said Merriman over the radio, calling for them to widen the formation. "I might explode." They could see a trail of vapor streaming from Merriman's plane. "I am losing oil," he said.

It had been two hours since they left Kamina. They were deep in enemy territory, and there was no ejection seat in the plane. Merriman's only hope was to find a place to land. At the rate that he was losing oil, he would fall out of the sky like a rock long before Kamina. And still, Merriman appeared his usual calm self as he lit up a cigarette.

García remembered a four-thousand-foot landing strip in Kabongo, still an hour from Kamina, but wide and open enough that Merriman might have a chance to bring his plane down—if the oil lasted that long. García took the lead and dropped down to search for barrels or drums beside the runway, any sign of the enemy's presence. It looked clear. He gave Merriman the go-ahead to land.

Merriman's T-28 descended slowly. He seemed confused. He was making a teardrop approach coming into the wind, a quarter mile from the runway. There would be no time to make another approach. Now it was clear to García that he had taken a hit in the oil return line between the propeller and the tank. He was about to lose his propeller. Still Merriman was coming in perfectly level and straight when suddenly, at eight hundred to one thousand feet, he lost all power.

The plane plummeted. A huge red cloud rose into the air.

"My God," thought García, "he's exploded." But it was only the red dusty earth of the fields. When it cleared, Varela and García could see Merriman's propeller fifty yards from the rest of the plane, spinning absurdly. And they could make out the mangled remains of the plane. The wings were twisted crazily, the fuselage crumbled. They could see Merriman's head, motionless, in the cockpit. Varela wanted to land but García talked him out of it. There was no way, he said, that Merriman could have survived such a crash. What good would it do to lose two men and two planes?

Back at Kamina, Ponzoa had begun to worry and had taken to the control tower waiting for some word. García radioed the tower. "Kamina tower, this is Tango flight. We have lost one of our airplanes."

Ponzoa recognized García's voice and called him by the Spanish word for "Baldy." "Calvo, is that you?" Then García broke the news that it was Merriman who had gone down. Ponzoa shook his head in disbelief. Merriman, his mentor and ace of aces, was too good to have been shot down.

When García and Valera landed, there were few words spoken. They had lost their commander, an American whom in such short time they had come to call a friend. He was not even supposed to engage in combat. In his logbook Ponzoa scribbled in Spanish, *"Tumbaron a Merriman"* (They shot down Merriman).

The next morning there was a stir at the entrance to Kamina. A beat-up old truck, driven by two locals, had something in the back they wanted to unload. It was Merriman. He had somehow survived the crash and been discovered by these two men who pried him out of the crumpled cockpit. Suspecting he had come from Kamina, they were determined to return him before the rebels found him.

Passing in and out of consciousness, Merriman was carried to the base hospital. But it was a hospital in name only. There were no doctors, no nurses, only two local nurse's aides. There was not so much as an aspirin to ease Merriman's pain. Merriman was placed on a bed, the blood wiped off with a clean, damp cloth. His eyes were bloodshot, his face lacerated. His shoulder bone, both ankles, and three vertebrae were broken. His chest and legs were covered with contusions. The force of the crash had been so great that the harness strap had cut a quarter inch into his flesh. Even the bezel of his Rolex watch had popped out on impact.

García, the son of a doctor, was deeply concerned. He remembered his father's patients, how they could sometimes be up and about the very day they were operated on and then suddenly develop a clot and die. What García noticed was that Merriman's skin had taken on a bluish tint. García understood that as miraculous as it was that Merriman had not died in the crash, his survival now depended on getting him back to the States or Europe where he could receive proper care. Immediately the Cuban pilots notified the embassy in Léopoldville asking someone to come and medevac Merriman.

Each time Merriman regained consciousness, he would plead with Ponzoa: "Gus, please send me home. I want to see my family. You can run the operation here yourself. I am feeling very bad. Please, Gus." Even his flier's pride was wounded. "You guys fly so long and nothing happens to you," he would say to the Cuban pilots clustered around his bed. "I go on the first mission and . . ."

But Ponzoa's appeals to Léopoldville went largely ignored. There was nothing they could do for Merriman but try to make him comfortable. Sometimes lucid, sometimes delirious, he would pass out for five or six hours. Ponzoa and the others could not understand why the Americans had not yet come for him.

But if the U.S. Embassy and CIA were concerned with Merriman's well-being, they were at least as committed to concealing the fact that he, an American, had taken part in combat and crashed. On July 25, 1964, the day before his crash, U.S. Ambassador McMurtrie Godley had sent a telegram to Secretary of State Dean Rusk advising that "we should indulge in no, repeat no, covert operations here that do not have Tshombe's [Moise Tshombe, the Congo's premier] and/or [Congo President Joseph] Kasavubu's blessing."

Adding to sensitivities was a State Department cable sent the day after Merriman's crash. It reported that rebels under Communist influence were now convinced that Americans had taken a direct hand in the conflict. They vowed to punish any and all whites found in the region. Thirty rebels had been killed and eighty wounded in one such attack in which Americans had allegedly participated.

A day later a military attaché in the U.S. Embassy referred to a Congo Army report that a "T-28 on its third mission made a forced landing 300 yards short of runway at Kabango [sic]," and that helicopters from Kamina were attempting to salvage the parts. "Pilot not badly injured," the embassy erroneously concluded.

"We are concerned," cabled U.S. Ambassador Godley, "about increasing number of reports that if T-28 or mercenaries used by GOC [government of Congo] against rebel-held areas in eastern Congo, rebels will retaliate by killing whites in areas under their control." That was July 28. Two days later Godley reiterated his concerns and expressed his growing opposition to the CIA's reliance on an air campaign. "While we here unable to completely evaluate contribution which T-28's may be making to security situation Katanga, own present impression is that aircraft alone cannot contain continuing rebel advance unless there are armed men on ground willing to stand and fight. This is not now the case in Katanga. Therefore suggest consideration be given halting T-28 operations temporarily until more dependable ground forces materialize."

Merriman, from a diplomatic and security viewpoint, was an embarrassment and a liability. On July 30 Ambassador Godley, in a cable classified "Secret," reported that the pilot of the downed T-28 was "Merriman, a U.S. citizen," but instead of expressing concern for Merriman's condition, he expressed relief that Reuters was reporting the pilot was Cuban. That miscue was courtesy of the Belgian consul general who was covering for the United States—for which Ambassador Godley later expressed his appreciation. Any further inquiries into the crash were to be referred to the Congo Air Force, which the United States had advised to "stick to Reuters story."

Ambassador Godley simply wanted the Merriman situation to quietly fade away. "Should pilot's nationality be revealed we will continue refer inquiries to CAF [Congo Air Force] but if pressed will emphasize non operational character of mission. Would hope that nothing be said by USG [United States government] officials." That message was passed on to the White House at 6:50 A.M. on July 30.

From the U.S. vantage point, Merriman's misfortune could not have occurred at a more inopportune moment, potentially inflaming as it did rebel passions against whites in the area and threatening to discredit U.S. denials of direct military involvement in the region. At that very moment the Congo seemed to be imploding. The very day the White House learned of Merriman's crash, a second cable, more dire than the first, arrived in Washington. "Security situation North Katanga continues to deteriorate . . . ANC [Congolese forces] and ex-gendarmes have fled . . . ANC troops deserting Kabongo . . . Fall of Kongolo will be further psychological shock. Defection of troops at Kabongo opens way for advance on Kamina . . ."

While the diplomats and covert planners fretted over the situation and continued their debate, Merriman lay in a hospital bed at Kamina, his condition worsening.

It was not until at least July 31—five interminable days of anguish—that a DC-4 was finally dispatched from Léopoldville to airlift Merriman out. But it was not to take Merriman home or even to Europe, but rather to a dismal and backward hospital in Léopoldville. So sensitive was the situation that Merriman was admitted into the hospital under the pseudonym of Mario Carlos in an effort to preserve the ruse that he was Cuban.

The days dragged on. His condition worsened. With nothing but pain to occupy his time, and no immediate prospect of a flight home, he tried to fend off depression. Ponzoa visited him in the hospital and was distressed by the care his friend was receiving. Aside from shots to help him sleep, Ponzoa saw little to indicate he was receiving appropriate medical treatment.

Ponzoa returned to Kamina. Even without Merriman the air campaign against the rebels had to continue. On August 4, Ponzoa and the other Cuban pilots strafed a train heading north between Kabongo and Pidi. They raked the locomotive and four cars with a murderous fire from their .50-caliber machine guns, as men dove off the train in desperation. Only then did Ponzoa and the others discover that the men were wearing uniforms and that it was a troop train of friendly Congolese soldiers. By then some fifteen soldiers were dead. In the chaos that was the Congo, the mistake went utterly unrecorded.

By then, Merriman had been lying in the Léopoldville hospital for five days. Until then, it might have been argued that his fate was subsumed by the larger concerns for the Congo. But on August 4 the Congo and Merriman's future would both be eclipsed by events halfway around the world. On that day two U.S. destroyers were said to have come under attack by North Vietnamese patrol boats. The incident, of dubious credibility, provided the impetus for what became known as the Gulf of Tonkin Resolution, the legislative basis for the Vietnam War. Provocation or pretext, it consumed all other concerns. Even Ambassador Godley found himself pleading for attention from a Washington that was, in his words, "preoccupied with Vietnam." But there was no one to plead on Merriman's behalf.

Two days later, on August 6, 1964, Merriman took up a pen and wrote his wife a letter. "Dear Darling," it began. "Our letters will probably be a little staggered while I am here so I will write as often as I can when I can. I received several of your letters today and spent quite a while going through them . . . by the way don't pay too much attention to my writing as I am not terribly coordinated at the moment. Also everything will be a little slanted." Indeed the words nearly veered off the page.

Merriman did not mention that he had been in a plane crash or that he was suffering. Whether it was to spare his wife worries or to avoid any breach of security is not clear. There were hints of a mishap and clear signs of growing resentment and disillusionment. "There are some people," he wrote, "I don't think I'll ever be able to like whether I want to or not. About the only one I know that is always straight is you." It had been two weeks since the crash and there was little hope that he would be sent back to the States anytime soon.

There was more than a touch of understatement in his letter. "Some of the work is exciting to say the least. Some of it I'll be able to tell you about when I come home. One thing you've probably heard by now is the fact that I've had an accident. Don't let this worry you. For a few minutes it was a near thing but everything so far has worked out O.K. and think everything will." Merriman was wrong. The Agency had apparently not yet made any mention of a plane crash.

As the letter progressed, Merriman's writing slanted more and more, the words themselves belying his fatigue. "I have to stop for now," he wrote, "so I'll use the rest of this page to tell you that I do love you so very very very much that you will never realize how much—I'll try to tell you how much when I come home—Your very own—John."

René García could scarcely believe that the United States would allow one of its own with such critical injuries to be left in a primitive Congolese hospital. On his first return to Léopoldville he visited Merriman in the hospital and saw that, aside from sedatives and pain-killers, little or nothing was being done for him. He went straightaway to the embassy and confronted an air force officer stationed there, imploring him to intervene on Merriman's behalf.

The officer's response: "René, to win a war sometimes you have to be a son of a bitch."

García was stunned. "I was always thinking there would be somebody with the decency to take care of the situation but there wasn't anybody to take care of anything. Maybe it was the fear of the press, I don't know why they didn't medevac him out. I knew we were expendable, we the Cubans, but it seemed then the American boys were expendable as well."

Two more weeks passed with Merriman lying in the Congolese hospital. Finally, on August 20, he was put aboard an air force cargo plane back to the States. Even then, the Agency was concerned that such a move not leak out. It was arranged that Merriman be transported under the name of an air force officer.

Somewhere high above Ascension Island, between one and three in the morning, John Merriman's weary and broken body at last gave in, as an embolism lodged in his lungs. That his death might well have been avoided had he been returned to the States weeks earlier is conjecture. Perhaps it was fitting that Merriman, who all his life had wanted nothing more than to fly, should have died in an airplane.

Not long after, it was said the family of the air force officer whose name Merriman had traveled under was notified that they had lost their son. After some moments of shock and a call or two, it was discovered that their boy was fine. But there was no such good news awaiting Val Merriman and her three sons.

On the morning of August 20 the telephone rang in their Tucson home. It was Syd Stembridge asking if he could come out and talk with her. A short time later he arrived. Val poured him a cup of coffee and the two walked out on the patio and took a seat. Stembridge's message was short and to the point. He said John had had an accident—exactly what kind was not said—but that he did not think it was life-threatening. If all goes well, said Stembridge, he would be flown to a hospital in Bethesda for an examination and then come home. If there was a problem, the Agency would fly the family to be with him. It was almost presented as good news. John was coming home early.

In preparation for his homecoming, Val prepared his favorite meal, roast turkey. While it was still in the oven the doorbell rang. It was Stembridge again, this time with Dot Kreinheder, Gar Thorsrude's personal assistant. Kreinheder went into the living room, where the boys were watching television. Stembridge walked Val onto the patio. He had bad news, he said. John, he said, had been in a Puerto Rico hospital, that his spirits were good, that he had eaten a solid dinner, and sometime around 11:00 P.M. a nurse had checked in on him. John had asked for ice cream, which he was given. At six the next morning, as the doctor made rounds, Merriman was dead.

Stembridge's arm was around Val's shoulder. When she calmed down enough to hear his words, he told her that Kreinheder would be staying with the family for a time and that the Agency had worked out an elaborate cover story to ensure that Merriman's death would not be linked either to the Congo or to the CIA. It was a story Val would be expected to tell John's parents, his friends, and his sons.

Merriman, so the cover story went, had been flying an airplane with a magnetometer to find minerals on the ground, and when he finished the job, the private firm for which he worked had asked him to fly to Puerto Rico to finalize a contract. When he arrived there, he rented a car and was to drive into the city, but on the way, exhausted from his trip, he ran off the road and crashed into a tree. From there he was taken to the hospital at Ramey Air Force Base. "I remembered every word of it," said Val Merriman.

John Merriman's children and parents were also told the cover story. It would be more than thirty years before Val Merriman would discover that the Agency had lied to her about the circumstances of her husband's death.

The Agency contacted a doctor who came out and gave Val Merriman a tranquilizer and left several others for her to take later. She hadn't asked for them but did what the Agency told her to do. She was so dazed by the medication that she remembers little of the days thereafter, except that either Stembridge or Thorsrude convinced her not to let her children attend the funeral. It was a decision she would forever regret.

The funeral was small, about thirty-five people. Thorsrude had flown in many of John's friends from Marana—Stembridge, Gearke, and many of the Intermountain pilots and smoke jumpers. Later there was a wake. Endless stories of Merriman's exploits as a pilot were told over drinks.

A few days later Merriman's final letter, the one written from his hospital bed in Léopoldville, arrived at the Merriman home.

. . .

For Val Merriman, John's death brought with it not only grief but a profound sense of isolation. "When John died, there was nobody I could talk to about this death. A wife that loses her husband in a car accident can go to a meeting with other widows and talk about what happened. I couldn't even tell my friends what happened. It's also pretty tough to lie to your children and your mother-in-law. To sit around telling them flat-out lies is pretty tough."

Not long after Merriman's death, the Merrimans began to receive monthly checks, which Val Merriman assumed were akin to workers' compensation. But these checks were drawn on an offshore bank and the Agency had instructed her to pick them up from a Tucson post office box. The last check arrived when Eric, Merriman's youngest son—four at the time of his father's death—turned twenty-one.

There were other ways, too, that the Agency tried to look after her. A local attorney working with the CIA arranged to take care of all tax, Social Security, and insurance matters. But the latter became more complicated than expected. Back when John Merriman was twenty-one and living in Alaska, he and Val had purchased a $3,000 life insurance policy that contained a double indemnity clause. If John Merriman died in a car accident, the policy would pay double.

Val Merriman knew that her husband had been in a plane crash in the Congo, not in a car crash as his death certificate recorded. But she had had no reason to doubt the Agency's story that his injuries had at first appeared minor and that his final day was spent in a Puerto Rican hospital attended by a solicitous medical staff. The grim truth—that he endured agonizing injuries that went largely unattended—would not be made known to her for three decades, and even then, not by the Agency. "It was the only story I had," she said. Still, she felt uneasy about accepting the insurance company's $6,000 that included the double indemnity payout. "John died in an act of war and I didn't want that to ever come back and haunt us," she said. "Keeping the money was not something that I or John would want me to do." So she returned the money.

But Robert Gambino, a senior security officer with the CIA's deputy director for plans, flew to Chattanooga where the insurance company was based and privately disclosed to the firm's president that Merriman had died serving his country. The company concluded that Val Merriman was indeed deserving of the proceeds, including the double indemnity provision. Even so, Val Merriman declined to accept it.

Finally there were individual acts of kindness about which not even Val Merriman was aware. At Marana, Merriman's death hit hard. His friend Don Gearke remembered that in the week before Merriman left he had been cited with a violation by the FAA for hassling a general's plane. The fine was still outstanding. Not wishing his widow to have to deal with such matters or to have Merriman's flight record blemished, he pulled some strings and had the violation quietly quashed.

In April 1965, eight months after Merriman's death, his widow was presented with a posthumous medal, the Agency's much-coveted Intelligence Star. It was a private ceremony held on the seventh floor of the CIA's Langley headquarters. Only Merriman's widow and parents were invited. The citation, signed by Director Central Intelligence John McCone, reads: "for his fortitude and courage in an overseas area of extreme hazard. Volunteering for an assignment which he knew to be fraught with danger and hardship, Mr. Merriman lost his life as a result of hostile action while engaged in an activity of great concern to the United States. His exemplary conduct served to inspire his associates and maintains the finest traditions of service to our Nation."

Later they lunched on filet mignon in a private dining room. The meal was abruptly interrupted as word was received that President Johnson wanted to meet Merriman's widow and parents. They were immediately driven to the White House, where Johnson received them. No record of that meeting would appear in White House logs or the presidential calendar, though the family was later permitted to pose for photos in the Rose Garden. Accompanying the Merrimans on their White House tour was Robert Gambino, the senior CIA security officer, and Syd Stembridge. (As if the scene were not already macabre enough, the

Merrimans were later joined by the wife of film director Alfred Hitchcock.)

President Johnson solemnly received the family in the Oval Office and expressed his condolences. He said that the nation honored this son and husband, that the country owed him a debt that could never be repaid. He never mentioned John Merriman by name, but his eyes were tearing. He said he took the loss personally and was saddened even further that he could not declare to the public what this man had done. He even referred to Sam Houston, the hero of the Texas war for independence. A few moments later McGeorge Bundy, Johnson's security adviser, introduced himself to the Merrimans, as did Lady Bird Johnson. The president then clasped the Merrimans' hands, squeezing firmly.

He turned to Merriman's father. "So you're from Tennessee?" said Johnson in an effort to infuse some levity. "We had some Tennesseans helped us out at the Alamo." The senior Merriman, a salty Chattanooga detective, was accustomed to speaking his mind. "Helped you out?" he fired back. "Hell, if you had more of us we would have saved your ass!"

For an instant Johnson, a man rarely at a loss for words, stood speechless. "You're okay," he said, then erupted in laughter, tears streaming down his cheeks.

Outside, a helicopter landed as the Johnsons prepared to leave for their Texas ranch. Before departing, Lady Bird handed Val Merriman a book on White House interiors. There was no inscription. A moment later the Johnsons were gone. Afterward the Merrimans were taken to the kitchen and served some finger sandwiches and iced tea. The two Merriman women, widow and mother, were then given an orchid corsage and led by a Secret Service agent on a rare tour of the upstairs residence.

. . .

After Merriman's death, Washington would continue to prop up Tshombe and later army strongman Mobuto. In the annals of the CIA the outcome in the Congo would be placed squarely in the win column, as Mobuto remained in the U.S. sphere of influence. He provided a share of his country's rich minerals (including tantalite, used in nuclear weapons) to the United States as well as a strategic base from which the CIA would launch later anti-Communist and counterinsurgency efforts in Angola.

For the people of the Congo, known as Zaire under Mobuto, it was not so clear a victory. For thirty-three years Mobuto's name was virtually synonymous with corruption and repression. Not since King Leopold II of Belgium a century before had the country been so plundered, its people so devastated. Mobuto became a billionaire, bankrupting his country. To describe the avarice and thievery of his regime, a new word had to be coined—kleptocracy. But though he betrayed his own people, in the Cold War era of "clientitis" he remained "faithful" to the West. As was said of many, he may have been a bastard, but he was our bastard.

Sidney Gottlieb, the eccentric CIA scientist who delivered poison meant for the Congo's Lumumba, died in 1999 at the age of eighty. He spent his final years caring for the dying, running a commune, and fending off lawsuits growing out of his secret CIA experiments decades earlier.

CIA Station Chief Lawrence Devlin, who had tossed the poison meant for Lumumba into the Congo River, later went to work for American diamond magnate Maurice Templesman, paramour and final companion to Kennedy's widow, Jacqueline Onassis. Devlin's courtship of Mobuto had proved most valuable.

As for the Cuban pilots who survived the Bay of Pigs to later fly with Merriman, they remained close comrades, though they took divergent paths. René García became Mobuto's personal pilot. From 1969 to 1985 he flew him everywhere, from Paris to China to North Korea to Disneyland. García watched as the diamonds from the mines of Katanga, the province in which Merriman had died while trying to prevent it from seceding, went to Belgium—except for the largest stones, which were lost to Mobuto's palace.

Gus Ponzoa would later fly for another CIA proprietary and ferry American weapons to an equally repressive U.S. client, the Shah of Iran. He is now retired and living in Miami.

Jack Varela, Merriman's wingman that fateful day, died in a Dominican prison where he was serving time on drug charges.

As for the Merrimans, John Merriman remains very much a daily presence in their lives. The oldest son, Bruce, joined the CIA in the Office of Security. Unbeknownst to him, his mother had gone to Gar Thorsrude and quietly persuaded him to promise that Bruce would never be placed in harm's way, a promise he honored. Bruce Merriman left the Agency after a decade.

The legacy of Agency service is often passed from parent to child, creating a kind of caste system in which sons and daughters are welcomed into the fold. Having been raised within the culture of secrecy, they need no reminders. Today Bruce wears his father's Rolex watch, the one whose bezel popped off in the crash.

Son Jon entered the 82nd Airborne just as his father had done before him. In 1980 he, too, interviewed for an Agency job. As a former fine arts major, he was asked if he was interested in the "manufacturing section," and, in particular, where forgeries and false documents are prepared. Then they asked if he was willing to break the law. "Which laws," asked Merriman, "foreign or domestic?" That question put the interviewers off and no job offer was received.

For years Jon pursued every lead that might shed light on his father's life and death. His den is a kind of living shrine to his father, about whom he speaks in soft and reverential tones.

Merriman's widow, Val, remarried—another pilot, David Folkins, who also flew for the CIA. Increasingly, as the Agency matured, it moved more and more into the role of extended family. But Val Merriman Folkins did not forget John. His portrait hangs in their bedroom. Her second husband had no wish to expunge him from their lives, or to allow John Merriman's sons to forget him. No one had to convince him of the honor and remembrance Merriman was due. And in her purse, just as she did the day of the funeral, Val continues to carry a picture of John Merriman. Not a day goes by when she does not speak with him, silently communing with his spirit.

The CIA's Syd Stembridge, who told Val Merriman the story of her husband's passing in the Puerto Rican hospital and of his request for ice cream, is retired now. He attended the 1977 wedding of Merriman's son Jon. But when the wedding pictures were developed, Jon noticed that the only pictures of Stembridge were of the back of his head. A consummate professional in security matters, he was a study in anonymity.

Stembridge will still not speak of the circumstances surrounding Merriman's death. "It's security reasons with me," he says. "Once you start down that road, I would say something and you will want to know why and that will lead to something else. I've just made it a policy. I knew John Merriman well, and I know John is resting easy if I abide by what he knew to be the rules of the game."

But in 1996 the Merrimans made a dramatic discovery. It came not by way of the Agency, but from Janet Weininger, daughter of the Alabama pilot Pete Ray, who died at the Bay of Pigs. As Weininger pursued her life-long search for answers about her own father, interviewing veterans of the Bay of Pigs, she came upon a pilot who told her the story of John Merriman. He asked her to help him track down Merriman's family. Later the Merrimans were introduced to the Cuban pilots who served with John Merriman. They told her of his suffering and of what they believed was the U.S. government's inexcusable delay in getting him proper treat-ment. They were convinced that Merriman had suffered needlessly and that, had he received proper care, he might well be alive today.

Val Merriman was appalled. She contacted several lawyers in an effort to sue the Agency for wrongful death, but each one declined to take the case. So thorough was the Agency's security that she had not a shred of pa-per to document the circumstances surrounding Merriman's death. What Val Merriman said she wanted was not money, but someone to say "I'm sorry."

That same year Merriman's son Jon was idly thumbing through a magazine when he came upon a photo of the CIA's Book of Honor. There on the open page he saw inscribed his father's name. No one from the Agency had bothered to tell the family that Merriman had been so honored.

The next year the Merriman family once again approached the Agency pleading with them to release the file on John. At a December 16, 1997, meeting, CIA officers told the family it would take a prodigious ef-fort on the Agency's part to retrieve the records. A few months earlier one of those same officers had said the file had been lost. But first the Agency insisted that the Merrimans sign a secrecy agreement pledging not to di-vulge whatever information they might learn. This they did.

It was only the latest in a series of bizarre negotiations between the CIA and the Merriman family. Several months earlier the Agency had made an even more unusual request. In return for any cooperation, the family would be required to tender their copy of Merriman's death cer-tificate, the one that said he had been in an auto accident in Puerto Rico. This, too, the family did.

The only thing the Merrimans came away with from that December 1997 meeting that they did not have before was Merriman's autopsy re-port detailing the awful extent of his injuries. Val Merriman could not help but remember when the CIA had told her John had not suffered and had received the best of care.

The Agency maintained that it had done all it could for John Merriman, that his delicate condition would not permit him to have been moved any earlier. The idea that it abandoned one of its own in the field strikes a raw nerve even today at an Agency that prides itself in getting its people out when they are in danger. But that's not how the Merrimans see it. "They let him die," says Val Merriman. "I really hope he didn't realize that. He thought the Agency was the greatest thing in the world. He was a flyboy. He would never have thought they would have deserted him."

CHAPTER 7

The Two Mikes

Alas, but Michael fell young:
Hee never fell, thou fallest my tongue.
He stood, a Souldier to the last right end,
A perfect Patriot, and noble friend,
But most a virtuous Sonne.

FROM AN ELEGY BY BEN JONSON

AT TEN O'CLOCK on a sunlit Sunday morning—October 10, 1965—two young men in khakis, both named Mike, hoisted themselves aboard an Air America chopper and lifted off from a tiny air base in Pakse, Laos. One was named Mike Deuel. The other, Mike Maloney. Both were said to be with the Agency for International Development, AID, helping to resettle displaced refugees. Their true purpose, stamped "Top Secret," would, for decades, keep the Central Intelligence Agency from speaking of their mission or even uttering their names aloud, though not for lack of pride.

From the vantage point of far-off Langley, these two young bulls—Deuel was twenty-eight, Maloney twenty-five—were as close to royalty as the CIA possessed. In their faces the Agency's leadership could read the CIA's proud past and what it took to be its illustrious future.

What set the two Mikes apart from other young covert operatives was that they were among the first sons of CIA career officers to take to the field. That Sunday morning flight—the first time the two Mikes would link up—was in itself of no great political or military consequence. But to the few at Langley who were cleared to know the names behind the code names and who were familiar with the lineage of these two men, it was something of an epochal event.

It marked the beginning of the end for that first generation of CIA officer who had come out of World War II and Donovan's OSS, and it ushered in a whole new era of clandestine warrior. By 1965, two full decades after World War II, the CIA's wartime veterans were entering their fifties and sixties. Balding and slower of step, they were sagelike presences in the halls of Langley, already cast in supervisory and support roles and, but for a defiant few, reluctantly accepting desk jobs. They understood it was time to leave the action to the "kids," as those of the successive generation were sometimes called. The old-timers had passed along their tradecraft and their vision of a world in peril, one whose salvation rested upon constant vigilance and sometimes desperate measures.

The two Mikes were the very embodiment of that legacy, eager to demonstrate their courage and their skills. Over time, the novelty of a second generation of CIA officer would fade. More and more sons and daughters, nieces and nephews, were drawn into the fold of clandestine service. It was no accident. Through summer jobs and internships, through preferences accorded the scions of Agency employees, and through the natural patterns of socializing among themselves, the CIA's intergenerational ranks swelled.

In time, they would come to form an unseen clandestine class and a culture all its own. Raised within a raucously open society and yet a breed apart, they were reared to believe in the indispensability of espionage and the virtues of secrecy. They came to accept what the wider population could not—that even the ultimate sacrifice must sometimes go unrecognized and unrecorded. As public suspicions of the Agency deepened in the aftermath of the Bay of Pigs and the quagmire of Vietnam, the CIA increasingly gathered unto itself its own sons and daughters. They, above all others, could be trusted and demanded little explanation.

Mike Maloney and Mike Deuel were a part of that second generation of CIA officer who came of age in the early and mid-1960s and who would leave their own unique hallmark on the clandestine service for decades to come. To understand this second generation of Cold Warrior and its vision of the world, you must first come to know the stock from which they came and why, for the two Mikes, clandestine service was not merely a choice of career but an honored birthright, foreordained.

. . .

Mike Maloney's father, Arthur, was born in Connecticut in 1914. To his friends he was known as Art or Mal. No one ever doubted that he had the makings of a tough son of a bitch. He was a barrel-chested, Camel-smoking Irishman with a square jaw, teacup ears, a boxer's nose, and wild, bushy brows. His skin was pinkish and quick to sunburn. He could be gruff and intimidating but in an instant erupt with a roguish laugh from which neither funeral nor High Mass would have been safe.

He attended West Point, where he was the very embodiment of gung ho, even as a member of the backup lacrosse squad. One admiring observer wrote: "A whack from a lacrosse stick spread Maloney's schnoz so he could smell his ears. That normally is an annoying injury in sport but to a B-team player who picks his teeth with the cleats of the varsity stars a smeared bugle is no worse than a bad, but brief, cold." Maloney took his soldiering seriously, but not himself. In the Academy's production of a musical comedy, he played an utterly ridiculous Romeo. He graduated from West Point in 1938 and one year later married Mary Evangeline Arens, a chestnut-haired coed with a will all her own. A year later they had a child, a son named Michael Arthur Maloney—one of "The Two Mikes."

But Mal Maloney's homelife, like that of his generation, was interrupted by World War II. Maloney, a crack paratrooper, would find himself in charge of the 3rd Battalion of the 507th Parachute Infantry Regiment, part of the fabled 82nd Airborne Division. At 2:30 A.M., June 6, 1944—D-Day—he was the first among his nineteen parachute troops to leap from the plane into occupied France. In addition to his own burly 200 pounds, he shouldered a carbine, a pistol, two knives, a land mine, four grenades, ammo, a watertight escape kit, $40 in French currency, a silk handkerchief map, a compass, and a file—350 pounds in all. Never before had he jumped with so little space between himself and the ground.

He landed in a pasture on the west side of the Merderet River. Soon after, his battalion commander was killed, and Maloney took charge. He was not yet thirty, making him by some accounts the youngest commander in the European theater. Seeing that his battalion was being pushed back under withering fire, he reorganized them and led them forward, personally taking a bazooka team to destroy an enemy tank. He showed complete contempt for his own safety. At Chef-du-Pont a bullet from a German sniper pierced his helmet, tore through the toilet paper he carried there, and exited out the other side. His shoulder holster was scarred by a second bullet that bounced off the barrel of his .45. Unshaven and with dried blood streaking his reddish beard, he was a forbidding presence, and damn proud of it. "I was probably the ugliest soldier in Normandy," he later boasted.

On July 7, 1944, on the forward slope of Hill 95 at La Poterie Ridge, a bullet tore through his right leg, grazed his groin, and ripped through his left leg, severing several nerves. A British doctor had him fully prepped and was about to amputate his right leg when Maloney persuaded him otherwise: "No fucking way," he barked. And though he had been told it was doubtful he would ever walk again or be able to have more children, he went on to be a father three times more (he already had two children) and took great pride in proving the doctors wrong. For a year he was in a stateside hospital. He received the Purple Heart, three Bronze Stars, and the coveted Distinguished Service Cross. Upon winning the latter, the *Hartford Times* ran a photo of Mal and his son Mike, as the two posed with the colonel's perforated helmet. The caption read: " 'And that's where it came out.' Little Michael explains the two bullet holes in the helmet of his daddy, Lt. Col. Arthur A. Maloney." Already "Little Michael" had been introduced to soldiering. Baptized in the chapel at Schofield Barracks in Hawaii, Little Michael was given a toy plane and a toy soldier for his first birthday.

In August 1946 Mal retired from the military as a full colonel. Few doubted that, but for his wound, he would soon have been a general. He worked for a time at Colt's Patent Firearms Manufacturing Company and later the Aetna Insurance Company, but he chafed at desk jobs and hankered for military life. "You couldn't keep him away from anywhere there was shooting going on," recalled his friend Major General Paul F. Smith. With the outbreak of the Korean War in 1950 Mal Maloney volunteered for duty but was rejected because of his bum leg. His beloved military wouldn't have him.

And so it was by default that he came to the CIA in March 1951. The CIA was as close as he could get to the front lines. It was never to be a perfect fit, but his paramilitary skills and command experience proved a valuable asset to the Agency, and he was promptly put to work first in the CIA's Office of Training and later the War Plans Division.

In 1957 Maloney received orders that he was to be transferred to Hawaii, where he would be under military cover—hardly a stretch for the colonel. He was to dress in uniform and report daily to a nonexistent entity within the Department of Defense, the so-called Pacific Research Office. His actual CIA position was to be chief of the war plans staff, Far East Division, under the deputy director for plans. Specifically he was to help draft contingency war plans should North Korea, China, or both suddenly reach beyond their borders.

But the flight to Hawaii was to be even more harrowing than that which dropped him over wartime France. Maloney, his wife, Mary, sons Mike, Dennis, and Timothy, and daughters Erin and two-month-old Sheila took off from Travis Air Force Base in California in a four-engine Military Air Transport C-97 on August 8, 1957. The destination: Honolulu. Just over halfway to Hawaii, Dennis, then fourteen, looked out the window and saw the propeller from the number one engine on the left wing fly off, loop over the wing, and strike the fuselage. Moments later the second engine on the left wing also died.

With still another thousand miles to the nearest landfall in Hawaii, the plane limped on, barely a hundred feet above the black Pacific. The captain ordered everyone to put on life jackets and sent out a distress signal alerting ships in the area to be ready to help if the plane should need to ditch at sea. In an effort to stabilize the aircraft, the pilot had the Maloney family and the other fifty-two passengers shunted from one side to the other. Finally the captain ordered the passengers to dump their luggage into the sea.

A rear door was opened and seventeen-year-old Mike Maloney, together with the other passengers, formed a line and passed along suitcases as well as fifty-three bags of mail, shoveling them out the back, low enough to hear them splash. Included in the jettisoned baggage was an entire wardrobe of new military uniforms that Mal was to wear as part of his military cover. For six hours the ordeal continued, as the plane skimmed above the waves. Mary Maloney swore that if the flight landed safely she would forever give up cigarettes and potatoes.

As they approached Hilo, the captain discovered that the landing gear had been damaged. Mal Maloney offered to climb down and crank it by hand, but the captain had a crew member do it instead. Finally the plane landed without incident. Mary Maloney would honor her oath never again to smoke a cigarette—though twenty years later she would eat potatoes after a doctor told her she needed the potassium. In 1958, a year after that traumatic flight, when Mike went off to Fairfield College in Connecticut, Mary Maloney insisted that her son take the cruise ship *Matsonia* to the States. No Maloney was taking another plane, not if Mary Maloney had anything to say about it. She would forever have a bad feeling about planes.

Nor was it the last trauma for the Maloneys in Hawaii. Mal Maloney enjoyed robust health, but he had acquired something of a shake or palsy. When he held a cup of coffee, it rattled against the saucer. His friends called it nerves. Whether it was a result of the war or something else, he was not always the best of drivers.

A year after arriving in Hawaii, shortly after noon on October 7, 1958, Mal Maloney struck a sixty-one-year-old woman who was crossing at the corner of Hotel and Punchbowl Streets. The woman died in hospital hours later. Maloney was charged with negligent homicide. The trial hung over the Maloney family for six months. The shock of the accident weighed heavily on Maloney. So, too, did the newspaper articles that drew attention to him, identifying him by his cover, as a Defense Department researcher. From the witness stand, Maloney described the accident to the jurors and concluded, "I will see it for the rest of my life."

On March 18, 1960, after six hours of deliberation, a jury found him not guilty. But the accident left a deeper scar on him than even the casualties suffered in combat.

. . .

Mal Maloney transferred back to CIA headquarters in August 1961. He was a familiar presence in the halls, the sight of his husky figure dragging his leg, braced and inflexible. Without the brace his left foot flopped in front of him like a flipper, and even with the brace he would on occasion stumble and collapse in a heap like a huge rag doll. Such falls would be followed by a moment of concerned silence, inevitably broken by Mal Maloney's own boisterous laugh as he gathered himself and got up. Except on the golf course where he occasionally cited his injuries in an unsuccessful bid for a few strokes' advantage, he never played up his wounds. Indeed, he disdained such attention. "Sympathy is a word between 'shit' and 'syphilis' in the dictionary," he would often declare until it became a mantra in the Maloney family.

Besides, at the Agency, such injuries were too common to merit special notice. In the years after World War II there were many men like Mal Maloney who loved the military but who, because of disabling combat injuries, were not able to return to active service. Like Maloney, they joined the CIA by default. Among these was one of Mal's dear friends, Ben Vandervoort, a fellow veteran of D-Day, who lost an eye and would later be played by John Wayne in the film *The Longest Day*. Another was the CIA's executive director, Colonel Lawrence K. "Red" White, who lost the use of one leg in combat. In the halls of Langley such injuries merely enhanced one's credibility. For Maloney and the others the curse of such injuries was that it had prematurely reduced men of action to bureaucrats and desk jockeys.

In Maloney's Washington home the medals were prominently displayed in shadow boxes. Framed on the wall was a handwritten note that read: "To Col. Arthur Maloney, a veteran of one of the truly great fighting units of World War II. With best wishes from a comrade of the ETO [European theater of operations]." It was signed by Dwight D. Eisenhower. Maloney also kept a yellowing newspaper article about the elite training given paratroopers. The headline read: "Silent, Clever, Deadly." Not one to romanticize war, Maloney penned under the headlines, "Noisy, dumb, scared."

But Maloney continually used his wiles to get as close to the action as Langley would permit. From November 1961 until May 1962 he was on temporary duty in Saigon, consulting on the growing U.S. efforts to contain the Communists. There he worked under Desmond FitzGerald, a legendary CIA covert warrior. In Saigon he also caught the attention of other future CIA standouts. Years later one of them would scribble a note to Maloney in the frontispiece of a book: "With fond memories of our time in Saigon—and the Irish wit and courage you supplied." It was signed "Bill Colby," Director Central Intelligence.

But the real focus of Maloney's attention by 1962 was not Vietnam but Cuba. In the aftermath of the Bay of Pigs in 1961, President Kennedy did not simply lick his wounds and walk away from the debacle. Instead, he and his brother Bobby, the attorney general, resolved to bring down Castro by any means necessary: to destabilize the country's economy, bankrupt it if necessary, and create such social unrest that the government would topple.

. . .

With the Kennedy brothers, it was no longer purely a matter of national security. It was personal. Castro had not only survived the Bay of Pigs but been emboldened by it, openly mocking the United States' effete and quixotic attempts to bring him down. A smoldering President Kennedy demanded action. Sam Halpern, a veteran Agency officer, recalls Richard Bissell summoning him into his office. "He told us he had been chewed out in the cabinet room of the White House by the president and attorney general for sitting on his ass and not doing anything about Castro and the Castro regime." Bissell related the president's order: "Get rid of Castro."

Halpern wanted clarification. "What do the words 'get rid of' mean?" he asked Bissell.

"Use your imagination," Bissell responded. "No holds barred."

In the year ahead the Agency did indeed use its imagination. There was even a short-lived plan to convince the Cuban people of Christ's Second Coming, complete with aerial starbursts. "Elimination by illumination," the scheme was dubbed by one senior officer. But such silliness gave way to more deadly plans, including a contract on Castro's life offered to the Mafia. The Agency was determined to create chaos in Cuba, with a mix of sabotage, propaganda, and, if need be, outright assassination.

The project was part of a broad-based action against Castro code-named Operation Mongoose.

The name was chosen by Halpern. He had telephoned a woman at CIA whose job it was to track those operational code names or cryptonyms already in use and provide a list of those still available, usually taken in alphabetical order from the dictionary. Only the first two letters, or digraph, were of any internal significance. In this instance, "MO" signified operations in Thailand and was chosen to mislead even those within the Agency. Halpern selected the word "mongoose," not knowing its meaning. (Years later he read Rudyard Kipling's story "Rikki-Tikki-Tavi" and learned a mongoose was a ferretlike creature famed for its speed and ability to kill cobras.)

The operation, under a unit designated simply Task Force W, commenced in October 1961. Mal Maloney was chosen to oversee a key component of that project—the selection of targets for sabotaging Castro's economy. This included copper mines, the sugar crop, and manufacturing concerns. Nothing was off-limits. "We were at war with Cuba," recalled one former member of the unit.

Maloney's sabotage efforts were interrupted a year later by the Cuban missile crisis of October 1962. He was then assigned a number of exotic roles. At the height of the crisis the United States had a broad contingency plan calling for the invasion of Cuba. At the CIA Maloney prepared an elaborate diversionary scheme designed to mask the true invasion points on the island. He oversaw an Agency program that was to parachute countless dummies on various landing sites. Each of the dummies was equipped with a timer that would set off firecrackers, in the hope that it would draw attention and fire away from U.S. troops landing elsewhere. As there was no invasion, the plan was put back on the shelf.

The Maloney family, of course, knew that Mal was with the CIA, but they had no inkling of what it was he did for the Agency. Early on, they learned not to ask. "If I told you," quipped Maloney, "I'd have to kill you." It was an oft-repeated line in CIA families, a way to laugh off the deadly serious consequences of a breach of security. As an inside joke, the Maloney's family dog, a white-and-brown-spotted beagle, was named Spook. But whatever it was that Maloney did, his son Mike decided he wanted to do the same. There would sometimes be friction between father and son, both of them husky, headstrong, and competitive, but there was also an abiding adoration.

. . .

If Mike Maloney's father was a man of action, Mike Deuel's was a man of words. His name was Wallace, but he was known to family and friends as Wally. He was a bookish figure with an owlish face, horn-rimmed glasses, and a slim frame, the sort of fellow pictured on the beach getting sand kicked in his face. He stood five feet ten, weighed 165 pounds, and had pale blue eyes and a ruddy complexion. As a child he had been pensive and sickly, suffering scarlet fever, diphtheria, mumps, whooping cough, and boils. His eyesight was poor and his later travels overseas would bring him dengue fever, ringworm, and, at age twenty-nine, a bout of pyorrhea. By age forty-one he had lost the last of his teeth.

More scholar than soldier, he loved his quiet Sundays when he would curl up with a literary classic or sit beside the radio engrossed in Puccini performed by his beloved Metropolitan Opera. He would never be mistaken for a warrior, but he had a kind of gumption that even warriors came to respect.

By trade he was a newspaperman, a world-class foreign correspondent for the *Chicago Daily News*. He had the good fortune in 1934 to be posted to Berlin even as Hitler consolidated power. Deuel would remain there for seven years. During that time he made a study of the Reich and published a book, *People Under Hitler*, a scathing account of German despotism. Columbia University Press placed Deuel among the fifteen American authors—along with the likes of Pearl Buck, Archibald MacLeish, and Sinclair Lewis—that Hitler would liquidate first if he conquered America. The Reich dubbed him "the worst anti-Nazi in the whole country." Author and friend William L. Shirer called him "brilliant."

In the Berlin of 1935 Deuel befriended a young United Press correspondent, a bachelor, with whom Deuel would often share meals and break the lonely tedium of a foreign posting. Later, in March 1942, Deuel wrote an effusive letter of recommendation for that correspondent who had applied for a position with the navy's public relations department. He hailed the young man's "personal charm," his intelligence, initiative, energy, honesty, and patriotism. That correspondent would become an integral part of the nascent OSS. His name was Richard McGarrah Helms, a future director of Central Intelligence. It was a friendship that would last for decades and profit Deuel in his second career with the Agency.

It was during his tenure as Berlin correspondent that Wally and his wife, Mary, had two sons. Peter was born in 1935 and Mike on May 13, 1937, in Berlin.

With the outbreak of World War II, Wally Deuel joined the Office of Strategic Services, the forerunner to the CIA. He was named special assistant to Wild Bill Donovan, the charismatic leader of the OSS. Not cut out for the derring-do of covert military operations, Deuel took on a variety of tasks, even working with Walt Disney on a cartoon propaganda project. He was later assigned to the PWD, the Psychological Warfare Division, where he helped to disseminate false stories designed to undermine Germany's will to fight. Among those Deuel would work with during the war was future CIA chief Allen Dulles.

At the end of the war Donovan asked Deuel to write the first history of the OSS, an internal document chronicling some of the service's missions and personalities. In August 1945 Deuel returned to the *Chicago Daily News* and was asked to write a series on the OSS. He prepared a generally glowing account of the OSS but suggested in one brief phrase that at times the espionage business called for the use of "subversion." In an otherwise flattering portrayal of the service, he wrote, "Some of the methods employed are not nice."

Constrained by both his lifetime secrecy oath and his bond of friendship with Donovan, Deuel submitted the article to the former OSS head for his approval, assuming it would be instantly forthcoming. But Donovan raised his eyebrows at the suggestion that his OSS had ever stooped to ungentlemanly behavior. Donovan pointed out that at that very moment, the FBI, the State Department, and the Navy and War Departments all had their knives out trying to gut his efforts to salvage elements of the OSS and create a postwar central intelligence apparatus.

The exchange that followed was recorded in an August 25, 1961, letter Deuel wrote to his son Mike, then a marine. Deuel recalled Donovan telling him that "if he and/or I admitted in print that we had used methods which weren't nice, this would be used as evidence that we were all wicked, dirty people whose agency should be abolished. 'Besides,' said Bill, looking his most virtuous, his most butter-wouldn't-melt-in-my-mouth, 'I defy you to name me one single case in which we used methods that weren't nice.'

"This, of course, was my cue to stammer and stutter and blush and pick my nose in well-simulated confusion, and pretend to cudgel my brains and then confess that, shucks, in actual fact I couldn't cite a single instance of OSS skullduggery.

"But the war was over, and Bill, for all that I adored him, already had a slight overdraft of his moral credit with me," wrote Deuel, "and I was a newspaperman again as of that day and occasion, and no longer a public servant, and Bill's righteousness was just altogether too Goddam silly, and so instead of making the obeisance expected of me, I said:

" 'All right, dammit, I will give you an example. I'll give you the example of Baron von ———, of the German diplomatic service, whom we suborned to the betrayal of his country's military secrets in time of war to an enemy—namely, us—by the threat that if he didn't give us what we wanted we'd expose him as a homosexual.'

"Bill beamed with gratification, highly pleased to be reminded of a coup of which he had always been particularly proud.

" 'But he was a homosexual, wasn't he?' said he.

" 'Certainly he was,' said I.

" 'And the threat worked, didn't it?' said he.

" 'Certainly it worked,' said I.

" 'Well, then?' said Bill, triumphantly."

Deuel ultimately won permission to publish the offending sentence, but without reference to any specific misdeeds.

. . .

Wally Deuel later took a job as diplomatic correspondent for the *St. Louis Post-Dispatch*, but in 1953 he was laid off. Thereafter he called upon his constellation of well-placed friends to help him find a job. Among these was a prominent fellow Illinois resident and future senator, Adlai Stevenson, and the then president of the Rockefeller Foundation, Dean

Rusk. But while there were many offers of assistance, no specific jobs materialized. Deuel's pride was hurt and his finances were frayed. He recalled that a decade earlier Allen Dulles had attempted to enlist his help in an OSS effort. Dulles was now Director Central Intelligence and eager to have Deuel on board.

In January 1954 Deuel took the oath of office, passed his final security interview, and signed a loyalty affidavit at CIA headquarters. He was a GS-15 with a starting salary of $10,800 a year, but he was jubilant, and once again intoxicated with the mystique of espionage, even though his career would rely more on his skills with a typewriter than a garrote or codebook.

On May 31, 1954, he wrote his friend Adlai Stevenson, "Dear Adlai: I have gone back to spying," a claim slightly exaggerated, but one in which he took enormous pride. "I thought I could take the stuff or leave it alone, but clearly it had a more powerful hold on me than I realized. Anyway, I'm with the CIA and having the time of my life. It's the most exciting and rewarding work I've done since I was Berlin Correspondent for the Old Daily News. It's like taking holy orders; you are vowed to silence, to obedience, to poverty and to long, long, long hours of extremely hard work. No vows of chastity, though."

To Dean Rusk, Deuel wrote: "I am back in the spy business . . . I am working for my favorite Dulles (Allen, of course) in CIA . . ." (The other Dulles, John Foster, brother of Allen, was then secretary of state.)

"The kids in CIA are simply terrific," he wrote another friend. "I never saw anywhere such a gang of brilliant, inspired, dedicated, hardworking, selfless men." Such effusiveness was the hallmark of those early years at the Agency, predating the revelations and allegations that would thereafter stain the Agency's name and create a more subdued and somber atmosphere.

But there was a strange irony to the idea that a man like Deuel who had made his living sharing his vision of events with the world was now bound to keeping his mouth shut. "The silence is the hardest part, of course," he wrote. "Imagine to yourself a Deuel unable to say anything about his work or anything about politics, either foreign or domestic. Imagine to yourself a Deuel whose garrulity is inhibited in any manner or degree whatever. What practical jokes life plays on us, sooner or later, doesn't it?"

At the Agency Wally Deuel held a variety of midlevel and senior positions. He was made chief of staff overseeing all current intelligence publications, including those that each morning went directly to President Eisenhower and, later, Kennedy. From 1957 until 1968 he served as deputy chief and then chief of Foreign Intelligence/Requirements, overseeing those branches that collected, edited, and disseminated the CIA's secret intelligence. He was later assigned to the inspector general's staff, traveling to more than twenty countries, examining the conduct of the Agency's far-flung stations and bases. He even undertook a covert assignment to Beirut, where he made a study of why the Lebanese press was negative toward the United States and what could be done to influence that press and plant stories more favorable to American interests.

In February 1961 Deuel's immediate superior broke his arm, and Deuel was asked to fill in as the CIA's representative to the Kennedy White House. There he attended meetings with Pierre Salinger, Ed Murrow, Walt Rostow, McGeorge Bundy, and other senior officials advising Kennedy on how to deal with the press on sensitive political and intelligence matters. At one such meeting, held on February 21, 1961, Deuel noted that the State Department representative advised Kennedy that the United States should have used the recent assassination of Patrice Lumumba in the Congo to its political advantage. The official argued that the United States "should have mounted a 'black' effort designed to convince world opinion that the Russians were responsible for Lumumba's assassination." Apparently the State Department official was unaware that the CIA had earlier ordered Agency operatives to poison the former Congolese leader.

At another White House meeting, on February 28, 1961, Deuel and others prepped Kennedy for an upcoming news conference. Kennedy was steamed at the CIA's apparent intelligence failures in the Congo, complaining that Agency reports were false or misleading. He turned to Deuel. "What's the matter—have you got only one man there in the Congo?" Kennedy asked.

"He smiled when he said it," wrote Deuel in a memo to Dulles. "He made it clear however that he meant his criticisms seriously."

In March Deuel was relieved of White House responsibilities. His replacement: his old friend Dick Helms.

But by May 1961 the White House and CIA were already the targets of fierce criticism in the wake of the Bay of Pigs debacle. Deuel understood that henceforth nothing would be the same. He wrote his son Mike: "We've been living—I won't say in a fool's paradise, but we've been living charmed lives all this time until now. Our immunity from exposure and attack has been partly luck, partly due to the laziness and lack of imagination of some editors and publishers, partly to self-restraint imposed by patriotism on the part of others, partly to trust in the Old Man [Allen Dulles], partly to the Old Man's skill in handling his public relations—and, above all, to the fact that we've had a series of fantastic successes. We've had a few failures too, but they either haven't amounted to much or we haven't been found out."

With the Bay of Pigs, all that had now changed.

. . .

Mike Deuel inherited his father's intellect, but something else as well. Where Wally Deuel had always been most comfortable standing on the sidelines as observer or adviser, his son Mike was determined to be a player. Wherever the action was most intense, that was where Mike Deuel wanted to be. Mike was what his father always hungered to be— not the scribe but the doer, living on the edge. His son was all of that— a romantic and roguish figure in whom his father could realize a lifetime of pipe dreams.

Physically Mike Deuel was not particularly formidable, but he had little regard for his own well-being and even as a child took pride in throwing himself in the way of the biggest kid on the playing field. More than once he ended up in the hospital, not because he was accident-prone, but because caution was a concept foreign to him. On March 14, 1949, the *Washington Post* ran a picture of eleven-year-old Mike Deuel smiling in his hospital bed after plummeting thirty feet from a two-story house to a concrete pavement. He suffered a concussion, a fractured elbow, and a cracked vertebra, but was delighted to have the time to build a model plane. Even then, he viewed fear and pain as elements to test his will.

On November 9, 1953, sixteen-year-old Mike Deuel was in a bruising football game when, in the second quarter, he became aware of a pain in his side. He felt tired and unable to run. But he played through the entire game without complaining, and it was not until that evening that he mentioned his discomfort. Not long after, an ambulance arrived to take him off to Garfield Hospital. There he would remain for the next four weeks with a ruptured kidney. Two operations later his only concern was that it not interfere with the next season's football.

His father, Wally, was attracted to those in power but also somewhat awed by it. Son Mike was utterly unintimidated by title or rank. In May 1950 he wrote a letter to U.S. Supreme Court Justice William O. Douglas: "I have recently red [sic] a slight story about your proposed vacation trip across Iran on horseback.

"Before I go any further I might introduce myself. I'm Mike Deuel, 12, my father is a foreign affairs correspondent for the Saint Louis Post Dispatch." Deuel went on to explain that he had all As and Bs in school, a taste for adventure, and would very much like to accompany Justice Douglas on his next trip abroad.

On May 8, 1950, Justice Douglas replied:

"My dear Mike, I greatly enjoyed your recent letter. I am glad far-away places, high mountains and horses interest you. There is a great joy in exploration. I hope you find time in your life for a lot of it.

"I am not sure that I will make another trip abroad this summer. Should I do so it would be a great pleasure to have you along. But there is a difficulty. I have a son just 18 years old. He was with me last summer in the Middle East and we had a wonderful time together . . . He has first claim to go, as you know. If I cannot take him, I don't know how I could take you. You understand, I am sure. I am very sorry for I think you and I would have a great time together. Yours Truly, William O. Douglas."

There was little that Mike Deuel did not excel at. Where natural talent failed, pure gumption kicked in. At Washington's Western High School he played fullback and made the All-Star D.C. team—while serving as president of the student council. Graduating in 1955, he went to Cornell as one of the school's twenty-five National Scholars.

At Cornell Deuel played lacrosse and eagerly awaited the day his team faced Syracuse and the chance to butt heads with that school's most fiercesome athlete. Butt heads he did, though in each collision he got the worse of the exchange. The player he was so determined to stop was named Jim Brown, and he would go on to become one of the greatest running backs in NFL history. Deuel's classmates watched in disbelief as the modest-sized Deuel time and again attempted in vain to stand his ground against the broad-shouldered juggernaut from Syracuse. Such pluck became the stuff of myth.

At Cornell's Sigma Phi fraternity Deuel was seen as a spirited and gutsy classmate, with a puckish, sometimes lusty playfulness. As editor of the fraternity newspaper his junior year, he once wrote an article describing the fiancée of a senior fraternity brother as "succulent and squablike"—apparently an accurate enough description. But the senior whose fiancée was so described was not amused by the phrase, and a short time later a repentant Deuel was observed on hands and knees, indelible marker in hand, blacking out each such reference from a stack of yet-to-be-distributed newsletters.

With prematurely salt-and-pepper hair cropped to a perfect brush cut, a devil-may-care smile, and squared jaw, he was a dashing figure—never more so than when he once returned to Cornell from the marines in full dress uniform, starched blue collar, white gloves, scabbard, and swagger stick. He was the very image of the sturdy warrior but not quite able to fully conceal the little boy's thrill to be in uniform.

Deuel chose the marines because he hoped they would meet his own standards of toughness. It was not that he spoiled for a fight—he did not—but he was constantly looking for ways to test his mettle. During basic training, when it was his turn to lead a platoon, he inadvertently took his men into an ambush. Instead of capitulating, he yelled "Charge!" He was named that month's outstanding platoon leader.

But as a Marine Corps officer, he seemed oddly distanced from the tasks at hand. To a Cornell classmate he wrote on July 16, 1960: "We still take orders from mean men afflicted with chronic flatulence and we still run until puddles of earnest sweat accumulate around us." He seemed mildly amused by the regimentation. "I'm drunk with power but clear of eye," he wrote his family in 1961. "My hair is short and so is my patience. When I say 'frog,' my men jump. When I say 'merde' they say how much and what color?"

But for Mike Deuel, not even the marines supplied enough action. In a letter home, typically candid and irreverent for Deuel, he wrote: "Life here creeps on in an undetectable pace, so much so that I am thrown back on my strong inner resources—tobacco, (awful) whiskey and pornography."

Hungry for more action, Deuel left the marines and in 1961 joined the CIA. He knew he was in the right place when an Agency lecturer told him: "You were brought into the service to provide new blood. Bleed a little." Instead of a cushy desk job, Deuel sought out the clandestine service and the most rigorous training the CIA offered. While nearly all clandestine officers passed through Camp Perry with its indoctrination courses and basics in tradecraft, Deuel applied to undertake the specialized program in jungle warfare.

On April 2, 1962, Deuel and the toughest of his Camp Perry classmates began what was called Paramilitary Course 3, at the Jungle Warfare Training Center, in the Canal Zone. By 1962 most of the old guard of paramilitary experts trained in World War II were now too old to undertake paramilitary operations, and most of the paramilitary training had been discontinued a decade earlier. At the very time when President Kennedy resolved that the United States would blunt Soviet and Chinese aggression whenever and wherever it showed up, the Agency was woefully strapped for so-called paramilitary knuckledraggers. To the outside world such a term might have smacked of ridicule, suggesting Cro-Magnon-like warriors, but to the Agency it was an honorific term recalling the glory days of OSS operations, of raw courage and finely honed survival skills.

The course Deuel and his fourteen CIA classmates found themselves in was billed as "realistic, rough, and hazardous." It was all this and more. The instructor was Eli Popovich, a former OSS operative who had, among countless hair-raising missions, rescued downed American crewmen from behind enemy lines in Yugoslavia during World War II. He had a well-deserved reputation for being afraid of no man and no terrain. Agency recruits would later recall him bagging a huge python, hacking it into steaks, and dining on it as if it were a tender fillet.

The course was designed to turn young CIA recruits into jungle warfare experts in a mere three weeks. Awaiting most of them were jungle assignments as case officers leading counterinsurgency movements in Southeast Asia, particularly the CIA's still-secret war in Laos. The course curriculum acquainted the CIA's junior-officers-in-training (JOTs) in such topics as "Effects of Heat," "Snakes and Animals," "Reconnaissance Patrolling," "Ambush and Counter-Ambush," "Evasion and Escape," and "Guerrilla Operations."

Even Popovich was astounded by the caliber of recruits. In a memo stamped "Secret" he noted: "Our JOT's, often called 'intellectuals' and/or 'Eggheads,' have demonstrated that they are not only intelligent young men, but also are capable of being physically and mentally tough when necessary to carry out the most difficult tasks under adverse tactical conditions . . . In spite of drastic change in climate, temperature, and humidity, and while being constantly harassed with cuts, bruises, bites from hornets, ants, and vampires [bats], and infections from black palm and sand box trees, they carried out their assigned tasks without undue gripes or complaints."

Not everyone finished the course. One man fell to fever. Another broke his leg on the "slide for life," a cable stretched across a river.

There was intense competition between the men, each one wanting not only to complete the course but to distinguish himself as the toughest, most resourceful and aggressive officer. Early on, Mike Deuel recognized that classmates Ralph McLean, Robert Manning, Andre LeGallo, and above all Richard Holm were his primary competitors.

But if the course brought out rivalries, it also imbued the men with a lasting esprit de corps. In the jungles of the Canal Zone were born friendships that would endure a lifetime. No greater friendships were forged than those between Deuel, McLean, Manning, and Holm. From the beginning, when Deuel and Holm entered the Agency as callow JOTs in June 1961, they had shared a special unspoken bond. They both adored sports, had a deep revulsion to Communism, were religious agnostics, and longed to make a difference in the world.

The two not only endured but reveled in the grueling jungle course, a program also given to elite military units. The CIA contingent was under cover as civilian employees of the U.S. Army Element, Joint Operational Group (8739). Each CIA officer was issued a false set of orders, fake IDs, and bogus medical records. Upon graduation the commanding officer of the exercise wryly noted: "There is a small group of civilians in this course from the United Fruit Company and although some of them have never been in uniform they have carried out their assigned tasks in this course as required with the rest of the class members in a manner that is worthy of praise and deserving of a fine hand." As the applause died down, the officer told CIA Training Director Popovich that Mike Deuel was the top man in the class, though his friends Holm, McLean, and LeGallo had slightly outscored him.

From the jungles of the Canal Zone, Deuel was dispatched to Langley to serve on the Laos desk, providing tactical and logistic support to the men in the field and acting as a transit point for outgoing orders and incoming intelligence. Deuel understood, as did everyone in the clandestine service, that Laos was center-stage in the struggle with Communism.

As far back as January 19, 1961—the day before Kennedy's inauguration—the incoming president and the outgoing Eisenhower had spent more time discussing the prickly issue of Laos than any other subject. Following a 1954 international agreement, Laos was to remain neutral, free of outside intervention and superpower meddling. But the Communists brazenly ignored such restraints, and the United States, in what came to be known as "the secret war," fought bitterly to repel them and disrupt the tide of men and matériel that flowed through the country along the Ho Chi Minh Trail and into the hands of the North Vietnamese.

"Laos," Kennedy once declared, "is far away from America, but the world is small . . . The security of all Southeast Asia will be endangered if Laos loses its neutral independence. Its own safety runs with the safety of us all—in real neutrality observed by all." Instead of neutrality, Laos would be decimated by undeclared war. Not since the Bay of Pigs had the CIA staked so much on a single foreign gambit.

Deuel seized the first opportunity he had to go to Laos. Four members of his JOT class volunteered for that country assignment. Among them was his friend and colleague Dick Holm. Both he and Deuel thrived in the primitive backcountry. To his mother and father Mike Deuel wrote: "After about a week starts a job big and responsible enough to inspire equal parts of pleasure and panic. In times past, this combination has been enough to overcome my habitual mental lassitude; there may be cause for optimism . . . But, now to my rude bower. Tomorrow, I must fight off wild Asian tigers and semi-wild Eurasian girls. Once more into the Breech?"

It was not only the job that captivated Deuel but the physical splendor of Laos as well. "This area is volcanic," he wrote. "A plateau dominates

Arthur "Mal" Maloney, a gritty and much-decorated veteran of the Normandy campaign, in his retirement at Hilton Head, South Carolina. A severe wound that forced him out of the military led him to the CIA. His son, Mike, would follow in his footsteps as a crack CIA paramilitary officer until his death in Laos. Arthur Maloney would never recover from the loss. *(Courtesy of Michael Maloney, Arthur Maloney's grandson)*

Art Maloney in battle fatigues during the fight to liberate France in World War II. A graduate of West Point, he was a soldier's soldier until a severe wound cut short his career and drove him to seek employment with the CIA. *(Courtesy of Michael Maloney)*

Mike Maloney and wife Adrienne shown at their wedding in 1963. Two years later he would be killed in a helicopter crash in Laos while on a CIA mission. He left behind a one-year-old son and another in utero. More than thirty years later the CIA still ignored his widow's repeated requests that her husband's name be added to the Book of Honor in place of a nameless star. *(Courtesy of Michael Maloney)*

Mike Maloney, wife Adrienne, and eleven-month-old son Michael in Virginia in the summer of 1965—just before Mike received CIA orders to ship out to Thailand for eventual assignment to the Agency's secret war in Laos. *(Courtesy of Michael Maloney)*

Mike Maloney in the summer of 1962 learning to be a paratrooper, as was his father before him. A second-generation CIA officer, he was determined to make his father, Arthur Maloney, proud of him. *(Courtesy of Michael Maloney)*

Wallace Deuel, a veteran newsman, OSS adviser, and senior CIA staffer, behind his beloved Underwood typewriter. By temperament he was a wordsmith, not a man of action. His son Mike was a covert field officer and paramilitary specialist killed in the Agency's not-so-secret war in Laos in 1965. *(Courtesy of Peter Deuel)*

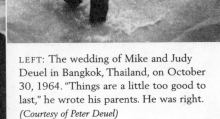

RIGHT: Mike Deuel fording a river in Laos. A covert CIA operative, he was working under cover of the Agency for International Development when he was killed in a helicopter crash in 1965. His Agency connection was kept a secret for more than three decades. *(Courtesy of Peter Deuel)*

LEFT: The wedding of Mike and Judy Deuel in Bangkok, Thailand, on October 30, 1964. "Things are a little too good to last," he wrote his parents. He was right. *(Courtesy of Peter Deuel)*

BOTTOM: Mike Deuel, one of the Agency's most gung-ho and promising young case officers. His superiors considered him headstrong, but a mission placed in his hands was considered as good as done. In Laos, his secret campaigns against the Communists were counted among the CIA's most successful. *(Courtesy of Peter Deuel)*

LEFT: Harlan Westrell, retired CIA chief of counterintelligence in the Office of Security, holds a photo of Hugh Redmond. For a time, Westrell found himself overseeing the Agency's handling of the case and working to assure Redmond's mother, Ruth, that the CIA had not forgotten about her son. *(Courtesy of the author)*

BELOW: At New York International Airport—Idlewild—the mothers of (left to right) Richard Fecteau, Hugh Redmond, and John Downey (Jessie Fecteau, Ruth Redmond, and Mary Downey) hold photos of their sons, each of whom was a CIA covert operative held in a Chinese prison. The date was January 1, 1957, and the three were on their way to China to visit their sons in prison. *(Courtesy of William McInenly)*

ABOVE: Hugh Redmond and his mother, Ruth, pose for a photo against the wall of a Chinese prison where Redmond was being held. After years of incarceration, the once-athletic Redmond would lose all his teeth and become afflicted with disorders of which he was forbidden to speak, even to his mother. *(Courtesy of William McInenly)*

RIGHT: A political cartoon from the July 11, 1970, *New York Daily News* that appeared after the Chinese reported that Hugh Redmond had committed suicide in one of their prisons. An accompanying editorial suggested what many already suspected—that Redmond had been murdered or died of neglect. *(© New York Daily News, L.P. reprinted with permission)*

SHAMEFUL SEALING

Ivan Berl King taken in 1978, the year he was killed in a secret CIA training mission in North Carolina. A legendary pilot, he had volunteered for the assignment even though someone else had already been slated to fly the ill-fated mission. Not even in death did his link to the CIA surface. *(Courtesy of Velma Waymire, his sister)*

ABOVE: The badly mangled fuselage and wing of the plane that crashed into a North Carolina cornfield the night of July 13, 1978, killing CIA operatives Ivan Berl King and Dennis Gabriel. Local police who responded to the crash were told it was a matter of some sensitivity and that it would be best not to dig too deeply. *(Courtesy of Velma Waymire)*

RIGHT: Dennis Gabriel with his son, Sean, at his side. Once hoping to be an Olympic decathlete, Gabriel was a seasoned CIA operative who had worked both the Mideast and Asia. He was killed along with CIA pilot Berl King in the July 13, 1978, crash of a small plane in North Carolina while on a secret training mission. His links to the Agency never surfaced. *(Courtesy of Dr. Ronald Gabriel, his brother)*

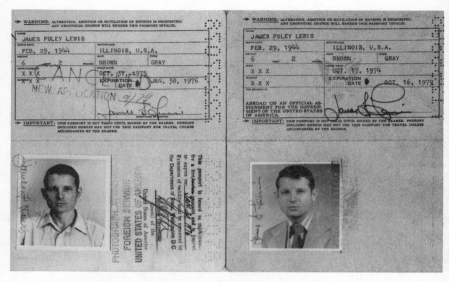

Two passport photos of James Foley Lewis. The earlier of the two passports was issued October 31, 1975, immediately after his release from a North Vietnamese POW camp. *(Courtesy of Antoinette Lewis)*

James Lewis in Laos, from a scrapbook he kept. *(Courtesy of Antoinette Lewis)*

James Lewis and his Vietnamese-born wife, Monique, who was also killed in the bombing of the Beirut embassy. It was her first day on the job as a CIA secretary. *(Courtesy of Antoinette Lewis)*

President and Mrs. Reagan at Andrews Air Force Base, where he met the plane carrying the coffins of sixteen Americans killed in the April 1983 bombing of the U.S. Embassy in Beirut. Here he is seen preparing to offer condolences to the families of those killed. *(Courtesy of Antoinette Lewis)*

William Casey, Director, Central Intelligence, presenting Antoinette Lewis with a posthumous commendation recognizing her son's service to the Agency. In the CIA's Book of Honor, his death is marked by an anonymous star. *(Courtesy of Antoinette Lewis)*

Barbara Robbins, a twenty-one-year-old CIA secretary working under State Department cover, was the youngest Agency employee to be honored with a star. Killed by a car bomb at the U.S. embassy in Saigon on March 30, 1965, she was twenty-one. Though she was never involved in covert operations, her Agency affiliation remains veiled in secrecy and her death is marked by a nameless star. *(Courtesy of Ruth Robbins, her mother)*

Barbara Robbins as a Girl Scout in 1955. Convinced that if the Communists were not stopped in Southeast Asia they might well take over the world, she volunteered for duty in Vietnam as a CIA secretary. *(Courtesy of Ruth Robbins)* south Laos and then drops from the plateau are sheer and green. Throughout the year, huge waterfalls drop down to the lowlands around the plateau . . ."

It was a raw existence that Deuel lived, working fifteen to twenty hours a day, seven days a week, then collapsing in exhaustion. But he never lost his sense of humor. In time he acquired an odd and exotic menagerie of pets, including cats, dogs, monkeys, and civets. "Chou," he wrote his parents, "is the horniest dog that God ever put on earth; he even stares at young girls. At age five months and height at the withers of $7\frac{1}{2}$ inches, he sired a litter out of a middle aged female who stands 15 inches high. I am lost in admiration." In time, his penchant for animals was jokingly referred to as "Deuel's Zoo."

But it was work that kept Deuel's mind focused. At times he saw his role in almost Wagnerian terms, but was always quick to puncture any sense of self-importance. In a letter home, twenty-six-year-old Deuel wrote:

"In fact there are no dramatic reports a'tall a'tall. All is prosaic, too much so . . . I dream of glory and future excitements. Of course when I get them, I'll probably ask for the next boat home but I think the time has not yet come for the dread assassin of the sea to become the sacred defenders of the home.

"Besides, the Creeping Red Menace still threatens which should justify continued gainful employment for citizens abroad (and at home). Of course before you can fight the Reds, you must survive local traffic and VD—and that's no easy thing."

. . .

At about the same time that Deuel arrived in Laos, a comely twenty-two-year-old CIA secretary named Judy Doherty was working back at Agency headquarters in Langley, Virginia. She was asked where she might like to be posted. She had grown up in the small coal-mining town of Bulpitt, Illinois, population 250. She had listed Paris and Rome and Lima, names out of a small-town fantasy. Some time later an Agency officer informed her she had been assigned to Bangkok, Thailand. She had never heard of it. In November 1962 she found herself working at the embassy there under State Department cover. There she met the dashing young

Mike Deuel, though she had earlier caught the eye of both Deuel and his friend Dick Holm, when all three were still at Langley. Judith Doherty was far too pretty to have escaped the notice of men like Deuel and Holm. "We didn't walk blindfolded up and down the halls," Dick Holm would say.

But it was Deuel who began courting Judy Doherty. "Saw my favorite secretary for two days in Bangkok," Deuel wrote his father. "She showed her normal distrust of my intentions which gives evidence of good sense on her part. I'm not sure whether she was relieved or not to see me go."

In late August 1964 Deuel "smuggled" Judy Doherty into Pakse, Laos, aboard one of the Air America planes at his disposal. His purpose was to give her a "cold-eyed look" at his lifestyle and to see how she might cope with it. His home was a farmhouse with high ceilings and many windows, a mix of French and Lao. His bed was a cotlike affair, a bamboo platform warmed by two blankets. Judy passed the test brilliantly. "She's so sensible that she's downright unromantic sometimes," he wrote. "This is good. Starry eyes would not be an asset."

"I'd swear an oath before the Commission of the American Baseball League to marry this one, she's that good," he wrote his father a short time later.

At 1:00 P.M. on October 30, 1964, Judy Doherty and Mike Deuel were married in the Holy Redeemer Church in Bangkok. Pat Landry, who helped oversee the CIA's Laos operations, was best man, and Dan Arnold gave away the bride. Deuel slipped a 1.4-carat blue and white diamond solitaire on her quivering finger. Both of them were so nervous that they would later laugh about the muscles twitching in their faces. After a brief honeymoon at the beach, the couple moved to Pakse in southern Laos. There Judy helped manage the Agency's base operations and plotted on a map the reported sightings of enemy convoys and movements of matériel and men.

"All in all," wrote Mike Deuel to his parents on November 29, 1964, "things are a little too good to last; we'll have to have some bad luck ere long. Meanwhile, the sun is shining and I'm making hay as fast as I can move, trying not to look too smug."

Deuel was fast becoming the romantic. In January 1965 his wife,

Judy, wrote: "After two and a half months, I was finally carried over the threshold last Thursday . . . Mike had arranged all sorts of surprises for me, including a new, red bicycle, two beautiful Italian rugs, some perfume." Awaiting her in the hall upstairs was a piano. "His last present for me," wrote Judy, "was waiting at the Moffett's house—a beautiful tan-colored horse, complete with English saddle. His name is Fahong, which means 'Thunder' in Lao."

But the stress of Mike's work took its toll. He was frequently gone on overnight missions and flying over rough country in all manner of aircraft piloted by the Agency's proprietary air wing, Air America. It was a harrowing beginning to a marriage, and Judy, a worrier by nature, could not help but fret. She feared that Mike could be hurt or killed, but she never spoke a word of it to him, believing it might jinx him or take his mind off his work. Nor did Mike discuss the risks, even after he had been involved in a couple of "minor plane crashes." Such crashes were common among the CIA officers in Laos. An errant water buffalo would stroll across the dirt runways oblivious to incoming planes. A sudden gust of wind off a mountain would toss the slow-moving STOLs—short-takeoff-and-landing aircraft—pitching them sideways like discarded toys.

Judy had her own brush with danger the night of February 3 during a casual visit to the Laotian capital, Vientiane. As she later wrote in a letter, she spent that night huddled on the floor of the U.S. AID vault, "lulled to sleep by the vibrations of mortars and grenades."

Judy Deuel's parents were concerned for the safety of both their daughter and their gung-ho son-in-law. But on February 16, 1965, Judy's parents received a letter from an Agency employee: "This is to assure you that Judy and Mike are perfectly safe and you have absolutely nothing to worry about . . . Mike is a very responsible and mature person in whom you can have full confidence. Judy and he are very much in love and very happy. Do not worry for them."

One day after the letter was written, Mike Deuel's close friend Dick Holm was returning from a mission in another part of the world. Deuel and Holm had both been sent to Laos in 1962 to work with the indigenous tribes in fighting against the Communists. But in August 1964 Holm, a French speaker, received orders that he was to be transferred to the Congo to help put down the Simba's rebel insurgency.

It was February 17, 1965, and Holm was in the rear seat of a T-28 flying with Cuban pilot Juan Peron in the northeast corner of the Congo near the border with Sudan. Peron had been trained a year earlier by John Merriman at the CIA base at Marana in Arizona. A second plane was piloted by Cuban Juan Tunon. The mission had been a machine-gun attack on a power plant in rebel-held territory. After a successful assault the weather turned nasty and both planes had too little fuel to make it back to base.

Peron crash-landed in a field of elephant grass. The left wing was ripped underneath and the remaining fuel caught fire. Peron jumped from the plane, assuming that Holm had also jumped. But as Peron ran from the plane expecting the .50-caliber bullets to go off, he heard Dick Holm's desperate screams. Holm was still in the burning aircraft. Dick Holm pried himself free and Peron carried him some distance from the plane seconds before it exploded. It was getting dark and it was raining. The two were in rebel territory. They spent the night under cover of bushes.

Peron did not yet know the extent of Holm's burns, but now, in the first light of morning, he could see his friend twisting in agony. Holm pleaded with Peron to kill him. Peron wrested away Holm's Walther nine-millimeter pistol from him, fearing he would shoot himself to end the pain. Peron could now plainly see the horror of Holm's burns—his flesh hung from his hands like an oversized pair of plastic gloves. His arms, too, were badly burned and his face swollen beyond recognition. Peron unsheathed his hunting knife and, without any anesthetic, cut off the burned flesh from Holm's limbs. He left Holm beneath a bush beside a stream and told him he would go for help. He swore he would return. Tunon, the pilot of the second plane, Peron would later learn, had been captured and cannibalized. Peron carried thirteen rounds in the magazine of his pistol, twelve for the enemy and the last one for himself. He was not going to allow himself to be taken alive.

By sheer luck, Peron wandered into one of the few friendly villages in rebel-held territory. There a young warrior of the Azande tribe named Faustino offered to help carry Dick Holm to safety. When Peron, Faustino, and two other villagers returned to Holm, they found him completely blanketed with bees. Holm was swollen from the stings and crawling in a vain attempt to escape them. The Azandes fashioned a crude stretcher from branches and limbs and carried the semiconscious Holm to the village. They fed him fruit and water and hid him by the riverbank, regularly salving his burns with snake grease.

Faustino and Peron took the village's only two bicycles and began what was to be an arduous eight-day journey through jungle and five-foot-tall grass. They headed for the base camp at Paulis more than 280 kilometers away. The morning after their arrival, they flew back to the village and picked up Holm. His flesh was now as black as that of the villagers who tended him—black from the pitchy snake grease that covered his burns. Holm was flown to Léopoldville and then on to the army's special-burn unit in San Antonio, Texas. There army surgeons marveled that he was still alive.

Months later, when the fighting in the area subsided, the air force sent a team to the Azande village to study the remedial properties of snake grease on burns. And the CIA, in an effort to express its gratitude to the village that showed Holm such kindness, sent in a C-146 fully loaded with new bicycles, medicines, tools, and sacks of rice for the villagers.

But for Dick Holm the ordeal was only just beginning. For the next two years physicians at Walter Reed Army Medical Center in Washington would treat his burns, perform skin grafts, and reconstruct portions of his hands and face. Holm had lost his left eye and was in jeopardy of losing sight in the other.

Mike Deuel was devastated by the news of Dick Holm's crash. Though he was a seasoned marine combat officer and had two years in the field with the Agency, this was the first time one of his close friends had been hurt. He brooded about Holm's condition, searching for some way to help him. Finally he sat his wife, Judy, down and told her he had been thinking about what he could do for Dick Holm. Deuel, then twenty-eight and married for less than a year, had an idea. "Would you mind," he asked her, "if I offered one of my eyes to Dick?"

Judy Deuel was speechless. "For heaven's sake," she said, "do you think that's necessary?" But Mike persisted. "It would be better," he argued, "if each of us had one eye than if one of us had two and the other had none." Judy was silent for a moment. "It's up to you," she said. A short time later Deuel wrote Dick Holm's father formally offering one of his eyes.

For months, senior CIA officers quietly made their pilgrimage to Walter Reed Army Medical Center's Ward Nine to visit Dick Holm. Among the visitors were Desmond FitzGerald and Dick Helms—who smuggled in a thermos of martinis. But none was more faithful than Mike Deuel's father, Wally, who spent each Sunday for nearly a year at Holm's bedside, reading aloud the Sunday paper and keeping him abreast of Mike and Judy's latest exploits in Laos.

After each visit Wally Deuel would dutifully send a detailed report to Mike and Judy of the medical and emotional progress their friend had made. One such letter, dated August 23, 1965, notes: "His morale's especially good these days because Dick Helms went out to see him Friday or Saturday and, of course, completely captivated him.

"The plastic surgeons are ever-so-gently nudging the ophthalmologists to get on with their eye operation so Dick [Holm] can go on outpatient status for the treatments still to come . . . The plastic men haven't decided yet whether to rebuild Dick's ears with wee pieces of a rib as the base, or to try to do it all with strips of skin which they would detach from his neck below the ears and roll up into suitable shapes for the ears.

"The only other medical development to report is that they've got Dick's right hand in a Rube Goldberg sort of contraption which holds each finger in a sling which in turn is suspended by a rubber band from a brace above the hand—the brace being held in place by a plaster cast on the forearm—all of which is supposed to help the fingers recover a considerably greater capability for use than they now have."

Seven months after the crash, observed Wally Deuel, "Dick's hands are still in such bad shape that he wouldn't be able to pick up a grape, even if he could see it."

In the months ahead Dick Holm underwent an endless series of operations, major and minor, providing him with new eyebrows, rebuilding the bridge of his nose, the corner of his mouth, and the skin between his thumb and index finger.

In September 1965 Judy Deuel wrote her mother-in-law a letter. "Have they found a cornea donor yet?" she asked timidly. "I'm kind of holding my breath on this question for obvious reasons."

After a series of operations, including a corneal transplant from an eye bank, Dick Holm's remaining eye began to improve. The doctors used the word "miraculous." Mike Deuel never had to make good on his offer, but neither was it soon forgotten.

. . .

By that summer the covert operations within Laos were expanding daily and more Agency case officers were needed. Mike Deuel was about to get some help and, if things worked out, even a replacement, allowing him to return to the States and begin another assignment, perhaps to Hong Kong or Taiwan.

In September 1965 help arrived in the person of Mike Maloney. Maloney, like Deuel, was a paramilitary officer, a quiet young man with a gleaming smile, deep-set dimples, and—from his father—full brows and a barrel chest. He was a soldier's soldier, every bit the man his father, Colonel Mal Maloney, hoped he might be. And like his father, Mike Maloney's first choice had been the military. But the military refused to take him because of asthma. And so, by default, he, too, had joined the CIA.

To break in the younger Maloney, Deuel invited him to Pakse, Laos. That Saturday night, October 9, 1965, the two young officers could get acquainted and Deuel would brief the new man on what to expect. Maloney's wife, Adrienne, was just getting settled in Bangkok. Later they planned to move to Pakse. It seemed a perfect match—the two Mikes, both young, gung-ho case officers, both the sons of CIA officers, both their wives pregnant.

Mike Maloney had married his college sweetheart, Adrienne La Marsh, on October 5, 1963. Already they had a one-year-old son, Michael, and the second child was due in four months. The Maloneys had just celebrated their second wedding anniversary. The Deuels were two weeks from celebrating their first. That night the two Mikes stayed up late talking about the mission and looking forward to a collaboration that seemed certain to mature into a friendship.

It was hard for Mike Maloney not to be impressed with the life Deuel and his wife, Judy, had carved out for themselves in Pakse. Their oversized French Colonial home featured four bedrooms, bright terrazzo floors, the spoils and artifacts of Laotian culture, food flown in from the commissary, a Vietnamese cook, a houseboy, a girl to keep things tidy, and in the upstairs hallway, the blessed piano—Deuel's gift to his wife.

The next morning, a Sunday, the two Mikes were scheduled to board a chopper, survey the region, make some payroll stops at area villages, and introduce Maloney to the tribal leaders with whom he would be working. Judy Deuel was slightly miffed that her husband had to work even on Sunday. She watched as the two Mikes piled into Deuel's Morris Mini and sped off on the drive across the river to the airstrip. They were scheduled to be back home about two that afternoon.

That morning Judy went by herself to a French Mass held in a small country church, then returned home. At two the men had not yet returned. She began to worry. She sat down at the piano, as she often did, to play a piece of classical music and drown out the voice of fear that often preceded Mike's belated returns. She had one eye on the ivory keyboard, the other on her watch.

It was three. It was four. It was five. Now it was dusk. She knew they would not choose to fly in such poor light. She could not help but suspect the worst.

Not long after, an Agency operations officer arrived at the house. He looked grim. He said that some villagers had reported seeing a chopper go down near a place called Saravane. The officer took Judy to the airport and there they waited for word of what had happened.

Back at CIA headquarters in Langley, a cable was received from Vientiane alerting the operations desk that Deuel and Maloney might have gone down. A plane was ordered up to search for the missing aircraft, but it was already dark and the area where the chopper was believed to have gone down was covered by a smothering double canopy of jungle. Even at noon such a search would have been taxing.

That night a message was sent to the Canal Zone, where Colonel Mal Maloney was stationed under military cover, and where he had been involved in training and paramilitary activities in South and Central America. The first call informed Colonel Maloney that the chopper carrying his son was missing and that there was little chance he had survived. He gently woke his children up and walked them out to the patio overlooking the canal. There he told them his worst fears. It was the first time his children had seen the big man weep.

At the first light of morning, October 11, the Agency dispatched a search team, some of them Lao, others seasoned American smoke jumpers trained at Marana Air Base in Arizona. That afternoon they spotted something through the trees and radioed for help. In Vientiane a medical officer at the embassy, Dr. Burton Ammundsen, was dragooned into a desperate rescue mission. He was told only that four U.S. servicemen had crashed in the jungle, that there was a chance they were still alive, and he was to do what he could for them. By the time the chopper carrying Ammundsen reached the approximate site where the wreckage had been spotted, it was sundown. Ammundsen was told he would be spending the night alone in the jungle and that the next day help would arrive.

Carrying leg splints and a medical bag, he was lowered by rope through the jungle canopy, beside a river. On the way down, the rope swung wide and smashed him into a tree. When he finally reached the ground, he attempted to find the wreckage but was unable to penetrate the dense jungle without a machete. Armed with only a flashlight, he spent the night on a small island just offshore. The next morning an Agency rescue team linked up with him and cut its way through the forest. The wreckage was less than a hundred yards from the river where Ammundsen had spent the night.

But it was evident that there was nothing for Ammundsen to do. The chopper had been badly mangled when it fell through the jungle. There were four bodies—the two Mikes, and those of an Air America pilot and mechanic. Three of the four—the mechanic, Deuel, and Maloney—had been killed instantly, thrown against the forward bulkhead. The pilot had survived the crash just long enough to crawl out of the fuselage. His body lay draped over the side of the chopper. When the rescue team reached the crash site, his body was still warm to the touch.

The bodies of Maloney and Deuel were taken back to Vientiane for identification. It was Ammundsen who witnessed the postmortem examination at a Philippine hospital across the street from the embassy. The men had broken necks and massive internal injuries. For Ammundsen it was a particularly grim task. Just a few weeks earlier he had examined Judy Deuel, monitoring her pregnancy.

Two days later the two young widows, Judy Deuel and Adrienne Maloney, were on Pam Am 2 on their way back to the States. The Agency had arranged for the wife of an Agency officer, Susan Gresinger, to accompany them. The women flew first-class, courtesy of the CIA. It was the first time the young wives, now widows, had ever met. Adrienne, pregnant, and clutching one-year-old Michael, sat next to Gresinger. Most of the flight she spoke of the comfort she drew from her Catholic faith.

Immediately behind her sat Judy Deuel. She spoke not a word and downed more than a few Scotches. Judy Deuel had been twenty-two when she met Mike, twenty-four when they married, twenty-five when she lost him. He had died two weeks shy of their first anniversary.

It was not long thereafter that an Agency employee drove out to Walter Reed Army Medical Center to break the news of Mike Deuel's death to Dick Holm. "It seemed like a heavy price that we were paying," Holm thought to himself. "The Agency, the directorate, us, my colleagues. I was part of that group. Why the best guys?"

· · ·

The deaths of Mike Deuel and Mike Maloney received scant attention in the newspapers. The brief obituaries spoke of two young AID officers killed in a helicopter crash. But one of Wally Deuel's journalist friends and former *Post-Dispatch* colleagues, conservative columnist Marquis W. Childs, wrote a panegyric to Mike Deuel. The headline read: "Commitment of Young American to Life Ends in Death in Laos." Childs, unaware that Deuel had been CIA and as much a warrior as a humanitarian, spoke of Deuel's selfless efforts to resettle refugees, extolling him as part of a generation of peace-loving Americans risking their lives in the cause of peace.

There was a grim irony in the CIA's choice of cover story, the idea that Deuel and Maloney and other Agency operatives in Laos were working for AID on refugee resettlement issues. The reality was that their real mission was adding to the refugee problem and creating an ever-greater need for AID's assistance. As the CIA succeeded in attracting more and more indigenous tribesmen into the ranks of its anti-Communist units, there were fewer and fewer men left home to plant and harvest rice and other food crops upon which the villages depended for their survival. In time, so many men were enlisted into the ranks of the CIA-backed units that there might well have been widespread famine had it not been for the intervention of genuine AID missions in the region.

For the Agency it was easy to obscure Deuel's and Maloney's deaths. Most of the nation was engrossed in the broader quagmire of Vietnam and Southeast Asia and by the antics of President Johnson, who was then at Bethesda Naval Hospital recovering from gallbladder surgery. Before being released, he was placed briefly under a sunlamp so he wouldn't appear so yellow to the awaiting press corps. Once released, he would ham it up for reporters, even baring his midriff to show off his scar.

But at Langley those cleared to know the true identities of the two young men and their fathers were decimated by the loss. On October 14, 1965—four days after the crash—Dick Helms penned a letter to his friends Wally and Mary Deuel:

"That your sadness has no limits is well understood by your friends, especially those who knew you thirty years ago even before Mike was born.

"This loss of an uncommon young man is so pointless, so impossible to rationalize. Yet I cannot help wondering whether Mike has not the best of it if the alternative might have been comparable to the kind of thing Dick Holm is going through. It is perhaps a blessing too that young Judith is pregnant. She has something of Mike which may make it easier for her to face the void immediately ahead.

"To you both there is nothing to say. I can only extend the hand of friendship and support which you so warmly offered me so many years ago . . ."

It was signed, "Sadly, Dick."

Five days later Helms wrote a second letter, this one to Mike Maloney's father, Colonel Arthur A. Maloney. "Dear Art," it began. "All of us are shattered by the death of Michael. Coming so suddenly and so unnecessarily, it had a shock that can only have been worse for you. These events seem so wrong and so unfair. These uncommon young men who are willing to go forth for their country unheralded and unsung are indeed the heroes of our modern age, and I feel sure that some day they will be understood and respected far more than they are now. It was ever thus."

The Deuel and Maloney families were deluged with such letters of condolence from those within the CIA's covert ranks. Despite the out-pouring, it was a delicate matter, balancing grief with the need to main-tain security. Even in such a moment as this, Art Maloney would thank Des FitzGerald for his kind note of condolence but scrupulously avoid any mention of the CIA. "The loss of Mike," he wrote, "brought forth a reac-tion by the company for which we will always be extremely proud and grateful." To the outside world the words "the company" would sound cal-lous and remote. But at Langley there were many unseen tears shed in the days after two of its favorite sons were lost.

. . .

On October 24, 1965, the day before Michael Deuel's funeral, the Reverend Russell Stroup delivered a sermon entitled "Pointing with Pride" to the congregation of the Georgetown Presbyterian Church. By then, America was already in the tumult of the antiwar movement, and Stroup seized the opportunity to show that there were young Americans who were a credit to the country. He remembered Mike Deuel coming to him as a high school student, on his own, saying that he wanted to join the church and to be baptized. It was Stroup who performed the baptism.

"Tomorrow at Arlington we will bury Mike Deuel," he told the con-gregation. "But the work to which he gave himself goes on. And there are hundreds and thousands of Mike Deuels who are carrying on the work, and there will be more. Those beautiful Americans. I am not ashamed of America."

Deuel was buried in Arlington National Cemetery in grave 156, sec-tion 35, just to the south of the Memorial Amphitheater and the Tombs of the Unknowns. A standard, government-issued stone, it reads:

MICHAEL

MCPHERSON

DEUEL

DISTRICT OF

COLUMBIA

CAPTAIN

USMCR

MAY 13, 1937

OCTOBER 12, 1965

In a letter to his aging mother, Wally Deuel described the funeral:

"Mikie was entitled to be drawn in the casket, covered with a flag, on an artillery caisson, by beautifully matched horses, and with a band playing funeral marches, from the gateway to the cemetery to the grave, and as Mary said, Mikie would have loved it—all by Marines in dress blues—but it was Judy's wishes that counted, and she said as little pomp as possible, which means no caisson, no horses, and no band, but the flag-covered casket driven in the hearse to the grave. Even so, though, it was almost more than could be endured, with a platoon of Marines lined up on the gentle slope above the grave, and six Marines to carry the casket from the hearse the short distance to the grave. The immediate family sat in chairs quite close to the grave—which was covered over with something green so it looked like grass. There's three volleys fired by the platoon on the slope above, then taps on the bugle, the six Marines at the casket fold the flag, in accordance with a special set of rules, and the Warrant Officer at the grave hands the folded flag to the widow. He said something to her—more than a few words—but we never have found out what it was."

As with the graves of so many covert CIA officers buried at Arlington, there was no hint that Mike Deuel had been with the CIA. His cover story went with him to the grave. Behind him, Deuel left a father, a mother, a pregnant widow, and little else—a bank account with $1,869.14 and his beloved 1952 MG valued at $200.

Wally Deuel managed to persuade AID to return to him the last three letters he wrote to his son, which arrived after Mike's death. In a thank-you note to the AID official, Wally wrote, "God knows what was in them, but probably something ribald or in some other way horribly inappropriate, and I am extremely grateful you didn't send them on to Judy."

· · ·

Six days after the crash, on October 18, 1965, a telegram stamped "Secret" arrived at Langley. It was routed to the director of Central Intelligence, the executive director, the deputy director of plans, and other senior Agency officials. It was from a Philip K. Radnor, chief of station, and recommended that one Karl W. Aufderheide, a GS-11, recently killed in the field, be awarded the CIA's Intelligence Star. But there was no Radnor or Aufderheide employed by the Agency. These were merely code names.

Radnor was really Philip Blaufarb, the CIA station chief in Vientiane running operations in Laos. Karl Aufderheide was Michael Deuel's code name in the field, a fittingly Germanic name for one born in Berlin.

Blaufarb had been keeping a close eye on Deuel, whom he considered headstrong and a little cocky, but one of the most reliable men he had. He summarized Deuel's work for the Agency in two paragraphs: "For two years Aufderheide has been in charge of a major paramilitary program involving tribal groups in South Laos. At the time of his death in a helicopter crash in the line of duty his program was expanding faster than any other program in Laos. The number of men under arms had doubled from 1,205 to 2,400 in the past year. As a result of Aufderheide's imaginative and resourceful direction, several new expansions and probes were underway and territory was being recovered from the enemy. Partially as a result of his efforts enemy morale in South Laos has been deteriorating in recent months and their hold over the indigenous populace weakening.

"Although the tribal elements with which he worked are exceedingly primitive, he succeeded by patient and diligent effort in training many of them to be acceptable and reliable reporters of enemy convoy movement, construction activity, etc. His dynamic and confident leadership was an inspiration to those who worked with him. He was never daunted by difficult or dangerous situations, and it was while visiting one of his teams in a remote mountain area to resupply them and boost their morale that he met his death. His performance of and dedication to duty were in the finest traditions of our service."

Eight months after the "secret" wire was received, at noon on June 28, 1966, the Deuel family—mother and father, widow and brother—gathered in a small conference room on the seventh floor of the CIA to receive the Distinguished Intelligence Medal on Mike Deuel's behalf. The medal was presented by Admiral W. F. Raborn, then Director Central Intelligence, but it was far more than a presentation ceremony. It was an assemblage of Agency legends and a gathering of the generations. Among those in attendance were Richard Helms, Desmond FitzGerald, William Colby, Ben DeFelice, Lloyd George, Theodore Shackley, and of course, Dick Holm.

It was later determined that mechanical failure, not enemy fire, had brought down the aged helicopter that killed Deuel and Maloney. Indeed, many of the aircraft in use in Laos were in desperate need of replacement. Not long after the crash, Blaufarb made a formal request that his men receive more modern aircraft. His request was denied.

. . .

Wally Deuel would never recover from the loss of his son, though he tried to put up a solid front and find meaning in the tragedy. In a letter to Blaufarb, he wrote on November 5, 1965:

"He [Mike] didn't want to be a violent-action man all his life, as you probably know. But he was determined to qualify as one, and see what violent action was like, and how good he would be at it, before going on to other things. So he did his damndest to get all the action he could, and the risk of getting killed in the process was, of course, what gave it its most especial savor and attraction.

"Thus there was nothing irrelevant or incongruous in his getting killed in the way he was killed, and, in this meaning of the term, nothing senseless. It was, on the contrary, exquisitely logical, in the bitter logic that always causes the killing of so many of his kind of the best youngest men.

"But of course this is damnably cold comfort to hearts, like Mary's and Judy's and mine, that are so very cold just now."

The outpouring of grief from friends and Agency colleagues was overwhelming. Among these was Ben DeFelice, the man who had taken it upon himself for two decades already to provide comfort to bereaved CIA families, from Hugh Redmond to the Merrimans. "You've been magnificent," Wally Deuel wrote him.

Dick Holm, Bob Manning, and Andre LeGallo, three friends dating back to the days of jungle warfare school three long years earlier, helped organize a trust fund for Deuel's daughter, Suzanne, born five months after his death. Through it all, Wally and Mary Deuel continued their weekly visits to Dick Holm and reported on his progress to Judy. On one such visit, on November 7, 1965, three weeks after Mike Deuel's death, Wally found Dick Holm alone in his hospital bed listening to a broadcast of a football game. Deuel wrote his son's widow:

"The plastic surgeons have operated on his left hand since we last saw him, removing the bent, charred stub which was all that remained of his little finger and which they could not salvage. They also cut down the palm of his hand between the knuckle and the wrist, so that his left hand is now only a three-finger hand, with a palm the width of three fingers, not four . . . The hand and forearm are bandaged up in the shape of a miniature Indian club . . ."

Deuel continued to monitor Holm's glacial recovery in excruciating detail, forwarding clinical assessments to his son's widow, Judy, after each such visit. It was as if he could do no less out of memory for his son, or perhaps it was that in some way Dick Holm, who had survived a plane crash and was one of his son's best friends, had become a son to him.

That was as it should be. On September 1, 1968, three years after Mike Deuel died, his widow walked down the aisle once more in marriage. The groom was Dick Holm. Wally Deuel would write: "The really grand and glorious news of this past year, though, has been that our beloved Judy (our son Mike's widow) has married one of her and Mike's and our oldest and most cherished friends, a guy who is everything good you can think of as a husband for Judy, a father for the baby (who adores him) and a son for us."

Years later Wally Deuel would confide in friends that almost anything could trigger in him a profound and disabling sorrow—the melody of "Taps," a familiar scriptural reading, even the sound of a young man on the street whistling gaily, as Mike so often did as he approached their Georgetown house. On October 31, 1967, upon learning that one of Mike's fraternity brothers had named his firstborn son for him, Wally wrote: "Mike will be vastly pleased, in whatever Elysian Fields he now roams, and Mike's Ma and I were so touched we darned near burst into tears when we got your telegram. Mike's friends are the noblest band of brothers . . ."

Wallace Deuel retired from the CIA on August 1, 1968, amid a flurry of bureaucratic awards and letters of appreciation from Dick Helms and others. His health deteriorated until he was, in his words, "chairbound." He continued to write regularly to Judy and Dick Holm, as he would to a son and daughter. On April 13, 1973, he wrote: "Behold comma it is I exclamation. I will not say I am alive and well and living in Washington D.C., because I sure as hell am not well, but I am alive, sort of, and I'm in Washington D.C."

He was then in his twelfth year of emphysema and had recently had a pulmonary embolism. But Deuel's "melancholy," as he called it, was brought on not only by his own physical deterioration but by a lingering sense of loss and by the spectacle of his beloved CIA in the throes of what appeared to be an act of self-destruction. It was coming under increasing public scrutiny and criticism, as was the entire U.S. government. Watergate had erupted. Ugly accounts of CIA excess were coming to light, an omen of even darker revelations to come. And then there was Vietnam.

Within the CIA internal dissension over the conflict in Indochina had taken a profound toll. At the height of the Vietnam War the Agency had occupied three floors of the U.S. Embassy in Saigon and dispatched, by one count, some seven hundred employees there. Wally Deuel's friend Dick Helms, Director Central Intelligence, had been buffeted by years of turmoil and by hostility from Presidents Johnson and Richard Nixon. His analysts' vision of prospects for Vietnam was deemed too pessimistic. The intense bombing of North Vietnam—even ten thousand sorties a month— would not break the will of the Communists or interrupt the flow of men and matériel, the CIA had concluded. "Not since the abortive Bay of Pigs invasion of 1961 had the Agency put so much on the line, and lost it through stupidity and mismanagement," wrote the CIA's former senior Vietnam analyst, Frank Snepp.

Public suspicion of the CIA deepened. Support for covert activities was waning. Sordid accounts would surface of domestic surveillance under Operation Chaos, of efforts to destabilize the government of Chile's Salvador Allende Gossens, and of the ruthless Phoenix Program in Vietnam, in which more than twenty thousand were killed. A malaise settled over the Agency from which it would not soon emerge. In February 1973 Nixon sacked Helms as CIA head, appointing him ambassador to Iran. Those who had spent their lives with the Agency and were proud of that affiliation were heartsick and in shock.

Two months after Helms was fired, on April 17, 1973, a disillusioned Wally Deuel wrote Dick and Judy Holm, then stationed in Hong Kong: "As for my former place of employment, not only is there nothing I can do about that, but I don't even know what's going on there. So far, I have heard reports only from an incredibly small number of people, people who are all without exception old, decrepit, out of touch as badly as I am—and plunged in the blackest despair . . . A fine basis for my trying to figure out what the hell is happening in Langley, wouldn't you say?"

Wally Deuel's health deteriorated rapidly. He passed in and out of consciousness, sometimes mistaking his son Peter for Allen Dulles, his revered leader at the Agency so many years before. On May 10, 1974, Peter arranged to accompany his father on an air ambulance from Maryland to Chicago. "I'm taking you home," Peter told him. Wally Deuel had had a tracheotomy and was barely able to speak, but he made his resistance known by shaking his head and whispering a soft "no." He had had enough.

Somewhere over Indiana, he died. He was cremated and his ashes scattered in a cemetery that borders an expressway. Each time Peter drives by he offers his father a respectful salute.

Mike Deuel's daughter, Suzanne, was born in the spring of 1966, two years before Judy Deuel and Dick Holm were wed. For them and for Wally Deuel it was a union that closed many a circle. But it was not without its secrets. Suzanne was raised believing that Dick Holm was indeed her biological father. For the first years of her life, the name Mike Deuel meant nothing to her. She had not yet picked up on the hints and anomalies, like the wedding photo of Dick Holm and Judith in which a baby girl is seen in the background.

Intuitively she sensed something was amiss. For years she was visited by a recurring nightmare in which she was speeding down a steep hill on roller skates. On either side of her was a figure in a children's red wagon. It was Dick Holm, but there were two of him. She knew one to be her father. But the other she knew to be a bomb which would detonate at her embrace. "Pick me," cried the one, "the other is the bomb." Suzanne could never tell which was which.

She could not be blamed for feeling as if she grew up in a world of deception. It was not until she was nine or ten that she remembers stumbling across a box of old records and memorabilia in the basement. For hours she dug through the crate fixated on photos of a man whose smile and eyes bore an uncanny resemblance to her own. She found his lighter, his ring, and newspaper accounts telling of a plane crash. She also found references to his burial at Arlington.

When she turned sixteen and got her driver's license, she secretly drove to Arlington National Cemetery and found her father's grave. After that, the nightmares ended. But whether because of secrecy constraints or the emotional scars left by Mike Deuel's premature death, Suzanne never felt comfortable asking her mother or Dick Holm about the man she had come to know as Mike. He would remain a shadowy presence throughout her adolescence, a face she could see hints of in the mirror but would come to regard as something of a taboo subject.

A second stunning surprise awaited her. It was not until she was in high school that the man she called "Father," Dick Holm, confided in her that he was not with the State Department, as she had been led to believe all those years, but that he was a covert operative with the CIA. Such deception of one's own children to maintain cover is often the hardest and most exacting act of dissembling a covert officer must face. Suzanne, like countless other children of CIA officers, at first felt deceived and then, for the first time, began to perceive a pattern where before there had been only confusion. Suddenly emerged a logic that accounted for a lifetime of mystery and secrecy.

A decade later, when she was living in Paris and engaged, she wrote a Cornell classmate of her father's asking if he might share with her some memory of Mike Deuel. That classmate contacted the entire fraternity house, who, one by one, poured out years of memories in letters sent to Paris. By the time Suzanne married she had come to know her father as few daughters ever do.

As for Dick Holm, after the crash no one would have thought any worse of him if he had retired on full disability. Instead, after two years of surgery and rehabilitation he was back in the field as a covert case officer—not to mention a spirited tennis player. He quickly rose through the ranks, becoming a respected CIA chief of station. Based in Hong Kong, he ran several covert operations across the border in the People's Republic of China. For Dick Holm, a man who once contemplated shooting himself to end the unbearable pain, life was once again good, with family, work, and a restoration to health. In a January 16, 1972, letter to Wally Deuel he had written: "All this and interesting work! You can see that life is treating me well. More than ample justification for my determination *not* to die in that damn Congo."

Holm's long-ago ordeal had become a part of the Agency's lore. Wally Deuel would relate how one day at Langley Dick Holm was speaking to some people in the hall when the director, Dick Helms, passed by, stopped, and said, "Hi, Dick." Holm's associates were astonished that the director would stop to say hello and would know him by name. Holm simply laughed it off. "Listen," he said, "if you'd cost him a million dollars, he'd know who you are too"—a reference to the medical expenses incurred in his two-year convalescence.

Holm was later named head of the Agency's Counterterrorist Center, overseeing operations to blunt terrorist activities worldwide. As a final plum assignment, prior to retirement, Dick Holm was made chief of station in Paris. It was his fluency in French that had taken him to his ill-fated Congo mission in 1964, and now that same proficiency was cited in rewarding him with Paris.

But in January 1995 a covert CIA operation in France was compromised, as it came to light that a female agent under deep cover had fallen in love with the French official she had targeted. Her mission had been to learn France's position in upcoming world trade talks. The United States was profoundly embarrassed as the tale of economic espionage against a close ally came to light. In March 1996 Holm was pressured to resign under a cloud. It was widely viewed within the CIA that, after years of loyal, even heroic service, Dick Holm had been made a scapegoat to save face for the Agency. His treatment further lowered morale within the CIA's covert ranks.

Six months later, in a transparent effort to boost sagging morale and extend an olive branch to Holm, he was invited to return to Langley, where he was presented the Distinguished Intelligence Medal. But by then it was too late. His reputation was stained. He had tried to defend himself publicly but found that while the Agency felt free to blame him publicly, it invoked its own rigid secrecy constraints on him, preventing him from discussing the case or restoring his good name.

· · ·

Mike Maloney's father, the colonel, stayed with the Agency until he retired in January 1972. He and his wife moved to Hilton Head, South Carolina, where he became a eucharistic minister, puttered about in the garden, and let his grandchildren stomp about the house in his leg brace.

But Mike's death continued to cast a pall over his days. "The spark went out of that man's life," remembers Mike's widow, Adrienne. In his last years Mal Maloney was stricken with Alzheimer's and had to be fed by others. A proud man, he died on August 18, 1994, at age eighty in the Avon Convalescent Home in Connecticut.

As for Mike Maloney's widow, Adrienne, she would never remarry. Four months after her husband died, on February 20, 1965, she gave birth to a second son, Craig Michael Maloney. She devoted herself to raising her two boys, Craig and Michael. In time, both boys toyed with the idea of joining the CIA. Craig formally applied but later withdrew his application. "I just came to the realization that I was doing it for the wrong reasons," he would say later. "I was chasing a ghost." His brother, Michael, filled out a CIA application but missed his interview because of flu. "I took it as a sign from God that I wasn't supposed to do it," he concluded. There would be no third generation of Maloneys in the CIA.

Adrienne Maloney, now fifty-seven, never put her young husband's death fully behind her. She had her wedding ring, which had been inscribed "FOREVER M.A.M. TO A.L.M.," set into the base of a gold chalice and given to a church to be used in sacraments. A few years ago she gathered up Mike's letters and put a match to them. Even that could not distance her from the loss. Much of that pain stems from watching her two sons growing up without a father. They knew only that he died in a helicopter crash and that they were not allowed to discuss his death or the circumstances surrounding it with anyone.

Their father's entire life was shrouded in mystery. Son Craig, who was in utero when Mike Maloney was killed, would lament that he had never seen his father's face. Adrienne would comfort him by saying that at least his father had felt him kicking inside her and had chosen for him his name.

There was one moment when the CIA seemed to relent in its otherwise all-encompassing invocation of secrecy. In 1993 the Maloney sons were permitted on one occasion to visit the Agency and were shown a scant few records, many of them heavily redacted, from their father's personnel file. Though the file jacket was stamped "Top Secret," it shed no light on either their father's life or his death. Anything sensitive had been removed. What was left were his college transcripts, his essay on why he wanted to join the CIA, and a few perfunctory application materials. But the visit meant something to the Maloney sons nonetheless. So, too, did the fact that their guide and companion at the Agency that afternoon was none other than Dick Holm. No one had to explain to him how much had been lost that October day in 1965.

For years Adrienne asked the CIA to inscribe her husband's name in the Book of Honor, believing it was something she should do for her two sons and for her husband's memory. As recently as 1996, while at an Agency memorial service, she asked then CIA Director John Deutch if he would examine the Maloney file and reconsider adding her husband's name to the book, thereby releasing her and her sons from the onerous burden of silence they had endured. "Why," she asked Deutch, "must it all be kept a secret after more than thirty years?"

"Why don't you write me a note?" Deutch told her. "Don't put down any explanation, no song and dance, just a note."

Adrienne Maloney did just that and sent it registered mail. Then, as before, the CIA did not respond to her request. Each time she attempted to follow up with a letter or phone call, the Agency told her that her letters had been lost.

Son Michael even wrote a poem for his brother, Craig, about their father and the burdens of a life enshrouded in secrecy. That poem now hangs on Craig Maloney's wall. It reads in part:

> *Faded Stories, Secrets Told,*
> *A Marble Star To Behold,*
> *Her Pictures Gathered In One Place;*
> *To Suffice For One So Bold?*
> *Track the Ghost Who Wears Your Face*
> *Through The Halls of Time and Space.*

"It's thirty years ago," says son Craig Maloney, "and I can't help but think of what kind of rhetorical crap and political crap it is that they can't release his name. His name deserves to be there. We write letters and they never go where they should. I think it's completely unjust."

Finally, in September 1997 an article in the *Washington Post* by this author identified Mike Maloney as one of the nameless stars. The same day the article was released, Adrienne Maloney received a phone call from the Agency informing her that the CIA had reconsidered her request and had decided that her husband's name could at last be inscribed in the Book of Honor. A short time later his name was added to the book.

But nowhere in the Book of Honor appeared the name of Mike Deuel, who sat beside Maloney on that same fateful helicopter on that same covert mission some thirty-five years ago. His daughter, Suzanne, and other family members had to content themselves with an unnamed star and shoulder the burden of an arbitrary code of secrecy. In this they were not alone. So, too, did the families of John "Lone Star" Kearns, Wayne McNulty, and John Peterson—all of them still nameless stars from the long-ago secret war in Laos.

That secret war dragged on for more than a dozen bloody years, but it was a secret for a short time only. So many men and supplies could not long be concealed. To some degree it was an act of legerdemain practiced upon the American public, whose patience and support of the Vietnam conflict were already flagging. To some degree, too, it was a feeble attempt to avoid international condemnation for violating a promised neutrality—one already flagrantly breached by the other side.

The two Mikes, Deuel and Maloney, were neither the first nor the last of the CIA paramilitary officers killed in the conflict. And like Deuel and Maloney, their Agency affiliations would be covered up.

Even as the two Mikes' brief collaboration ended, the Communists were expanding their vast network of roads and resupply routes, creating a major artery for the North Vietnamese war effort. A "Secret" CIA intelligence assessment provided to Lyndon Johnson seven weeks after Deuel and Maloney were killed notes that the Communists were moving largely at night and that they had concealed the roads with overarching trellises and vines, making them virtually invisible.

Even years later Dick Helms and other senior Agency officials would extol the efforts of its men and women in Laos and speak of the CIA's costly campaign as if it had been a success. And those in the jungles and mountains who fought the covert war in Laos continue to say "We won our war," contrasting it with the Vietnam conflict, which was bitterly lost to the Communists following an unseemly withdrawal.

But in the eyes of history it is a meaningless distinction, an expression of wounded pride. No sooner did Vietnam fall than Laos followed suit. On December 3, 1975, the Lao People's Democratic Republic formally came to power.

Many could argue—and did—that Mike Deuel and the others who died in Laos died for naught, that their efforts failed to sway events. But though the mission ultimately failed, their grit is still quietly celebrated at Langley by the aging few who knew them, particularly those from the Agency's class of 1961. They remember Mike Deuel not as a casualty of war, but as the standard-bearer of their class and generation. "I want to make a difference," Mike Deuel would often say. In that, he spoke for them all.

CHAPTER 8

Homecoming

IT WAS dubbed "the Summer of Love," though it began in the spring. That April 15, 1967, some 300,000 demonstrators, among them Rev. Martin Luther King, Jr., activist and pediatrician Benjamin Spock, and folk singer Pete Seeger, came together for a peace march through New York City in protest of the undeclared war in Vietnam. For the CIA it was to be a particularly trying year. An article in a magazine called *Ramparts* drew national attention to the CIA's secret funding of American student groups, educational foundations, and voluntary organizations operating overseas. In response to the public outcry that followed, President Lyndon Johnson set up a commission to investigate the scope of CIA involvement in such groups. It would be the first of many such revelations to rock the Agency, whose natural instinct was to close ranks, further isolating it from the mainstream of American culture.

That same year, budgetary cutbacks at the State Department reduced the number of cover positions available to CIA case officers. Congress was taking an ever-greater interest in intelligence matters. Concern was growing over the Agency's ability to conceal its more ambitious covert operations. Though more than half the Agency's personnel and budget continued to go to the clandestine service, the era of expansion was coming to an end. In June 1966 Richard Helms had been named Director Central Intelligence, but his attentions and energies would be largely consumed by the steadily unraveling situation in Southeast Asia. And not even Langley was immune to the upheaval in political and social values that was sweeping the country.

In such times it was easy to forget the fate of Hugh Redmond, John Downey, and Richard Fecteau, who, a generation earlier, had disappeared behind China's dreaded "bamboo curtain." They had long before been consigned to history. But for Redmond's family the summer of 1967 would be remembered as the summer they received his last letter.

There was nothing foreboding or even memorable about the two-page letter, except, perhaps, as the family would later observe with grim pride, that it was dated July 4, 1967. "It just dawned on me that today is the Fourth of July when I wrote the date above," Hugh Redmond wrote. "Did you have a big celebration with fireworks and all?" It closed, as his letters so often did, with a gentle reminder: "Don't forget to buy ice cream for the children. Very best regards to you all, Love Hugh." And there was this final postscript. "Please send a bottle of aspirins."

As months passed without further word from him, his mother, Ruth, and sister, Ruthie, grew despondent. They feared that something terrible had happened to him. But if something terrible was happening to Redmond, it was also happening to all of China. It was called the Cultural Revolution. The convulsions it caused China made the unrest in America look tame by comparison. Its object was to foment revolutionary fervor, as millions of Red Guards waving Mao's *Little Red Book* unleashed their fury against any and all institutions that promoted stability or the preservation of cultural values. Redmond was an incidental victim of that typhoon. He was sentenced not to death, but to silence.

But long before that last letter, there was evidence that the years of imprisonment, many of them spent in solitary confinement and shackles, had taken their toll. Redmond could still fend off the crude attempts at indoctrination, but he was now more vulnerable to the corrosive realization that day by day his life was trickling away. His father had died an invalid in 1959. Redmond's own body, despite a strict regimen of exercise, was deteriorating, and his knowledge of the world beyond his cell was increasingly gleaned from books. With so much time on his hands, worries were magnified into obsessions.

Not the least of these centered on his wife, Lydia, or Lily, as he called her. She appeared to have inexplicably stopped writing in July 1959. Whether any letters from her were among the correspondence intercepted by the Chinese is not known. Month after month Redmond waited to hear from her. Finally he wrote his mother asking her to find out what had happened to his wife. Ruth Redmond knew the answer. Lydia Redmond had divorced her son. But his mother could not bring herself to tell him. She feared it would shatter him. Instead, she chose to ignore his inquiries and avoided the subject completely.

But the more he pressed, the more she was forced to hint at the answer. She had always detested her daughter-in-law, a woman whom, no matter how irrational her judgment, she secretly blamed for her son's imprisonment. Two years would pass without a word from his wife. For Redmond these were years of anguish.

Then, on November 28, 1961, Lydia sent Redmond a letter and a belated birthday card. She told him she was living in Washington, D.C., working on her music and teaching. Redmond drew little comfort from her words. "From her letter," he wrote his mother, "everything is the same as it was and she is still my wife, no mention of divorce, etc. etc. Naturally I am more confused than ever and do not know what to think. Please make a new investigation. This thing must be cleared up. I can't tell what the score is. All she said in her letter was that she was sorry for not writing for so long . . . I don't like this in between, in again, out again, off again, on again game." By February Lydia was again writing regularly, with what Hugh Redmond viewed as nothing more than a casual apology for the two-year hiatus. The silence had driven Hugh Redmond to the brink of despair.

Each of Redmond's monthly letters to his mother was now spent pleading with her to find out the truth about Lydia and whether she was in fact still his wife. He was losing patience and uncharacteristically lashed out at his mother and at the world at large. In a June 1, 1962, letter he berated her for sending him a copy of *Redbook* magazine. "This is a disgusting magazine," he wrote. "For addled-brained adolescents and harebrained women. Some of the books you send are very poor. I know that you don't read them yourself, but please ask that the book shop use a little discretion. No more books about queers and fairies and pansies if you don't mind. I don't know why those kinds of books are even published."

His anxiety over Lydia was compounded by myriad other frustrations and by the awareness of how little control he had over his own life. He had entered prison a proud young man. Now he was destitute, reduced to a single pair of tattered underpants, shoes nearly without soles, and a relentlessly insipid diet. He inhabited a vacuum. For months he had been asking his mother for vitamins, unaware that she had been including them in each package but that they were being pilfered by the Chinese. This, too, infuriated him.

But the underlying cause of his angst remained the status of his marriage. "Please let me know what happened to Lily," he wrote. "Is she remarried? If so what is her new name? I have been waiting now for nine months to find out. Don't you think that it is about time that you let me know what is going on?"

In June Redmond wrote his wife telling her that he had met someone new in prison and was going to marry her upon his release. It was a pathetic and desperate ploy to smoke out the truth. "Naturally this is not true," Redmond confided in his mother, "but I thought that she might at least in anger write me an honest account of her activities if she thought I intended to marry someone else. After all I have been a prisoner more than eleven years so I don't know any women."

Ruth Redmond was torn. She feared that telling him the truth might be the coup de grâce. Withholding it any longer would drive him even deeper into depression.

In June 1962 she wrote Redmond all that she knew of Lydia. The truth was that Lydia had divorced her son in Mexico years earlier. On June 21, 1960, Lydia, then thirty-two and working in a clerical job at Georgetown University, had married a man ten years her junior. His name was Gerasimos Koskinas. He was an immigrant from Greece who made his living as a driver. It had been a civil ceremony at the Arlington County Courthouse in Virginia. On the marriage application Lydia had listed her place of birth as Harbin, China. The maiden name she gave was unfamiliar to the Redmonds or to those once assigned to her case at the CIA.

But within two years that marriage, too, was troubled. It was not until September 1962 that, according to Hugh Redmond, Lydia finally wrote and spelled it all out—the Mexican divorce, her marriage to a younger man, the problems surfacing in her new marriage. There was even a suggestion that he come to her aid, that he challenge the Mexican divorce on the grounds that he had been unaware of it. Such a protest would nullify the divorce and subsequent marriage. But Redmond wanted no part of it. He was devastated.

A few weeks later, in an effort to bring his spirits up, Ruth Redmond arranged, with the cooperation of the CIA, to visit her son in China a second time. Even as one arm of the Agency helped her make travel arrangements and secretly channeled funds to her, the rest of the organization was engrossed in matters even more grave.

At noon on October 19, 1962, Ruth Redmond crossed into mainland China for her second visit. World tensions were never higher. The Cuban missile crisis had begun five days earlier.

Ruth Redmond was permitted four visits with her son. The first of these was on October 22—the very day that President Kennedy went on television to announce to the nation both the presence of Soviet missiles in Cuba and the U.S. quarantine of shipping to that island nation. On her way to the prison that day she saw Chinese militia conducting exercises in the public parks. From every building hung banners that declared "Cuba Yes, Yankee No!" The frail sixty-year-old cafeteria worker from Yonkers found herself in an alien and hostile land readying itself for a nuclear Armageddon.

But even that sobering reality did not prepare her for what awaited her at the prison. In the intervening four years since she had last seen her son, he had gone from a young and vital man to one whose face was now prematurely creased with age and worry. His right eye and cheek were afflicted with a nervous twitch or spasm—a tic she would call it. His lower right eyelashes were missing. Distraught over his condition, she pleaded with the Chinese to allow her to extend her stay an extra day so that she could be with her son on his forty-third birthday. They refused. So she gave her son his birthday gift a day early. It was a wristwatch, a way to measure the passage of time in lieu of any other.

In their final meeting Hugh Redmond seemed curiously upbeat. He repeatedly used the phrase "when I get home," not "if I get home."

A year later Ruth Redmond returned for yet another visit. This time she detected what she called "a vacant look in his eyes." Twice he had been taken to the infirmary for treatment of a condition he was not allowed to mention. His clothes appeared to be falling off of him. When she handed him a new pair of shoes, the guards laughed. They knew his routine, that he would walk fifteen miles a day, pacing about in his tiny cell. But if the walls of the prison seemed to be closing in on him, his intellectual limits were receding. He had taught himself Chinese, Russian, French, and Spanish. As soon as he mastered one language, he would go on to another, fearing that the ennui of prison life would otherwise catch up with him. He asked his mother to send him a copy of Gibbon's *Decline and Fall of the Roman Empire*. And as she was about to leave, he told her he had but one dream—to come home.

For a time after that, his letters came at the rate of one a month. Most contained lists of books he wished to read—*The Romance of Leonardo da Vinci*, by Dimitri Merezhkovsky; *The Agony and the Ecstasy*, by Irving Stone; *The Creative Process*, edited by Brewster Ghiselin. But by 1966—with the eruption of China's Cultural Revolution—incoming letters were increasingly censored, or confiscated in their entirety. Packages no longer arrived. The war in Vietnam was raging and America was seen as the incarnation of evil. Hugh Redmond, its agent, would be made to shoulder the full weight of that animosity.

One of the last letters he received brought news that his mother had suffered a stroke. She was now fragile and birdlike, paralyzed on her left side, and barely able to speak. Redmond wrote his sister suggesting that she make flash cards with one hundred of the most common words to try to teach his mother how to speak again. He also asked that she be provided a typewriter and be taught to peck with one finger. His mother's letters had been a vital link to the world beyond his cell.

But even then, Redmond could steel himself and show flashes of humor to console his mother. On December 7, 1966, he wrote: "I had an accident a few days ago. Sitting reading, I suddenly sneezed, (a sneeze that Dad would have been proud of.) It would have shaken the bats off the rafters in the attic if I had been in the coal bin. When I stood up I saw that it [his belt] had broken, snapped right in half, so now I have to use a piece of string to hold my pants up . . . I don't know what my waist size is. That depends on the time of the year. Sometimes I am not an eagle's talon in the waist, other times I barrel up with a banker's bulge."

Years passed without a letter from Redmond. Occasionally diplomats in Hong Kong would report unconfirmed sightings of him from missionaries and businessmen recently released from Chinese prisons. Some described a man who fit his description but who appeared to be too old to be Redmond.

In the spring of 1968 Ruth Redmond sent a letter to Chinese Premier Chou En-lai pleading with him to provide some information of her son. "If he is ill or unable to write would you not relieve a concerned mother's mind by having the prison authorities inform me of his condition," she wrote. There was no reply.

In August 1968 the CIA, working through Yonkers attorney Sol Friedman, hatched a final desperate plan to win Redmond's release. After years of refusing to offer a ransom for Redmond's freedom, the Agency concluded that there was no other alternative. It devised an elaborate scheme designed to keep the Agency's role a secret and to maintain the decades-long denial of any connection between Redmond and the CIA. With Friedman's help it would appear that thirty-two anonymous sponsors had contributed money to a fund aimed at winning Redmond's release.

If pressed for the sources of those funds, Friedman stood prepared to provide the names of leading sports figures and celebrities of the day. Among those who had apparently consented to appear as donors and lend their names to the ruse were baseball great Jackie Robinson, and boxer Rocky Marciano, and even an NFL coach. The Agency would provide $1 million.

Advertisements of the ransom were placed in capitals around the world, wherever the Chinese had diplomatic representatives. But apparently unaware of the CIA plan, the U.S. Treasury Department, in August 1968, issued a warning that it would be illegal for an American citizen to transfer money to China without a special license. Undaunted, Sol Friedman, then chairman of the Yonkers Citizens' Committee for the Release of Hugh Francis Redmond, went to The Hague and Paris in mid-November 1968 to meet with diplomats and others close to the Beijing regime, hoping to pique an interest in exchanging Redmond for cash. There were no takers and the plan was abandoned. Two more years of absolute silence followed.

· · ·

On July 10, 1970, the Chinese issued a press release from Shanghai that contained two simple statements of fact. The first was that that day they were releasing James Edward Walsh, a seventy-nine-year-old Catholic bishop whom they had been holding for twelve years. For an instant the U.S. consulate's office in Hong Kong was jubilant.

Then the consular staff read the second part of the message and were staggered.

On the evening of April 13, 1970, according to the Chinese, Hugh Francis Redmond had slashed himself with an American-made razor blade. He had severed "the artery of the medial aspect of his left elbow and the arteries of his wrists and mortally wounded himself." The Chinese said they had rushed Redmond to the hospital but that it was already too late. He had lost too much blood to be saved.

Redmond had lived nineteen of his fifty years behind bars.

Even in death, Redmond was branded by the Chinese as a "United States imperialist spy." He had, according to the state-run New China News Agency, been sent to carry out "espionage sabotage in Shanghai, Peking and Shenyang and thus committed grave crimes." The Chinese said Redmond's body had already been cremated and that the Red Cross had been instructed to "inform the culprit Redmond's relatives of his death."

A cable from the Chinese Red Cross asked that no more letters or packages be sent to him. There was no explanation for the three months that had elapsed between Redmond's alleged suicide and the announcement of his death. At 10:30 A.M. on July 30, 1970—even as an exhausted and unshaven Bishop Walsh was released—an urn said to contain Redmond's ashes was turned over to representatives of the American Red Cross.

It happened on the same Lowu Bridge where, three times before, Redmond's mother had crossed from Hong Kong and the New Territories into mainland China. The handover of the urn that midsummer day was otherwise unremarkable, part of the routine monthly exchange in which Red Cross representatives passed on food parcels destined for American prisoners held in China. Three days later the Redmond family asked that Hugh Redmond's ashes be returned to the United States. The urn was shipped by air to New York.

Redmond was finally on his way home.

For the Chinese it had been a brilliant but cynical ploy, releasing the aging bishop at the same time that they announced Redmond's death. In newspapers and radio reports nearly everywhere but Yonkers, the freeing of Bishop Walsh eclipsed news of Redmond's death. The Chinese had held Redmond for longer than any other American prisoner. They had interrogated him, subjected him to prolonged isolation, and attempted in every way they knew to break him. Yet now, by veiling news of his death in the announcement of Walsh's release, they were being praised for showing compassion. At the State Department many interpreted the release of Walsh as a gesture to the West, an invitation for improved relations.

President Nixon, already anxious to improve ties with China, later met with Bishop Walsh at the White House. The talking points were supplied by the office of Henry Kissinger, special assistant for national security affairs. At the meeting no mention was made of Hugh Redmond.

But at Langley and in Yonkers there was anger and disbelief. Why would Redmond, having endured nineteen years of imprisonment with unbending defiance, suddenly capitulate and take his own life? Why had the Chinese waited three months to tell anyone of his death? And why had they been so eager to cremate the body, if not to conceal the actual cause of death?

None of this made much difference to Ruth Redmond. She was now seventy-two, the victim of three disabling strokes, the last and most devastating of which occurred on April 30, 1970—two weeks after Hugh's death. She was now confined to a wheelchair, paralyzed on her right side, and barely able to speak. For three months she had been living at the Hudson View Nursing Home. She was no longer able to recognize even her closest friends.

On Monday morning, August 3, 1970, Yonkers said good-bye to Hugh Francis Redmond. All flags were lowered to half-mast. The funeral cortege, escorted by six policemen on motorcycles, left the Flynn Memorial Home at 10:15 A.M. and headed for the Church of St. John the Baptist. Along the way, it paused in front of the Hudson View Nursing Home on Ashburton Avenue. As the funeral procession passed by, a frail old woman in a wheelchair could be observed waving to the procession from the window of the sunporch. It was Redmond's mother. She was described that day as "dressed in a soft pink nightgown under a cotton robe, her hair coifed and a tinge of rouge upon her cheeks and lips." Weighing a scant eighty pounds, she watched with dry eyes. It was whispered by those familiar with Ruth Redmond's suffering that it was a blessing she was in her condition. The stroke had dulled her mind and memory, sparing her the final pain of her son's death. What passed before her window that morning might just as well have been a slow-moving parade.

Some who lined the street saluted as the procession passed. In the church two hundred mourners listened as Rev. Bernard Quinn read the eulogy. "After his long life of suffering and serving God, Hugh Francis Redmond has begun his eternal life in heaven." In the sanctuary the urn containing his ashes was covered with a white linen doily.

Four former mayors—all who had been in office through the nineteen years of Redmond's imprisonment—served as honorary pallbearers. Redmond's friends, middle-aged men and women who had not seen Redmond since their youth, gathered in the church. Sol Friedman, who had headed the Yonkers civic group campaigning for Redmond's release, gave the graveside eulogy. "Today," he began, "we bury the ashes of Hugh Redmond. For certain, no one can ever bury the indomitable spirit and courage of this man . . . Never once could the Chinese government extract a confession of an admission of guilt from him."

After a final blessing, the silence was shattered by a four-gun salute from the color guard of the Veterans of Foreign Wars Post 7. A bugle wailed "Taps," and a perfectly folded flag—the one that now gathers dust in a nephew's cellar—was presented to Redmond's sister.

His ashes were buried in a silver and lead urn on a hillside in Yonkers's Oakland Cemetery beneath a modest granite tombstone featuring a cross and wreath. The inscription reads: "His Country Above All Else." Next to him lay his father, Hugh Redmond, Sr.

Three years later his mother was buried beside him.

Neither the CIA nor the Redmond family was ever persuaded that Redmond had committed suicide. Nor was there any way of proving that the ashes were actually those of Hugh Redmond. Testing them would have revealed nothing except perhaps that they were of human origin.

Redmond's death alarmed the Agency and put new urgency into efforts to free Fecteau and Downey, who had spent eighteen years in prison. There were reasons now to be hopeful. Even as Nixon prosecuted the war in Vietnam, he sought rapprochement with China. In March 1971 he lifted passport restrictions on travel to that country. On April 6 the Chinese invited the U.S. table tennis team to the mainland, in what came to be known as Ping-Pong diplomacy. Years of glacial hostilities were rapidly melting away.

What might Redmond have thought if he could have
July 1971—a year after his death—Nixon's national se
Kissinger, would secretly visit China and agree to share ser
gence reports with Premier Chou En-lai? Might he not hav
what had been achieved by his years of refusal to admit he was a spy? And
what had the Agency to show for so many sacrifices in its covert war
against that country? Beijing would claim that of some 212 Chinese
agents who parachuted into the mainland in the early 1950s—with CIA
help—half had been killed, the other half captured.

Fecteau was luckier. On December 13, 1971—two months before
Nixon's scheduled trip to Beijing—he was at last released. He was flown
to Valley Forge Military Hospital in Pennsylvania. There he was placed
under observation and given a battery of medical tests. The Agency dispatched Ben DeFelice and one of its psychologists to the hospital.
Fecteau, then forty-three, had never been outgoing or gregarious, even before his capture. But after years of solitary confinement, he was painfully
withdrawn. DeFelice was there not only to assist him in dealing with bureaucratic matters but, perhaps more important, with Fecteau's emotional
reentry.

Just three days after Fecteau's return to the United States, DeFelice
got permission to take him on a drive through the surrounding countryside and towns. Fecteau had never before seen a shopping mall. He was
bedazzled by the colors and contours of cars. They stopped for a burger at
a fast-food restaurant. It was all so new, so alien to Fecteau. Afterward,
DeFelice scribbled down some notes of the experience. He called it his
"Rip Van Winkle piece," after the fictional character who slept for twenty
years and awoke an old man, his wife dead, his daughter married, and the
portrait of King George replaced by that of George Washington. So it was
for Richard Fecteau. His infant twins were now women, and he had
missed the presidencies of Eisenhower, Kennedy, and Johnson.

One pleasant surprise awaited him. The puny salary he thought was
due him had grown, after years of Agency investments and promotions,
into a hefty sum. Fecteau declined sizable offers from publishers and
movie studios to tell his story, fearing it might jeopardize his Agency colleague Downey's chances for release. Fecteau later remarried his first wife,
Margaret, and became assistant athletic director at Boston University.

On February 21, 1972, Nixon arrived in China for his historic meeting with Premier Chou En-lai and Chairman Mao Zedong. In the very city where Hugh Redmond rotted away in prison, the two leaders issued a joint statement on February 27, known as the Shanghai Communiqué, agreeing to normalize relations.

A year later, in February 1973, Nixon held a press conference. The last question asked was about Downey. At the Agency Downey's friends were convinced that the question was planted and the answer rehearsed. Nixon seized—if not created—that opportunity to finally acknowledge what the Chinese had known for two decades: that Downey was a CIA operative. That was all that the Chinese had been waiting for.

On March 10, 1973, the White House announced that Downey would be released so that he could be with his mother, who was then in critical condition in a Connecticut hospital, suffering from a stroke. Two days later, on March 12, the Chinese let Downey go. He, too, walked across the Lowu Bridge to Hong Kong, after twenty years in prison. He cut a stark figure in Chinese blue pants and blue shirt, an overcoat slung across his arm and a black suitcase in his hand.

At Langley it was a time for quiet celebration and perhaps some soul-searching as well. Privately some within the Agency believed that Downey and Fecteau—and perhaps Redmond too—might well have been released many years earlier, and that their ordeals were avoidable.

Steven Kiba had been an American radioman in a B-29 when he was shot down over North Korea in 1953. He was briefly imprisoned with Downey and Fecteau in Beijing. Just prior to his release in 1955, a Chinese commissar told him that Downey and Fecteau could be released if the U.S. government admitted they were spies.

Upon his return to the United States, Kiba was debriefed by CIA officers. During those sessions in downtown Washington he spoke of the Chinese offer to release Downey and Fecteau if the United States would admit they worked for the Agency. Kiba was told never to mention that he had met Downey or Fecteau and was advised to "forget about the whole period." He was stunned that the CIA officers showed no interest in pursuing the subject. Instead, they told him that "it looked pretty hopeless for them and seemed to indicate they would never get out."

Eighteen years later the United States admitted what was clear to the Chinese from the beginning. And just as Kiba had suggested, freedom followed soon after.

Upon his return to the States, Downey acknowledged that he had told the Chinese what he knew during his imprisonment and interrogation. Still the Agency, in recognition of his ordeal, offered him a position at Langley. Downey declined. "You know I just don't think I am cut out for that kind of work," he jested. He dismissed his two decades in a Chinese prison as a "crashing bore." At age forty-three he entered Harvard Law School. Today he is a judge in Connecticut.

It is said that he was the last of his Yale class still on the books as an Agency operative. Everyone else had left. One had gone on to become a photographer, another a clothier, and yet another a lobsterman in the Solomon Islands. Downey and Fecteau and Redmond had stayed on the Agency rolls long after most of their peers had departed or retired. It was partly a matter of bureaucratic fiction and partly out of deference for their long suffering.

Nor was Redmond forgotten. In 1972 Yonkers renamed Cook Field, a thirty-five-acre recreational site, Redmond Park in honor of their native son.

As for Redmond's wife, Lydia, she is in her seventies, divorced, and living in a Virginia suburb outside of Washington, D.C. She says the CIA lost interest in her the moment she divorced Redmond. She rails against the Chinese. "They are just butchers, butchers sitting on top of butchers," she says. "They have never changed." She has no interest in speaking of Redmond or seeing his letters. "I know all the gruesome details and I have enough letters to last me a lifetime." She has never been to Redmond's grave, nor has she an interest in doing so.

Redmond, Fecteau, and Downey had all paid a profound price for what in hindsight may be viewed as fictions created by government. The United States would not acknowledge what the Chinese already knew: that all three men were spies. Nor would Washington recognize the Communist regime, even if it meant blotting out a quarter of the world's population. Instead, it acted as if mainland China were represented by the effete and exiled Nationalist government on Taiwan. Covert operations against the mainland had been a part of that greater fiction, accepting the most profound acts of personal sacrifice and heroism in a vain effort to modify Chinese political or military conduct.

One last lingering remnant of that fiction remains. The U.S. government has yet to publicly acknowledge that Hugh Francis Redmond worked for the CIA. To this day he remains a nameless star in the Book of Honor.

Only in Yonkers, among the elderly, is his name remembered and revered, and by a nephew who dutifully returns the scant artifacts of Redmond's life to a small mahogany chest destined again for the basement.

CHAPTER 9

Honor and Humiliation

This is neither a Boy Scout game nor a boxing bout
fought by the Marquess of Queensbury Rules. It is
a job to be done.

ALLEN DULLES

BY THE EARLY 1970s more than a decade had elapsed since the Bay of
Pigs. Finally it appeared that the CIA might again enjoy some measure of
credibility as the Cuban fiasco faded into history. But new and more trying ordeals were already taking shape. Cumulatively they would create a
crisis of confidence in the CIA from which it would not soon recover. By
1974 the long-festering war in Vietnam was coming to an end. A short-
lived and illusory peace was all there was to show for so much sacrifice.
The end would be immortalized as a frantic scurry aboard a final chopper
out of Saigon on April 30, 1975, and the spectacle of a Communist
takeover.

On many fronts the public felt it had been deceived. Watergate, the

begun on June 17, 1972, with a break-in of
Committee headquarters. It was followed by the ar-
all but one of whom had worked for the CIA and
went back to the Bay of Pigs or before. Other former
ld later be implicated, leading many to muse that the
y of Pigs was upon Langley still. On August 9, 1974,
Presid̲ ̲ard Nixon resigned in disgrace. With Nixon gone, the CIA
would take unwanted center stage.

Investigators on Capitol Hill and in the press began to unravel the
CIA's most sensitive secrets, digging into a past that would chill even stalwart patriots and challenge time-honored myths of America's moral superiority. Millions, it was learned, had been spent on toppling duly elected
foreign governments. Tens of thousands of Americans had been subjected
to illegal CIA scrutiny. Former Agency officers were writing books, threatening to tell all. Détente and its relaxation of tensions with the Soviets un-
dermined support for covert operations and called into question the need
for extreme measures.

As if external wounds were not enough, Langley had long engaged
in its own bloodletting. The self-destructive hunt for Soviet moles inside
the CIA, led by the brilliant but obsessed James Angleton, was finally
brought to an end with his forced retirement in December 1974—but not
before the careers of honorable officers had been ruined and vast resources squandered chasing phantoms.

Ahead lay devastating Senate and House hearings. Out of these
would come revelations that would forever alter Americans' view of the
CIA and, in the minds of at least one generation, brand it as a rogue
agency—"uncontrolled and uncontrollable," to use the words of Senator
Frank Church. An incredulous nation learned that for years the Agency
had been reading Americans' mail, spying on its own citizens, experi-
menting with LSD and deadly toxins, plotting to assassinate foreign
leaders, and destabilizing other governments. William E. Colby, director
of the Central Intelligence Agency, horrified the clandestine service by
voluntarily assembling a list of Agency actions that violated its charter.
To the outside world it was known as the Family Jewels. Inside the
Agency it was called the Skeletons. Nothing so demoralized Langley as
the perception that it had been betrayed by one of its own, a career in-

telligence officer, an OSS veteran, and the overseer of the controversial Phoenix Program.

Out of that would come a vast expansion of congressional oversight and a prohibition of assassinations. Few would be exempt from accountability. In 1973 a Senate committee asked former Agency director Richard Helms if the CIA had had a role in the coup attempts to bring down Chile's President Salvador Allende. "No sir," he replied. Four years later, when the truth emerged, Helms was slapped with a $2,000 fine and a two-year suspended prison sentence for misleading Congress. "You now stand before this court in disgrace and shame," a federal judge told him. It was a rebuke that, in the public's mind, might just as well have been meted out to the entire Agency.

By the mid-1970s and for decades thereafter, the CIA would be the focal point for every conspiracy theory. The excesses of such accusations were matched only by the CIA's own bizarre and often harebrained schemes. For those inside the Agency who revered it and remembered those who had recently died in its service in Southeast Asia, the mid-seventies were years of high honor and excruciating humiliation. Many Agency veterans remained unbowed and resentful. Among these was Richard Helms.

"Some political commentators lamented the fact the CIA was not the Boy Scouts," an indignant Helms would reflect. "Those of us who worked in the CIA were surprised—we had always assumed that we had been expected to act otherwise. The CIA was damaged, almost crippled, by that dark period in its history." Citing the patriot Nathan Hale, whose statue graces a CIA walkway, Helms would say, "Intelligence is necessary to the public good, and, by being necessary, becomes honorable." At Langley "necessary" and "honorable" had been allowed to become synonymous.

It was against just such a darkening backdrop that CIA officials gathered in the spring of 1973 in an attempt to craft some sort of memorial for the many Agency men and women who had died in the line of service. Up until then, there was no monument, only a secretive gathering of men assembling under the sterile-sounding name of the Honors and Merit Awards Board. It was they who determined who would posthumously receive what, if any, medal or honor. Most such honors and commendations would be presented to the surviving spouse, then quickly retrieved and placed in the deceased's personnel file, deep within the vaultlike chambers of Langley. Such deaths, shrouded in secrecy, were deemed a private matter between the family and the Agency representative. That was usually a job for Ben DeFelice, who for two decades comforted the bereaved and provided them with whatever bureaucratic and personal assistance might be needed.

But in the grim days of 1973 and 1974 senior Agency people seized upon the idea that something more was needed, something both to recognize the personal sacrifices of its officers and, equally important, to provide a focal point for the CIA community at large. Such sacrifices in the aggregate, it was thought, might inspire and uplift an increasingly demoralized organization. For a guide, they looked naturally enough to the State Department, which had, over the years, lost scores of men and women in service overseas.

Adopting State Department rituals and criteria was a first step. But Agency officials soon recognized that most of those the CIA would honor would be from the clandestine ranks. That posed unique security problems. At the State Department there was a large plaque at the end of the main lobby listing its honored dead. For years the CIA had quietly salted in among the ranks of the State Department's casualties some of its own covert officers killed in the line of duty. Among these were the names of Douglas S. Mackiernan, "Killed by Gunfire Tibet 1950," and William P. Boteler, "Killed by Grenade Nicosia Cyprus 1956." It was an odd way to do Agency casualties honor, but the only way that the CIA knew. Besides, since those men and women had died under State Department cover, not to include them on that wall would attract unwanted attention and raise suspicions about their true employer and mission. It was a dilemma that would continue for decades.

Creating an Agency memorial would require the organization to first define the criteria for inclusion. Those deemed worthy would then be the subject of an elaborate declassification review to determine whose name could be revealed and whose must remain a secret. Like the State Department, the Agency concluded that such a death must be "of an inspirational or heroic character."

But at the CIA the precise criteria for inclusion were deemed so sensitive that they were classified and would remain so. Unlike the State Department, the Agency concluded that death need not occur outside the United States, though it must occur while in pursuit of an Agency mission. Excluded were deaths occurring from disease, earthquakes and other natural disasters, and simple auto and plane crashes occurring in the ordinary course of one's private life. On this they agreed. But such a provision excluded numerous Agency officers who perished in the field from exotic circumstances to which they would not otherwise have been exposed but for their CIA missions.

Initially they also agreed that those honored should not be limited to CIA staff employees but should include those who died while under contract to the CIA. This was a point of considerable sensitivity in 1973. Scores of pilots and crew members from Air America, the proprietary air wing of the CIA, had died in Southeast Asia while on Agency business. Excluding them from the memorial would have been seen as drawing an untenable distinction between the sacrifices of those who died in service to country, based solely on employment status and bureaucratic hairsplitting. (Yet in the end, such a distinction was invoked, to the consternation of countless Air America families who felt their loved ones' sacrifices were belittled by the CIA.)

There was also an early consensus as to the words that would appear above the memorial.

Finally, after consultation with a noted private architectural sculptor, Harold Vogel, there was agreement that all the deceased would be recognized with a star. Some other instrument, perhaps a book, could provide the years in which the officers were killed. But one thorny question remained: what exactly would such a memorial look like? For this, they relied largely on Vogel.

In some ways he was the perfect choice. An experienced sculptor, he was widely respected and had the sort of forceful vision that would cajole the Agency into reaching a firm conclusion as to the design. Even more important, Vogel brought to the project the sensitivities of a man only too familiar with the causes and values for which these covert operatives had been said to have given their lives.

The son of German immigrants, he was born in the United States. But following the stock market crash of 1929, he and his family returned to Germany. As a teenager Vogel grew up under Hitler's Third Reich. When it was discovered that his father carried a U.S. passport, his mother was locked up, his father dispatched to Russia, and he, though only fourteen, was interned at a labor camp near Nuremberg. There Vogel was assigned to assist a Russian explosives expert whose job it was to dismantle Allied bombs that failed to detonate. Vogel knew he was utterly "disposable." Another lad forced to perform the same task completely disappeared after a bomb he was dismantling went off.

It was unimaginable to him then that he would survive those years, much less return to the United States and eventually design the frame that held the Declaration of Independence at the Capitol, an LBJ memorial, and other prominent public commissions. But none would prove more challenging than that at the CIA. Problems arose early on. Months after the Agency contacted him, he heard nothing from them and assumed that they had selected someone else. In fact, the Agency was conducting a security check of Vogel and was troubled when it was discovered that he had relatives living in East Germany. Only when the Agency satisfied itself that he was not a security threat did they contact him again. That was in the spring of 1974.

Then came the conundrum of how to pay homage to people whose identities were, due to compartmentation, largely unknown even within the CIA itself. Early on, Vogel, unfamiliar with the Byzantine ways of the Agency, felt as though he had stumbled into some sort of Alice in Wonderland landscape.

Much of the idea for a "book of honor" in which to record the names of the fallen must be credited to Vogel. But as originally envisioned by some at the Agency, the Book of Honor was to contain not just some of the names but all of them. For this reason, Vogel would be asked to design a way to display the volume, albeit closed and under lock and key.

Vogel designed a lecternlike affair of Carrara marble to be fastened with rods into the wall. The book would be placed within the lectern and sealed with a bulletproof plate of glass secured with a stainless-steel frame and a solid lock. Each of four sets of keys would be carefully accounted for. The lectern itself was constructed on a slant so that those who were in wheelchairs could appreciate the beauty of the volume. But because the book was to remain closed, a premium was placed on its outward appearance.

For this Vogel went to New York and selected the finest black Moroccan goatskin for a cover. This he embossed with a 22-karat gold-leaf emblem of the Agency. The cost of the book was $1,500, the lectern $4,300, plus thousands of dollars caused by subsequent Agency revisions.

But there was a problem. Who, the Agency representatives asked, would record all the names, including those still classified? Vogel did not possess the requisite security clearance. Indeed, because the identities were compartmented on a need-to-know basis, no one individual might be entrusted with them all. So the Agency gathered together three of its in-house calligraphers and decided to divide the names among them. But when the calligraphers were informed that they could not make a mistake on the one-of-a-kind handmade rice paper, they withdrew from consideration. That left Vogel.

"Well," said Vogel, attempting to make light of the situation, "you could blindfold me and then I wouldn't know what the hell I wrote." The Agency representatives were less than amused. The entire concept underwent yet another revision.

This time it was decided that only those names cleared for release would be included in the Book of Honor. The others would be marked only by a star and the year of death. No other clues to identity or mission or circumstances of death would be included in the book. Now the concept called for the volume to remain opened, and the costly cover would be unseen. On the top two pages, hand-lettered in black India ink, were to be written the names and stars. Beneath these two pages and supporting them was a series of blank sheets to give the book heft. With each passing year, as more and more names were to be added, a blank page would be taken from the bottom, inscribed, and placed on the top.

More than a year had passed between the time the Agency had first approached Vogel and the time an agreement was reached on the precise design of the project. For Vogel the final step came in July 1974, as he chiseled the letters of the inscription into the marble:

IN HONOR OF THOSE MEMBERS
OF THE CENTRAL INTELLIGENCE AGENCY
WHO GAVE THEIR LIVES IN THE SERVICE OF THEIR COUNTRY

The actual cutting of the first thirty stars was left to Vogel's sixty-one-year-old assistant, Lloyd "Red" Flint. It was Flint who manned a carbide-tipped chisel fastened to a tiny air hammer. Delicately he incised each five-pointed star into the marble wall, careful not to cut so deep as to crack the seven-eights-inch-thick slabs of Vermont Danby marble. Hundreds of CIA employees came and went through the cavernous lobby without taking any notice of this man in the work coat, his face to the wall, absorbed in his task. To them, he was virtually invisible, just another workman. A quiet man with no more than an eighth-grade education, he seemed almost a part of the wall itself. But for Flint, the carving of the stars, and the knowledge that each one represented a life lost, was more than just a job.

Five years earlier Flint had himself been a CIA employee with a top secret clearance. At times his responsibilities were as sensitive as any of those who passed by him. With the blessings of some former OSS officers, Flint had joined the Agency in 1952 and would remain there until his retirement seventeen years later. During that time he would operate the Agency's "Bindery," an innocuous-enough name, suggesting that he put together books. But Flint's work was more esoteric. He was assigned to Technical Services and operated out of the basement of a nondescript downtown Washington edifice known as the Central Building, part of the complex that once served as OSS headquarters. It was far enough from Langley to escape suspicion and sat atop a hill near the State Department, providing easy cover stories for Agency personnel.

There Red Flint used his skills to create a panoply of counterfeit documents to be used by covert operatives, some of whom might well be represented by the very stars he carved. Among his output he could count bogus license plates for clandestine officers driving through the streets of Taiwan, phony passports carried into East Germany, and innumerable leaflets disseminated throughout the Far East. His trained eye looked for minuscule "checkpoints" that the Communists buried in their documents to tip them off to his and others' CIA counterfeits. He helped provide officers with "pocket litter," the scraps of paper, store receipts, theater stubs, and other indigenous junk and refuse that might convince interrogators, when they stopped and searched an officer on hostile streets, of the person's bona fides and could mean the difference between life and death.

For Flint, as for many others, the wall of stars expressed not so much losses suffered by an institution as it did the losses endured by family. Indeed, Flint's own stepson would spend his career in the clandestine service. The Agency was, increasingly, a family affair.

. . .

By the fall of 1974 the Book of Honor and the wall of stars were completed, and the criteria for inclusion well settled. But only a few months after the chisels had been put away and the dark lithochrome applied to the last of the original stars, the Agency suffered yet another casualty. He, too, would eventually be honored with a nameless star, though the circumstances of that death diverged from all the others and, to the few familiar with the facts, would remain a lingering mystery.

His name was Raymond Carlin Rayner. Unlike his peers in the Book of Honor, Ray Rayner was not engaged in classic espionage. He ran no agents and, in the CIA's bureaucracy, did not even report to the Operations Directorate that oversaw the clandestine service. Rayner reported to the far more mundane director of administration. His last assignment was as far from the popularized vision of spying and James Bond as one could imagine. Ray Rayner's final job was warehouseman.

His story begins in 1951. He was then twenty-one and still living at home, the youngest of three brothers born and raised in Brooklyn. He was soft-spoken and possessed a deep soothing voice, an easygoing manner, and a wry sense of humor. And he was tall and well built. His hair was a mix of gold and red, his complexion ruddy, marked by freckles. His father, Edward, had been a truant officer who died when Ray was twelve. His mother, Helen, was a schoolteacher.

In high school Ray had been a solid student, his name appearing often on the honor roll. But since graduating from Brooklyn's St. Francis Preparatory School on June 24, 1948, he had had a series of dead-end jobs, including selling Bibles door-to-door and even a stint as a chimney sweep. His mother fretted what would become of him and called his older brother Bill asking for his advice.

That phone call ultimately put Ray Rayner on a very different career path, for Bill Rayner and his wife, Barbara Ann, both worked for the CIA. Barbara Ann was a secretary in the Agency's Office of Communications recruited at age nineteen straight out of Immaculata Junior College in June 1950. The Agency in those years seemed partial to Catholics, drawn to true believers and staunch patriots. With a top secret clearance, Barbara Ann Rayner would sometimes find herself clicking away at the typewriter keys reading the U.S. war plan in response to a Soviet nuclear attack. At night the typewriter spools were locked in the safe, and even innocent typographical errors were deposited in the burn basket beside her. Her husband, Bill, joined the Agency in 1951, assigned to the signals center. Once again, Agency employment was a family matter.

Bill suggested to his younger brother, Ray, that he apply to the Agency. And so he did. On his application Ray was asked why he left his previous employment. Remembering his work as a chimney sweep, he is said to have written, "Low pay, dirty work." After that, the phrase became a family joke, a way to decline unwanted chores. "No thanks," the Rayners would say. "Low pay, dirty work."

With his brother and sister-in-law vouching for Ray, his acceptance into the CIA was nearly a foregone conclusion. In 1951 Ray Rayner joined the Agency and within a year found himself shuttling between a couple of small rock outcroppings off the Chinese mainland known as Quemoy and Matsu. His cover was as an employee of Western Enterprises, a thinly veiled CIA front organization based in Taiwan. Given the risks and the demands of travel, Western Enterprises relied on young single men. Rayner's job was to covertly man a radio and keep an eye on what was then known as Red China.

He returned to the States just long enough to wed Margaret Mary "Peggy" Tully, a girl who grew up two blocks from him. The wedding was on April 11, 1953, in Brooklyn's Church of St. Agatha. His in-laws would always find it hard to understand what Ray did for a living, given his ever-changing cover stories and constant transfers. Like many Agency employees, he would have to endure in silence his relatives' doubts and criticisms, unable to share with them his true profession or accomplishments. In 1961 the Agency presented Ray with his ten-year pin, which he was required to keep locked away out of sight. Ironically it was given to him at the very time that his father-in-law was pressing him to get a "steady job."

Every few years, Ray would be transferred to yet another foreign post—Frankfurt, Germany, Indonesia in the mid-1960s, and in 1970, Banbury, outside of London. His specialty was communications. By all accounts, he was quiet though not reclusive, and had a streak of mischief about him. His sister-in-law would long remember when she and her husband, Bill, were preparing to return to the United States from Southampton aboard the passenger liner *Queen Elizabeth II* in July 1970. Ray Rayner and his wife, Peggy, not content to see them off at the pier, were hoping to briefly board the ship and then exit before it set sail. But at the pier, Ray was informed that without a boarding pass he could not gain way to the gangplank—and passes were no longer available.

Rayner ducked into a nearby pub where he sought out the acquaintance of a small man enjoying a last pint before boarding the *QE II* with his wife to see off a friend. Rayner, while charming the man, caught sight of his boarding pass sitting on the bar. He coolly put his cold mug of beer over the pass, raised it for a drink, and deftly pocketed the pass in his inside breast pocket. With that, he bid adieu to the man and boarded the ship to say his farewells.

Once on board, Rayner shared his tale of chicanery with his brother and sister-in-law. "You didn't!" said a disbelieving Barbara Ann. As he later exited the ship, he caught sight of the same little man from the bar, this time pleading his case at the gangplank. "I had a pass," he argued furiously. "My wife will kill me."

· · ·

It was in 1973 that Rayner, then forty-three, his wife, and their five children were assigned to Monrovia, Liberia, on Africa's west coast. Liberia was a notorious hardship post, and Ray had misgivings about the assignment. The country had a reputation for being a lawless place.

Monrovia, and particularly the Monrovia to which Rayner and his family would be exposed, was a world unto itself, rife with risks, seen and unseen. Only seven years earlier, his family had been evacuated from Jakarta, Indonesia, when that country slipped into chaos. Ray had stayed on with the rest of the CIA contingent. But at least Liberia would take him away from a Washington sinking ever deeper into the scandals of Watergate and CIA excesses. For that, at least, he might count himself among the lucky ones.

On paper the U.S. Embassy staff in Monrovia was unusually large for so small a nation. True, Liberia had enjoyed a special relationship with the United States, dating back to the 1840s when it was resettled with freed American slaves. And the country had a certain strategic importance, as Firestone had one of the world's largest rubber plantations there. But that did not account for the scores of American communications specialists working there under State Department cover. In truth, the communications people, as many as 150, were CIA officers, assigned to run the Area Telecommunications Office, or ATO, a central relay station through which nearly all message transmissions passed between the African continent and Washington. Much of that communications traffic was classified. The ATO had both a transmitter and a receiver, and maintaining the facility required a constant and significant store of replacement parts.

That's where Ray Rayner came in. Under cover as a State Department employee, Rayner was in CIA logistics, overseeing a gigantic inventory of antennae, receivers, transmitters, and innumerable tiny parts imperative to the continued operation of the ATO. The Agency warehouse was a dingy and dark structure on a small islandlike spit of land known as Bushrod Island. This was Rayner's domain. His office was located under a roof garden, and when it rained, he would constantly have to move his files around trying to keep them from the raindrops that were splashing on his desk.

He and the other CIA workers under State Department cover lived together in a community known as Caldwell a few miles from town. It was geographically isolated and socially inbred. CIA families passed their time almost exclusively with other CIA families. The work of maintaining the ATO was exhausting—and reminded many of watch duty in the military. To amuse themselves in their time off, they created a yacht club and dubbed it "the Watch Standers Club." There they and their families swam, boated, fished, and shared Sunday cookouts featuring barbecued bar- racuda.

But even when off duty, they had to be circumspect. Nature was not always friendly in West Africa. The Rayners' backyard went down to a swamp. In the wet season, when two hundred inches of rain fell, the croc- odiles from the St. Paul River would enter the swamp and come up onto their backyard and the yards of the neighbors. Children had been known to trip over a croc or two. One CIA officer, after learning that his child had had such an encounter, fetched his gun, shot the beast, skinned it, and kept the trophy in his freezer.

There were snakes too, deadly mambas, which would sun them- selves on the driveways and whose neurotoxic bites could disable their victims in seconds. Some were found hanging in the palms, others slithering through the lawns. The CIA's orientation had warned against sitting on logs or going barefoot. But that was little comfort to the CIA officer who came home to find a mamba shedding on his living room floor.

There was also the constant threat of burglars and break-ins. So widespread were these that every CIA family in Caldwell paid a local to sit in a chair in the front yard twenty-four hours a day and watch for in- truders, known as rogues. These local guards would invariably fall asleep, but their presence gave some false sense of security, enhanced by the pres- ence of "rogue bars" on the doors and windows of the families' homes. But not even the local custom of cutting off a finger or the ear of a burglar seemed to deter intruders.

And just as deadly were the ennui, the insidious boredom, and the lure of vice that crept into homes already sorely taxed by the headaches of living where electricity and water were sporadic, where nothing worked, government corruption festered, and cynicism spread like fungus.

The Agency people, always drawn to acronyms, had a name for the cumulative adversities they faced. They called it WAWA. It stood for "West Africa wins again." Nothing could resist its corrupting influence. It was said that in such a clime even aluminum rusted. Neither was the soul exempt. To combat such fatalism, a few strayed with their neighbors' spouses. Others buried themselves in work. Still others drank. Ray Rayner, by all accounts, was neither unfaithful nor slavish in his devotion to work. Whether his taste for drink exceeded that of those around him was at times a matter of whispers.

As Thanksgiving 1974 approached, the Rayners were planning a trip, a chance to get away. The night of November 23, a Saturday, Ray Rayner was said to be awakened from his sleep by the sound of an intruder, a rogue. He went to investigate and was bludgeoned over the back of his head with a heavy metal object, later thought perhaps to be a flashlight. The intruder fled. Rayner was alive but disoriented and badly shaken. For whatever reason, he did not go to the hospital that night but stayed at home.

In the morning the community of Caldwell was already abuzz with stories of the intruder. Visitors to the Rayner home found silverware strewn about, the house in disarray, and a disoriented Ray Rayner. As he walked down the house's narrow hallway, he seemed to stumble, bouncing from wall to wall. "Like a pinball," remembers one visitor. He lay on the couch, speaking but making little sense. His condition was deteriorating.

He was taken by ambulance to the ELWA Hospital, a tiny forty-five-bed clinic run by evangelical Protestant missionaries and situated thirteen miles from Monrovia on a bluff overlooking the Atlantic Ocean. ELWA stood for "Eternal Love Winning Africa," as if faith alone might be the antidote to the poisons contained in that other acronym, WAWA. Rayner was taken into private room A, where he was examined by the hospital's lone physician, Dr. Robert Schindler, who diagnosed him with what he described as "a subarachnoid hemorrhage." Rayner's brain was bleeding. Unless Schindler could soon bring down the swelling, Rayner would die. A plane was on standby to take Rayner to a hospital in Germany, but to survive the flight, the pressure on his brain would have to be reduced.

Schindler was not a neurosurgeon and he had no pretensions of being able to perform such a procedure unaided. The closest neurosurgeon was in Abidjan, hundreds of miles away. The hospital, while the best the region had to offer, did not even have a single working telephone. While Ray Rayner lay in a hospital bed, his wife, Peggy, paced the halls with her friend Barbara Teasley, wife of another CIA officer. Peggy Rayner was trying to make sense of what had happened. She spoke of their retirement plans now in jeopardy after twenty-three years of CIA service. Rayner lay unconscious. "I can't talk to him," she lamented. "I can't tell him that I love him."

At Langley there was a desperate effort to come to Rayner's aid. A radio link was set up between Washington and the ELWA Hospital, and a Bethesda neurosurgeon was brought in in an effort to talk Dr. Schindler through the complex procedure. The radio link was open and families in Caldwell clustered early that morning around radio sets on their porches, listening as a doctor an ocean away gave surgical instructions on how to operate on Rayner's brain. They sat in rapt silence, six and eight to a group, their ears to the over-and-out radio. The conversation detailed Dr. Schindler's struggle to save him. The bleeding was deep down in the base of the brain. Things were not going well. "I am losing him, I am losing him," they heard Schindler say. Then there was a prolonged silence. "He is gone," announced Schindler.

The time was 2:40 A.M. eastern standard time, November 26. On the porches of Caldwell, some cried. Others made the sign of the cross.

The next day, November 27, 1974, Ray Rayner's body was loaded aboard Pan American flight 187 for New York. His bogus diplomatic passport, number X070360, was returned to the CIA. And on December 2 he was buried in Brooklyn's Holy Cross Cemetery, in St. Joseph section, range 31, plot 203.

Rayner's death was the lead story in the Liberian *Star*, under the headline "U.S. Embassy Official Dies." But in Washington his death created not a ripple. That week, all eyes were on President Gerald Ford's meeting in Vladivostok with Soviet leader Leonid Brezhnev. The two had agreed to put a ceiling on offensive nuclear weapons. Détente was the news of the moment. Ray Rayner had been too minor a player on that grand stage of geopolitics and espionage to warrant even a nod from the hometown paper—which was as the CIA wished it to be.

. . .

In the days and weeks ahead, as the boat rides and cookouts resumed in Liberia and life in Caldwell returned to its old ways, the shock of

Rayner's death faded. But it was not long before rumors surfaced, rumors questioning the account of Rayner's death, suggesting that it had something to do with his drinking. Over games of bridge, housewives expressed doubts about the very existence of an intruder. The implications of such idle speculation were unspeakable. No one, they pointed out, had been brought to justice. Maybe such gossip made them feel better, gave them some comfort to believe that the rogues who stalked their homes by night meant them no harm and only coveted their possessions. Perhaps it was the only way they could make sense of an otherwise senseless loss.

The Agency dispatched an investigator to examine the circumstances of Rayner's death. His findings were stamped "Secret," but those who read it say it contained no surprises, no whiff of scandal or doubt. It concluded that Rayner had died as his family had said. And the rumors were just that, baseless.

Rayner's widow, Peggy, and the children returned to the States. Peggy would fall ill and die at the age of forty-nine. The death certificate would list the disease, but her in-laws would always believe that a broken heart was at least partially to blame. To this day, Ray Rayner's five children feel duty bound to honor the secrecy under which their father lived and died, fearing that to do otherwise would compromise national security. The Agency has given them little reason to believe that even after twenty-five years of rigid silence the veil should be lifted.

Equally irrational was the guilt that dogged Rayner's older brother Bill. For years he blamed himself for intervening in his brother's future and securing for him that first position in the CIA. But for his help, Bill Rayner reasoned, his little brother might yet be alive. But the search for reason or blame was futile. If Rayner demonstrated heroism deserving of a nameless star in the Book of Honor, perhaps it was not for what happened on that single fateful night in November 1974, but rather in recognition of what he had faced day in and day out—a different kind of enemy, one less identifiable than those produced by the Cold War, but no less fearsome. Perhaps it was this thing they called WAWA. West Africa had won again.

CHAPTER 10

Privation and Privilege

MACK CHAPELL remembers it well, that Thursday night, just after 9:30. The date was July 13, 1978. The skies over rural North Carolina, undiminished by city lights, were shimmering with summer constellations. The closest community, a crossroads called West Eagle Spring, was miles away. Chapell, worn out from a day in the fields, had just put his feet up to watch television in the den of his farmhouse. Suddenly from outside came a deafening boom. Chapell jumped up, got into his pickup truck, and raced over the half mile of rutted road in the direction from which the sound had come. He had a suspicion what had caused such a ruckus but was praying he was wrong.

Just days earlier he had given some fellows from the army permission to use his private airstrip, a 2,500-foot stretch of sand and grass that bisected his fields. They had said they wanted to practice night maneuvers. As Chapell drew closer to the airstrip, his headlights fell upon the broken tail section of a plane rising above the shoulder-high stalks of corn. The tail number was N-76214. He turned off the ignition, got out of the truck, and headed for what little he could see of the plane. But when he was no more than fifty feet from the wreckage, he was intercepted by three or four burly soldiers, members of the Special Forces.

"Get back! Get back!" they yelled at him. "It's going to explode!" The air was heavy with the smell of fuel, and the soldiers were running around in utter confusion. They were cursing at each other, arguing over what to do with the bodies and where a helicopter should take survivors. Only moments earlier these same men had been concealed in the shadows of the cornfields waiting for this very plane which now lay scattered in pieces.

Chapell could only listen and look from afar. He saw a blanket stretched out on the ground and, beneath it, the outline of a man's body, a small man it seemed to him.

About that same time, miles away at the Moore County Sheriff's Office, a breathless call came in over the radio: "Code six . . . Code six"— a plane crash. Timmy Monroe sped to the scene along with a rescue squad. By the time they arrived, Special Forces had secured the area and cordoned it off with ropes. Guards were posted to prevent anyone other than Special Forces from getting near the wreckage. Special Forces soldiers were combing through the debris searching for survivors.

Not far from the site, an officer with a flashlight came upon the beginnings of a blood trail. He followed it as it wove through some fifty yards of cornstalks until he came upon a man badly broken and unconscious, but alive. Others at the scene were now going through what was left of the fuselage. They found three bodies, and yet another survivor— one of their own from Special Forces—clinging to life. He would die hours later.

It was no great mystery what had happened to the aircraft. The sheared-off top of a towering oak told the tale. The plane had come in low—too low—struck the tree, and flipped nose-first into the ground, cartwheeling and ripping off both wings. The fuselage had split wide open right behind the cockpit. Two of the dead were found fastened into their seats in a cockpit that was torn open like a tin of sardines.

By morning the entire site had been completely cleared by army tractors, virtually swept clean. It was as if the crisis of the night before had all been little more than a bad dream. A few local reporters asked questions and were deftly shunted to Special Forces press officers who gave them the names of those on the plane and nothing else. A few paragraphs appeared in area newspapers along with the names of the dead and the lone survivor. The plane, it was reported, had been on contract from Coastal Air Services to the Army Institute for Military Assistance, a parent organization of the Green Berets. It was said to have been a routine flight, part of an elaborate annual training mission for Special Forces known as Robin Sage.

Sheriff's Deputy Bobbie Hudson filled out the investigative report with what little information he could glean. The plane, a twin-engine Special Light Otter, had been coming in for a low-level landing. There had been five persons aboard the plane. Among the fatalities were a Dennis Gabriel, Walter S. McCleskey, and a "John Doe, name unknown." On this John Doe's person were found a set of car keys and a black watch. Nothing else. It was the body of John Doe that Chapell had seen beneath the blanket. Also killed was a soldier named Luis Lebartarde. The lone survivor was listed as a "Civilian Gov. Employee name unknown." Nothing to attract special attention.

But attached to the typed report was a handwritten note to the sheriff. It read: "Officer on the scene Lt. Harry Pewitt HQT US Army Special Forces Ft. Bragg, N.C. states *Highly Classified* operation. Civilian plane contracted to the Army for this operation suggest you not release any information . . ." Yet another note to the file read: "Classified: CIA & Army Mission." Under orders from the Central Intelligence Agency, nothing more than the names of those who died that summer night would ever be revealed.

The secret was not how the men had died, but rather how they had lived. Their exploits filled entire folders, all of them stamped "Top Secret." The CIA connection was something the Agency was determined to conceal from public view. For decades the cover-up succeeded.

. . .

Four hundred miles north of the crash site, at CIA headquarters in Langley, Virginia, news of the downed plane struck hard. Within minutes the phone beside James Glerum's bed began to ring. It was the middle of the night and Glerum, still half-asleep, reached for the receiver. It was Agency headquarters. Bad news. Berl King and Denny Gabriel were dead.

Alex MacPherson was not expected to live through the night. The names needed no amplification. Glerum knew them well. Each had long been a cornerstone upon which the Agency had depended for its most daring covert missions. Glerum, as chief of Special Operations Group under the CIA's deputy director of operations, understood the loss not only in human terms but for what it meant to the Agency. To lose three of its very best in a single catastrophic accident was devastating.

Glerum was himself one of the Agency's most seasoned veterans. It was his job to maintain the CIA's capability to wage covert paramilitary actions. There had been none better than King, Gabriel, and MacPherson. Together and individually, their lives circumscribed much of the Cold War's hottest and most secretive history. The less notice the crash received, the less the chance that the secret lives of these men would become public.

It was almost unthinkable to Glerum and his colleagues that men who had faced death so many times should die on American soil and in what appeared to be an exercise, perhaps nothing more than a generic rehearsal for some future exploit. That exercise had been part of a broader effort to ensure that elements within U.S. Special Forces retained the exotic skills the CIA might need to supplement its own thinning ranks of paramilitary officers. Crack military units—the elite of the elite—had to be ready to do the Agency's bidding whenever the White House gave its nod to covert ops.

Once again, Agency morale was at a low point. As Director Central Intelligence for less than a year, George Bush had been wildly popular within the Agency, perceived as a man who held the reigns loosely, was loyal to a fault, deferred to career officers, and dragged his heels when asked to reduce staff or give up information damaging to the clandestine service.

He was followed in March of 1977 by Admiral Stansfield Turner, a man viewed by some Agency veterans as somewhat imperious and determined to keep a firm hand upon the CIA. His detractors say he was better at giving orders than listening to the needs of his subordinates. To them, he seemed outright suspicious of the old hands at Langley and too eager to implement so-called reforms and cutbacks in staff.

Under Turner's watch, technical collection of intelligence prospered at the expense of human intelligence. From the clandestine service, some

820 positions were cut, among these some 200 veteran covert operatives and 600 staff slots, many through attrition. Turner had no interest in shielding the Agency from its own past transgressions and viewed those transgressions as evidence that early directors had permitted too much freedom and too much compartmentation. He excoriated Langley for its inhumane treatment of a Soviet defector named Yuri Ivanovich Nosenko and expressed disgust at the vestiges of earlier drug-testing programs. For this, too, he was reviled by some career case officers. In the dramatic draw-down of manpower that immediately followed the post-Vietnam years and the subsequent cutbacks within the Agency, experienced officers like those aboard the flight that went down in North Carolina were nearly irreplaceable.

But that night the Agency's most immediate concern was breaking the news of the men's deaths to their families. King and Gabriel had been together at the controls that fateful night, sitting side by side in the cockpit of the twin Otter, linked by years of shared history. It could be said without fear of contradiction that no two men ever had more in common *or less* than Berl King and Denny Gabriel. And therein lies a story.

. . .

The body that lay beneath the blanket that night, listed simply as "John Doe," was that of Ivan Berl King, the pilot of the plane. On the death certificate filled out two days later, the cause of death was given as a "ruptured thoracic aorta" due to massive trauma. Death had been "immediate." King was fifty years old. In the space marked "occupation" were written the words "U.S. Gov't Emp.," and under "kind of business or industry" was scribbled a single word, "Gov't." The medical examiner and North Carolina investigators knew nothing more of King, and that was how the Agency wanted it.

It seemed only fitting that a man whose life was so intensely private should have no less private a death. Berl, as he was known, rarely spoke of himself or of his background, not only because of security restrictions but because it was a life studded with hardship. While the public image of the Agency is often sculpted by the sons of privilege who oversee it—Ivy Leaguers like Allen Welsh Dulles, Dick Helms, and George Bush—it is the Berl Kings of the world who often as not carried out their orders, individuals of quiet courage steeled by years of early want. They were not only content to be invisible, they would not have had it any other way. Berl King was one of these.

He was born on June 27, 1928, and grew up in a hardscrabble corner of Arkansas. He was one of fourteen children born to Mabel and William Isiah King. His father was an itinerant Baptist preacher, a circuit rider, who hitchhiked to churches too small to have their own pastors. The elder King received nothing for his services and, but for a $21-a-month veterans pension, seldom brought so much as a penny into the home. He was gone more than he was there. So much the better perhaps for the family, given the frequency with which he reached for the belt and razor strop. It was left to Berl King's mother to make do by taking in others' laundry, often working until midnight.

The family home had neither electricity nor indoor plumbing. For a time, when Berl was a toddler during the Depression, the family moved to the Ozarks. There three-year-old Berl contracted typhoid fever. For an entire month he lay in his mother's arms as she rocked in front of the fireplace, getting up only to relieve herself. He recovered but was so weakened that he would have to learn to walk all over again. After that, he seemed to be a magnet for every childhood malady. Like all but two of his siblings, Berl had white hair as fine as the silk of corn.

The family returned to Nettleton, Arkansas, in the spring of 1938 and to a tiny three-bedroom house. Fifty feet from the front door ran the railroad tracks, and as each passenger and freight train rumbled past, the windows of the King home rattled in their panes. Berl shared a bed in the north bedroom—the coldest of the three and farthest from the wood and coal heater. In that same bed slept three of his brothers, each one sleeping toe-to-head. His mother had made the mattress out of cotton and ticking made available from a government program. To tie it off, instead of buttons, which were far too precious, she used rounds of felt cut from a discarded hat.

There was seldom meat on the King table. Most meals featured fried potatoes. Occasionally the boys shot a squirrel or blackbird. There were no birthdays celebrated and no exchange of presents, not even at Christmastime. But Christmas was marked with what the King family called "a feast." On that day they dined on chicken.

Early on, Berl had to pitch in, picking cotton and strawberries in the fields, toting ice at the local ice plant, and working a paper route. He wore nothing but hand-me-downs and did his homework by kerosene lamp. In elementary school he had few friends. He said little in class and was painfully shy. The more he could stay unobserved, the happier he was. Never did he complain about his circumstances.

In high school he began to gain self-confidence, in part from success on the basketball court, then in the classroom. He was an avid reader. His favorite writer was John Steinbeck, whose stories spoke of the life of the poor with an authenticity that King recognized at once. A romance in high school ended badly. Though other women would come in and out of his life, he would never marry. He told a sister he wanted to be sure that he could adequately care for a wife. He never wanted to see another woman endure the hardships that his mother did. He graduated from high school in 1949 and observed the occasion by buying himself his first suit.

No sooner out of school, King enlisted in the navy. During the Korean War he was stationed aboard an experimental ship that would fire a salvo of rockets into North Korea, then withdraw and reload. He was proud of his service but hated life at sea. He likened the experience to being a cork that bobbed up and down the entire time. He never got over his seasickness.

After service, in 1954, Berl moved to California and went to work in the sheet metal department of Douglas Aircraft, where his brother Clarence worked. All the while he was putting money away toward flight school. Whenever he had enough saved, he would take another lesson. He adored small planes. For a time he was a pilot for Pat Brown, who was then running for governor. Later he flew commuter flights between Los Angeles, Las Vegas, and Reno.

But King was not one to be content flying the air equivalent of a bus route. He wanted to see the world, he was deeply patriotic, and he was not afraid of taking risks, especially when he could be compensated for his daring. Nor was keeping his mouth shut a burden. It was second nature to him.

By temperament he was perfectly suited for his next employer—Air America, the CIA's proprietary airline. For years, King flew countless covert missions over Laos and Vietnam. Mostly he flew Twin Beech

Volpars on low-level photo reconnaissance missions. Many of these flights put him over the Ho Chi Minh Trail. King reported to Jim Rhyne, one of Air America's most senior pilots. But Rhyne and King were more than colleagues, they were friends. Even among the rough-and-tumble cohorts of Air America, the sangfroid of these two low-flying pilots was the stuff of fables.

Berl never discussed his work with his family and they never asked. Still they worried for him and with good reason. Sometime in 1963 he was shot while flying a mission over Laos. The bullet pierced his right thigh and arm. He came home to convalesce and stayed with his brother Clarence, then a policeman living in California. Only Clarence knew the truth of Berl's wounds. The rest of Berl's family was told that he had been involved in a motorcycle accident.

No sooner had he mended than he was back in the air. It was duty, not money, that motivated him, but the money was deeply appreciated, as if he could use it to correct his own grim past. In 1966 he purchased a new home for his mother and father in Nettleton, Arkansas, right next to the home he had grown up in. It was one of his great pleasures in life to know that his mother would at last have some measure of comfort.

But that peace was shattered in February 1969 when one of King's younger brothers, David, was killed by a sniper in Vietnam. King's sister Velma pleaded with Berl not to go back to Southeast Asia after David's death, but Berl was determined. "Sis," he told her, "I have to. I don't know if you realize how close the Communists are to the United States, and how many of them have infiltrated the government and what a mess everything is in."

By the time that the war in Southeast Asia was winding down, Berl King had become one of the unspoken heroes within the ranks of Air America, a pilot who time and again had survived flying through storm and enemy fire, over fog-enshrouded mountains, and in planes whose airworthiness was often suspect.

It was only fitting that on June 30, 1974, it was Berl King who piloted the very last Air America flight out of Laos. In a modified Twin Beech Volpar, with a short-takeoff-and-landing capability, King prepared to fly from Udorn to Bangkok to Saigon. The Air America base manager in Udorn, Clarence Abadie, watched pensively as King lifted off on course "Tango zero eight." At the bottom of this last flight order, Abadie scribbled a few lines of tribute not only to King but also to the other pilots with whom he had served:

"So ends the last sentence of the final paragraph of the saga that may have an epilogue but never a sequel. It has been to each participating individual an experience which varied according to his role and perspective, however there is a common bond of knowledge and satisfaction having taken part in something worthwhile and with just a slight sense of pity for those lesser souls who could not or would not share in it. This last flight schedule is dedicated to those for whom a previous similar schedule represented an appointment with their destiny."

With the end of the war in Southeast Asia there was suddenly a huge glut of former Air America pilots, "kickers," and crew members looking for jobs with the CIA, but the Agency was loath to take them, fearing that their former affiliation with Air America—by then widely identified as a CIA proprietary—would compromise the security of future covert operations. The Agency's James Glerum, chief of Special Operations Group, had to get special dispensation from his superiors to carve out two exceptions to the Agency's ban on Air America pilots, arguing that they possessed extraordinary flight skills. One of these was Berl King, who was brought into the CIA on staff following the collapse of South Vietnam. The other was Jim Rhyne, King's friend and superior.

Less than four years later it was Rhyne who would deliver the eulogy for King following the North Carolina crash. No one understood better than Rhyne the risks that King had taken during his career. Years earlier, in January 1972, Rhyne had been in an Air America Volpar on a mission dropping leaflets along the Chinese border hoping to get information on a missing U.S. C-123 that was believed shot down by the Chinese. Rhyne's plane came under intense ground fire. Bullets ripped through the aircraft. One of them shredded the control wires connected to the rudder. There were but two thin strands of cable left, and these Rhyne plied deftly, guiding the disabled aircraft home. But the same eighty-five-millimeter rounds that had ripped apart the cables had also shredded Jim Rhyne's leg. There would be no saving it.

That should have been the end of Rhyne's covert career, but six months after his leg was amputated at the knee, he was back flying for Air America. He would go on working covert operations well into his sixties. The Green Berets even bestowed upon him an honorary beret, and his work for the Agency was often among the most sensitive. As Director of Central Intelligence Stansfield Turner is said to have remarked in mock disbelief, "You mean I sent a one-legged man on this mission?"

But there was something else that connected Rhyne to King and the fateful North Carolina crash. It had been Rhyne who was scheduled to fly the aircraft that night, and only at King's insistence did he relent. King was not quite as familiar with the precise landing setup as Rhyne, and his death was, ironically, perhaps the result of his own meticulous precision with the aircraft. His approach was exactly as was called for, but for a foot or two more of altitude. All of this Jim Rhyne reflected on as he prepared to read his brief eulogy for King at the Farmer's Union Funeral Home in Jonesboro, Arkansas. The date was July 19, 1978, and Rhyne, supported by his prosthesis, stood close by his friend's body, enclosed in a casket the undertaker's catalog listed as "Roman Bronze."

"I am here today to represent and speak for Berl's many friends, fellow pilots, air crews and associates," Jim Rhyne began. "Among these professionals of the aviation community both overseas and throughout the country he was known and respected for his outstanding airmanship. As a friend, he was sincere, understanding and generous. As a man he was courageous in the face of danger, calm and resolute in times of stress and kind and helpful to those less fortunate.

"Berl had been flying for many years and had logged over 18,000 hours. Much of his flying was done under difficult, primitive and hazardous conditions in southeast Asia. Berl was one of the best of an elite group of pilots known throughout commercial aviation for their versatility, experience and performance in a demanding and dangerous profession. With his passing the select ranks of these intrepid men are irreversibly thinned. The loss is irretrievable. The hard unforgiving school of unique flight operations is of another time—an era past. Men of his caliber, skill and dedication are rare. The pipeline for their development is virtually gone. Berl's image stands proudly as an example for those few who have the fortitude, persistence, and skill to follow him as a true professional. Those of us who honor him today will always remember him as such. Now that he has left, his spirit continues to serve as it will forever. God rest his soul."

King was buried beside his mother, Mabel, in the Jonesboro Memorial Park Cemetery. His father is buried in another cemetery—in keeping with his wishes, close to his son David, killed in Vietnam in 1969. On Berl King's simple gravestone are written the words "RDM3 US NAVY KOREA." There was nothing from the quarter century after the Korean conflict that the family felt it could safely refer to on the stone.

But for the siblings of Berl King, his death brought neither peace nor answers. Clarence King, his older brother who was in law enforcement, attempted to piece together what had happened. He was stymied at every turn. A senior Agency official made it clear that no one was to make inquiries, including the family. "They wanted us never to open our mouth to anybody and we've never been any different," recalled Clarence two decades later. "We were not to talk about this, period."

The family was not even free to select which attorneys could close Berl King's estate. Instead, the Agency provided the names of three Washington-area lawyers who had been cleared by the CIA. The first attorney demanded that the family give him a checkbook and leave the rest to him. Suspicious, the family went to the second attorney on the Agency's list. A short time later he was found dead, floating in the Potomac River. Finally they turned to Jim Rhyne to handle the estate. King's family asked Rhyne if there was any risk that the family could be sued either by survivors of the crash or by the decedents' families. Rhyne assured them they would never hear from anyone again. What he did not mention is that the families of the two military men killed in the crash, Luis Lebatarde and Walter McCleskey, were never told it was a CIA flight.

Like many families who have lost loved ones in the CIA's clandestine service, it is often hard to separate paranoia from reality, so enveloped are their lives in secrecy. King's entire funeral had been photographed, and only certain people were allowed to attend. Clarence King says he was warned by an Agency employee to be careful what he said on the phone, that his and his siblings' telephones were tapped by the Agency. He was also told that for a time he would be followed by someone from the CIA's security section, that he would do well to simply ignore the person and go about his life. So long as no one mentioned the CIA to the press or public, there would be no problem. Some months later the Agency returned King's wallet to the family. It had been cleaned out of all but a driver's license.

Not long after the crash, Clarence and sister Velma went to pack up King's belongings at his northern Virginia home. It was clear to them that the CIA had already been through the house making sure nothing sensitive was left behind. It was an eerie feeling as if everything had been set up by the Agency—it was all too perfect.

King's bed was still turned down just as it had been when he got up the morning of the flight. His sandals were by the bed, as if awaiting him still. There were only hints as to the nature of his life and travels—Persian rugs, an opium scale of teak in the shape of elephants, a cigarette lighter presented by the president of Thailand. In an effort to identify his assets, the family called King's stockbroker. The moment the broker learned it was with reference to Berl King, she told them to call from another phone, that King's phone was bugged.

Members of King's family are still not completely convinced that Berl was even aboard the ill-fated aircraft. His sister Velma believes that, with the Agency, anything is possible, and knowing her brother's devout sense of duty, she does not put it past him to disappear at the CIA's request and to continue a life of covert operations under a pseudonym. She knows how wildly unlikely all this sounds, but no more so than much of her brother's life in the shadows. "There will always be a tiny bit of doubt in my mind," she says, twenty years after the crash. "I have become so jaded about our government since all this happened. I have become very skeptical. They tell you what they want you to know whether there's a grain of truth or not. A lot of times, they don't tell you anything."

. . .

Seated in the cockpit next to Berl King that July evening in 1978 was Dennis Gabriel, a tall, broad-shouldered figure with thick black hair, muscles upon muscles, and a torso that formed a perfect "V." The two men, King and Gabriel, had known of each other for a long time, their paths first having crossed more than a decade earlier in the Far East. Both men were quiet, self-effacing, but supremely confident of their skills. Both were unflappable.

But that is where any similarities ended. Where King had grown up in abject poverty, Gabriel was the son of privilege. His father, Philip Louis Gabriel, was a wealthy California industrialist, a Christian émigré from Lebanon, whose financial interests ranged from automotive components to a television studio. Denny Gabriel grew up with a cook, a housekeeper, and gardeners. He attended private Catholic schools. At eleven his parents divorced, and Denny, who was close to his mother, seemed to withdraw into himself. Early on, he demonstrated an interest in a life of travel and adventure. He read the stories of Jack London and talked of becoming a fighter pilot like his two uncles.

Despite scoring a hefty 146 on the IQ test, he showed no particular gift for academics. After a stint at Berkeley, he transferred to Washington State University, majoring in political science and French. To these he would later add Arabic and Spanish. Intensely private, he seldom gave even a clue as to his personal goals or feelings. Physically he was a remarkable specimen. At six feet two and 220 pounds, he excelled in the competitive Pacific Coast Conference in both discus and shot put. He possessed an explosive strength tempered by uncommon gentleness.

Gabriel had grown up in California. By 1961 he had set his sights on training for the 1964 Olympics in the decathlon. He graduated from Washington State on June 3, 1962. During his senior year he was approached by a CIA recruiter, and in 1963 he entered the Agency through a program code-named IU Jewel, one of the major Agency recruitment efforts of the decade. Most of those who entered the Jewel Program came out of the military, particularly Special Forces. But some, like Gabriel, were recruited right off the college campus, based on their unique interests and skills, be it trekking, mountain climbing, hunting. All were rugged outdoorsmen. Gabriel had it all—a rugged physique, a black belt in judo, a fearless demeanor, and a pilot's license.

Denny's roommate those first months with the Agency was Bill Miller, a solid six feet one inch. But Gabriel could literally lift Miller over his head without the slightest strain. Denny neither drank nor smoked and constantly watched his diet. Like Berl King, he was painfully shy at social gatherings, and though he possessed the looks of a Hollywood movie star, he winced when invited to parties and squirmed if ever the center of attention. Besides, he was already dating Renier Barnes, a vivacious redhead whose own gregarious ways more than offset his own awkwardness. Renier, also an employee of the Agency and fluent in Portuguese, Spanish, and French, would become his wife on December 30, 1967, at St. Thomas Apostle Church. (The Agency confiscated all the wedding photos except those of immediate family.)

Gabriel's entry into the Agency was intense and exhausting. For eighteen weeks he trained at Camp Perry, taking courses in indoctrination and tradecraft. From there, Gabriel elected to go to Panama and the jungle warfare school, where he learned such arts as knife-throwing, tracking, and living off the land.

Later he was one of twelve Agency recruits sent to mountainous Camp Hale in Colorado for cold weather survival training. Then came three more months studying parachute rigging at Arizona's Marana Air Base, where he was a contemporary of John Merriman's. Denny was packing a parachute on a long table when the news came over the radio that John F. Kennedy had been shot.

A year later he was in Vietnam. Twice he was involved in minor plane crashes. While in Vietnam, he received the Vietnamese Medal of Honor from Vice-President Nguyen Cao Ky. From Vietnam, Gabriel was assigned to Laos. Like Maloney and Deuel, he trained and organized the indigenous peoples to resist the Communists and to monitor and disrupt any convoys of men or matériel moving along the Ho Chi Minh Trail. Denny Gabriel had begun in the Agency's Ground Branch but eventually switched to aviation. His missions remain classified to this day.

What is known is that for nearly a year in the early sixties, he worked with the Nagas, a tribe indigenous to northern India along the Tibetan border. There he trained the Nagas for cross-border operations against the Chinese, part of the Agency's effort in support of Tibetan independence. He was also active in helping the Nagas bury caches of provisions, arms, and radios for later use against the Chinese. He might also have taken part in an Agency program to smuggle nuclear detection systems across the border. When Gabriel returned from the Tibetan border, he brought back a couple of six-foot-long native spears, the grips wrapped in fur. And he returned with one less tooth—pulled by a Punjabi dentist without benefit of anesthesia.

For much of the late 1960s Gabriel was based in Thailand and affiliated with Air America. So far from the States, he could only read and wonder what was becoming of his homeland—the assassination of Martin Luther King, the race riots, the demonstrations against the war. The year 1969 was an annus mirabilis—former CIA director Allen Dulles died, the secret war in Laos was a secret no more, and a massacre by U.S. troops of some 450 villagers at a hamlet called My Lai was making the news. When American astronauts set foot on the moon on July 21, 1969, Gabriel had his ear pressed to a shortwave radio in Bangkok.

Throughout those years his father did what he could to keep him apprised of events at home, routinely sending him American magazines as well as care packages of gourmet foodstuffs, including one of Gabriel's favorites, Lebanese goat cheese, though it often spoiled en route. But the life of a covert officer was taking its toll. Gabriel was working seven days a week and was constantly on the move. U.S. policy in the region was also galling to him, as he watched his fellow Agency officers and American troops risk their lives while the U.S. government waffled on its commitment to the war and pursued seemingly contradictory policies of pacification, war-making, and distribution of relief.

In October 1968 he wrote: "I have had it in the East. When I leave here this time I will never come back. If I do it again it will be to the Middle East. I have finally got this part of the world and this stuff out of my system. The Middle East should prove interesting and right up my alley. Anyway, that's for the future."

In December he wrote his father: "I am getting a little weary of this. It will be almost eight years when I finish here (13 months) and plan to stay in the States awhile and relax." From Bangkok in June 1969 he wrote: "When I finish here I should be in the states a couple of years before I go again. And when I go it's going to be where I want or no place. Since 1962 I have been around the world many times, now I am going to be selective."

His entire career within the Agency remains shrouded in secrecy. But in addition to his covert missions in the Far East, he is known to have taken part in ultrasensitive missions in the Mideast, calling upon his skills as both an Arabist and a paramilitary officer. Evidence of one such mission may be found today in a California safe-deposit box. There is stored more than a mere token of appreciation from one beneficiary of Gabriel's efforts.

In 1964 Gabriel was presented a one-of-a-kind Rolex watch from the ruler of Jordan, King Hussein. Gabriel had trained and set up an elite corps of bodyguards and officers to protect the king at a time of great peril to him. The watch, 18-karat gold, is studded with diamonds and the face is adorned with the king's crest. On the back, in Arabic, are inscribed the words "Deepest Gratitude." Gabriel's brother, Ron, has kept the watch in the safe-deposit box. One day he will give it to Gabriel's son, Sean, now twenty-seven.

In the mid-seventies Gabriel lived in McLean, Virginia, with his wife and son. He would frequently disappear on month-long TDYs—temporary duties—overseas, particularly in the Mideast and Central America. He became increasingly active in training other paramilitary officers. More than once he declined senior administrative positions, knowing that a desk job was not for him.

But if he had had a mind to, he could easily have retired at forty to a life of comparative ease. With a personal real estate portfolio worth $2 million to $3 million, he had no financial motivation for continuing a career as a covert operative, though those who worked with him had no idea either of his rarefied background or of his own financial position. He continued to take pride in being as gutsy as anyone the Agency could put in the field. He was never an ideologue, but he remained a stickler for individual freedom and hostile to any foreign power he viewed as a threat to personal liberty. It was as simple as that.

The night Gabriel died he left on his desk a résumé rife with the fictions and inventions of a covert operative. His bogus cover ID said he was a civilian employee of "The Department of the Air Force, Service and Support Group, Detachment Eight, AFESPA, Bolling Air Force Base." He listed himself as a "GS-13 Operations Officer." Also among his possessions was a bogus business card from Jim Rhyne.

Dennis Gabriel is buried at Rose Hills Memorial Park in Whittier, California, space 4, lot 2713, beside his father. On his gravestone are listed the dates of birth, July 14, 1939, and death, July 13, 1978. He died one day shy of his thirty-ninth birthday. At the funeral on July 19 Ron Gabriel offered a few brief thoughts on behalf of Denny, who was both his brother and his closest friend. "Please remember his loyalty and gentleness to his family," he said. "His quiet service to country . . . God bless us as He did him and make the living worthy of the dead."

. . .

From the North Carolina crash site, Special Forces officers had followed the trail of blood deep into the cornfields. There, buried beneath a heap of cornhusks was a man, broken and twisted. His name was Alexander MacPherson, and he was swiftly medevaced by helicopter first to an army hospital and later to Cape Fear Hospital in Fayetteville. For five days MacPherson lay in a coma. When he came to, he found himself lying naked on a hospital bed, a large light overhead, and two massive tubes, each as big as a garden hose, coming out of his chest. The ribs on the right side of his chest had been smashed, the broken bones driven back out through his lungs. His legs were scarred and bruised, his skull fractured. His arms were laid out flat, his hands sandbagged on either side to prevent the slightest movement.

He had no idea where he was or what had happened to him. From the tubes that went in and out of him he surmised that he had been shot. "Oh my God," he thought to himself, "you mean I've got to go back to that place again?" "That place." What place was that? he wondered, through a mind-numbing fog of sedatives. He felt little pain. That would come later.

This man lying in the bed was an enigma for the hospital staff. It was not clear what was keeping him alive. And whenever he spoke, he spoke in flawless German. The hospital brought in a German nurse to tend to him.

MacPherson would remain a mystery patient. At five feet eight and 180 pounds, he was in remarkably robust physical condition for a man of forty-eight—the product of a lifetime of mountain-climbing and an unwavering daily regimen of swimming and hiking. But then, the doctors and nurses had no idea what sort of man they were dealing with—the ultimate CIA paramilitary officer.

Within a few short months MacPherson—or Mac, as he was known—would be back in an airplane parachuting again, many high-risk missions still ahead of him.

There are few major hot spots where MacPherson had not been. To a long succession of CIA heads, among them Dick Helms, William Colby, Bill Casey, and Stansfield Turner, he had been viewed as one of the Agency's most reliable operatives. Paratrooper and rigger, anti-Communist and counterterrorist, he had worked behind enemy lines on at least three continents over the course of as many decades. In his North Carolina home are photos, plaques, and medals from a career spent under cover. Not the least of these is a citation, with accompanying gold medallion, that reads:

"The United States of America, To All Who Shall See These Presents, Greeting. This is to certify that the President of the United States of America authorized by Act of Congress has awarded the Airmen's Medal to Alexander MacPherson United States Air Force For Heroism Republic of Panama on 20 of August 1964. Given under my hand in the city of Washington this 29th day of April, 1965."

MacPherson smiles coyly when asked what mission won for him this distinction. There is nothing in the newspapers or the history books to suggest that anything of consequence happened on that day in Panama— which is exactly as MacPherson wants it. "Don't bother trying to find out anything," he says. "You'll just be spinning your wheels. You'll never find out."

Eight years later, in 1973, the CIA presented him with the prestigious Donovan Award—the reason for that recognition also remains a secret. And he may be the only CIA person to have twice received the Exceptional Service Medal from the Agency. What do they mean to him? "That I was there and forgot to duck," he says, laughing. Among his memorabilia is a photo of him with President Ronald Reagan. Everywhere are clues, but none of them add up to anything that would shed light on his clandestine career.

And even after he formally retired from the Agency in 1986, he went on for another eight years to serve in a variety of sensitive positions, particularly in the Mideast gathering intelligence on terrorist organizations. Like the movie character Zelig, his presence is barely discernible in the background of many historical frames. Among the places he is known to have served are Jordan, Sudan, and Ethiopia.

Tom Twetten, former head of the CIA's clandestine service, remembers him well. "He's a crazy guy," he says. "Crazy," as in daring beyond words. "He did some extraordinary work from time to time and in between times he was a royal pain in the ass." Twetten encountered MacPherson in India in the late seventies, where he apparently left some Indians with the impression he was a four-star general. Later, Twetten recalls, he was instrumental in somehow stopping Palestinians from coming over the border from Syria and firing rockets into Israel. Toward the end of the Cold War he worked behind the Iron Curtain on a mission involving the cooperation of half a dozen governments. That operation is still deemed so sensitive that Twetten will not even hint at its purpose.

But even as MacPherson's career winds down, he will not acknowledge that he is or ever was with the CIA.

Little is known of his background. He was born in Chicago in 1930 or 1931 and was educated in Scotland and Germany, where he studied electrical engineering. He lived in Europe for sixteen years. Given his thick Scottish brogue, he could easily be mistaken for a native of that country. But he also speaks Spanish, French, German, and Russian, and is known to be conversant in an Eastern European tongue or two as well as Arabic. During the 1950s he served as an Air Commando with the U.S. Air Force, a precursor to the elite Special Forces. In the course of his career he has been shot at by Katyusha rockets, AK-47s, a variety of small arms, and even SA-7 missiles.

He has routinely parachuted from altitudes of thirty thousand feet and higher where sixty-below temperatures can freeze a man's eyeballs, where the slightest gap in the filling of a tooth can reduce a man to desperate agony, and where, if the joints are not scrupulously purged of gases, the jumper will exhibit symptoms associated with diver's bends.

In his world—as well as Berl King's and Denny Gabriel's—expertise and survival were never more than a hairbreadth apart. And still there was a place for luck. The crash in North Carolina was not the first such downed aircraft MacPherson is known to have crawled away from.

MacPherson knew both King and Gabriel. He had flown with them many times in the days of Air America. But in an odd way he knew very little of either man. That was how he wanted it. "I have purposely cut myself off from these kinds of things, much as I thought these guys were really great. Even when I worked with them I really didn't try to know them too well. It would have made it tougher to do the job we were trying to do. I have made it a point of not getting to know the people I work with. It is one of the cardinal rules I have followed. When engaged in work, I operate on a need-to-know basis, not just nice-to-know."

Today MacPherson wonders at the young stock of Agency officers coming through the ranks and worries for them. One young man, intent upon a career as a paramilitary officer, saw in MacPherson a kind of mentor and expressed an interest in accompanying him on an assignment.

"Do you think you could live in a foreign country?" MacPherson asked the young man.

"Yes," he said boldly.

"Smile," responded MacPherson. The young man smiled a toothy smile. "No," persisted MacPherson, "open your mouth." Inside, Mac-Pherson was looking at some $20,000 worth of American orthodontic work. "Every time you open your mouth," he said, "you will be telling people where you come from. You can still make the trip but we will have to knock out a few teeth and things like that," he said half jokingly. "Living in a foreign country, you have to have absolutely impeccable credentials, right down to the last tooth." Any mistake can be fatal.

After so many brushes with death, MacPherson remains almost at ease with the idea of his own mortality. "I really absolutely no longer fear death. I've sort of been there," he says. "I came within a whisper of dying." That is not to say that he is ready to die. More than death, he fears being crippled. From his earliest mission to his most recent, he does not get on a plane or embark on any mission without first intoning the same silent prayer that he learned from his school days in Europe, a prayer that dates back more than 350 years to the English Civil War. "Lord, we are about to go into battle and I know that most of the day I will forget about you. Please don't forget about me." That prayer has served him well.

He has known many men who have died. Some are represented by nameless stars in the CIA's Book of Honor. And he has known many men who, like himself, have survived against the odds, among them Dick Holm, whose crash in the Congo in 1965 left him disfigured. MacPherson and Holm have been friends for twenty years, though the two of them have never spoken a word to each other of their respective plane crashes. MacPherson believes in honoring those who perished, not in dwelling on near misses. He is fond of citing lines from Laurence Binyon's poem "For the Fallen" that appear in a place where many British SAS soldiers are buried:

> *They shall not grow old*
> *As we that are left grow old.*
> *Age shall not weary them*
> *Nor the years condemn.*
> *At the going down of the sun*
> *And in the morning*
> *We shall remember them.*

Just what the three CIA officers—King, Gabriel, MacPherson—were doing that July night more than twenty years ago remains something of a mystery. Relatives of Berl King and Denny Gabriel each have their own theories based in part on hints from CIA colleagues and in part from the irrepressible need to find some transcendent meaning in the loss of a loved one.

The King family was given to believe that that night's operation was preparation for a specific hostage rescue mission. Perhaps. Denny Gabriel's brother, Ron, a medical professor, is convinced that that night was a practice run for the insertion of a CIA team into Cuba, where it was suspected that a Soviet brigade was present. In fact, some months later the presence of such a brigade was confirmed, nearly scuttling the SALT II treaty. Also plausible. Hardest of all to accept is the idea that it was merely a routine training exercise, a fluke accident oblivious to consummate skill and courage. One man who knows the truth about that night's mission is Alexander MacPherson. The lone survivor, he's not saying a word.

PART THREE

Chaos and Terrorism

CHAPTER 11

Indestructible

SUNDAY EVENING, April 17, 1983, had been a festive time for CIA employees stationed in Beirut. Thirty-nine-year-old James Lewis, a veteran covert operative, and his Vietnamese-born wife, Monique, had invited Agency colleagues to their apartment for a dinner as only Lewis could prepare. A gourmet chef, he had spent hours fixing the meal—nothing but the freshest ingredients, the best spices, the perfect wine. The Agency's top Middle East specialist, Robert C. Ames, was in town on temporary duty, and there was a sense that what was happening here made this shattered capital city, once likened to Paris, some sort of epicenter—a place of deadly intrigue, espionage, and ancient rivalries. In short, Jim Lewis's kind of place. Monique, too, had special reason to celebrate this evening. The next day was to be her first on the job, working as a CIA secretary in the embassy. It was spring, a time of hope even in Beirut, and a time for Jim Lewis to put his culinary skills to the test on behalf of friends old and new.

Across town somewhere, other preparations, no less elaborate, were under way. Two thousand pounds of high explosives were being readied. The target: the U.S. Embassy, Beirut. For the driver of the truck that would carry the massive bomb and steer it squarely into the embassy's glass and concrete facade, there were preparations of another kind to be made, for whatever promised glory might await, it would be not in this world, but in the next.

The Beirut embassy had come to be the gathering point to which many seasoned CIA operatives had made their way. Over the years, these same individuals had come to know one another and to share a common history. Like a pooling of mercury, they had been called upon to go their separate ways over the years, but inevitably would be drawn together again in places such as Beirut where the stakes were high and so, too, the rewards. What the Agency could not yet know was that Beirut was the face of its own future, a place where hostilities would have little to do with the Cold War, where the enemy belonged to no foreign embassy, wore no uniform, and would hide behind not a border of barbed wire but a smile.

The Agency operatives in Beirut each had their cover, their bogus stories, their mundane tasks that they hoped would shield them from suspicion. Jim Lewis was listed as an embassy political officer. His wife, Monique, was said to be a State Department secretary. Kenneth Eugene Haas, the Agency's thirty-eight-year-old chief of station, was also listed as a political officer. Recently married, he had served in many sensitive posts—Bangladesh, Iran, and Oman among them. Frank J. Johnston was carried as an econ officer, as was Murray J. McCann.

Fifty-nine-year-old William Richard Sheil was said to be a civilian employee of the army. A veteran of Vietnam, he had made a name for himself as a superb interrogator, a man who relied on honey, not horror, to wrangle information from his subjects. Deborah M. Hixon, a thirty-year-old from Colorado and daughter of an airline pilot, was said to be a foreign affairs analyst with State. Phyliss Faraci, forty-four, was an "administrative assistant," under cover with the State Department.

Less than twenty-four hours after the Sunday evening dinner, all but one of them would be dead.

. . .

James Lewis bore little resemblance to the fictional James Bond, but in Lewis, 007 would have more than met his match. A lanky six feet two, he had boyish good looks, a full head of dark hair parted perfectly, kind eyes, and an easy smile. He was most comfortable dicing onions in the kitchen, listening to a French chanteuse, or sipping a good Bordeaux. He might as easily have been taken for a fresh-faced teacher at a prep school as one of the Agency's premier covert operatives.

A personable fellow, he thrived on entertaining and mixed easily with diverse peoples, but even those who worked with him daily would later reflect that they knew almost nothing about him. It was not a dark reclusiveness, but a talent for appearing open and guileless, all the while giving up nothing of himself. But those who underestimated him did so at their peril—literally. Fluent in Arabic, French, and Vietnamese, he was an expert with an M-14, a .45, a parachute, and scuba gear. He was as capable of underwater infiltration as dropping silently from the skies. His work for the Agency had taken him to every country in Southeast Asia and most of those in Europe and the Middle East.

From earliest boyhood, James Lewis had but one ambition—to be a soldier. Not just any soldier, but a paratrooper. There was no great mystery to his attraction to the military. His father, James Forrest Pittman, had been a paratrooper in the 101st Airborne. Lewis was born James Forrest Pittman, Jr., on February 29, 1944. His father was overseas fighting World War II. Little Jimmy would be nineteen months old before he would first set eyes on his father. Forrest, as his father was known, returned to his rural hometown of Coffeeville, Mississippi, and like many of his generation, was greeted as something of a local hero. His three sons and daughter would sit wide-eyed listening to his accounts of combat far beyond the confines of Yalobusha County.

But in 1952 Forrest simply walked out on the family. He was never to return again. A heavy drinker and a poor provider, he vanished. Lewis's mother, Antoinette—Toni to her friends—moved to Gulfport, Mississippi, and struggled to raise four young children. Much of the burden fell upon the slender shoulders of the oldest, Jimmy, then aged eight. Neither as a child nor as an adult would he permit himself to speak of his father, but the lingering pain of that loss would define the landscape of his life for many years to come. Already a sober child, Jimmy learned to hold his emotions tight within, sharing them with no one. He was as slow to show affection as he was to show pain. It was not that he did not feel both, as would later be abundantly clear, but that he would not allow himself to show any vulnerability. And so, even as a child, he became practiced in the art of deception, accustomed to living with secrets and self-containment—liabilities in all but a spy's trade.

To his sister and two brothers, he was seen as the consummate leader, a boy who squared his shoulders and naturally assumed command in every situation. An aunt would always think of him as "indestructible." His military demeanor and self-discipline provided a way to conceal the hurt behind a facade of spit and polish, and at the same time, to obliquely express his adoration for the father who had disappeared. It was no coincidence that Jimmy and his two brothers would all become paratroopers in their father's image.

Lewis took it upon himself to watch over this cadre of three younger siblings, not as a protector or ersatz father, but as a drill sergeant, demanding obedience and seeking to toughen them up. His sister, Susan, recalls him leading the three of them out on "a combat expedition"—that was what he called it—into a neighboring swamp. Deep into the morass, Jim Lewis announced that the others would have to fend for themselves. He disappeared, leaving his siblings to find their own way home. Hours later when they appeared, safe but exhausted, he reviewed them with pleasure. "Oh, you made it back," he said, confident that he was whipping them into shape.

The world as he knew it was plenty tough. To win his love, one first had to pass muster. When he took his little sister and brothers to the movies, he insisted they walk "ten paces" behind him. It was simply a privilege of rank.

Though a mediocre student, he had a voracious interest in geography and military affairs and was said to have read *The World Book Encyclopedia* nearly cover-to-cover. Other times he buried himself in comic books featuring square-jawed soldier heroes invulnerable to fear or pain. His favorite hangout was the local army surplus store with its camouflage gear, its footlockers, machetes, vests, and other accoutrements of war—all of his father's vintage.

As a child he was not a troublemaker, though at times he would do something that would unsettle his mother and reveal something of the turmoil within. At age twelve he ran away to New Orleans, but, ever dutiful, he left a note for his mother, who notified the police. A day later he was returned to the house. Another time he and his sister pilfered three dollars from a collection box at a local church. His mother found out and had them return the money to the preacher along with an apology. In 1959 his mother married George Lewis. He promptly adopted fifteen-year-old James, who changed his name to James Foley Lewis, the Foley being his mother's maiden name. Enraged that the family was moving to Phoenix, he took a stick and shattered the glass in the French doors of the dining room—perhaps the only such outburst he ever allowed himself to have. But after the move, by all accounts, he settled down and seemed to flourish.

By high school, Jimmy stood six feet two, a rangy kid intent upon putting muscle on his lanky frame. Often he could be found pumping iron in the garage until his face flushed with exhaustion. In a vain attempt to bulk up, he devoured a high-calorie concoction that resembled a pasty mix of flour and water. If others saw him as indestructible, that was how he had come to view himself as well. He once told his brother Tom, "The day I start to get weaker is the day I want to die."

Tough as Lewis was, he was never a brawler, though on one occasion as a teenager he was seen going out with a businesslike look on his face and a six-foot length of steel chain wrapped menacingly around his narrow waist. In high school he was an active member of ROTC. To school he wore only button-down shirts in gray and white, a self-styled uniform, which his sister ironed each morning in exchange for a ride for her boyfriend. The essence of gung ho, he scrupulously followed events in Vietnam, tracking each development on a map of the country that hung in his bedroom.

A leap-year baby, Jim Lewis enlisted in the army on his eighteenth birthday, February 28, 1962. Lewis had his eye on wearing the Green Beret of Special Forces. He instantly distinguished himself, first in training, then in combat. His quiet manner, boyish good looks, and unflappable courage led some to compare him to World War II Medal of Honor winner Audie Murphy.

By early 1967 Lewis was in command of an elite unit of Vietnamese tribal Montagnards, known as Mike Force. Their mission was to stave off impending disaster, to defend or relieve Special Forces when they found themselves under siege or about to be overrun. "Indefatigable" was how one of his commanding officers would later describe Lewis. "His enthusiasm, aggressiveness, cheerfulness, and energy were not only hallmarks of his personality but they were so contagious that the simple, uneducated, and very suspicious native tribesmen in his unit were infected with the same qualities . . . The empathy and compassion which Captain Lewis felt for the Vietnamese people was genuine and sincere. They recognized this rare quality in him and responded to him when no other 'outsider' could make any headway in dealing with them. He comes very close to possessing that unique ability to be all things to all men."

Time and again Lewis proved himself in the field. On April 3, 1967, as a second lieutenant in the 5th Special Forces Group (Airborne), he was wounded. For this he would receive the Purple Heart. Just seven days later he was back on a mission deep within hostile North Vietnamese territory. As the head of a Special Forces reconnaissance platoon he and his men were moving through a dense jungle when they came under intense automatic-weapons fire from three sides. Instead of retreating or hunkering down, he led his men on an attack of Viet Cong positions and drove them back. "His fearless leadership contributed greatly to the defeat of the hostile forces and prevented serious casualties to his men," read his citation for the first of an extraordinary four Bronze Stars he would receive. Add to these an Air Medal, a Gallantry Cross, and innumerable other medals, ribbons, and commendations.

A notebook he carried, though somewhat encoded, reveals something of his life in the field. On one page he wrote:

Message from Catcher to Chestnut

VNSF [Vietnamese Special Forces] have planned an operation and Camp Commander has approved. They have requested that the following items be given to them for the operation:

4 PRC-10 Radios

1 LMG W/1000 RDS Ammo

50 or more Carbine Mags

20 Bar Magazines

20 Hand Parachute Flares

Both USSF [United States Special Forces] This location

Have agreed that the Items are Necessary
For the Successful Completion of the Patrol
      Over "Break"

Elsewhere in the notebook are references to tapes of music he carried with him. One tape featured an eclectic mix of Patsy Cline, Brenda Lee, and Sarah Vaughan. He even jotted down some random meals. One such entry read: "Lunch = 1 duck egg . . . 1 pat rice . . . 5 glasses milk."

Many of James Lewis's military operations with Special Forces had been conducted under the direction of the CIA. By the spring of 1969 he had decided that he would apply to work for the Agency directly. With his background in Special Forces, his familiarity with Vietnam, his gift for languages, and his reputation for both valor and discretion, he was exactly what the Agency was looking for.

In a May 21, 1969, letter of recommendation to the Agency, one of Lewis's superiors, Colonel Eleazar Parmly IV, wrote: "I can personally vouch for Lou's courage under protracted periods of intense personal danger. Aware of the impropriety of over-statements in letters of this type, I would classify Lou as fearless or, if he experiences any fear there is absolutely no manifestation of that fear in his actions, thinking, or attitudes. His presence instills calm and his tall, muscular, tiger-like physique not only furnishes physical strength in times of stress but also generates an increased sense of confidence, resolution, and strength in his men and his leaders. When everyone else is worried and jumpy, Lou can break the tension by a natural gesture or expression or a pertinent but humorous remark. He is always in the advance guard of his unit when there is danger and he never draws back from the defensive point because of the risk to his own person."

In 1970 Lewis was brought into the CIA under the Jewel Program, which sought out those with unique paramilitary skills. The Agency returned him to Southeast Asia's jungles, where he was made all too familiar with desperate situations, particularly in Laos. There his code name was Sword. On January 26, 1972, James "Sword" Lewis wrote: "I have been at Long Tieng since before Christmas. I took 2500 people from Savannakhet up there to help out. I now have 1500 left. Things are pretty bad, nobody can or will help us now. Every soldier in Laos is committed and we are still being pushed back. Long Tieng will be our Dien Bien Phu. We will make it or break it there. I can't complain about my guys . . . but I just don't know how much longer we can hold. The Viet Minh have 130 mm artillery and tanks, we have rifles. The Air Force can't knock out the enemy artillery. All those fine weapons systems the U.S. has spent millions on are about 95% ineffective, the ultimate weapon is still the infantryman."

. . .

By the end of 1974 even the most stalwart supporters of the war in Vietnam had come to recognize that loss was inevitable. The United States had put its military and political prestige on the line, and the CIA, in support of that policy—sometimes reluctantly—had committed untold resources to help hold the line against Communism in the region. To those Agency operatives in the front line, neither the drawing-down of the U.S. military nor the proximity of an end to the conflict brought any relief.

On the contrary, as the mission became more desperate, the demands upon them increased. One of the final missions of the CIA was to assist in waging a delaying action. The final mission was to monitor the inexorable advance of North Vietnamese troops, if for no other reason than to provide U.S. planners with a timetable for the evacuation of those South Vietnamese who had been intelligence or military assets and who would otherwise be imprisoned or executed by the North Vietnamese. In those final frantic months it was the unenviable task of men like James Lewis to chronicle defeat.

In the spring of 1975 James Lewis was acting as an adviser and observer attached to a Vietnamese general named Nghi. Lewis was said to be in the command bunker of an air base that was overrun. The army, beating a chaotic retreat before advancing North Vietnamese troops, was in disarray. Lewis and others attempted to escape by night.

Near a place called Phan Rang, some 160 miles northeast of Saigon, a B-40 rocket landed near Lewis. He found himself in a ditch beside the road, trying to stanch the flow of blood from his wounds. It was there that Lewis fell into enemy hands and was taken prisoner. The date was April 11, 1975. He would eventually be taken to the notorious Sontay prison, twenty-five miles northwest of Hanoi. Five years earlier, on November 21,

1970, that prison had gained a kind of fame when American Special Forces staged a daring raid on the camp in an effort to rescue American POWs said to be held there.

Instead, the elite commando unit found the camp deserted, and though they returned unharmed and were later decorated, the raid was emblematic of a war in which even the utmost of valor often could not produce results.

Sontay prison was a remnant of old French colonial days. The buildings were of concrete and red tile in a U-shape. Around the camp was a high wall and on top of that ran a perimeter of wire. Even without the wall and wire there was little hope of escape and nowhere to escape to. For several months Lewis appeared to be the only prisoner in the camp. When a group of missionaries and an AID worker were later imprisoned there, they were forbidden from speaking to Lewis. To them he was merely a shadowy figure whom they would occasionally see shuffling across the compound's courtyard under the watchful eye of a guard.

For months, thirty-one-year-old Lewis languished in a cell at the largely abandoned prison camp, its earlier American inmates having long since been released. His few possessions included a mirror and a comb.

Lewis tried to convince his captors that he was a civilian employee of the embassy, a State Department consular officer. But his captors were not taken in by his cover story. Agency comrades of Lewis suggest that the State Department inadvertently did something or said something following his capture that further compromised his cover.

For this he would pay a dear price. At Sontay Lewis endured relentless interrogation and torture. For months he was made to live in solitary confinement in a tiny concrete cell. Above him, night and day, burned an agonizingly bright light. Overhead was a loudspeaker blaring Vietnamese music twenty-four hours a day. Sleep was all but impossible. He was given nothing but a small bowl of rice and a smattering of unrecognizable greens—no meat, fish, or other protein. Already lean, he sloughed off thirty-plus pounds. Nor did his captors ever treat the wounds he suffered from the rocket attack. These he was left to minister by himself, relying on the medical training he had received as a Green Beret. After several months' isolation, dysentery, and sleeplessness Jim Lewis had been pushed beyond the point that even he could tolerate.

There is some dispute within the ranks of the Agency as to whether he was ever technically "broken" by his tormentors, but this is largely a matter of semantics. The simple fact is that Jim Lewis, the toughest of the tough, finally talked. The consummate soldier, he later came to regard his capitulation as an act of betrayal and weakness for which he would long reproach himself.

Back in the United States his mother, Toni, was receiving sporadic reports from the CIA indicating that her son had been taken prisoner, but as the months dragged on, and the information they provided became more and more scant, she began to get angry, fearing that the Agency had written off her son as the final casualty of the war. There were many in government then who were only too eager to blot out all memory of so ignominious a defeat.

Again and again the Agency urged Toni Lewis not to speak to anyone about her son's situation, suggesting that it might imperil him. Toni Lewis was by turns first trusting, then suspicious, then resentful. She began to wonder whether the Agency's constant request for silence reflected its concern for her son's well-being or for its own tarnished image.

Finally, in the late fall of 1975 Jim Lewis's situation improved markedly. His bowl suddenly held more food. The grueling interrogations ceased. His captors even fitted him out with a new shirt and heavy blue work pants. He was given a new pair of shoes. A trained intelligence officer, Lewis must have sensed that his release was imminent, that he was being fattened up so that it would appear that he had been treated in accordance with the strictures of the Geneva Convention. But before he was released, he and the other prisoners were taken to a museum in Hanoi replete with displays documenting what was said to be the inhumane war waged by the imperialist United States against the country of Vietnam. On October 30, 1975, Jim Lewis found himself on a C-47 cargo plane headed for Vientiane, the Laotian capital. Then it was on to Bangkok and finally California.

For several days Jim Lewis convalesced in a hospital bed. Though he was somewhat emaciated, he appeared to be in good spirits, the same tough and indestructible James Lewis that he had always been. But his family could sense that he had been changed by the experience. Try though he might to keep his emotions in, they were now nearer to the surface, and the months alone in solitary had, for the first time, given him a chance to reflect on his own mortality.

For many years Lewis's sister, Susan, had been working to reestablish ties with their father, Forrest, and one by one, Lewis's brothers and sister had come around to a kind of reconciliation with him. But not Jim Lewis. Not once in all the years since childhood would he permit himself to speak of him. Each time that Susan gingerly broached the subject or suggested that perhaps it was time for Jim, too, to make his peace and reconnect, Lewis had dismissed it out of hand.

But on November 19, 1975, only days after his release from Sontay prison, Lewis, who was then staying with his sister, asked about his father for the first time. "Susan," he said, "I want to get in touch with Forrest."

Susan told him she had an address for him. Lewis asked her to go to the store and buy some white typing paper. When she returned, he went upstairs to the guest room, fed a sheet of paper into an old manual typewriter, and began to write a letter to the man he had not seen or spoken to since he was eight years old. He was now thirty-one, a veteran of wars, overt and covert, and as battle-hardened as any man of his generation. For three hours he composed the letter. When it was done, he came downstairs and hesitatingly asked Susan to read it and make sure it was all right. It was so unlike Jim Lewis to seek the counsel of his younger sister.

Susan sat down to read the three-page letter but could barely get past the first two words. It began "Dear Daddy." After twenty-three years of burying the pain, Jim Lewis had become a child again.

"I guess that you will be a little surprised to receive this letter after so many years," he wrote. "I guess that you know that I just got out of prison in North Vietnam a few days ago. While I was there I had a lot of time to think about things. I realized that there were a lot of things I had neglected to do over the years that I really wanted to do, but for some reason . . . I had left these things undone. I resolved that if I ever got out, there were several things that I would do immediately. The first and most important was to write this letter.

"It's hard to explain why I waited so long. The reason is not because I was bitter about you leaving us so long ago. I really believe that it was for the better for both you and Momma. Although I didn't understand it when you left, and it took several more years before I did understand, I really believe that you and Momma were not right for each other and as a result of the separation both of you have found happier lives than if you had remained together. As for me, I guess that I missed the things that most children get from a father who is always there to take care of them, but in the long run I think that growing up on my own gave me something that would serve me much better in my adult life.

"Growing up on my own taught me independence and to take care of myself and not to depend upon others. Before you left home you taught me to be tough, you made me learn to shoot your shotgun even when I had to stand up against an old pine tree to keep it from knocking me down each time I fired it. You taught me not to be afraid of anything by making me ride the wildest horse we had until I overcame my fear. I learned not to be afraid of hard work in the cotton fields behind our house in Coffeeville. All these things have served me well since I left home when I was 17 and joined the Army. Most of the past thirteen years of my life have been spent fighting in Indochina, and those traits I got from you got me through a lot of hard times over there.

"I guess that the reason I never got in touch with you was because I was just so engrossed in what I was doing over there that I lost almost all contact with my family. I've been very poor in keeping in touch with Momma, Susan and everyone else. I can't explain very well why I haven't contacted you, but I can assure you it wasn't because of any bitterness on my part."

Lewis spoke of his sister's recent "reunion" with her father in Coffeeville and of how much he, too, yearned to return and have a reunion of his own. "I'd really like to go back there and see you and all the rest of the family. Susan and I have been talking about going to Coffeeville this summer if it's all right with the rest of the family and you. I hope that we could all have sort of a reunion there this summer. It may seem strange, but I always think of Coffeeville when I think of home. I was only there for a short while, but I think of it as my hometown."

At the time, Lewis was engaged to a twenty-one-year-old Vietnamese woman named Hang. "I want her to meet you," he wrote.

He spoke sympathetically of the accident his father had recently suffered. He had been working on a shrimp boat out of Galveston, Texas, and a thick rope had become wrapped around his ankle as the boat pulled out, mangling his leg. A short time later it had to be surgically amputated from the knee down, and he was fitted with a prosthesis. Jim Lewis wrote that he was glad to hear that his father was now doing better.

"You can write to me at Susan's address. I will be here long enough to receive a letter from you, and as soon as I get to Washington I will write and send you my address . . . I'll be waiting to hear from you, and plan to stay in close contact with you in the future." The letter closed simply, "Love, Jimmy." It had taken a lifetime to utter those words.

But unbeknownst to Jim Lewis, his letter would be lost in the mail. His father recovered from the physical injuries of the boating accident, but not from the emotional scar of losing his leg. Always a man doubtful of his own self-worth, Forrest Pittman sank deeper and deeper into drink and self-pity. He considered himself to be useless. He lamented the breakup of his family, and the decades of silence between him and his eldest son, James, weighed upon him. On August 21, 1977, Forrest Pittman drove to his favorite place, the boat landing on Enid Lake. There he took his own life with a .22-caliber pistol shot to the head. He left no note. He was sixty years old.

Jim Lewis was never to receive a reply to his letter, or to see his father again. The courage it had taken him to break his long silence had been for naught. At the burial of James Forrest Pittman in Coffeeville, his eldest son was nowhere to be found.

It was not long after the death of Forrest Pittman that a letter arrived at the home of his sister. It was Jim Lewis's "Dear Daddy" letter. Nearly two years had elapsed since it had been mailed, then suddenly, without explanation, it appeared in the mailbox. Forrest Pittman's sister Elizabeth wonders to this day how that letter might have changed the lives of both Forrest and his son James had it arrived on time. "We wished that letter had been delivered," she says. "If Forrest had gotten the letter it might have changed his thinking." It might, she believes, have persuaded him not to take his own life. And had Forrest answered the letter, as his sister Elizabeth says he surely would have, it might have given Jim Lewis the sense of peace that had so long eluded him.

Both men yearned for a reconciliation. As it was, father and son would go to the grave mistakenly believing that the other no longer cared.

. . .

Jim Lewis underwent a slow and difficult reentry into society following his release from Sontay prison. It was his nature to seek refuge in work, but the Agency understood that he would first have to come to terms with his prison experience. He returned to Washington, and, having survived interrogation as a prisoner, he submitted himself to a far friendlier but grueling debriefing at the hands of fellow CIA officers who needed to determine the extent to which his prison confessions may have compromised security. Agency colleague Larry Baldwin recalls meeting a dispirited Lewis in the halls of headquarters at Langley.

Baldwin had known him as "a man of great bravery." The Lewis he encountered now was subject to more introspection. "He felt he had failed himself and failed the Agency." But Baldwin and his Agency colleagues knew better. Many of them had been trained in the art of interrogation, learning how to prey upon a man's worst fears, to exploit his anxieties and feelings of vulnerability. They knew that no man, not even the steely James Lewis, could long withstand a concerted effort by skilled interrogators. Colleagues went to great lengths to reassure him that he had not been weak, but merely human.

The Agency provided Lewis with psychological counseling and a period to "decompress." In 1976 and 1977 it paid for him to attend George Washington University, where he got his bachelor's degree in French language and literature. When he had completed his academic course and the Agency's "rehabilitation" program, he was ready to be reassigned. But rather than simply throw him back into an international post, they sought something less stressful and more familiar: Chicago.

It was an unconventional assignment and politically sensitive. In 1977 Lewis moved to Des Plaines, a suburb northwest of Chicago. At that very time, the Senate and House were conducting hearings into CIA abuses and instances of domestic spying. Now here was James Lewis, a covert CIA operative, setting up shop in America's heartland, still assigned to the Agency's Operations Directorate, East Asia Division. On his résumé, years later, he would write that he spent those two years with the State Department in Washington.

In Des Plaines he married Monique, a soft-spoken Vietnamese woman whom Lewis had met in North Carolina during one of many returns to Fort Bragg. Monique, then thirty, had been educated in Switzerland and France, spoke fluent French, and had a degree in pharmacology. She was a woman of considerable beauty and intelligence but asked few questions of her husband and his work.

The only hint of what Jim Lewis was doing in Chicago comes from his sister, Susan, who found herself momentarily a player in CIA intrigue. For years she had kidded her brother that she was fully capable of doing the kind of shadowy espionage work that he did, never imagining that he would take her up on it. Then one night Jim Lewis called and asked if she wanted to play a small but key role in one such mission. "Of course," said Susan. Not long after, she was asked to fill out some government forms and to provide her brother with a photograph. To assist in the scheme, she would need some marginal clearance.

The full details of the mission were never revealed to her, but this much her brother shared with her: He had persuaded an "Arab student" in Chicago to routinely monitor and report on some activities, presumably within the Arab community or among other Arab students. In exchange for the intelligence the student provided, the Agency was paying him a $1,000 monthly retainer. Lewis had told the student that he lived in California with his girlfriend. That was the role Susan was to play. Lewis asked her to give him the name of a girl, the first one that came to mind. "Janet," she blurted out. Fine, Janet it would be.

Susan was to purchase a telephone with an unlisted number and keep it out of sight. This she did, hiding it in a desk drawer. No one was to have the number except for Jim and the student informer. When the student called, she was to answer the phone as "Janet" and say that Jim was not at home but that she would take a message and have him return the call. A few days later Lewis called to test the system. "Susan?" he said. "The phone is working."

"No," said his sister. "This is not Susan."

"Susan?" Lewis repeated with growing impatience.

"No," she repeated. "This is Janet."

A miffed Lewis had to admit his sister was even more savvy at this business than he had expected. But several months passed and not once did the caller from Chicago telephone. The phone was eventually removed and the subject was never spoken of again.

Meanwhile Lewis continued to live with his wife, Monique, in a huge Victorian house on River Street in Des Plaines. There he had dinner parties for his Washington contacts and would routinely retrieve vintage bottles of wine from his ample wine cellar. In his spare time, he played an active role in the army reserve, completing a course in psychological operations, advancing to the rank of major, and winning a Certificate of Achievement from Headquarters Company, 12th Special Forces Group, in Arlington Heights, Illinois. The certificate was in recognition of his efforts in recruiting "intelligence analysts and target area language experts for the 5th Psychological Operations Group." No matter how many years he was with the CIA, Jim Lewis would always see himself as a soldier.

In late 1979 he began to prepare himself to return to a covert post in the Mideast. First he would need to undergo rigorous Arabic-language training. After completing an intensive course at the Foreign Language Institute in suburban Virginia he was assigned to Tunis to complete his language training. But in the summer of 1982, as events in Lebanon heated up, the Agency cast about for an experienced case officer with solid nerves and a knowledge of Arabic to gather intelligence on the deteriorating situation in that country.

Already it had a reputation as a hazardous post. Five years earlier, on June 16, 1976, U.S. Ambassador Francis E. Meloy, U.S. economic counselor Robert O. Waring, and the ambassador's bodyguard and chauffeur, Zohair Moghrabi, had been assassinated. Their bullet-riddled bodies were later found at a construction site. In September 1981 the French ambassador had been murdered. In December of that year a bomb had killed sixty-four people at the Iraqi Embassy, including the ambassador. In May 1982 twelve people were killed and twenty-seven injured at the French Embassy. It was no secret that Beirut was a place of peril. But if that was where the Agency needed Lewis, that was where he would go.

On August 13, 1982, Lewis arrived in war-ravaged Beirut. His intelligence-gathering mission was linked to the arrival seven days later of eight hundred U.S. marines, part of a multinational force to supervise the withdrawal of Palestinians from the city.

It began as a temporary assignment. Beirut was a volatile place, and spouses of Agency officers were not yet permitted to accompany them. Still Lewis was bent on setting his mother's mind at ease. Four months after arriving in Beirut he wrote: "Everything is fine here. The war (in the Beirut area) is over and I have survived as usual (not even a scratch)."

The temporary assignment became a full tour of duty, and the prohibition on spouses was lifted. Lewis and Monique found a temporary apartment in a commercial area of the city, an easy ten minutes to the embassy. Monique had not yet started working. She spent the days at home studying Arabic and preparing meals. "Just a note to let you know that we are fine here in Beirut," Lewis wrote his mother and father. "Guess that you have been seeing the worst on T.V. and have the impression that things are worse than they really are. There has been no anti-American action at all here. There are incidents taking place in the surrounding mountains and in the City itself from time to time. However, we feel safe and are at ease . . . Our maid, a Tunisian girl, has arrived and as usual is really making life easy for us. Monique says that she doesn't think that she can remember how to iron a shirt anymore."

. . .

It was a few minutes after one on the afternoon of April 18, 1983, when a truck with a tarp over it was observed making its way purposefully toward the U.S. Embassy, along the Corniche, the main thoroughfare that runs along the Mediterranean in Beirut. One pedestrian would later note that it was so laden down with cargo that the tires bulged beneath the weight.

At the very time the truck came in sight of the embassy, personnel were finishing lunch in the cafeteria. Thirty-seven-year-old Richard Gannon, the State Department's regional security officer, or RSO, was at his desk reviewing security procedures. Gannon was a tall and gangly figure with gentle eyes and a coal-black mustache. Across from him sat his superior, Dave Roberts, the regional director of security who had flown in from Casablanca.

Gannon's job, making sure the embassy was secure, was an impossible task. The embassy was housed in an aging eight-story structure, originally a hotel, that was built up against the Corniche. It provided a spellbinding view and a deadly vulnerability. Gannon had been fretting about the exposure of the embassy ever since arriving in country eight months earlier.

Tensions had been running high for months. The Israelis had invaded Lebanon on June 6, 1982, and there was an uneasy standoff between their occupying forces and various Palestinian and Syrian forces. On September 15, 1982, the Israelis had entered Beirut. The next day, at the camps of Shattila and Sabra, some six hundred Palestinians, most of them women

and children, had been massacred by Phalangist militia who, it was suspected, had been given the green light by the Israelis.

To many in the strife-torn country who saw Israel as merely a U.S.
proxy, the ultimate blame for the invasion, the massacre, and the subsequent strife rested with America. In a part of the world where revenge is axiomatic, it was only a matter of time. Already, American
David Dodge, acting president of American University Beirut, had been
kidnapped.

It was the job of the CIA station in Beirut to try and make some
sense of the bewildering intrigue and animosities that periodically
erupted. Almost daily, CIA Station Chief Ken Haas briefed Ambassador
Robert S. Dillon on what the Agency had learned. An energetic and as-
sertive figure, Dillon would listen carefully but quietly hunger for more
definitive information. Haas adopted a secretive mien even with the ambassador, perhaps because there was sometimes little of substance to pass
along. The country was in fragments, and many of the traditional tools of
Agency tradecraft had proved peculiarly ineffective.

The CIA in Beirut had many objectives: find out what had become
of the hostage David Dodge, gather intelligence on the growing threat of
Shiites, the role of Syria, Iran, the Palestine Liberation Organization, and
the Maronites. There was trouble brewing in the Bekáa Valley, but pene-
trating the tight ethnic and familial units there had proved nearly impossible. The Agency had woefully few "assets" in the area. In addition, Haas
and Lewis were continually getting requests from Washington to chase
down Israeli intelligence reports, many of which proved to be bogus or
self-serving. "Your friends are just as unreliable as your enemies,"
Ambassador Dillon would conclude.

For months security officer Gannon had made no secret of his concerns for the embassy's safety. On October 1, 1982, he had sent a
telegram out under Ambassador Dillon's name, the subject of which was
"Public Access Controls." Gannon had met with some resistance. There
were concerns of cost. To the uninitiated, the embassy might have appeared well fortified. Stern-faced marine sentinels stood watch, and
heavy masonry walls appeared impervious to attack. In case of trouble,
inside there were steel doors with armor rings that could be closed to
seal off the building, as on a ship. In the entryway concealed holes could

be used to flood the area with tear gas. The windows were covered with Mylar, a plasticlike material designed to prevent the glass from becoming a hail of deadly projectiles.

But so grave was the concern for security that in February Washington had sent out a team of experts to examine the building. The embassy had asked for sweeping security improvements. The team made numerous sketches detailing what would later be made obvious—that the embassy, for all its precautions, was virtually indefensible, pressed as it was against the Corniche without any buffer to protect it from attack.

But the team from Washington faced financial constraints. No sooner had they left when the embassy sent off a telegram to the State Department pleading its cause. "We thought we had a special case," recalls Robert Pugh, then deputy chief of mission. The essence of the cable was "we need it all and we need it now."

But by mid-April, after the Israelis had pulled back and a multi-national force had come on the scene, there was a kind of lull in the violence that raised hopes. Spring itself seemed to promise a relaxation of tensions.

All such buoyancy of spirit would soon come to an abrupt halt. As the explosives-laden truck turned into the embassy driveway and gunned the accelerator, Ambassador Dillon was in his eighth-floor office, one hand holding the phone, the other awkwardly putting on a thick red marine T-shirt in expectation of his afternoon jog. Three floors below him, virtually the entire CIA station was assembled for a staff meeting—James Lewis, his wife, Monique, Phyliss Faraci, Frank Johnston, Bob Ames, William Sheil, and Deborah Hixon were all there.

Dick Gannon's back was to the sea, a roll-down metal shutter raised to let in the afternoon light. In Gannon's in-box was a handwritten memo, what he called a note to himself, laying out the vulnerabilities of the Beirut embassy. It read in part: "Post has increasing concerns with deteriorating security situation in Beirut . . . Ability of LAF [Lebanese armed forces] or local law enforce. to prevent such attacks is non-existent. May only be a matter of time before U.S. is includ in list of opportune targets. With avail explosives, suffic. motive and in absence of any deterrent (effective law enforcement) U.S. interests could be target w/ minimal risk . . . What might we face . . . 1.) Car bomb/package bomb at Chancery." Like Cassandra,

Dick Gannon's prophetic warnings went largely unheeded, lost in the welter of bureaucratic concerns and budgetary restraints.

At precisely 1:06 P.M. his worst fears were realized. The truck carrying the bomb drove into the building and simultaneously detonated a ton of high explosives. Cars were tossed into the air, a blinding fireball rose up, and a murderous shock wave scaled the front of the building, bringing down its midsection as if it were no more than a house of cards. Some of those in the adjacent cafeteria closest to the explosion were blown through the wall. Support pillars disintegrated. Black smoke engulfed the entire building, air conditioners were blown inside of rooms, walls collapsed, and safes flew open. Canisters of riot control gas erupted, mingling with the black smoke and dense debris, making breathing even more difficult. Flying metal cut a tree in half, and heat from the blast melted nearby traffic lights. So great was the force of the blast that it was said the helicopter carrier *Guadalcanal*, several miles offshore, felt a shudder.

Amid a landscape of twisted metal, concrete, and broken glass, the wounded and disoriented stumbled about in utter shock.

Security officer Gannon and his boss, Roberts, were blown to the floor. Roberts, who had been facing the window, was cut by flying glass. In the next room a secretary was screaming.

On the eighth floor Ambassador Dillon had slipped the heavy T-shirt halfway over his head at the moment of the blast. The shirt absorbed the glass that was blown in and saved his face, if not his life.

But much of the worst damage occurred in the upper floors, which collapsed and pancaked one atop the next.

Within minutes the frantic search for survivors began. From the street there was a grim vision of a body literally hanging over the edge. It was that of CIA officer Frank Johnston. Pinned between slabs, he was being crushed to death. A military team reached him and pried up one of the slabs just long enough to loosen its grip and free him. Johnston lived just long enough to ask that his wallet be given to his wife, Arlette.

On the upper floor where the CIA station had been meeting— where Monique had been enjoying her first day on the job—there was now nothing but air and the dismal view of seven floors of concrete, steel, and glass reduced to rubble far below. Jim Lewis, Monique, Bill Sheil, Deborah Hixon, Phyliss Faraci, Bob Ames, station chief Ken Haas—all lost. Cranes carefully lifted slabs searching for survivors. From inside the wrecked building a rescuer yelled into a bullhorn, "If anybody can hear me, please call for help." He was met with utter silence.

Scenes of horror would forever etch themselves on the memories of those combing through the debris. From the cafeteria emerged a worker carrying a plastic bag containing human hands.

It would be two, even three days before their bodies would be found. The awful duty of identifying the bodies fell to Deputy Chief of Mission Robert Pugh. Among the bodies he identified were those of Jim and Monique Lewis, Bob Ames, and the other CIA officers. "They were not mangled," he remembers. "They looked very much like themselves. They had been suffocated by debris and dirt. It looked almost as if they had died in their sleep."

Of the entire CIA Beirut station only one covert officer had survived. His name was Murray J. McCann. At the time the bomb detonated he had been out of the building on a personal errand—taking a second look at an oriental rug he was considering buying.

And, unknown to even the embassy, there was yet another covert CIA officer in Beirut that day. He was Alexander MacPherson, the veteran of clandestine missions who five years earlier had crawled away from the fiery North Carolina plane crash that had killed Berl King and Dennis Gabriel. MacPherson, then under deep cover, was on temporary duty in Beirut and had scrupulously avoided contact with the embassy lest it compromise his cover. Standing a mile or so from the embassy, he heard the deafening blast. Once again he had proved to be the consummate survivor.

In all, seventeen Americans and thirty-three foreign nationals had died in the embassy bombing.

While the search for survivors continued, security officer Gannon and the CIA's McCann bumped into each other amid the confusion. McCann was worried about classified documents strewn about in the rubble. He wanted to sift through the documents and try to preserve that which was needed, getting rid of the rest. But Gannon was convinced there would be no time for such a procedure.

"Burn everything!" he barked to the marines standing nearby. The soldiers gathered up armfuls of classified materials and dumped them into fifty-gallon drums, then set them on fire. Armful after armful of sensitive

.s was put into the flames, while an officer stirred it with a stick, ..aking sure that nothing survived the blaze.

In the immediate aftermath of the bombing, the State Department was besieged by reporters asking for the identities and biographies of those killed in the attack. Without time to coordinate stories with the CIA, State released thumbnail sketches of the victims based upon the cover stories provided. Reporters were told, for instance, that CIA operative William Sheil was a civilian employee of the army, but there had been no time to give the army a heads-up. "Sheil?" said an army spokesman. "We have no William Sheil."

There would be many attempts to remember the dead. Five days after the bombing, President Ronald Reagan boarded a helicopter for the flight to Andrews Air Force Base to meet the arrival of a cargo plane bearing the bodies of sixteen Americans killed in the bombing. Seven of the coffins held CIA officers. Among them were the bodies of James and Monique Lewis. It was a cold rain that fell that late afternoon as the Lewis family huddled together inside the hangar, their eyes on the flag-draped coffins.

An angry Ronald Reagan spoke of the loss and declared: "Let us here in their presence serve notice to the cowardly, skulking barbarians in the world that they will not have their way." But such resolve was of little use without the underlying intelligence needed to bring the guilty to justice. Even as he spoke, Lebanese authorities were rounding up anyone who might be a suspect. Even some who were bodyguards to the U.S. ambassador were swept up in the net and beaten by their interrogators. But ultimately the call for accountability would go unanswered. Reagan would later speak of that afternoon's trip to Andrews Air Force Base as "one of the saddest journeys of my presidency." The nation, too, watched on television in an extraordinary outpouring of public grief.

Six days later, on April 29, the CIA conducted its own ceremony for the victims of the bombing. This one was held in the Agency's auditorium and was closed to the public. Such losses were viewed as intensely familial. It began with a playing of the national anthem and a scriptural reading from Romans 14: "None of us lives as his own master and none of us dies as his own master. While we live we are responsible for the Lord and when we die, we die as his servants. Both in life and in death we are the Lord's . . . Let us then make it our aim to work for peace and to strengthen one another." Then William J. Casey, Director Central Intelligence, spoke of the heroism of those who had died. He cited the lines written at Thermopylae, where in 480 B.C. the Greeks, though ultimately defeated, heroically resisted the Persians. "Go, passerby, and to Sparta tell that we in faithful service fell."

A year later, in his private office on the Agency's seventh floor, Casey would present to Lewis's mother, Toni, posthumous medals for her son's valor. The citation for the Certificate of Distinction for Courageous Performance reads: "In recognition of his superior performance with the Central Intelligence Agency from August 13, 1982, to 18 April 1983. During this period of civil anarchy and turmoil at an overseas location, he demonstrated exceptional devotion to duty under conditions of grave personal risk. His professionalism was a constant source of strength and encouragement to his colleagues and upholds the finest traditions of the Operations Directorate. Mr. Lewis' flawless efforts, commitment to excellence and unstinting courageous service reflect credit on himself, the Central Intelligence Agency and the Federal service."

Even in a posthumous commendation to the mother of a fallen covert officer, the Agency would not put in writing the country of service.

But it was the letters of condolence from Jim Lewis's colleagues within the covert ranks that moved Toni Lewis most deeply. "I—and many others—regard Jim as one of the true latter-day American Heroes," one colleague wrote. "Unfortunately, the world may never become fully aware of the depth of his experience and service and sense of duty. I hope that you can take comfort in knowing that there are many who not only know of Jim's gallant history, but who will also remember him as a model for our own lives." Another covert officer wrote: "Your son was a friend and colleague for the past twenty years . . . Our sorrow, frustration, and anger over his loss in Beirut cannot be expressed to you in a way that will soften the blow or dull the pain . . . All of us have learned to create a reserved place in our hearts for memories of men like Jim—to be brought occasionally to the forefront of our thoughts, carefully burnished, and recalled with a mixture of sadness and pride. Remembering Jim's efforts to make a difference in this world will help us continue."

. . .

The Agency lost more staff operatives in the Beirut bombing than at any time since the Vietnam conflict. Many of those individuals were among the most skilled the Agency had. Casey would later call Bob Ames, the CIA's senior Middle East expert, who was killed in the blast, "the closest thing to the irreplaceable man." Casey said he had "the keenest insights into the Arab mind of any individual in government." Ames had been something of an idealist. He had believed that "things need not always end in disaster."

But the loss in Beirut could not be measured in lives alone. Its psychological impact would be felt for years to come. Just as James Lewis, the "indestructible" one, had been killed, so, too, the Agency would find itself faced with a new and profound sense of vulnerability. It was a feeling shared by the entire foreign service.

Before Beirut there was a feeling that, in the words of diplomat Robert Pugh, "embassies were sacrosanct, that they were safe ground." True, other American embassies had been targeted in the past—Teheran and Saigon among them—but the sheer magnitude of the Beirut assault was stunning.

After that day in April 1983, the term "diplomatic immunity" had a different, almost anachronistic ring. The violence of the world would no longer stop at the embassy door or respect the lives of those engaged in representing nations. After Beirut, embassies worldwide underwent renewed security exams and hardening against attack. But no amount of protection could fend off a terrorist willing to sacrifice his own life to take the lives of others. It was often observed that the United States had to be vigilant all the time, but the terrorist only had to get lucky once.

The old world and the rules by which it lived were dissolving quickly, but in the Oval Office and at Langley—as well as in the Kremlin—the old guard was having its final days. In Washington two aging Cold Warriors called the shots. President Reagan, who had spoken of the Kremlin as "the evil empire," was determined not to allow Soviet influence to expand even by a single inch. William Casey, a shrewd and combative former OSS veteran, now Director Central Intelligence, was committed to restoring pride to the Agency and reenergizing the clandestine service. With Reagan's unflagging support, Casey's CIA was the beneficiary of a multibillion-dollar buildup. Thousands of new officers were brought into the Agency, so many that future DCI Robert Michael Gates would say they were "stacking people like cordwood in the corridors."

Under Reagan's watch, Casey launched ambitious new covert operations and engaged the Agency in numerous superpower proxy wars. Support was given to the Contras in their effort to topple the Sandinista regime in Nicaragua. Military aid, including Stinger missiles, was provided Afghan guerrilla fighters seeking to expel a Soviet aggressor. At Langley the Cold War showed little evidence of winding down. Even after so many years of scrutinizing the Soviets, tensions ran high and intelligence was much less than perfect.

On September 1, 1983, the Soviets shot down a Korean commercial airliner, KAL 007, killing all 269 people, including 61 Americans. And in November 1983 the Soviets actually believed that the United States was possibly preparing a preemptive nuclear strike against them. The attack, they believed, was to come under cover of a planned NATO command post exercise known as Able Archer. The Kremlin's military was placed on heightened military alert, and it was not until many months later that Casey's CIA came to understand that the Soviets viewed such a strike as potentially imminent. "The hottest year of the last half of the Cold War— the period when the risk of miscalculation, of each side misreading the other, and the level of tension were at their highest—was 1983," reflected Robert Gates, then the Agency's deputy director for intelligence. He would remember 1983 as "the most dangerous year."

But even then, the specter of a new and faceless enemy, that of the terrorist, stalked the Agency. It was suggested by some that the Cold War had provided a kind of unwritten understanding between Moscow and Washington that we would not kill their case officers and they would not kill ours, as if espionage were subject to Robert's Rules of Order or some higher code of chivalry. Not so, though it is true that direct attacks on one another's case officers rarely if ever occurred. This was less the result of mutual respect or restraint than simple pragmatism. "We coexist," KGB Director Vladimir Krychkov once remarked. "They work, and we work." Once a case officer was identified by the other side, be he CIA or KGB, it was easier to monitor his or her comings and goings than to assassinate him and risk a replacement who might take months or years to identify, and who in the interim could wreak havoc. Besides, the consequences of assassinating the other side's case officers working under diplomatic cover could indeed be grave.

No such concerns applied in the post-Beirut era. The object was not to gather intelligence, but to create chaos and spill blood. Men and women of superior training and valor were as likely to be incidental victims as intended targets. Indeed, it was the very randomness of such mayhem that gave acts of terrorism their potency.

Within months of the bombing terrorists struck again. On October 23, 1983, Islamic Jihad targeted the U.S. Marines barracks. Two hundred and forty-one marines and fifty-eight French paratroopers were killed. In December a Mercedes dump truck heavy with explosives rammed the gate of the U.S. Embassy in Kuwait. Between 1984 and 1986 some eighteen Americans were taken hostage in Beirut. Station Chief Ken Haas was succeeded by William Buckley, winner of a Silver Star in Korea and a man whose Agency career spanned four decades. He would be kidnapped and tortured. In 1991 his remains were discovered in a plastic sack beside the road to the Beirut airport.

. . .

In time, Jim and Monique Lewis and the other CIA officers who died in the Beirut bombing would be accorded nameless stars in the Agency's Book of Honor. But nearly two decades after the bombing, the names of the dead remain classified. As in other cases, the Agency maintains that identifying its casualties, even decades later, would endanger foreign nationals who may have provided the CIA with intelligence. But the oft-invoked argument wears thinner and thinner as the years wear on and bereaved families are asked to bear their losses in continued silence.

Such secrecy takes on a life all its own. The family of Barbara Robbins understands this well. In 1965 Barbara was a fresh-faced twenty-one-year-old CIA secretary, working under cover of the State Department in the U.S. Embassy in Saigon. She was at her desk when she heard a commotion outside. She rushed to the window to view the disturbance at the very moment that a Viet Cong car bomb detonated. She was impaled by the iron grating surrounding the window and died instantly.

Her father, Buford Robbins, was a quiet and patriotic man who made his living as a butcher in a Denver suburb. His daughter, he argued, had been no more than a secretary. She had no covert role to play, no agents reporting to her, no one who could be endangered if the truth of her employment were to be revealed after so many years. The burden of three decades of silence weighed upon him. He wanted only that he live long enough to see his daughter's name inscribed in the CIA's Book of Honor where only a star appeared. He died in 1998, his dream unrealized. Barbara Robbins's name does, however, appear on a bronze plaque in the State Department, where more than thirty years later her cover story is intact.

Nearly two decades after the Beirut bombing, the emotional scars for some have yet to heal. The lone survivor of the CIA Beirut station, Murray McCann, whose errand the day of the bombing saved his life, is still trying to put the horror of that day behind him.

"It's ancient history," he says, "and I just don't want to talk about it." In 1993, on the tenth anniversary of the bombing, he honored those comrades with a few brief remarks at the Wall of Honor, recognizing their sacrifices but not uttering their names aloud. Security forbade it and besides, there was no reason to. Before him sat the families of the deceased. He had done what he could to comfort them. He even told Jim Lewis's sister, Susan, that when her brother Jim's body was found, he and Monique were holding hands.

The family of James Lewis has much to remember him by. They have the medals presented by Director William Casey. Lewis's brother Donald has the stainless-steel Rolex watch Jim was wearing at the time of the blast, its crystal scratched from the impact of his fall. His mother still has a box of Lewis's personal effects that he brought with him when he was released from Sontay prison—the simple shirt and pants, a green beret, a cracked mirror, a razor, a comb, and his field notebook. And then there are his many books—art books on Monet and Degas, and cookbooks for French, Creole, Indian, and Chinese cuisine.

But perhaps the greatest onus of the Beirut bombing fell on two survivors of the blast, Deputy Chief of Mission Robert Pugh and embassy regional security officer Richard Gannon. Today Pugh lives in retirement in an antebellum home in Mississippi, deliberately far from Washington. He still remembers the wife who, day after day, stood at the sidewalk in front of the bombed-out Beirut embassy waiting for word of her husband, an embassy employee. Nothing was ever found of him, not even a trace.

Richard Gannon would, for years, be haunted by the tragedy and by the gnawing feeling that he could have done something more, that the disaster might have been averted or at least mitigated. "In hindsight," he says, "I should have taken a stand. I should have said, 'We either make this something secure and do these things or I want a plane ticket out of here.' I didn't do that and that was costly—worse than costly."

Gannon alone had found himself wanting. State Department experts concluded that no security enhancement could have adequately shielded the building against a two-thousand-pound explosion in the hands of a suicide bomber. Indeed, State determined that many of the 136 U.S. embassies worldwide were similarly vulnerable.

And yet, for all the horror that Bob Pugh and Dick Gannon had endured at Beirut, each would soon have to face an even more grievous ordeal in the years ahead. As with lightning, there was no immunity to terrorism. Not even for those already struck once.

CHAPTER 12

Deadly Symmetry

AS THE Boeing 747 lifted off from London's Heathrow Airport into a calm December sky, thirty-four-year-old Matt Gannon had every reason to believe that good fortune rode with him. He had survived the perils of yet another clandestine assignment in Beirut, arguably the CIA's most hazardous post. With his swarthy complexion, thick black mustache, and gift for Arabic, Gannon had demonstrated once again his talent for blending into Mideast cultures, even one so wary of outsiders. He had exited unscathed, his cover intact, his superiors enamored with his performance. Just hours before takeoff, the CIA's Beirut station chief had sent a glowing cable to headquarters at Langley, a further testament to an already gilded career. The classified missive read in part:

"Matt's performance during his three-and-one half week TDY [temporary duty] in Beirut was outstanding. He produced 24 intelligence reports in as many days, several of which were multi-section studies of terrorist organizations or facilities in Lebanon which added substantive information to our knowledge of these subjects. He met seven different assets, bringing back on stream all of our Arabic-speaking assets that had been unexpectedly abandoned after [name deleted] was prevented from returning to Beirut . . .

"In short Matt made a major contribution to our operational and reporting mission which could not have been equaled by many other officers in the service. His operational judgment was consistently sound, his instinct for intelligence was unerring and, most important, his willingness to work the eighty to ninety hour weeks that characterize Beirut operations meant that he left with a series of major accomplishments during a relatively brief TDY. He is welcome back any time."

As a token of the Agency's appreciation, Langley had granted Gannon's request to leave Beirut a day earlier than scheduled. But it was sheer luck that Gannon had been able to book a flight at that late date and at the height of holiday travel. It was just three days before Christmas. As he reclined in his seat some 31,000 feet above the Scottish countryside, he could at last breathe easy with the knowledge that Beirut and its insidious dangers were behind him. For a time at least, he could put out of his mind the agony of American hostages that had so haunted him and his Agency colleagues and whose liberation had preoccupied him in Beirut. Within hours he would be back in Washington. There he would again hold in his arms his twenty-seven-year-old wife, Susan, and his daughters, four-year-old Maggie and Julia, not yet one. In particular, he had been anxious to get home to help his wife with Maggie, who was autistic and had yet to utter her first words. But Maggie's hard-fought progress in recent months meant so very much to him.

"We (I should say Susan) are working with her every day & we see the gains in her better behavior. Julia is a little doll, walking and beginning to talk—growing up way too quickly." Those were the words he had written four days earlier from Nicosia, Cyprus. That letter was now tucked into his garment bag. It was written to his brother Dick Gannon—the same Dick Gannon who five years earlier, as a State Department employee, had overseen security at the U.S. Embassy in Beirut when it fell to a terrorist car bomb. The two were not only brothers but best friends, and now they shared something else in common: they both inhabited a world overshadowed by the threat of terrorism. Matt had decided to mail the note from the States. It was written on a festive Yuletide card produced by UNICEF to benefit "the world's children."

Now less than an hour out of London, Matt Gannon could finally relax. Lulled by the monotonous drone of the engines and the promise of a quiet Christmas at home, Gannon had much to look forward to. It was the evening of December 21, 1988. The flight was Pan Am 103.

. . .

Matthew Kevin Gannon's story neither begins nor ends with that evening's flight, but straddles a critical moment in the CIA's history, a time of profound change. When Gannon joined the Agency in 1977, it was still fixated on containing Communism, as it had been for three decades. But with the gradual implosion of the Soviet Union and its waning capacity for mischief, the Agency found itself facing new and unfamiliar enemies. The superpower struggles of the Cold War, for all the human suffering and vast resources that were expended in that titanic contest, had imposed a kind of constraint on their respective client states. The world that Matthew Gannon and his colleagues in the clandestine service were to inherit was even more treacherous and uncharted a territory.

Terrorists and ultranationalists, some equipped and trained by Washington or Moscow in the era of proxy wars and realpolitik, could care less about the finer points observed in the Cold War. To them, DMZs, safe havens, and diplomatic immunity were meaningless. Old refuges presented fresh targets.

The new struggle played itself out in all the venues heretofore largely forbidden—civilian aircraft, cruise ships, city buses, embassies, hospitals, department stores, marketplaces, even funerals. For all its well-earned reputation for Machiavellian measures, the CIA's clandestine service was filled with choirboys compared with some of the predators they now faced.

The bombing of the U.S. Embassy in Beirut in April 1983 served notice that one era was ending and another beginning. Within three years the Agency established a Counterterrorist Center, or CTC, an interagency entity that combined cutting-edge hardware with old-fashioned human cunning. For the first time, the fire wall between CIA operations and analysis was torn down in the interest of providing the most current data to those in the field. CTC's single-minded purpose, its raison d'être, was to stave off the sort of catastrophe that had cost so many lives in Beirut and elsewhere.

But even as the CIA geared up to wage war with myriad shadowy cells of terrorists, some of them enflamed with visions of a jihad, or holy war, the Agency found itself under new constraints—increasing congressional oversight, a prohibition on assassinations, closer scrutiny of its budget, an aggressive U.S. press, and a residual public revulsion to the cowboy tactics revealed in the course of stunning public hearings on Capitol Hill just a few years earlier.

"The playing field," itself an expression of an earlier age, was uneven at best. American society in the late 1970s and early 1980s demanded of its covert operatives that they respect both law and morality even as they went up against often diabolical foes who openly embraced chaos and horror.

Upon just such a field strode Matt Gannon, a perfect gentleman by all accounts, dispatched to the front lines of the war on terrorism. Matt Gannon lived on the very edge of a dilemma that would plague the CIA and the nation for years to come: can those who operate within the tenets of a civilized society effectively combat the unchecked powers of fanaticism? Gannon's brief life suggested that the answer was a qualified "yes." His death, to many, represented a portentous "no."

. . .

To a stranger, there was nothing in Matthew Gannon's early years to suggest that he would become a spy in the Mideast, or that a life of intrigue would suit him. A calm and easygoing Southern California boy, he spent much of his childhood in San Juan Capistrano. Slow to anger and gentle by nature, he was one who, when a playmate pulled a toy out of his hands, would turn away and find something else to occupy him. As an adolescent he was neither a risk-taker nor possessed of particular physical prowess. But throughout those same years Gannon was immersed in the virtues of service and sacrifice that would define his personal and, later, professional values.

Born on August 11, 1954, the eighth of ten children, Matthew Gannon came from a devoutly Catholic family where commitment to others was seen as a natural extension of the catechism itself. Most of his siblings found their way into positions that served others. In addition to brother Dick, who chose the State Department's Diplomatic Security Service, two other brothers would go into law enforcement. Among his sisters, two became grade school teachers and a third, a nurse.

Despite years of Catholic schooling, Matt Gannon was never religious, at least not outwardly. But what he lacked in public expressions of piety, he made up for in his own deeply held belief that individuals owed something to each other. Of course, he would have cringed at any such baldly altruistic talk. Faith for him demanded action, not words.

Gannon attended the University of Southern California and the University of Grenoble. His senior year he studied at the University of Tunis. It was there that his fascination with the Arabic language and cultures was first whetted. It appeared that an academic with Agency contacts, recognizing Gannon's passion for distant cultures and his natural discretion, suggested he consider the clandestine service. So Gannon did just that in 1977, undergoing the basic training program at Camp Perry on the way to becoming a case officer in the Operations Directorate.

Not long after completing the course, on September 24, 1978, Gannon was dispatched to Egypt to study Arabic at the American University Cairo, where he enrolled as a student. His Agency checks were deposited into his Washington bank account, but no one in Cairo knew he was with the CIA. He was not to go near the U.S. Embassy. It was his first experience living with a cover story.

He immersed himself in studies of Arabic, Mideast history and culture, and Islam. He routinely left the confines of the campus to explore the crowded streets of Cairo. Often he would visit the main mosque, al-Azhar, where he would stand in the shadows and observe. He would tape the sheikh's services and play them over and over throughout the week, until he had memorized them and mastered the accent. As a break from studies he took a modest role in a play produced by the university. It was a Henrik Ibsen play, *An Enemy of the People.*

"In a sense I feel as though I've steeped myself in so much work in several areas so as not to have time to feel alone or at a loss," young Matt Gannon wrote.

His first formal CIA posting overseas was to Sanaa, Yemen Arab Republic, a natural assignment for a junior case officer. It was well off the main path of covert activities but a perfect place to observe and test a young recruit. Gannon's time was divided between the mundane consular duties that devolved upon him as a part of his cover, and the evenings spent in covert matters, including his attempts to recruit and run agents. Hints of his philosophy seep out in the letters he wrote to his brother Dick.

Gannon recounted one planning session that apparently preceded a covert operation. "There was a long complicated discussion of a pending op, in which one of the participants, after three hours of debate, finally said that the issue had been tossed back and forth too long, that to think about something too much, to intellectualize a problem for too long, is detrimental in that it rules out acting out of instinct. He advised that action come 'clean' . . . fortunately we did and everything is fine. Had we not gone ahead the other night, the chance would have been irretrievably lost. We gambled and won, the point being, I guess, is that decisive action is oftentimes required without agonizing over the decision itself."

No one who knew Matt Gannon doubted his patriotism or devotion to duty, but for him there was also the lure of Arabic cultures. He took an almost childlike pleasure in "going native." He spoke Arabic, devoured the local foods, and melted in with the people on the street. He treasured his copy of T. E. Lawrence's *The Seven Pillars of Wisdom* and was not above fantasizing a role for himself like that of Lawrence of Arabia, who roused the Arabs to rebel against the Turks during World War I.

"It was hard to imagine he was Irish Catholic," his brother Dick mused. While others dreamed of cushy assignments in Paris or London, Gannon longed for Baghdad and Beirut. On a home visit from Yemen, he showed up unannounced at his sister Cabrini's door, dressed in full Yemeni garb—from the headdress to the billowy white pants and tunic. With his roguish mustache and dark complexion, his sister momentarily failed to recognize him. Gannon could scarcely contain his delight.

His brother Dick remembers that on one visit home he noticed

ABOVE: Portrait of Matthew Gannon
(pictured in front row, flanked by sisters, to
his right Cabrini, to his left Julie)
and family taken in California circa 1967.
(Courtesy of Richard Gannon)

RIGHT: Matthew Gannon at sister Cabrini's
wedding in California at the Mission
San Juan Capistrano in 1987.
(Courtesy of Richard Gannon)

ABOVE: Matthew Gannon with his daughter, Maggie (in plaid jumper), and Molly, brother Richard Gannon's daughter. Taken in Alexandria, Virginia, in 1987, a year before Matthew's death. *(Courtesy of Richard Gannon)*

RIGHT: Richard Spicer in a casual moment in 1982. Two years later, on October 18, 1984, he was killed during a secret CIA mission to resupply Nicaragua's Contra rebels. The Agency still will not acknowledge he worked for them, and some in Spicer's family remain unconvinced he is actually dead. *(Courtesy of Carroll Spicer)*

ABOVE: The grave of James E. Spessard in Williamsport, Maryland. Killed in Angola, Spessard was interred in the same cemetery where his widow, Debbie, works to this day.
(Courtesy of Debbie Pappas, his widow)

LEFT: An unidentified worker at the CIA chiseling into the wall at CIA headquarters a star to honor James E. Spessard, killed in Angola in 1989. After a decade, his death is still wrapped in secrecy and marked by a nameless star.
(Courtesy of Debbie Pappas)

LEFT: James Spessard on his wedding day in 1981 standing beside his father, Kevin Spessard. *(Courtesy of Debbie Pappas)*

BELOW: Wedding photo of James and Debbie Spessard (1981) flanked by grandmothers. *(Courtesy of Debbie Pappas)*

RIGHT: Pharies "Bud" Petty in a casual moment. A decorated Vietnam veteran, he never questioned military or CIA orders, though he expressed apprehension about the Angola mission that was later to claim his life in 1989. His death was surrounded by unanswered questions and his coffin is empty. *(Courtesy of Losue Hagler, Petty's sister)*

BELOW: The remains of the six CIA operatives killed in Angola in 1989 were quietly returned to Dover Air Force Base. The caskets were wrapped in cardboard containers bound by string and carrying the warning "Handle with Care." *(Courtesy of Losue Hagler)*

ABOVE: Two hearses pull out of a hangar at Dover Air Force Base, taking with them the charred remains of CIA operatives killed in Angola in 1989. Other caskets, wrapped in cardboard and carrying the warning "Handle with Care," can be seen awaiting the arrival of additional hearses. *(Courtesy of Losue Hagler)*

RIGHT: CIA operative Larry Freedman, a veteran of Vietnam, Delta Force, and numerous covert actions for the Agency. The photo was taken in Somalia only days before his death. *(Courtesy of Sylvia F. Doner, his sister)*

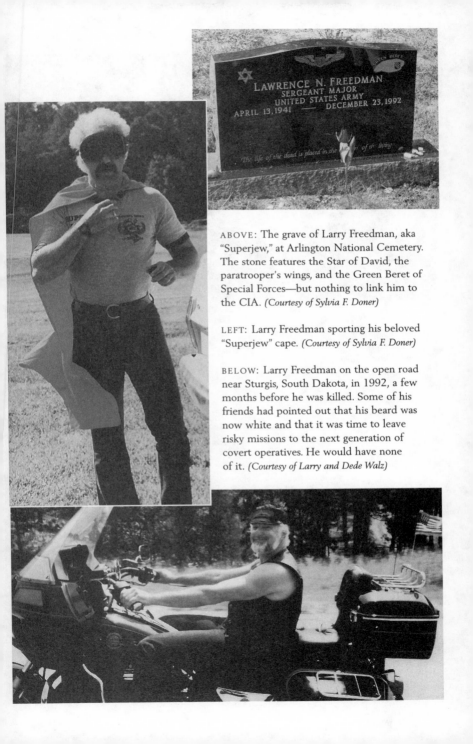

ABOVE: The grave of Larry Freedman, aka "Superjew," at Arlington National Cemetery. The stone features the Star of David, the paratrooper's wings, and the Green Beret of Special Forces—but nothing to link him to the CIA. *(Courtesy of Sylvia F. Doner)*

LEFT: Larry Freedman sporting his beloved "Superjew" cape. *(Courtesy of Sylvia F. Doner)*

BELOW: Larry Freedman on the open road near Sturgis, South Dakota, in 1992, a few months before he was killed. Some of his friends had pointed out that his beard was now white and that it was time to leave risky missions to the next generation of covert operatives. He would have none of it. *(Courtesy of Larry and Dede Walz)*

ABOVE: Larry Freedman's longtime friends gather to reminisce about him, still laughing at his wild antics. Even years after his death, they are not quite convinced he is dead. From left to right: Petey Altman, Kenny Gold, Wynne Crocetto, and Paul Weinberg. *(Courtesy of Sylvia F. Doner)*

RIGHT: A letter from Marine Lieutenant General R. B. Johnston offering condolences to the Freedman family and extolling the work Freedman had done in Somalia. *(Courtesy of Sylvia F. Doner)*

Combined Task Force Somalia
UIC 43605
FPO AP 96609-3606
24 December 1992

To the Larry Freedman Family:

There are many young Marines and Soldiers who can take credit for the early success of our operation in Somalia. But there are also a number of very special people like Larry who made the most significant contribution by performing missions that gave us the highest possible guarantee that our troops could enter the major relief centers safely. I cannot underscore how important was the performance of Larry and his fellow team members. They courageously put themselves in harm's way and took personal risks on behalf of our entire force. The news of Larry's death was a great shock to all of us in Somalia, and yesterday proved to be a very solemn time for all of us -- it dramatized the inherent risks of this operation. I know I speak for every man and woman in uniform here in Somalia in expressing to Larry's family our deepest sympathy.

Our prayers will be with you during the difficult days ahead.

Most sincerely,

R. B. Johnston

R. B. JOHNSTON
Lieutenant General, U.S. Marine Corps

that Matthew's teeth were stained a yellowish brown. He asked if he had taken up smoking. Matthew laughed it off, explaining that the stain was the result of chewing *qat* leaves, a mild stimulant commonly used in Yemen in the afternoon, particularly as men gathered to talk business or politics.

But if Gannon could maintain a laserlike focus on work, he was considerably less adept at the management of his own personal affairs. Notoriously absentminded, he was so preoccupied with Agency work that all else suffered. Some of those who spoke with him were convinced that he failed to hear a single word so lost was he in his own thoughts and Agency business. He rarely found time enough to even trim his mustache, which was often unruly and in dire need of scissors. Accounts of his forgetfulness and distractibility are legion. On the way to Dulles Airport before leaving the country for an extended foreign posting he casually turned to his brother Dick and declared, "By the way, I forgot my clothes in the dryer." As always, Dick Gannon baled him out, sending the clothes through the diplomatic pouch.

Gannon was sometimes slow to pay bills, and on one occasion he wrote a flurry of checks on an account that had long before been closed. In Amman, Jordan, he took his typewriter to a shop to be repaired and forgot about it for more than a year. He took little notice of the necessity to file tax returns on time, and once, it was said, he had to be literally locked in his Agency office to get him to do his expense reports. Once, in a rush to catch a plane at Washington's National Airport, Gannon flashed his diplomatic passport at a parking attendant and left his car for an entire week in a lot reserved exclusively for Supreme Court justices and other VIPs.

He accumulated a formidable collection of unpaid District of Columbia parking tickets, which brother Dick paid off. One July evening in 1978, a year after joining the CIA, Matt Gannon was driving his brown Datsun 210—still with California plates—through Georgetown, going the wrong way down a one-way street. Coming from the opposite direction was another car that happened to be a police cruiser. When the officer asked for Gannon's registration and license, the policeman discovered that both had expired. The car was towed to an impound lot. Once again Dick Gannon came to the rescue.

That was just Matt Gannon's way and it endeared him to his friends and family, who felt a certain responsibility to keep an eye on him, lest things got out of hand.

Only rarely did his inattention to personal detail spill over to his work. One such instance occurred in July 1980 as he landed in Dhahran, Saudi Arabia. It was not until the next morning when Gannon flew to Jidda that he discovered he had left his passport at the airport in Dhahran. He managed to convince a security officer in Jidda to issue him a tourist passport so he could return to Dhahran and pick up his diplomatic passport—which established his cover identity as a State Department employee. His superior was none too happy with the mishap.

As a young officer, Gannon was virtually oblivious to material needs. His first year at the Agency his room in suburban Virginia was furnished with only a desk and a sofa purchased at a yard sale. When he ate or studied, he simply pulled the sofa up to the desk. At night the sofa was his bed. There was something of the Inspector Clouseau about Matt Gannon. Those who worked with him took it in stride. Gannon himself had long ago come to accept such contretemps as a minor though noisome character flaw—one that he was readily able to accept in himself.

. . .

From Yemen, Gannon was assigned to Jordan. It was a move that would profoundly affect the course of his life and that of one of the CIA's most venerated and senior case officers, Tom Twetten, then chief of station in Amman. It was the summer of 1981. The Agency had notified Twetten that, barring objection, it would be posting Gannon to his station. Twetten was a twenty-year veteran of the Agency, a courteous man with a scholarly bent, a love of old books and maps, and a manner that suggested he might be well suited to the university. It took no leap of faith to picture him lecturing on the early Ottoman Empire.

Twetten had been raised in Spencer, Iowa. His family was in the furniture business and he had studied psychology at Iowa State. After a graduate degree from Columbia University and a hitch in the military, Twetten joined the CIA in 1961. He had been a part of that most remarkable class of junior-officers-in-training. His classmates included Mike Deuel and Dick Holm.

One of Twetten's early memories of the Agency was when he and his fellow JOTs were taken to meet Director Allen Dulles, an august figure only recently humbled by the Bay of Pigs. Dulles asked who among the junior officers was named Mike Deuel and commented that his father, Wallace Deuel, was a stalwart of the Agency. Decades later Twetten could still remember the pang of envy that his peer was so well wired in with the Agency brass. Already there were hints that Twetten, brilliantly invisible, had his ambitions.

The arc of Tom Twetten's career began in Africa. One of his earliest postings, from 1966 to 1967, was in the north of Libya, where he was under cover as a consular officer in Benghazi. There Twetten kept an eye on the Russians and East Europeans in town, one of myriad such sideshows in the global Cold War. In the same town was a young and ambitious lieutenant in the Libyan military. His name was Muammar Gadhafi. The two men, Twetten and Gadhafi, never met face-to-face, though in the years ahead their paths would cross in deadly ways. Libya would long remain a focal point of Twetten's career.

On June 7, 1967, the Arab-Israeli War erupted, and Egyptian President Gamal Nasser called for a pan-Arab uprising. Twetten and those in the U.S. consulate knew they were in for trouble. Seventeen U.S. embassies across the Mideast were attacked. The first to come under assault was Benghazi, where Twetten was stationed. On the way into town Twetten heard the news on the radio and went straight to the consulate, knowing that a mob would soon form. A dozen Americans worked in the embassy, including three Agency employees—Twetten, the lone case officer, a secretary, and a communicator. A week earlier Twetten had begun shredding sensitive CIA documents, convinced that either Nasser would attack Israel or vice versa.

No sooner had Twetten ordered the doors of the consulate barred than the assault began. The first wave came over the roof of an adjacent building. A signal corps officer standing watch on the roof announced he would shoot anyone who attempted to bring down the U.S. flag. Twetten relieved him of his .45 and put it in the safe. Then Twetten removed the embassy's remaining classified materials and stuffed them into self-destruction barrels containing a kind of nitrate charge to incinerate the papers. The barrels were placed on the second-floor balcony, where they were to be ignited if the mob attacked.

Then Twetten doled out the embassy's six gas masks to the secretaries and gathered together the consulate's tear gas grenades. As the perimeter of the embassy was breached and the mob came in, Twetten and the others lobbed the grenades down the stairwells and retreated into the vault, sealing it off and stuffing wet rags beneath the vault door. There Twetten and eleven other consular employees hid while the mob torched the curtains, destroyed furniture, and attempted to set the walls on fire. Within minutes the rioters withdrew, unable to withstand the tear gas. For six hours Twetten and the others remained hidden in the vault.

When they emerged, the consulate was a shambles. There was fire in the streets as the mob torched cars. Twetten stood at the window and watched as someone put a wick into the gas tank of his year-old MG Sprite and blew it up. As he and others ignited the barrels containing classified documents, black smoke enveloped the consulate. A cheer went up from the crowd below, mistakenly believing the consulate itself was on fire. It was an unintended deception that may have saved Twetten's and the others' lives.

A year later Twetten left Libya, never to return again. But Libya remained on Twetten's priority list. On September 1, 1969, Gadhafi and others mounted a successful coup and overthrew Libya's King Idris. At the time, Twetten was the Libya desk officer at CIA headquarters in Langley. Any cables from the field or operations against a Libyan passed through Twetten's hands. Above him was a branch chief and a division chief.

At the time of the coup, there was no immediate announcement of who the new leader was. That was learned about a week later. Initially Gadhafi was viewed by U.S. Ambassador Joe Palmer as someone the United States could readily work with. But soon enough it became clear that Gadhafi had other plans. He shut down Wheelus Air Force Base and prepared to nationalize the oil industry. The days of wishful thinking were over.

About a year and a half after Gadhafi came to power Twetten was summoned to the seventh-floor office of the deputy director of operations, the man who oversaw all covert activities worldwide. His name was Desmond FitzGerald. He was a figure like Allen Dulles and Frank Wisner and Dick Helms, of Olympian stature in the eyes of the Agency's clandestine rank and file. "It was like a phone call from God," remembers Twetten. "I went up to his office with a good deal of trepidation, having never before even seen the man let alone been in his office." FitzGerald invited Twetten to take a seat.

"What do you know about the Black Prince?" FitzGerald asked.

The Black Prince, so called because of the darkness of his skin, was a relative of King Idris. Twetten knew a good deal about him, none of it flattering. Twetten told him that the prince allegedly had been known to import Greek prostitutes for entertainment on the weekends, that he supposedly frequented the American PX and bought up numerous watches pledging to pay for them at a later date, and that he shamelessly exploited his royal connections.

"Well," asked FitzGerald, "what do you think of him leading a coup against Gadhafi?"

"I can't think of anybody who could be worse," answered Twetten.

"Thank you very much," said FitzGerald, accepting the fact that the Black Prince was, in Twetten's words, "the wrong horse."

And that was the end of it. The CIA would not again weigh mounting a coup to dislodge Gadhafi. A year later Twetten learned that it was the Israelis who had proposed arming the prince and organizing the tribes in the south into a Bedouin march to overthrow the Libyan leader. It was, said Twetten, "a harebrained scheme."

But as it turned out, the Agency might have been overjoyed to have the Black Prince in power, or for that matter, just about anyone else but Gadhafi. Those within the CIA who were fighting terrorism would come to regard him as the devil incarnate. And in the end, none would have better reason to do so than Tom Twetten himself.

. . .

As chief of station, Twetten had the authority to block Matt Gannon's move to Amman, but there was no cause to do so and nothing on the face of Gannon's file to suggest that he was anything other than a standout. When the two of them finally met in Amman in August 1981, Twetten saw in the callow young case officer great promise. If there was any reservation about Gannon, it was a tiny one and left unspoken.

Twetten wondered to himself if perhaps this well-heeled lad of gentle demeanor might not be a tad too nice, maybe a little soft in the center, indecisive. Would he, Twetten wondered, have the stuff to make the tough decisions called for in the Mideast?

Gannon for his part must have felt a twinge of awe for this station chief who had already garnered for himself a reputation for extreme coolness under fire and exceptional tradecraft as a spy.

It was not long after twenty-eight-year-old Gannon arrived in Amman that he found himself distracted by a pretty twenty-year-old who frequented the embassy. She had brown eyes, auburn hair, and pale skin. Her name was Susan, as in Susan Twetten, daughter of his boss, the CIA's chief of station. In the Agency, as elsewhere, it was not a good idea to court the boss's daughter, particularly given the personal and security complications such a relationship could entail.

Besides, Gannon was already involved with a woman named Susie who was then planning to visit him in Amman. "The past week has been tough . . . Have landed myself in a real spot," Gannon wrote his brother Dick on November 6, 1981. "Have begun to see Susan Twetten the daughter of the Embassy Political Officer [Gannon referred to Twetten by his cover position]. She teaches at a kindergarten here having arrived in early October. Am trying to sort myself out, taking a step back . . . at the same time, I decided to tell Susie NOT to come out as we had planned in early December, just four weeks away . . . The fact that I am drawing myself into seeing someone else doesn't help in the least . . . in the meantime, I feel like burying myself in my work . . . not seeing anyone, but I have made a commitment here and have to work that out some way . . . Why I bring this on myself, I don't know. I'll keep in touch on how all works out, or doesn't work . . ."

Dick Gannon did not have long to wait to hear how things worked out. Three months later, at a February 11, 1982, embassy party hosted by the Twettens, it was announced that Matthew and Susan were engaged. In a letter to Dick Gannon written eight days after the party, Matt Gannon wrote: "I have joined Susan in the catechism classes! I know you are shaking your head as I have been deemed a 'lost cause' for quite some time." And in a vain effort to muzzle his brother from telling his bride too many of his foibles too early, Matt wrote: "I want you to promise that you will tell only a certain number of stories about me to Susan, preferably only ones dealing with the parking tickets! We can leave passports and finances for another visit!"

Less than four months later, on June 3, 1982, Matthew Gannon and Susan Twetten were married at Holy Trinity Church in Washington, D.C.

As a parent Tom Twetten could not have been more pleased with his daughter's choice for a husband. But as CIA chief of station, Twetten regarded the union between his daughter and Matthew Gannon as potentially nettlesome. After that, Twetten would sometimes go to absurd lengths to avoid even the appearance of furthering his son-in-law's career. As Twetten rose through the Agency's senior-most ranks, Gannon's own innate talents distinguished him as a rising star in his own right. Inside Langley, there was inevitably the sense that Matthew Gannon had been anointed for great things, be it by pure merit, by blood, or by a combination of the two.

Early on, Gannon's obsessive devotion to Agency work and the travel that went with it put a strain on the new marriage. "Matthew has been very busy at work, staying at the Embassy for long hours and then doing work-related activities in the evenings," Susan wrote three months before the wedding. "He has a very bad cold now, which is probably due to a lack of sleep and good meals. He is also a bit stubborn in this area. (There, I've told!)"

Marriage did not alter his work habits. Less than two weeks after the wedding, Susan, then twenty-two, wrote Dick Gannon from Amman: "We have settled into as much of a routine as one can settle into when living with Matthew . . . He's off to Paris next month. I will stay here with the cat and plants."

Matthew Gannon, like many case officers, seemed wedded first to his work and second to his family. "Came down with a mild case of typhoid fever on 6 September," he wrote. "Basically two weeks out of the office. Susan tried to keep me in bed, but work here has been a bit heavy lately, and I couldn't afford to drop it altogether." But he, too, fretted about the impact of his work on his marriage.

Four months after the wedding, he wrote his brother Dick, then stationed in Beirut: "I worry that I don't see her enough during the work

ot the best way to start off." Like all case officers, he had to
th the nocturnal life of running agents while during the day he
fill his responsibilities as an economics officer, his cover in
Amman. Sometimes the pressure of the two jobs was more than even he
could take, fraying nerves and patience. "The embassy here appears sometimes like the monkey cage at the San Diego Zoo," he wrote, "everyone
running in different directions, and no control of the show. Susan told me
I had better start running again BEFORE I come home from work to get
out all the frustrations. She has a point."

The letter, dated October 7, 1982, closed, "Hope all is well, Dick,
and Beirut is not proving too dangerous." Gannon was by all accounts an
excellent intelligence officer, but it was something more than intelligence
that troubled him about Beirut. Call it a premonition. "The tension is in
the air," he wrote, "and Palestinians are rightfully angry at our support for
Israel . . . Amman though is not a high risk place for Americans; but
Beirut, what worries me is the unexpected event, the sniper, car bomb,
mine. You are the best Sy [security] has to offer," he wrote his brother,
"and I am pleased, in a sense that you are in Beirut, but the unexpected
incident, despite all planning, is really unsettling. We're praying for you."
Six months later the Beirut embassy toppled and Dick Gannon narrowly
escaped with his life.

From the summer of 1983 until the summer of 1986, Matthew
Gannon was based in Damascus, Syria, a country long suspected of supporting terrorism. Nowhere in the Mideast could one be sure to avoid the
ravages of terrorism. On October 7, 1985, an Italian cruise ship, the
Achille Lauro, was seized by four Palestinian hijackers and held for forty-
four hours.

Among those passengers looking on in horror was a sixty-nine-
year-old American named Leon Klinghoffer. Disabled by a stroke, he
was confined to a wheelchair. Terrorists put a machine gun to his wife's
head and forced her to leave him. A short time later she heard two
shots. Klinghoffer's body was dumped into the Mediterranean, along
with his wheelchair. The notion that an old man in a wheelchair could
be so coldly executed became one of the defining images in the war on
terrorism, erasing any lingering illusions about the nature of this new
enemy.

Worse yet were the denials that followed Klinghoffer's murder.

"News about the death of the crippled American passenger was fabricated by the American media to smear the image of Palestinian fighters," declared Abu Abbas of the Palestine Liberation Front, to which the terrorists belonged. "This American could have been dead in his cabin out of fear or shock." The Palestine Liberation Organization groused that the United States was making "an ado" over Klinghoffer's death and refuted suggestions he was murdered. "Where is the evidence?" demanded Farouk Kaddoumi, the PLO's foreign policy spokesman.

The evidence, Klinghoffer's body, washed ashore a week later near the Syrian port of Latakia. Two bullet holes left little doubt as to the cause of death. But still there was the need for someone from the U.S. Embassy in Damascus to claim the body and oversee its preparation for a return to the United States. Such unpleasant tasks as this fall to those assigned to the consular affairs section, which is precisely where Matthew Gannon was working under cover. Despite the misgivings of some within the Agency that his going to claim the body might attract unwanted press attention, he volunteered for the assignment. It was the first time, but not the last, that he would face the casualties of terrorism.

. . .

Though a generation apart, Tom Twetten and his son-in-law, Matthew Gannon, shared much in common. Both entered the CIA as young men profoundly committed—some would say obsessed—with work. Both had come into the Agency in troubled times. Twetten joined in 1961, three months after the Bay of Pigs. At an orientation program an Agency officer had declared that the CIA would never fully distance itself from that fiasco. Twetten momentarily wondered why, if that was true, he had bothered to join so mortally wounded an institution. Gannon had joined in 1977 as the Agency was mired in scandal and investigations into the excesses of the past.

In the mid-eighties Twetten and Gannon shared the drive together from their homes to Langley, leaving in Twetten's VW bus at 6:00 A.M. and often not returning until 8:00 P.M. Both men had brilliant futures to look forward to and both would suffer intensely personal losses at the hands of terrorists. That their paths should cross and their families unite was less a matter of serendipity than the realities of the clandestine service, itself a kind of extended family doubly bound by a culture of secrecy and a distrust of outsiders. By the time Susan Twetten took a part-time job at the Agency, it had become the center of their personal and professional lives.

. . .

As the years passed, young Matthew Gannon gathered for himself an enviable record and established himself as one of the foremost Arabists within the Agency. His ascent through the ranks seemed foreordained. Tom Twetten's career also thrived. In the summer of 1975 he had been made deputy branch chief of North Africa, overseeing operations in Libya and Egypt. Later he was chief of station in Amman. In 1982 he returned to Washington and was made chief of operations of the Office of Technical Services, the vast support arm of the Agency that provides everything a spy in the field might need—instruments of secret writing, bugging devices, disguises, concealable cameras, and other exotic gear. In 1983 he was made deputy chief of the Near East Division, once again overseeing Libyan operations, among others.

In the ensuing years, hostility and suspicion between the United States and Libya deepened. Each seemed destined to provoke the other.

In March 1986 a daunting thirty-ship U.S. Navy task force conducted exercises in the waters just off Libya, an action seen as taunting Gadhafi. On March 25 U.S. and Libyan forces clashed as Libya fired missiles on U.S. planes and the U.S. responded by attacking Libyan patrol boats and a missile site. The United States did not have to wait long for Libya's response.

On April 14, 1986, a West Berlin discotheque frequented by U.S. servicemen was bombed. Two American soldiers were killed and 229 were wounded. President Reagan, relying on U.S. intelligence reports, announced that there was "irrefutable" evidence that the bombing was the work of Libya. The United States had been waiting for just such a provocation to unleash a retaliatory strike.

The disco bombing gave the White House and CIA license to exact the most punishing attack on Libya, exposing Gadhafi's vulnerabilities, degrading his terrorist training facilities, and perhaps even destabilizing his regime. The army barracks in particular were selected as a target in the hopes that the troops would turn their wrath against Gadhafi.

A key participant in those consultations was Tom Twetten, then deputy chief of the CIA's Near East Division. Twetten and his staff provided intelligence that helped focus American targets in Tripoli, including Gadhafi's living quarters, though it was the air force that selected the sites and the National Security Council that gave ultimate approval.

Nine days after the disco was bombed, the United States launched Operation El Dorado Canyon. Dozens of U.S. Navy A-6 Intruders and A-7 bombers as well as air force F-111s pummeled Libyan airfields, command posts, and training centers in Tripoli and Benghazi. The CIA was banned by law from any direct assassination attempt on a foreign leader, but the bombing of Gadhafi's Tripoli residential compound could be understood as little else but an attempt on his life. Indeed, Twetten would later acknowledge that that was precisely what a senior Pentagon planner had in mind. Reagan himself had declared that Gadhafi was "this mad dog of the Middle East." And if there was any ambiguity left, a senior U.S. official was quoted as saying, "We all know what you do with a mad dog."

In the massive U.S. air assault Gadhafi's adopted eighteen-month-old daughter, Hana, was said to have been killed; two of his sons, aged four and three, were injured; and his wife was left shell-shocked. Gadhafi, for all his ruthlessness, was said to be shattered by the loss and more intent than ever to exact revenge upon his tormentor, the United States. "Child-murderer," Gadhafi branded Reagan, who had authorized the attack. But Gadhafi decided to bide his time before retaliating.

In 1987 Twetten was chief of the Near East Division and taking an active role in all intelligence operations against Libya. During this period he was intent not to take any action that might create the appearance of favoritism or particular interest in his son-in-law's career. Gannon was assigned to the Counterterrorism Center, taking him somewhat outside of Twetten's direct line of authority.

An Arabist by training with nearly a decade's experience in the Mideast, Gannon was a major asset to the center. Those who knew him were amused that Twetten had gone to such ends to avoid meddling in his career. Gannon's self-effacing brand of courage and his chameleon-like ability to adapt to life in the Mideast had long since ensured a meteoric rise within the CIA. For that, he needed no help from his father-in-law or anyone else.

. . .

By the summer of 1988 Gadhafi and Libya seemed to slip off the front pages of the news. The focus of the fight against terrorists had moved from Tripoli to Beirut, where American hostages continued to be held. At that point the Agency suspected that support for such terrorism came from Iran.

Tensions with that country ran high in the summer of 1988. On July 3, 1988, officers aboard the U.S. Navy cruiser *Vincennes*, deployed in the Persian Gulf, believed they detected an incoming Iranian F-14 and fired a surface-to-air missile to intercept the aircraft. The target proved to be not a fighter, but a civilian Iranian airliner, an Airbus A300. Flight 655 was blown apart by the missile and disintegrated midair. Two hundred and ninety passengers and crew members were killed. Once again Iran railed against the United States as "the Great Satan," and once again there was a feeling of waiting for the second shoe to drop—for Iran to take its revenge.

Five months after the downing of Iran's flight 655, the CIA's Counterterrorism Center needed an Arabic-speaking case officer to send to Beirut on temporary duty. A CTC officer informed Twetten that his son-in-law had been selected for the assignment.

"I am not a part of that decision," Twetten responded. "He's your officer." In his mind he knew he had no other choice. "It's all a sham if I intervene and say, 'No, you can't send Matthew to Beirut,' " he told himself. But there was no one in the Agency who understood better the perils of Beirut. Terry Anderson, a correspondent for the Associated Press, had by then been a hostage for more than three years, along with other Americans, including agronomist Thomas Sutherland and university administrator David Jacobsen. And they could be counted among the lucky ones.

The CIA's Beirut station chief, William F. Buckley, was not so fortunate. He had been seized by gunmen four years earlier, on March 16, 1984. A man who had quietly supported war orphans in Vietnam, Laos, and Beirut, Buckley had been widely admired by senior Agency officers and was a favorite of CIA head Bill Casey. For fifteen months Buckley was tortured and interrogated. He is believed to have died in captivity on

June 3, 1985. Six more years would pass before his remains would be recovered.

At Langley and at the Oval Office, the hostage issue had long been an obsession. The murder of Buckley had convinced the Agency that the other hostages were likewise in imminent peril. Frustrations grew. So, too, did comparisons with the Iran hostage crisis that came to define the Carter administration as weak and ineffective. Reagan's victory had in part been in revulsion to the humiliating spectacle of American hostages paraded about day after day. But in Lebanon, despite its best efforts, not even the location of the hostages was known to the CIA.

It was precisely such frustrations that led the administration and several within the CIA to appeal to Iran, which was believed to have sway over the captors. The plan that was concocted called for a trade of arms for hostages. Specifically the United States secretly sent TOW missiles to Iran in the hope of securing the hostages' release. The plan had a second aspect: proceeds from such sales would be diverted to fund the Contras in Nicaragua in their fight against the Sandinista regime, despite a congressional ban on such support. In November 1986 the scheme erupted into a public scandal known as Iran-Contra.

It would nearly bring down the Reagan administration and once again fix in the public mind the idea that the CIA was out of control and contemptuous of congressional oversight. Fending off congressional investigators and reporters would consume massive amounts of CIA Director William Casey's time and flagging energy. On May 5, 1987, just as the congressional Iran-Contra hearings were getting under way, the once-indefatigable William Casey died of a brain tumor. His successor as Director Central Intelligence was William H. Webster, a former federal judge and director of the FBI. Selected for his reputation for probity and candor, it was hoped that he might restore credibility to the Agency and hold a firmer reign over Langley. In the wake of Iran-Contra he fired two CIA employees, demoted another, and sent out letters of reprimand to four more. By then it had become a recurrent and all-too-familiar pattern at Agency headquarters, wherein men of action—a Dulles, a Helms, a Casey—are eventually followed by more disciplined administrators—a McCone, a Turner, a Webster—who are expected to pick up the pieces and restore credibility.

But the American hostages in Lebanon would long remain in captivity, some of them chained for upwards of a thousand days. It was their plight and the threat of even more terrorism that drew Matt Gannon to Beirut. In late November 1988 Gannon set off, traveling via Cyprus. For the next three weeks he worked relentlessly to reestablish contact with agents who provided him with critical intelligence on terrorist organizations in and around Beirut. But as Christmas drew near, Gannon thought of his family in suburban Maryland, of the burdens his wife faced without him, of his two daughters, Julia and Maggie.

He had been scheduled to fly out on December 23, but as exhausted as he was, he asked the Beirut chief of station if he might leave a day early. His request was granted and Gannon arranged to fly to Frankfurt and then on to London and New York. He booked his flight on Pan Am 103. Some weeks before the flight the United States had received what it considered to be credible threats that there would be an attack on a civilian airliner and the warning was posted to State Department personnel, though not to travelers at large. Even if Matt Gannon had been made aware of such a warning, it is doubtful he would have given it much notice. Such a risk would have paled in comparison to those he faced daily in Beirut.

The plane, named *Clipper Maid of the Seas*, was twenty-five minutes late in taking off from Heathrow, not unusual given the volume of travel at the Christmas holidays. Seven and a half hours later Matthew Gannon could look forward to landing at New York's John F. Kennedy Airport. Pillows were puffed up and in the galley flight attendants prepared to serve dinner. Sitting in business class, Matthew had room enough to stretch out.

Then, at precisely 7:03 P.M. GMT, the plane simply disappeared from the air controllers' screen at Prestwick, southwest of Glasgow. At 31,000 feet above the Scottish countryside it had blown apart. Moments later debris and body parts rained down on the village of Lockerbie. Matthew Gannon was one of 259 passengers and crew members who died. It was later speculated that many of the passengers did not die in the blast but rode their seats down in a terrifying six-mile descent. Eleven residents of Lockerbie also lost their lives.

· · ·

Early in the afternoon of December 22 Twetten was in his Agency office when the phone rang. His secretary answered the call. It was the

Counterterrorist Center. The message was brief. Pan Am 103 had gone down and Matthew Gannon was believed to have been on board. Twetten was at his desk when the secretary passed along the dreaded message. He asked that she inform him the moment anything more definitive was known, then he called his wife, Kay. He may also have called his daughter, Susan, that afternoon. He cannot now recall. "You're looking at a defense mechanism," he says. "I don't remember much of that afternoon. I know I made a decision that the moment there was any confirmation that he had indeed left Beirut a day early I would go home." And home he went.

A senior Agency officer wrote to those who needed to know: "It is with profound regret and sadness that I advise that Matthew Gannon was on board the PA 103 flight which crashed yesterday. Although as of this writing remains have not been identified, there is no chance he survived."

Twetten's superior, Deputy Director for Operations Dick Stolz, later asked if Twetten wanted his son-in-law buried in Arlington National Cemetery. Matthew had not been in the military, but the Pentagon had extended certain burial privileges in the past to CIA officers killed in the line of duty. Twetten left the decision to his daughter Susan, who said a burial in Arlington would be an honor. The arrangement was made between Stolz and senior Pentagon officials. "I doubt my position had anything to do with it," Twetten would reflect years later. "I didn't think it was appropriate to lift a finger myself." A consummate stickler for the rules, Tom Twetten was determined not to meddle in his son-in-law's career—even in death.

On the government-issued gravestone was written:

MATTHEW

KEVIN

GANNON

AUG 11 1954

DEC 22 1988

FGN SVC OFF

The abbreviation stood for "Foreign Service Officer." He had died under State Department cover. Now it was chiseled in stone.

. . .

Not long after the crash of Pan Am 103, Matthew Gannon's brother Dick received a letter of condolence from Robert Pugh, who had been the number two ranking official at the Beirut embassy when it was bombed. He knew how much Dick Gannon had already suffered as a result of the car bombing of the embassy and its unspeakable aftermath. Pugh understood only too well the irony that Dick Gannon's brother Matt should have survived the perils of gathering intelligence on terrorists in Beirut only to perish at the hands of terrorists while aboard a civilian airliner. There was no safe haven. Dick Gannon, already touched once by terrorism, had now to endure that much more pain again. Pugh's letter meant a great deal to Dick Gannon.

On April 20, 1989, Dick Gannon wrote Pugh, thanking him and his wife, Bonnie, for their kind expression of sympathy at the loss of his brother: "Matthew was a wonderful brother—he is never far from my thoughts. He leaves his wife, Susan and two beautiful daughters, Maggie age 4 and Julia age 1. They appear to be bearing up well. Our family and Matt's friends attended a funeral Mass at Holy Trinity Church in Georgetown where he and Susan were married in the summer of 1982. Matt was buried in Arlington on January 5th not far from some of our colleagues from Beirut."

Just five months after Dick Gannon wrote his letter—on September 19, 1989—a DC-10, UTA flight 772, was blown up over Africa by a terrorist bomb that had been tucked in the forward baggage compartment. The aircraft disintegrated, spreading wreckage across the desert of Niger in a scene all too reminiscent of Lockerbie, Scotland. Some 171 people lost their lives. Among the fatalities were 7 Americans. And among these was Bonnie Pugh, wife of Robert Pugh, then U.S. ambassador to Chad. It was now Dick Gannon's turn to write a letter of condolence to Pugh. Both men, twice struck by terrorism, shared a common bond that neither would have wished upon his worst enemy. But there was something not yet known to either man that would link their tragedies and point to the same sinister hand that may have been ultimately responsible for both Pan Am 103 and UTA 772.

. . .

In October 1989 Dick Gannon and his wife, Betsy, made a sort of pilgrimage to Lockerbie. They went through a series of trailers lined up side by side where the yet-unclaimed belongings of the deceased were set out on tables, organized by type of item. On one table were rows and rows of shoes, on another glasses, on another shirts, and on yet another pants. It was a grim scene, curiously neat. Each item had been meticulously laundered and folded or arrayed in rows by the townspeople.

Dick Gannon saw nothing of his brother's among the articles, but then a local constable escorted them to a table with a bag. Inside were many things Dick Gannon instantly recognized to be Matt's—a Catholic missal, its delicate pages damaged by exposure to the rains, a check for $43 protected in a plastic sleeve, a plaid flannel shirt Matt often wore.

The constable befriended them and drove them to an open field where sheep grazed on rolling green hills and the grass was high. It was a peaceful place beside a narrow country lane. The officer helped the Gannons as they stooped to clear some open slats in an old wood rail fence. He walked them well out into the pasture to a place undisturbed by the business of death and reclamation that still absorbed the town. This was the precise place, he said, where he had found Matthew Gannon's body.

. . .

The loss of Matt Gannon had hit particularly hard on the sixth floor of the old headquarters building at Langley where the Counterterrorist Center was located. The first reports of the crash had come not from some CIA agent in the field or satellite imagery, but from CNN. The entire CTC staff had congregated around the television in the so-called Fusion Center, the communications hub with other agencies, particularly the State Department's Office of Counterterrorism and the FBI. They had all watched in disbelief. First came the report that the plane was out of contact with Heathrow. Then came the haunting live pictures of wreckage strewn across the Scottish countryside. They had lost one of their own. The room filled with the sound of sobbing from those who had known Matt Gannon and who had worked so closely with him.

Now came the leviathan task of finding out who was responsible for bringing down Pan Am 103. It would be a couple of days before explosive residue was found on the debris signaling that an "improvised explosive device," or IED, had brought down the plane. Almost immediately the CTC set up a Pan Am Task Force, commencing what was to be one of the most intensive intelligence operations in the history of the Agency. The five officers assigned to the task force often worked around the clock. Twetten purposely kept his distance from the daily investigative operations, but everyone on the task force understood that his desire to solve the case went well beyond a professional interest. More than once the CTC ran into a bureaucratic snag and it was Tom Twetten who quickly cleared the way.

Initially the CTC presumed that the attack on Pan Am 103 was in retaliation for the July 3, 1988, downing of the Iranian airliner by the U.S. naval vessel *Vincennes*. Suspicions were strong within the CIA that the Iranians had worked with the Popular Front for the Liberation of Palestine–General Command, or PFLP-GC, a view that Israeli intelligence also promoted.

But two breakthroughs in the investigation pointed to a far different culprit. The first clue came from an analyst assigned to the task force who determined that the device used to trigger the Semtex explosive on Pan Am 103 bore an uncanny resemblance to that used to bring down the civilian aircraft in West Africa—the terrorist action that had claimed Bonnie Pugh's life.

That attack had been linked to the Libyans. The digital electric timers were traced back to a Swiss firm that had allegedly sold its products to the Libyan military and Jamahirya Security Organization, the country's intelligence service. In the case of Pan Am 103, a large brown Samsonite suitcase stuffed with clothes was believed to contain a portable radio cassette tape player that held the explosive. That suitcase had been transferred from an Air Malta aircraft to Pan Am 103 in Frankfurt, Germany, and then onto the Boeing 747 in Heathrow, the continuation of that flight. It was thought that little more than a pound of high explosive placed in the forward cargo hold had brought down the 600,000-pound jumbo jet.

A second, more serendipitous break reportedly came from within the ranks of the Libyans themselves. A code clerk stationed in a Libyan embassy in Europe cabled a cryptic message on a frequency readily accessible to the CIA. In what one senior CTC official said appeared to be a deliberate effort to contact the Agency, the code clerk claimed that the

Libyans were behind the bombing. The message offered a detailed account of how the decision was made within Libya.

In 1991 the United States and Britain charged two alleged former Libyan intelligence officers, Abdel Basset Ali Megrahi and Lamen Khalifa Fhimah, with the bombing of Pan Am 103. But the two had sought asylum in Libya, whose government steadfastly refused to turn them over to prosecutors to face trial. It was not until April 5, 1999, more than a decade after the bombing of Pan Am 103, that the two suspects were finally turned over to authorities to be tried under Scottish law in the Netherlands, the result of a carefully brokered deal with Libya.

. . .

More than a year after the downing of Pan Am 103 a farmer walking through a field in Scotland came upon the remnants of a suit bag lodged in a tree. Inside the bag was found the note that Matthew Gannon had written to his brother Dick, dated December 18, 1988. "You won't believe this," it began, "but I've spent the last three weeks in Beirut. The Embassy needed an Arabic speaker so I volunteered." Matthew Gannon spoke of his wife, Susan, and daughters Maggie and Julia. "I couldn't have taken this TDY if Maggie hadn't improved so much in the last 6 months," he wrote. "We (I should say Susan) are working with her every day & we see the gains in her better behavior. Julia is a little doll, walking and beginning to talk—growing up way too quickly." The letter ended, "Love, Matthew."

There was this postscript: "We didn't tell Mom and Dad I was in Beirut because they would worry too much." The letter was handwritten and the ink had blurred and run from exposure to a year's worth of rains that had washed over it. In time the letter found its way into the hands of Matthew Gannon's widow, Susan, and ultimately to his brother Dick, to whom the letter had been written.

For months thereafter, pieces of the plane and personal items turned up. The emotional wreckage caused by the crash was strewn over several continents and seemed to be without end.

At 2:30 P.M. on January 9, 1989, just weeks after Gannon's death, the CIA held a memorial service for him in the auditorium known as the Bubble, directly across from the old headquarters building. Scores of covert officers, analysts, senior administrators, and members of the

Counterterrorist Center filed somberly down the aisles and took their places. Tom Twetten escorted his daughter, Susan, into the auditorium. At the entrance was an enlarged photographic portrait of her husband. It was more than she could take. But for Tom Twetten's taking her by the arm and propping her up, she would have collapsed in grief.

In the memorial ceremony's printed program was a picture of a smiling Matthew Gannon, and beneath it, fittingly enough, were words from the Koran: "And God gave them a reward in this world and the excellent reward of the Hereafter. For God loveth those who do good." There were so many ironies surrounding his death, not the least of which was that Matthew Gannon had been among those within the Agency most sympathetic to the interests and causes of the Arab world. In killing him, they had slain not an enemy but an ally.

Susan Gannon would remarry in 1993, five years after the downing of Pan Am 103. She and her father, Tom Twetten, and mother, Kay, invited the entire Gannon clan to the wedding. The night before, there was a festive square dance at a farm outside of Washington and the sound of fiddles filled the air. Amid such merriment there was no mention made of Matthew Gannon, nor was there need to. Those who had known him simply exchanged knowing glances or paused an extra moment in each other's embrace.

As for Tom Twetten, the only setback to his otherwise charmed Agency career came as a result of his position as CIA liaison to a National Security Council staff member named Oliver North. It was North who oversaw the scheme to sell arms to Iran in the hope that it would win the release of American hostages.

"I like to call myself the chaperon for Ollie North," Twetten would joke years later. "I didn't aspire to the job but I got it anyway." For his reluctant role, Twetten would be called to testify some twenty-seven times, four of them to a grand jury. Six years after the calamitous operation was exposed he was still being called to testify.

But his Agency career was intact. On January 1, 1991, at the age of fifty-five, Twetten was named deputy director for operations. As DDO, Twetten was the nation's spymaster overseeing an estimated $1-billion empire that included all of the CIA's worldwide covert operations, safe houses, overseas stations and bases, and a network of communications facilities.

Twetten's seventh-floor office at Agency headquarters had a distinctly Middle Eastern flavor reflecting his scholarly interest in the region. On the walls were portraits of men in turbans and prints of antique maps, including one of Jerusalem and another of Turkey dated 1705. Under the coffee table was a Bedouin's camel saddlebag. Twetten had tried unsuccessfully to reclaim the desk of Wild Bill Donovan, the founder of the OSS, but settled for a standard wooden desk. On it were three STUs, secure telephone units, as well as a buzzer system by which the three Directors Central Intelligence under whom he served as DDO—Webster, Gates, and Woolsey—could ring him directly. Twetten could also have rung the director, but such an action was understood to be forbidden by Agency protocol.

These were good years for Twetten. After a lifetime of undercover work he seemed relaxed and comfortable with his new authority. Though sober and serious, he could also be playful. One Halloween, after being placed in charge of all CIA spy operations, he had a "spook party" for his friends and colleagues at the Agency. Twetten gave instructions that guests were to arrive by passing through a neighborhood graveyard. Twetten, dressed as a ghoul, had dug a hole on his property, and as guests arrived, he rose ominously from the makeshift grave to greet them.

But such moments of levity were rare. On June 2, 1993, still as deputy director for operations, he stood before the CIA's Wall of Honor and delivered the commemorative remarks for those who died in the line of service. Among those honored by a star on the wall—but never named—was his son-in-law, Matt Gannon. It was hard for Tom Twetten to deliver his remarks. His eyes filled with tears and his voice choked with emotion, but he never faltered.

After thirty-four years, Twetten retired from the CIA at the end of September 1995. Today he lives in a rustic 1840s home built on the edge of Little Hosmer Pond in the north of Vermont, a quiet place by a tiny spillway where children sometimes look for frogs. From inside his den, Twetten can watch the mergansers searching for fish. Once a week he visits Montreal to study the art of rebinding fine leather books, his second passion. Downstairs, in his library and bindery, are his precious books: a copy of *The Essays of Elia*, by Charles Lamb, dated 1896, beside it *New Improvements of Gardening*, dated 1739, and an undated copy of *Christian Lyrics*.

Once one of the most powerful figures in the CIA, he now contents himself with socializing with locals who know little of his background and could care less. In a sense, in retirement, he is again under cover. At a recent village barbecue at the Albany Church five miles from his home a woman patted him on the back for the fine 140-foot stone wall he erected, but scolded him lightly for a house she deemed too large. Twetten only smiled. He could not be further from power, or the violent world in which terrorists and those who stalk them live and die.

For Twetten the battle with Gadhafi and terrorism is over. The Agency in which he had risen to the senior-most ranks, working together with the U.S. military, had played a key role in the bombing of Tripoli that cost Gadhafi his eighteen-month-old daughter. Two years later Twetten's own Agency would conclude that Libyan agents had brought down Pan Am 103, costing Twetten his son-in-law, widowing his daughter, and leaving his granddaughters fatherless.

Terrorism and the war that sought to contain it had created a deadly symmetry in the lives of two men who had never met and had even less in common—Muammar Gadhafi and Tom Twetten. "It's an irony that certainly has occurred to me," says Twetten. "I have never thought of it as a grotesque irony. It's never occurred to me for more than two seconds that there was a causal link. The Libyans aren't that good. Their timing was entirely accidental."

Twetten is right. There is no evidence to suggest that the Libyans targeted Pan Am 103 because Matthew Gannon, Tom Twetten's son-in-law, was on board. It was a chillingly simple act of random violence. "It's fairly easy for me to dismiss the connection," says Twetten. "I have never permitted myself to feel any remorse or responsibility for his death. This is not a part of my baggage. I had so much authority over so many lives that I don't think I'd be among the sane if I permitted all the connections with all the people I had who are no longer living. I am saved some of that in terms of rationality because I didn't send Matthew to Beirut. This was the blessing of making sure that there was no potential nepotism."

As for Matthew Gannon's brother Dick, he remains with the State Department. Far from retiring, he took on the ultimate job for a security officer—overseeing the security of the new U.S. Embassy in Moscow. In his Virginia office just across the Potomac is a picture of Matthew cradling a small kitten and standing before a large wall map of the world. He is wearing a conservative white button-down shirt and a striped tie, but with his long hair and drooping mustache he has the hint of a desperado about him.

A decade after his brother's death, Dick Gannon still sorely misses him. He is envious of his mother's faith and the comfort it has afforded her at the loss of Matthew Gannon, aged thirty-four.

"God," she concluded, "must have wanted him awful badly."

CHAPTER 13

Damage Control

Give sorrow words: the grief that does not speak
Whispers the o'er-fraught heart, and bids it break.

SHAKESPEARE, *Macbeth*

WHAT Debra Spessard remembers clearly is helping her husband, Jimmy, pack on the morning after Thanksgiving 1989. She remembers folding his jeans and T-shirts and laying them out for him to put in his brown leather suitcase. She knew he was going to Zaire and she knew that, even in November, it would be sweltering.

It was a morning like many before it, full of the rituals of leaving. She watched as her husband emptied his wallet of any identification cards that might conflict with the pseudonym under which he was to work overseas. Out came the Social Security card, the credit cards, driver's license, even the family photographs—anything that might betray him. He sifted through his passports, selecting the right one for this mission's cover story. He was to be a civilian employee of the Defense Department. It was not the first time he had used that cover.

But on this morning he broke from the familiar pattern and removed even his gold wedding band, setting it gently in a small wooden box in his top dresser drawer. Inside the ring were engraved their initials: "DKS to JES." Never before had he done that, and the divergence, slight as it was, unnerved her. Even before that, Debra had sensed some higher element of risk to this mission.

He said he would be gone two weeks. "Is this necessary?" she asked, trying to mask her apprehension. She was still grieving over the loss of her father and was feeling needy. She was dreading Jimmy's absence. "Yes," he nodded, and that was the end of it. She knew not to ask for any particulars.

That morning she would have to steel herself as she and the boys, Jarad, aged five, and Jason, seven, drove Jimmy to the tiny Hagerstown, Maryland, airport to see him off. There he again broke with habit. Once out of the airport door, instead of making directly for the plane, he turned and walked back to the fence where Debra, Jarad, and Jason were waving. He gave his wife a final good-bye kiss. "I love you guys," he said, and boarded the tiny aircraft for the first of several flights on his way to Africa.

Jimmy Spessard was not a spy in the traditional mold of the clandestine service. He didn't even work for the CIA's Operations Directorate, which oversaw covert activities. Instead, Jimmy was chiefly answerable to "S&T," the Science and Technology Directorate that kept those in the field supplied with whatever electronics and paraphernalia were needed. After six years in the navy working with Terrier and Harpoon missiles Jimmy Spessard had emerged as a bona fide "techie."

A small-town boy, he had grown up in a crossroads called Halfway, so named for its position between Hagerstown and Williamsport, Maryland. The son of a railroad brakeman, he had spent mornings before school working at a nearby asparagus farm. He had been an Eagle Scout and an active member of the Grace United Methodist Church and was considered by his pals as something of a good-time Charlie. He joined the navy straight out of high school but was hardly gung ho. He signed his letters home as "A POW" and wrote "Go Navy (go somewhere else)." He married his childhood sweetheart and for a couple of years worked as a traveling salesman peddling copy machines and calculators. He lived a life so ordinary it bordered on the humdrum—until, that is, he linked up with the Central Intelligence Agency in the early 1980s.

For the next six years he commuted an hour and a half each way to Warrenton, Virginia, to an office at Computer Data Systems, a company that provided a wide array of high-tech electronic gear to the CIA. His work for the Agency took him to Athens, Amman, Ankara, Bangkok, and innumerable other far-flung outposts. A part of his duties involved the testing, delivering, and installing of complex surveillance systems destined for CIA stations in U.S. embassies abroad. From each trip he would bring back a lapel pin and a miniature flag, gifts for his sons.

Throughout those years he worked for the Field Support Branch on contract to the Agency. His specialty was something called "collection and signal processing equipment." In the summer of 1989 he apparently became a full-fledged employee of the CIA. It was hardly the stuff of spy novels, but a slipup or blown cover could prove messy, even deadly, for himself or those with whom he worked.

In November 1989 Spessard received an unusual set of orders. He was to go to Zaire and then on to Angola, part of a covert mission of particular sensitivity. It was the last chapter in the Cold War. An anemic Soviet Union was so absorbed in its own woes that it was scarcely capable of or interested in meddling in the sort of proxy wars that had come to characterize the post–World War II era. Just two weeks earlier the Berlin Wall had fallen. Bulgaria's dictator had resigned. So, too, had Czechoslovakia's Communist Party general secretary. At Langley there was a mix of disbelief and euphoria, a sense that history and destiny had, at long last, proved them right. But some fires were slower to burn out. Among the most persistent was that which engulfed Angola, where Spessard was headed. It was as if the rest of the world was embracing its future while Spessard was assigned to the past.

The country, which gained independence from Portugal in November 1975, had long been the subject of a brutal civil war. Early on, the CIA heaped covert paramilitary support on an organization known as the National Union for the Total Independence of Angola, or UNITA, led by Jonas Savimbi. Scores of CIA operatives were assigned to the Angola Task Force. But Congress was in no mood for CIA adventurism, fearful that it might lead the United States into yet another Vietnam. Saigon had fallen only months earlier. In June 1976 Congress passed the Clark Amendment banning all covert action in Angola. It was said to be the first direct congressional interference with a covert action and it would stand for a decade.

But the ensuing decade since gaining independence had bankrupted Angola and rendered it one of Africa's most desperate economies, its 10 million people utterly sapped by civil war and outside intervention. During those years the upper hand seemed to shift back and forth between UNITA and the leftist MPLA, or Popular Movement for the Liberation of Angola. By the early 1980s Soviet aid was said to total several billions of dollars, and an estimated forty thousand Cuban troops were in country. South Africa stood firmly behind UNITA, helping to stave off defeat.

In the summer of 1985 the MPLA with Soviet aid and Cuban support had launched an offensive and UNITA was pushed back. On August 8 of that year, Congress lifted its ban on covert support to Angola. Three months later Reagan signed a presidential finding providing covert lethal assistance to UNITA. The Agency even dispatched one of its operatives to Savimbi headquarters. He would live in a thatched hut for years. Matériel and weapons soon flowed into the country. In February 1986 the National Security Council approved the covert shipment of TOW antiarmor and Stinger antiaircraft missiles to Savimbi.

For years the CIA continued its secret resupply of UNITA, determined not to allow a Marxist regime to prevail. To do this, the Agency relied on the support of Mobuto, leader of neighboring Zaire and one of the world's most corrupt leaders. Mobuto had long enjoyed the CIA's favor and had allowed the clandestine resupply effort of Savimbi to operate out of one of Zaire's remote air bases—Kamina. It was the same base from which the CIA's John Merriman had taken off in his fatal flight against leftist Congolese guerrillas some twenty-four years earlier. Headed by a CIA base officer, Kamina provided a barracks, showers, and even rental movies to the crew that manned the huge cargo plane that made the perilous nighttime flight into and out of Angola. Still there was an undeniable sense of isolation at the base. There were no telephones. The link to the outside was by radio to Kinshasa, formerly Léopoldville.

Spessard's first mission in aid of Savimbi's troops was, after many delays, scheduled to take off on Monday, just three days after his departure from Hagerstown. While the precise nature of the equipment he was to deliver to Savimbi is not known, those familiar with Spessard's work say it would probably have been used to help UNITA locate hostile forces by getting a fix on their transmissions.

The lumbering cargo plane that would take him into Angola was to be one of the "Gray Ghosts," so named for their slate-colored paint. The plane had four seats in the front—for a pilot, copilot, navigator, and loadmaster. The fuselage was largely open for cargo. On board that night was a seasoned crew of six. Even by Agency standards, it had a distinctly international flavor. Heading the team was Pharies "Bud" Petty, a veteran Agency pilot who, at least on paper, presided over a Florida firm called Tepper Aviation, located in Crestview, just off Eglin Air Force Base. The other crew members were all ostensibly employees of Tepper. The CIA often uses such contracts as a mask to conceal its activities from public scrutiny, suspicion, and ultimately, accountability.

Petty, then forty-nine, was a husky six-footer with a full head of hair, hazel-blue eyes, and an easy, soothing manner. He was a shadowy character with an illustrious war record and a deep, some would say unquestioning, trust in government. Whatever his country asked of him he would do. In 1955, at age fifteen, he had joined the navy using a family Bible that contained an altered birth date showing him to be three years older than he was. A year later he stood on the deck of the aircraft carrier USS *Badoeng Strait* and shielded his eyes from the flash of a nuclear test, part of Operation Redwing in the Pacific Ocean. As ordered, he would dispose of his radiation-contaminated clothes, but never, even years later, second-guess the wisdom of exposing the troops to such a test.

By the time he reached Vietnam he was an army pilot, his dazzling record capped off with a Distinguished Flying Cross, a Silver Star, a Bronze Star with Oak Leaf Cluster, and an Air Medal with V Device. As fire team leader with the 334th Armed Helicopter Company he had led a devastating air raid that sank 174 sampans, some of them apparently loaded with ammo. In 1977 he retired as a major. He never spoke of Vietnam thereafter. But for years it invaded his sleep.

In 1981 Petty had gone to work for the Agency, living for a time in

Washington, D.C. Later he moved to Florida and set up a series of dummy companies and Agency proprietaries that provided the CIA with planes and crews. During the mid-1980s he played an unseen role in what would come to be known as Iran-Contra. He was a part of that tight-lipped circle of pilots and crew associated with St. Lucia Airways as it ferried missiles to Iran, supplied anti-Communist insurgencies, and engaged in other Agency-sponsored activities.

That November night, as the plane lifted off from Kamina Air Base in Zaire, Bud Petty was in the cockpit as pilot or copilot. There was none steadier. Still, his family had fretted about this mission. "Don't worry," he had told his eldest sister, Joyce, "this is my last trip. I'm tired."

He had seemed to think himself invincible, but he was savvy enough to understand that even the best are at risk. He took what precautions he could, always mindful of security. Several times he had told his sister Losue that if she should ever receive a collect call from someone named Grant Eugene Turner, she would know it was from him. The name was a corruption of his wife's maiden name, Gracie Tyner.

The aviation mechanic that night was thirty-three-year-old George Vincent Lacy. Raised in Lawton, Oklahoma, he had only recently signed on to Tepper. He came from a family in which service to government was a given. His father was a twenty-year army man and his uncle had died in the crash of an air force jet. As with so many others, working for the Agency was a family business. His older brother had spent a career serving Langley. But extended trips overseas were tough on George Lacy and harder still to explain to his fiancée.

Two Germans were also on board that night. One was forty-nine-year-old George Bensch, the other forty-one-year-old Gerhard Hermann Rieger. Bensch was a mechanic. He had moved to the States just two years earlier. Before that he had serviced St. Lucia's planes in Europe as they set out on covert Agency operations. Rieger, the flight engineer, was the father of two sons. Both men had been born in West Germany.

The last member of the crew was a Brit, forty-four-year-old Michael Atkinson. A hulking six feet four, he might easily have passed for the Marlboro Man. Born in Yorkshire, England, he had made his home for over a decade in the British West Indies on the lush island of St. Lucia.

Formerly the captain of a three-masted schooner, Atkinson was now a pilot. And though he had flown with St. Lucia Airways, the Agency proprietary, he had little interest in ideology or fighting the Communists. What he lived for was adventure, be it on the sea or in the air. He also had to think of providing support for his two sons, Oliver and Jason, and his wife, Madeleine, then pregnant with a third child.

Also on board were eleven of Savimbi's men and a fuselage full of supplies, including crates of ammo. So secretive was the operation that even at Kamina the men lived under aliases. When airborne, flight records listed them not by name, but by number. The two nightly flights were simply designated "Flight One" and "Flight Two." Even Savimbi was referred to only by an Agency code name. All knowledge of the operation was compartmented on a need-to-know basis.

The destination was a remote gravel airstrip in Angola. Landings kicked up huge clouds of dust. From there, it was nearly an hour to UNITA's base camp. Sometimes Savimbi himself would meet the plane, shake hands, and give out wooden carvings in appreciation. In the past, most such flights had been "touch-and-gos," meaning that the engines were never shut down, and once the cargo had been unloaded, the plane would take off again for Zaire.

Spessard's flight represented the first resumption of the resupply effort in many months. It took off without incident and for the next five hours was tracked closely by the Agency, which was in constant communication with the aircraft. It was an Agency communications officer in Kinshasa who first reported that he had lost contact with the plane.

· · ·

At eight o'clock that Monday night, November 27, 1989, in Hagerstown, Maryland, Debra Spessard was in her kitchen. Her mother was giving her a perm. The doorbell rang. It was a man in a black suit carrying a briefcase. He may or may not have given his name. Debra Spessard cannot remember. What he had to say made everything else melt away. Jim Spessard's flight, he said, was missing.

The next morning at eight he called back. James Spessard, he said, was dead. There was little else he could or would tell her. The area where the plane had gone down was remote. The Agency had not yet been able to reach it.

It was only later that the Agency determined that the Lockheed L-100–20 Hercules cargo plane had been on final approach to the airfield near Jamba, Savimbi's headquarters. It was too risky to turn the runway lights on until the last seconds and the pilot was forced to rely on instruments. In the utter blackness of night, there was no hint of a horizon by which to steer. It was already too late when he discovered he was coming in too low. He attempted to circle but the wing clipped a treetop and the plane cartwheeled into the ground. Almost immediately the fuel and ammunition aboard exploded in a fireball that consumed the aircraft, its crew, and its cargo. One Savimbi warrior, no older than sixteen, had been lying down on the cargo near the tail. He was thrown clear and survived almost unscathed.

Spessard, Petty, Lacy, Rieger, Bensch, Atkinson, and Savimbi's men perished in the crash. Many of the bodies were burned beyond recognition.

Soon after the crash, an Agency team composed of a dozen people—investigators and medical examiners—was on-site. They recovered the bodies, the black box, and remains of flight instruments, and scoured the area for anything of a sensitive nature that could prove awkward for the Agency. Anything not consumed by fire was retrieved.

The six coffins arrived at Dover Air Force Base without any of the usual ceremony or public spectacle that awaits many of those who are killed overseas in service to country. A photo would record that a nondescript cargo plane delivered six crates. "Handle with Care" stenciled on their sides and bound by white cord.

Five of the caskets—those of Petty, Lacy, Bensch, Rieger, and Atkinson—were flown to Florida via yet another nondescript cargo plane which was promptly taken inside a hangar at Tepper Aviation. The five identical silver eighteen-gauge steel caskets, all of them sealed, were placed in hearses and driven to the Twin City Funeral Home in Niceville, Florida.

For the next two days there were visitation hours as mourners passed by the caskets, each in its own room. Funeral director Joe MacLendon was struck that many of those who passed by the caskets were not attired in the usual black suits but wore instead weathered leather jackets and appeared, to use his word, "tough." They reminded him of the character Indiana Jones. He wondered if some of those in attendance were mercenaries.

From Florida the caskets would go their separate ways. But first there was paperwork to be done and regulations regarding the transfer of bodies that had to be satisfied.

For funeral director MacLendon this was not so easy. There were no accompanying death certificates. What scanty records arrived from Dover were largely illegible. Under the entry "Circumstances Surrounding Death" was written "Unknown." So it was with "Place of Death" and "Date of Death." There was no information to be had, no contact with the government, only a check from Tepper Aviation to cover the cost of the funerals.

In an effort to oblige the widows, MacLendon dummied up the necessary documents, made up what information he didn't know, and had them notarized. And with that, the caskets went out.

George Lacy's remains were flown by private plane to Oklahoma and interred in a family plot in El Reno. George Bensch's body was returned to Walldorf, Germany. Michael Atkinson's casket was returned to the island of St. Lucia. There, following his widow's request, the Cricks Funeral Home drilled holes in the casket and attached iron weights to it so that it might be buried in the sea he so loved. A small flotilla of fishing boats escorted the coffin three miles out of Rodney Bay. The swells were high and the mourners thought it only fitting that on such a day they would bury a man unfazed by rough weather. Then, with words of blessing from a Methodist minister, the coffin was lowered into the Caribbean.

Petty's and Rieger's final journeys would take an even more unusual twist.

Back in Hagerstown, CIA officers asked the Spessard family to provide dental records to help them identify Spessard's remains. Spessard's family was in the cemetery business, but even for them it was a grim assignment. They asked to view the body. They wanted to make sure that the remains were indeed those of James Spessard. But the Agency refused. The remains, they were told, were in a body bag within the coffin and were simply "not viewable."

But Debra and other family members were insistent. Years earlier Jimmy Spessard had tattooed on his chest the little yellow bird known as Woodstock from the cartoon *Peanuts*. They asked to see that the corpse had such a tattoo. The Agency refused their request. The family asked if a picture could be taken of the tattoo. This, too, was denied. They could not even pick out the casket.

A day later three Agency employees, two men and a woman, showed up at the Spessard home, which was now filled with mourners. The three arrived in a black car, dressed in black and carrying black briefcases. They asked Debra Spessard and her brother if they could go somewhere where they might be alone and be free to talk. Debra Spessard led them to the basement rec room, where she and her brother took a seat on a sofa.

If the Agency was concerned with Spessard's loss, it was also concerned with just how it was going to conceal the circumstances of that loss from the public and press. Damage control was foremost on their minds. They asked Spessard's widow if she would be willing to tell friends and any reporters who might make inquiries that her husband had been working for a private company and was moonlighting for a few extra dollars at the time he was killed. That way his link to the Agency might remain a secret.

Debbie Spessard said she would not lie about the circumstances of her husband's death. "If Jimmy was going to die for his country," she told them, "it isn't going to be perceived that he died for a paycheck." The woman from the Agency asked again, all the while holding Debra Spessard's trembling hands. Twice more, Debra Spessard refused. She eventually agreed to provide any reporters with a telephone number the Agency had given her which would shunt reporters off the track of the CIA.

At the Pentagon, three days after the crash, briefer Pete Williams was fending off reporters' questions. Williams was asked who was on the flight, what it carried, and which government agency, if any, it was affiliated with. "The only thing I know," he told reporters, "is what the army put out, which is that the person named James Spessard—S-P-E-S-S-A-R-D—was an army civilian employee, but that's all I know about it."

The CIA, when asked about the flight, issued its usual line, delivered by spokesman Mark Mansfield: "As a matter of policy, we never confirm or deny such reports," he said.

. . .

The crash had been catastrophic for the Spessard family. For the Agency, too, it was viewed with grave alarm. The timing could not have been worse. Just two days after the crash, President George Bush was to meet with the Soviets' Mikhail Gorbachev for a much-touted summit in the Mediterranean off Malta.

And only two days prior to the Angola crash the U.S. government had made much of a plane that had crashed in eastern El Salvador that was revealed to be carrying Soviet arms destined for leftist rebels in that country. The twin-engine Cessna that originated in Nicaragua carried some twenty-four SA-7 antiaircraft missiles in its belly. Its crash and the subsequent publicity surrounding it had provided a propaganda bonanza and potential leverage in the upcoming summit.

The United States could argue that the Soviets were still dirtying their hands in anachronistic proxy wars long after America had chosen to take the high ground, repudiating such nefarious intervention in Third World conflicts. An indignant Bush administration had even lodged a formal protest with the Soviet Embassy. Among those most eager to mine the propaganda benefits of that crash was CIA Director William Webster.

The crash in Angola threatened to expose U.S. hypocrisy and put the United States and Soviet Union on an equally equivocal moral footing in the eyes of the world. No one understood this better than George Bush, who as president was acutely sensitive to such developments on the eve of a summit. But as the only president to have also served as Director Central Intelligence he was sympathetic to the risks of covert operations. The CIA and State Department did what they could to mislead and distract the press and to ensure that the Angola crash got only minimal attention.

In the recent past the CIA had been quite successful at that. Just three months prior to the Angola crash, the Agency had lost one of its own in another African plane crash and managed to completely conceal its link to the fatality despite a flood of national and international press attention.

On August 7, 1989, a high-profile U.S. congressman, Mickey Leland, a Democrat from Texas, on a humanitarian and fact-finding mission in Ethiopia, had been en route to a refugee camp. His twin-engine plane crashed into a cliff during a violent storm. All sixteen passengers and crew were killed. Among the retinue of U.S. officials accompanying the congressman was twenty-five-year-old Robert William Woods. He was said to be a lowly third-level vice-consel with the State Department in the embassy at Addis Ababa.

But Woods was not what he seemed to be. A brilliant young man, he had attended Harvard as a National Merit scholar, graduated cum laude with a degree in history, was a licensed pilot, and, for the preceding two years, had been a covert officer of the CIA. Woods had volunteered for Ethiopia though he understood well its many dangers.

Just prior to leaving he had asked an attorney to draft a will. The attorney had said he was busy and that surely it could wait until Woods's scheduled return to the States in January—when Woods was to be married. What, after all, was the rush? Woods was but twenty-five. But he insisted and it was done before his departure. And not long before leaving, Woods took his fiancée, Colleen Healy, for a stroll through the Forest Hills Cemetery in Kansas City, Missouri. "This is where my grandfather is buried," he pointed out, "and this is where I want to be buried, beside him," he said. And so he would be.

But the Agency was intent upon making sure that no one linked him to Langley. The presence of an Agency operative assigned to Ethiopia was seen as extremely sensitive. The United States had withdrawn its ambassador nine years earlier, in 1980, and had operated only a skeleton embassy staff in Addis Ababa. Ethiopia had aligned itself with Moscow and Libya, and the United States had adopted a policy of encirclement, arming Somalia, Kenya, and Sudan.

The Agency had reason to fear that Woods's death might generate unwanted attention given the interest in Leland and the prominence of his family. His father, Dick Woods, was senior vice-president and general counsel to the Federal Reserve Bank of Kansas City.

But in the end, Woods's death was utterly eclipsed by the attention given Congressman Leland's loss. Woods's name would later be added to the State Department wall, continuing the fiction of his cover story, and another nameless star was written into the Agency's Book of Honor. His family even established a fund in his name at Harvard. But the secret of his CIA employment was intact.

. . .

Three months later the Agency faced an even more complicated situation in Angola with multiple fatalities and a volatile political situation. But while Langley fretted about keeping a lid on the accident, the Spessard family concerned itself with funeral arrangements for thirty-one-year-old Jimmy Spessard. Given Spessard's six years in the navy and his death in the performance of governmental service, the family had hoped that the Pentagon would provide the services of Arlington's famed Old Guard and a military funeral. But the military cited rules that the Guard would not attend funerals beyond a thirty-mile radius from Arlington. The Spessards were heartsick. They appealed to the Agency. Their concerns went all the way to the top. Director Central Intelligence Webster, a former judge and FBI head, personally got involved and used his clout to persuade the Pentagon to waive its restrictions and to allow the Old Guard to make the long drive up to Hagerstown. They arrived by bus, somewhat bewildered by the distance and the occasion. "I don't know why we're here or who he was," one member of the Guard was heard to say.

When it came time to lift the flag off the casket, fold it, and present it, they mistook Spessard's grandmother for the widow. At twenty-six, Debra Spessard simply seemed too young to be a widow. Spessard's grandmother accepted the triangular flag, then promptly passed it to her daughter-in-law, who sat beside her.

At the funeral, mourners signed a book, a maroon leather-bound volume entitled "Precious Memories." The book contained a number of curious entries. It said that Spessard had died in Zaire, continuing the cover story given to the press. Even odder were the signatures of those who attended the funeral. Many who were covert employees of the Agency simply signed their first name and the first letter of their last name. Others intentionally penned names that were illegible. Among these were three of Spessard's pallbearers who were Agency colleagues.

Spessard was buried in Greenlawn Memorial Park, the cemetery where Debra Spessard works and which is owned by her family. His grave is a few short minutes' walk from her desk. Before his interment, the gold wedding ring he had removed the morning of his departure was allowed to be placed in the coffin.

All along the way the CIA did what it could to conceal its link to Spessard and to the resupply effort of Savimbi. Days after the crash, CIA officers appeared at Spessard's home. They went down to the basement rec room and carted off Spessard's entire computer system. It was never to be returned.

Within a week of the crash a letter arrived at Debra Spessard's home. By all appearances it was a personal letter. It was from a Patsy Hallums and the return address was her home. But Hallums was a CIA employee, and inside the envelope was a letter of condolence from none other than William H. Webster, Director Central Intelligence. It was dated December 11, 1989, and read in part:

"Jimmy was a dedicated and conscientious employee who enjoyed the highest respect and admiration of his colleagues.

"He was one of the most energetic members of the staff who took the time to lend his help to others. Often, this meant going out of his way for a colleague with a work-related or personal problem. He spoke often of his family and was known to his friends as a devoted husband and loving father. Your husband's warm personality and quick smile will be missed by those who share in this tragic loss.

"I hope you will derive some peace and comfort in knowing that he served his country and this Agency well . . ."

Later a packet of letters from his Agency colleagues arrived. The return addresses had all been snipped off. Any mail sent by the CIA or its employees carried a stamp. A postage meter carries an identifying number and, along with it, the risk of being traced.

A month after the crash, on the morning of December 19, 1989, the Agency dispatched a van to Hagerstown to pick up the Spessard family and drive them to Langley for a meeting with Director Webster and a memorial service. They were escorted to the director's private elevator and taken to the seventh floor. On the way up, their escort told them a series of peculiar stories about the director's dining room, including one that involved a Saudi official who had requested and was granted a serving of boa constrictor. (Never happened, say senior Agency officials, though several members of the Spessard family recall being told the tale.)

Once inside the director's office, Webster asked how Spessard's two sons were coping. He expressed his regrets, asked if there was anything he might do, and then presented Debra Spessard with the Intelligence Star, awarded for "courageous action."

The citation read: "James E. Spessard is posthumously awarded the Intelligence Star in recognition of his exceptional service to the Central Intelligence Agency from July 1989 to November 1989. His voluntary acceptance of known dangers in the execution of his duties reflected the highest standard of professionalism and dedication to the mission of the Agency. Mr. Spessard's significant contributions to the overall mission of the Intelligence Community are justly deserving of commendation and honor, reflecting great credit on himself, the Central Intelligence Agency, and the Federal service."

Webster said that ordinarily he would not allow such an award to leave the premises, that it would be placed in a vault, but that he had made an exception. Debra Spessard could keep it, so long as she showed it to no one. In a moment of unusual candor he also admitted he did not know Jimmy Spessard.

A moment later Webster was interrupted and abruptly excused himself without explanation. His aide said he had been called away to the White House for consultation. Nothing more was said. The next day the United States launched a military action against Panama and toppled the regime of Manuel Noriega.

But the strangest events were yet to come. Several months after the funeral, two Agency employees paid a visit to the Hagerstown cemetery. In the cemetery office they showed a video of the crash site to Debra Spessard and her brother. The video lasted several minutes and showed that the plane had broken into three parts and that all around it the trees and grass were charred.

While the tape ran, one of the Agency officers read from an official report. "Every third word had a big black mark through it, so much of it was classified," recalls Debra Spessard. "The blacked-out part was like every other line." Afterward she asked if she could keep the tape. That would not be possible, the Agency men explained, and left, leaving nothing behind.

. . .

On December 7, 1989, in Dothan, Alabama, the body of pilot Bud Petty was said to be laid to rest with full military honors in the Memory Hill Cemetery. Family members had huddled around the flag-draped casket as a twenty-one-gun salute sounded. Then he was lowered into grave number 1, lot 405, in the cemetery's Garden of Chimes. It had been a moving tribute to Petty, as was the obituary that appeared in the local paper. Never mind that the obituary said he had died November 29, two days after his actual death, and that there was no mention of the place or cause of death.

His casket had arrived in Dothan sealed, with instructions that it was not to be opened. Men in black suits came down from Washington with a single message for the Petty family: "Don't talk to anyone from the newspapers." After a while, the Pettys had been told so many varying accounts of the crash that they weren't sure what the truth was. Some even suspected Petty was still alive.

Six months later, in Hagerstown, Maryland, Debra Spessard received a phone call from a woman who identified herself as Teresa Petty, Bud Petty's daughter. She was sobbing and said that she suspected her father's coffin had been empty. She was convinced she had been lied to. She had no proof to back up her accusation, but she was certain she and other family members had been duped. Then her grief gave way to anger. She said that the Agency had concluded that the plane had gone down due to pilot error. She said her father was too good a pilot to let that explanation stand. Later her family challenged that finding and the Agency seemed to amend its findings, in part to mollify Petty's survivors. There was talk of a faulty altimeter or other instrument.

Teresa Petty was not alone in believing that her father's coffin was empty. Bud Petty's eldest sister, Joyce, was also convinced, as was Petty's first wife, Doris, whom Petty divorced in the late 1970s.

But Petty's widow, Gracie, who worked closely with him at Tepper Aviation, will not speak of such matters. She says that she knows nothing of the CIA, that her husband merely worked for Tepper Aviation, and that the company had a "government contract."

"It's not a subject that I talk about," she says. "Bud's been gone ten years. I quit living after that. He was a wonderful man and a wonderful memory and I really don't care to rehash any of it. I wouldn't talk about Bud even if President Clinton called. I have my own memories and that's all I care about. If it don't bring him back I don't care." End of story.

Well, not quite.

In the Byrd Funeral Home in Dothan, Alabama, is a file with Bud Petty's name on it and inside is an affidavit that reads: "Before me this day personally appeared Gracie T. Petty who is being duly sworn, deposed, and says that they have full knowledge that the casket which is being brought to Byrd Funeral Home, Dothan, Alabama is only representative of their next of kin for the express purpose of memorializing their missing relative and that they fully understand there are no human remains or personal artifacts contained within such casket."

What Petty's daughter, Teresa, and others had suspected was true. The casket was empty. "I wanted Bud to be buried with dignity," Gracie would later tell Petty's sister Joyce. The Agency had apparently chosen to tell only Petty's widow. The same grim word would be given to the widow of Gerhard Rieger. His casket, too, was empty.

There was a hard irony to the way things turned out for the Petty family. Bud was not a man given to pithy sayings, but one thing he often told his children was that when adversity struck, it was important to "put it behind you and go forward." The peculiar circumstances surrounding his own death and the subsequent deception proved hard to leave behind.

"My brother was very honest with me," says sister Joyce. "He would not have wanted us to be lied to so that we would go on wondering—that we would be wondering ten years later if he was alive or dead. He would not want to be mourned for this long. He would have wanted us to get on with our lives and he would know we could not do that if we were not told the truth."

It has been no less hard on Alton Petty, Bud's father, now eighty years old. "Everybody was closemouthed and did what they was supposed to do," he says. "The whole stinking mess was shoved down our throat. All of us are afraid to talk to anybody. Most of it is rumor. I have no facts that I can believe. When you lose a son and you can't prove it, you just wonder and start grabbing at straws."

The Spessards were somewhat more fortunate. In time, they made a kind of peace with Jimmy's death. Debra Spessard later remarried. Some time after her husband's death she received a photograph from one of her husband's Agency colleagues showing a workman chiseling a nameless star into the CIA's Wall of Honor—a star for Jimmy. To this day her sons do not know that their father was with the CIA and was killed in service to country. The burden of secrecy has been upon them all.

. . .

There are other memorials to Spessard, Petty, and the other crew members who died aboard the Gray Ghost flight. Shortly after the crash, Jonas Savimbi was said to have erected an obelisk with a plaque dedicated to their memory. There is stands today amid thorn trees and high grass on the Angolan savanna not far from where the plane went down. And at Agency headquarters in Langley, along the path where the statue of Nathan Hale is to be found, the men and women of the CIA's Africa Division planted a small sapling in their honor—a tribute without names. In the Agency's Book of Honor, each is a nameless star.

But perhaps the most curious memorial service was one the Agency itself observed some two years after the crash. As if to make sure that no public link was forged between the Agency and the dead, the ceremony was held not at CIA headquarters, but rather at the Fort Myer Chapel in Arlington Cemetery. It was 11:30 the morning of August 7, 1991, and the families of the deceased, many of whom had never before met one another, gathered in tribute to their sons and fathers and husbands. Medals and awards were presented.

Petty's widow received a vaguely worded and undated certificate that read: "The United States of America honors the memory of Pharies B. Petty. This certificate is awarded by a grateful nation in recognition of devoted and selfless consecration to the service of our country in the Armed Forces of the United States." Never mind that Petty had been out of the military for a dozen years. But at least it was signed—"George Bush, President of the United States."

Mildred Lacy, the aging mother of aviation mechanic George Lacy, accepted a round metal that featured an eagle on the front and the words

"In Recognition of Distinguished Service." On the obverse was inscribed "George Vincent Lacy 1989."

A short time later she received through the mail a second award, named the Alben W. Barkley Award. The citation reads: "The United States of America presents the Alben W. Barkley Award to George V. Lacy in recognition of distinguished public service to the people and goals of the United States of America. Mr. Lacy is presented this award posthumously following his ultimate sacrifice in the line of duty serving his country. His individual contributions can never be forgotten and his public spirit will live on as a standard of excellence that future public servants will try to emulate. The dedication, selflessness, and commitment with which he served reflect great credit upon himself, his family and the United States of America."

What made the award so curious was not only that it made no mention of either the CIA or Lacy's mission but that, according to what Mildred Lacy was told, it was the first and only time the award would be made—that is, only those six on board the ill-fated Gray Ghost flight would ever receive it. Why it was named for Alben Barkley, Harry Truman's vice-president, was never explained to the relatives of the deceased. And there was an odd irony in suggesting that Lacy's contributions would never be forgotten, that they would become "a standard of excellence" for "future public servants," given that his name, his mission, and his fate were all completely veiled in secrecy.

There was nothing in any of the medals, honors, or certificates that showed the CIA's hand was behind it all. It was as if the bereaved, who had themselves made a stunning sacrifice, could not be trusted with anything that revealed the truth.

"All the medals and the talking will never bring my son or the other boys home," says Lacy's mother, Mildred. "They are gone. All we have is our memories and our thoughts every day of our son and what they had gone through when this happened. That's something nobody knows."

As for the people of Angola, like so many others caught in the undertow first of colonialism and then the Cold War, a happy ending is not yet in sight. A cease-fire between the government and UNITA lasted from May 1991 until October 1992, when UNITA refused to recognize the results of an internationally monitored election. A decade after the crash that killed Spessard, Petty, Rieger, Bensch, Lacy, and Atkinson, and two decades after the CIA's involvement in that civil war, Savimbi remains restive. The new millennium dawns with Angola's people facing still more violence and upheaval.

So it was to be for the CIA as well. Africa would soon account for still more nameless stars in the Book of Honor.

CHAPTER 14

The Last Maccabee

TRUTH, it is said, is the first casualty of any war. But in Somalia truth was the second casualty. Larry Freedman was the first. The Pentagon conferred that dubious distinction upon him when it reported that on December 23, 1992, he had been killed by a land mine and that he had been a civilian employee of the Defense Department. The first part was true enough. Freedman was dead. The second part was a lie.

Back home in the States, Freedman's death was reduced to a terse obituary and a fleeting item on the evening news. Those wary of America's foreign entanglements, especially those labeled "peacekeeping missions," cited his death as a kind of "told-you-so." He had become kindling in the debate, the ante lost in a hand that should never have been played. On the Pentagon's casualty list even his name was misspelled. They left out the "d" in "Freedman."

Of course, Freedman had no interest in geopolitical debates. Never one to question America's role abroad, he had stood ready, decade after decade, to be one of the nation's sharpest, and if need be, most deadly instruments of foreign policy. He lusted after action like he lusted after everything else. As for recognition, he had long since made his peace with anonymity. It went with the territory he had chosen for himself, as much as his sniper's rifle and scope. He had lived an explosive life and yet a life of stealth. It was only fitting his exit be one of fire and flash, and steeped in deception.

In the public's mind Freedman was at most a glancing thought, a fifty-one-year-old grandfather who died far from home and close to Christmas. He was just another faceless bureaucrat, a "civilian employee of the Department of Defense." Truth and Freedman now shared a common grave. And that was exactly how the CIA wished it to remain.

. . .

Mention Larry Freedman's name even today, nearly a decade after his death, and a mischievous smile creeps across the faces of those who knew him. It is as if they suddenly remembered a bawdy story too risqué to repeat but too delicious to forget.

Six years after his death, Freedman's longtime friends from Philadelphia gather in the Bucks County, Pennsylvania, home of his sister, Sylvia Doner. Within moments all semblance of sobriety vanishes, replaced by a convulsive hilarity. Like Freedman, they are Jewish, streetwise, and, even in their mid-fifties, not to be pushed around: Petey Altman, Kenny Gold, Paul Weinberg. Also here is Wynne Crocetto, who first set eyes on Freedman at seventeen and was forever smitten.

Weinberg was the first to meet Freedman. That was in kindergarten. They were both born to raise hell. "We even flunked twice so we could graduate together," Weinberg says. True enough, but it would not have taken much on Freedman's part to fail. Bright as he was, he was no student.

Back then, the gang hung out at the Pit, a bowling alley in the Mount Airy section of Philadelphia. To them, Freedman was known affectionately as Gus. At ten he had seen the movie *Cinderella* and was enamored with the antics of a fat mouse by that name who always seemed to get caught either by the cat or the broom. Freedman could identify with that.

Whatever defied common sense he took to be a personal invitation. A high school gymnast and diver, he was always looking for something more daring. He found it one night at the Ascot Motel in Atlantic City when he dove off a third-story balcony into the horseshoe-shaped swimming pool. "The edge was his favorite place," says his sister, Sylvia.

At five feet nine he was powerfully built, coiled like a spring wound a little too tight. He was utterly fearless. He never spoiled for a fight, but woe to the fool that pushed him too far. All such encounters were short and decidedly one-sided. But mostly he tested his body against gravity and his own limits of endurance. Often he would do handstands on the backs of chairs, on balconies and railings. He did it not for the attention, but for the pure rush of adrenaline. He was an odd mix of Tarzan and John Wayne, both of whom he idolized.

As an adolescent he took a keen interest in weapons, particularly bows and arrows, not the kind of rubber-tipped playthings sold in toy stores, but the real deal: deadly steel-tipped broad arrows launched from a fiberglass longbow. He would put paper targets on neighborhood trees and drive the arrow clean through the bull's-eye and deep into the living wood. His eye was unerring, his approach unnervingly silent. These were gifts that would serve him well in later years, but as a boy got him into considerable hot water.

At thirteen he and two of his buddies walked into an Esso gas station on Stenton Avenue and attempted to rob the place. Freedman was armed with his bow and arrow, drawn and trained on the owner, who dismissed the boys with a laugh. Just how many times Freedman ran afoul of the local constabulary is a matter of some dispute. Suffice to say, he could be a handful.

His parents would learn to be flexible but not when it came to attendance at temple. On March 27, 1954, Freedman was bar mitzvahed in a Conservative synagogue. From the pulpit he read from the Talmud with deep conviction. It was no act. In later years he could be vulgar, even downright raunchy, but never profane. About the same year he was bar mitzvahed he and his buddies were summarily kicked out of Boy Scout Troop 99.

To the outside world Freedman and his ilk might easily have been mistaken for juvenile delinquents, but there was nothing thuggish about them. It was themselves, not others, they usually put at risk. Occasionally they fought with the Oxford Circle boys, but it was nothing more than fists. They covered one another's backs. Between them grew an uncommon camaraderie and a raw but abiding sense of honor.

Freedman was the lead dog, adored, almost worshiped, by his co-conspirators. For all his excesses, he was, at heart, quiet and gentle, capable of casting a spell over other rebels. They would be drawn to him as to an outlaw Pied Piper.

But his parents were not to be envied. Again and again he tried their patience. His father, Leroy, gave him a '54 Buick Special. Freedman could not resist pushing the big V-8 to the max. Soon after, he rolled the car, then secretly had it repaired in a garage at night, at his sister's expense. His father never found out.

But like his patron mouse, Gus, Freedman seldom got away with anything. One day he returned home and announced that he had gotten a part-time job in a neighborhood pharmacy. His parents were elated. At last he was doing something productive. One night the family decided to surprise him and pick him up at work. There they learned Freedman had been fired three weeks earlier. Vintage Freedman.

From high school he went to Kansas State University. It was the only school that would have him. Friends say he majored in class avoidance and bedding coeds, but he did in fact have a genuine interest in veterinary medicine and a soft spot for any suffering animal—something that would later haunt him.

At college, to the delight of coeds, he would leap from stairwell to stairwell, deftly catching the railing, except when he did not. It was just such a maneuver that once opened his head and left some to wonder whether he really thought he could fly. Such kamikaze stunts won for him a kind of Superman moniker which was later amended to "Superjew," a title he proudly clung to for the rest of his life.

It was about this time that he came upon one of his abiding passions—motorcycles. There was nothing that gave him more pleasure than endless hours cruising on the open road. Regularly he would ride from Kansas to Philly for nothing more than the excuse of a milk shake, then head back forty-five minutes later. His friends remember him dismounting his thunderous blue Norton and proudly picking the bugs out of his teeth.

He still had the Buick but showed it little respect. One time he drove from Kansas to Philly through a deluge. When he arrived at home he was completely soaked. His family couldn't understand why until they looked out the window. Freedman had sawed the roof off his car to make it a convertible and had been driving something akin to a portable pool.

Ivan Doner, now married to Freedman's sister, remembers the time in 1963 when he first set eyes on Freedman, then twenty-two. He was wearing tight jeans, black boots, a T-shirt with sleeves rolled back to reveal rippling biceps, and long hair slicked back. He was the very picture of a greaser. It was easy to feel intimidated in his presence.

It wasn't long before Freedman flunked out of college. It came as a surprise to no one. Wild and undisciplined, his prospects seemed dim at best. The exuberance of youth, to put a polite spin on whatever it was that torqued Freedman's overheated engine, seemed destined to doom him as an adult. And then something happened that would change the course of his life. He found the army.

. . .

On September 30, 1965, with the war in Vietnam on full boil, Freedman enlisted at a recruiting station in Fort Jackson, South Carolina. Within six months he had maneuvered himself into a position as a medic-in-training. Instinctively Freedman had sought out the one unit that would impose upon him the discipline he needed, and yet place him among others who shared his infatuation with the edge—Special Forces. Twenty-four-year-old Lawrence N. Freedman was about to don the Green Beret.

One of the most wrenching experiences of his entire military career came early on and not on the battlefield. As part of his training as a medic he was to take a puppy that had been anesthetized and remove one of its legs. For a man who had aspired to be a vet it was almost too much to bear. Even twenty years later he spoke of the experience haltingly as one of the most traumatic events in an often violent life.

But whatever focus he had lacked in the civilian world promptly resolved itself in the military. Freedman discovered that he was born to be a warrior. He had at last found a place where his vices could be turned to virtues, his abandon into valor. Even among the elite of the elite, he determined that he would distinguish himself. He saw himself as one in a long line of Jewish warriors—the last Maccabee.

And distinguish himself he did: two Bronze Stars, a Purple Heart, numerous Good Conduct Medals, the Humanitarian Service Medal, the Defense Meritorious Service Medal, and a chestful of other decorations.

His first Bronze Star dated back to May 23, 1968. Freedman was a senior adviser heading up a team of Vietnamese civilian irregulars on ambush patrol along a North Vietnamese infiltration route. He and his men suddenly found themselves about to be outflanked.

The citation spells out what happened next. "Sensing the enemy's plans, Sergeant Freedman left cover, and although under murderous enemy fire, ran from position to position redeploying his men and directing their fire. The friendly positions began receiving mortar fire from minimum range.

"Spotting the muzzle flash of the weapon, Sergeant Freedman ran from cover and made his way to within 50 meters of it. Opening fire with his rifle he killed two of the enemy gun crew and caused the remainder to abandon their weapon and run . . . Sergeant Freedman's actions prevented heavy friendly casualties and were instrumental in the victory over a numerically superior enemy force. Sergeant Freedman's personal bravery and devotion to duty were in keeping with the highest traditions of the military service and reflect great credit upon himself, the Special Forces and the United States Army."

Piece by piece, Freedman assembled all the essential components of the ultimate soldier. In the years ahead he underwent advanced training in parachuting, martial arts, intelligence, and weaponry. He honed his skills as a sniper until he became one of the army's most accurate and deadly long-range shooters.

But Freedman was not immune to the emotional toll of Vietnam. He told one friend, Nick Garber, how he was firing his weapon to repel an attack while all the while drowning a Viet Cong soldier in a shallow rice paddy with his booted foot. Not until the soldier ceased struggling did he raise his foot. Such images were not easy for him to put out of his mind. On his first visit home from Vietnam his family took him to a nightclub. Freedman sat quietly, declining drinks and answering questions with a stiff "yes" or "no."

But through it all, his eye for women never flagged. In Vietnam he had met a slender Vietnamese woman named Thuy, then with two children. He married her, adopted her children, to be named Michael and

Linda, and together, they had a third child, David. But the marriage was ill-fated. They had little in common and less and less to say to one another. The marriage ended long before the divorce.

There is no doubt he was an incurable flirt, but his approach, like everything else about him, could be highly unconventional. How he met his second wife, Teresa, is a case in point. It was 1978. He had been checking out a woman who lived in an adjoining lot. She was petite and shapely, with long black curls and green eyes. One day as she was hanging her laundry he perched over the back fence and struck up a conversation with her. She seemed to be wilted as if in pain. He asked how she was doing.

"I just had a hysterectomy," she explained.

"Oh, I just had a vasectomy," he fired back cheerfully. "We'll have to have a sterilization party." He and Teresa married on May 10, 1981, though it, too, would be a turbulent marriage.

With women he was usually the perfect gentleman, romantic to a fault. But he could also be obnoxious and randy. A video captures him chairing a solemn meeting of officers at Fort Bragg. In walks a young lady bearing a surprise birthday cake for him. It is decorated with a menorah made of icing.

"Happy birthday!" she bubbles as she places it before him.

"Great Gugamugal!" thunders Freedman, feigning disappointment. "I told her I wanted a blow job!" Even the officers at the table momentarily fainted away in shock.

But it was never Freedman's intent to offend. It was just his way of testing for reactions, of seeing whether the person would pass muster or fold in a fit of embarrassment or pique. Often it was the first step toward a friendship.

· · ·

By the late 1970s Freedman had already established himself as a consummate soldier. But it was now peacetime, a state Freedman was not quite as comfortable with. He preferred action and sought it out at every turn. On March 28, 1978, he became a team member of one of the military's most elite and shadowy units, the recently formed Special Forces Operational Detachment-D. Today it is known as Delta Force, the legendary counterterrorist group, though the military is still reluctant to acknowledge its existence.

Trained in CQB, close-quarters battle, Freedman's superquick reflexes were refined and readied for overseas hostage rescue and extraction missions. With his medic's skills, his talents as a sniper, and his combat experience, he was a valued component of Delta Force. There are many in the military who are crack shots, but the perfect sniper, of which Freedman was one, is a rarer breed. It is said of Freedman that he could hike for two days through a jungle with a ninety-pound rucksack on his back, set up his scope and rifle without pause, and focus for three days on a window waiting for his target to show himself for a second only. His concentration was unflagging and lethal.

At training exercises he wowed even expert marksmen. At close range his weapon of choice was a Colt .45 that had undergone a "combat conversion," meaning the magazine would load quicker and the trigger was "tuned" to release without unwanted "creep." His body, too, was a finely tuned weapon. Each day he ran five miles, pumped iron, and practiced martial arts.

In Delta Force, Freedman was at last among peers, part of a warrior class, a full cut above the rest. But these soldiers exhibited none of the swagger of a John Wayne. They were content to be known as "the quiet professionals." They strove for invisibility.

Within the subdued ranks of Delta, Freedman maintained a somewhat higher profile. Still known as Superjew, he would literally show up at parties and other affairs wearing a red cape emblazoned with a large Hebrew letter, a gift from sister Sylvia. Freedman's escapades could be counted on to provide welcomed comic relief.

But sometimes he would make a few too many waves. "He pulled some crap on me and I had to hammer his ass," recalls one of his superiors from Delta. But Freedman was too talented to dismiss. Most of his offenses were peccadilloes that momentarily irritated the brass but cumulatively endeared him to them. His commanding officers remember him as a silent tiger in the field, a man ready at a moment's notice to go wherever asked and do whatever was required. "You knew he would always be there," said retired general Richard Potter, who was three years with Delta. "You may not like how he got there but you knew he would be there."

General Peter J. Schoomaker, commander in chief of the United States Special Operations Command, was in the field with Freedman and remembers him with affection and respect. In an otherwise low-key unit he was something of a firecracker. And he had a streak of vanity.

"I would say he was narcissistic," recalls Schoomaker. "He's the kind of guy that always tries to stay pretty, like his fascination with his hair. He was always a lady's kind of guy and always upbeat.

"He was one of the guys you could count on being there and also one of the guys who would have a good time. You had to jerk him up every once in a while to get his attention. He was a confident kind of guy who needed to be led well. Otherwise he'd lead you."

Freedman's missions, all of them still classified, took him to Africa, the Mideast, and the Far East. More than once he undertook covert operations in Ethiopia, a country that was said to be special to him. There was a sketchy story told of him helping a girl in Turkey to come to the United States. He promised to one day look her up in the States. He took out a dollar bill, tore it in half, and presented her with one of the halves. Five years later, in the United States, he presented her with the other half of the bill, redeeming his pledge.

He was even consulted in the design of the presidential limo and tested the armor plating on other vehicles used by ambassadors and visiting heads of state. Who better to test such defenses than a man who, given the order, would be the perfect assassin?

Freedman was extraordinarily closemouthed about his missions, but there was one instance in which a personal indiscretion identified his place of operation. Sometime in the mid-1980s he visited his sister, Sylvia, and called aside her husband, Ivan Doner, a physician. "You have to do me a favor," he said somewhat sheepishly. "When I was in Ethiopia I performed a transgression over there."

Doner understood instantly what Freedman was saying. He had had sexual intercourse with a local and now was worried about AIDS. Fearing both the personal and the security repercussions of his actions, Freedman asked that Doner do a blood test and assign him a pseudonym for purposes of the exam. The test came back negative and the usually steely Freedman exhaled a sigh of relief.

The major missions he and Delta Force undertook were often performed in conjunction with the CIA. It was an uneasy relationship between Delta and the Agency. Increasingly the Agency came to view Delta as its paramilitary arm, a role Delta did not relish.

Freedman and the men of Delta knew they could rely on each other. The Agency, on the other hand, had demonstrated a propensity to distance itself from anything that could go awry and seemed to be planning escape routes from responsibility even before operations commenced. "They'll have you crawl way out on a limb and then saw off the branch," said one former Delta Force leader. "They've done it many times." Often, too, Agency intelligence was inadequate or flat-out wrong. Freedman and his teammates came to be deeply suspicious of the Agency—and yet, when called, they went without hesitation.

It is nearly impossible to judge the efficacy of Delta's missions, so shrouded are they even years later. Sadly the one most daring operation and the one for which Delta will long be associated would come to haunt Freedman as it did the others. The code name was Operation Eagle Claw.

. . .

It was the spring of 1980. For six months the nation watched with revulsion as fifty-three American civilians were paraded about as hostages, humiliated at the hands of their Iranian captors. With apparent impunity the Ayatollah Khomeini and his followers taunted the United States as "the Great Satan." President Jimmy Carter saw his political standing and authority dwindle with each passing day. The crisis would define his presidency, cast America as a kind of impotent giant, and embolden other fanatics to strike at U.S. targets.

But in the deepest, most secure recesses of the U.S. intelligence and defense communities an elaborate plan was afoot to liberate the hostages. It would soon be payback time, a chance to regain face and show that the United States would not abandon its citizens. Perhaps not since the Vietnam War had a covert mission of such daring been undertaken. Completely cloaked in secrecy, a key part of the operation was placed in the hands of the country's most select military unit, Delta Force.

And among those chosen from that crack unit was Larry Freedman. It was to be Delta's first real mission, a chance to prove its mettle and demonstrate that two years of training had not been for naught. It was the moment that Delta Force had been waiting for. It was the moment Larry Freedman lived for.

On the night of April 24–25, 1980, Freedman was aboard an EC-130, part of a larger group of modified Hercules aircraft and RH-53D helicopters known as Sea Stallions. They were to rendezvous at a prearranged refueling site inside Iran, code-named Desert One.

Dressed in a black field jacket, Levi's, boots, and a naval watch cap, Freedman sat quietly as the massive plane droned on through the night toward its destination. On his right sleeve was a strip of tape concealing a small American flag that he was to peel off once in Teheran as a sign to the hostages that he was part of a rescue team. In his mind he went over and over the welter of intricate steps that lay ahead. He and the rest of the team were convinced that the plan would work. Just get them to Teheran and leave the rest to them.

Freedman had been assigned to the "Blue Element." He was to be a "blocker," making sure that the crowds that could be expected to assemble outside the U.S. Embassy in Teheran, where the fifty-three hostages were being held, did not make it past him. With his sniper's rifle and the support of a machine gunner, he was to provide a delay, if need be laying down deadly fire, while the hostages were removed and led to safety. Few in the operation would be more exposed to risk.

But of the eight Sea Stallions assigned to the mission, three either never made it to Desert One or were stricken with mechanical problems. It was decided that there were no longer enough choppers to make the operation work. The radical change in temperature from the cold of a desert night to the heat of daytime was deemed certain to ground another one or two choppers. That would leave just three to ferry to safety Delta, a Defense Department contingent, the fifty-three hostages, and the assault unit that was to storm the Foreign Ministry Building, which housed another three hostages. In all, 178 people would have to be carried out. It was cutting it too close.

The decision was made to abort.

On the ground at Desert One a Sea Stallion was repositioned for its return. Close by was the EC-130 with Freedman and his fellow Blue team members aboard. As the chopper moved to get into position, its rotors ripped through the cockpit of the EC-130 and instantly set off an explosion, igniting both aircraft. Suddenly the desert went from night to day, and the mission was transformed into a tragedy. Colonel Charles Beckwith would remember the Redeye missiles eerily "pinwheeling" through the desert night as on the Fourth of July.

Freedman and others of his team escaped the flames and leaped to safety, rolling in the sand to put out the flames that licked at their clothes. Freedman returned to the aircraft to help carry away one of the crew who was badly injured and screaming for help. But trapped inside the inferno, now fed by hundreds of gallons of fuel, were eight members of the rescue mission.

Four hours and fifty-six minutes after landing at Desert One, Freedman and the others were forced to abandon the site and head for the safety of the Indian Ocean. The flight back was nearly silent. Freedman and his fellow team members sat sullenly, some with tears sliding down their cheeks. They had come to rescue Americans and show that the United States would not abandon its citizens. But behind, on the desert floor, amid the twisted and burned-out wreckage of Sea Stallion and Hercules, were eight charred corpses. It was the most dramatic defeat since Vietnam. The enemy had been sand and night and, perhaps too, a lack of fundamental coordination. America's humiliation was now compounded by horror.

Such was the legacy of Operation Eagle Claw. But while it was an unambiguous fiasco, it also made Delta even more determined to play a frontline role in any future covert rescue and extraction operation. Freedman was convinced that had Delta been in control of the operation, they could have pulled it off. In this he was not alone.

In time, his grief gave way to rage. The aborted rescue mission was a subject he disciplined himself not to dwell on. Rarely would he speak of it and only to those who had played a role in the operation. The pain, the injury to pride and profession, the loss of friends, dogged him as nothing else would.

. . .

In October 1982 Freedman left Delta Force. His subsequent military record grows more murky with each passing year as he descended into increasingly sensitive and compartmented operations. On November 5, 1982, only weeks after leaving Delta, Pentagon records note he was an "infantry man (special project)." A year later he became a "special projects team member." None of those operations have come to light.

By December 1, 1984, his record clarifies somewhat with the notation that he had been made noncommissioned officer in charge of the Interdiction Branch, a position he held until 1986. In those years he trained Delta and other Special Forces units at Fort Bragg in many of the arcane arts he had mastered. In the "interdiction" course he taught advanced marksmanship, judging distances, camouflage and concealment techniques, observation skills, and how to "deliver precise rifle fire in support of special operations." It was the Special Forces version of Sniper School.

That same year he attended a birthday party for his old Philadelphia friend Petey Altman, who was turning forty-four. Altman had been smoking pot and was stoned. Freedman avoided him throughout the evening until Altman finally cornered him. Freedman glowered, and it was clear to Altman it was over drugs. "It occurred to me that here he was literally risking his life to stop this stuff and here I was at the other end of the pipeline being the retail consumer," recalls Altman. "That summer I gave it up altogether."

As Freedman approached his forty-fifth birthday, his career took a turn. He temporarily left the field for a classroom at the U.S. Army Sergeant Major's Academy at Fort Bliss, Texas. There, for the first time, he got a great report card. His transcript declared: "He is a true professional of the highest caliber and has exhibited the potential to succeed in any position at any organizational level within the Department of Defense." In August 1986 he returned to Fort Bragg as a sergeant major.

He continued to train Special Forces at Fort Bragg's John F. Kennedy Special Warfare Center and School, passing along to the next generation his skills and knowledge acquired over two decades of combat and covert missions.

But he was hardly the professorial type. He ached to get back into the fray. Talking about it was fine but no substitute for the real thing. Still running five miles a day and pumping iron, he was fit and trim and ready for action. But who would deploy a forty-nine-year-old grandfather?

He thought for a time of becoming a mercenary, perhaps working for Israel and the Mossad, the counterpart to the CIA. "You're Jewish, but you're not Israeli," one of his senior officers cautioned him. Freedman next decided to make a run at the Drug Enforcement Agency (DEA). He had had experience in the field fighting drug operations. It seemed a perfect fit. But the DEA was not interested in someone of Freedman's age for field assignments. Freedman was crushed.

So it was by default that he turned to the CIA. A friend of his from Delta had recently joined the Agency and knew firsthand Freedman's capabilities. On February 31, 1990, Freedman retired from the military after twenty-five years in Special Forces.

With hardly a break in service, he joined the CIA. For the Agency it was something of a coup. There were few employees at Langley that possessed Freedman's paramilitary skills. In 1947 when the Agency was founded, virtually all employees of the clandestine service were veterans of military service. The early 1950s saw an influx of men seasoned in battle on the Korean peninsula.

But by 1990 those in the Agency who had served in the military were in the distinct minority, and many of those still there were either too old or ill-conditioned to meet the physical demands of a covert paramilitary officer. Even at fifty Freedman carried a chiseled physique, a young man's stamina, and a wide array of skills rarely found in one person.

But for Freedman it was not the perfect fit. Once out of the military, he grew a ponytail and sported a full white beard. At Langley he was constantly being pushed to get a haircut. But more than that, something about the culture of the Agency put him off. He continued to harbor some distrust dating back to his days on Delta Force.

Like Freedman, the Agency itself was going through a period of self-doubt and reexamination. In 1991 William Webster resigned after four years as head of the CIA. The Agency had come under criticism from both the Bush White House and Congress. Specifically cited were intelligence failures connected to the 1989 U.S. invasion of Panama, the collapse of the Soviet economy, and the Iraqi invasion of Kuwait a year later. In November 1991 Webster was replaced by Robert M. Gates, a veteran Agency analyst known as something of a hard-liner.

For Gates and the Agency there was little time to reflect on the past or celebrate the collapse of its archenemy, the Soviet Union. The CIA was faced with nothing less than redefining its future. Its raison d'être—the

Cold War—was history. If Langley did not quickly embrace a new mission, it risked being identified as an anachronism and disemboweled, not unlike the fate of the OSS in the immediate aftermath of World War II. That was the same situation Larry Freedman found himself in as a warrior in middle age having consecrated himself to fighting Communists.

But Gates was an unabashed believer in the CIA's accomplishments. He counted the Agency's multibillion-dollar support of the mujahedin against the Soviets in Afghanistan as one of its finest hours. Even Angola, decimated by war and superpower intervention, he put in the Agency's win column, as one more strain on the Kremlin. That the Agency helped prop up, even install, many despotic regimes was simply a necessity of containing Communism. He would later muse that the CIA had "ended up with some strange and often unsavory bedfellows. Most you wouldn't bring home to Mom." But it was the future, not the past, that preoccupied Gates and the thousands of overt and undercover Agency employees. The CIA's resources, once directed against Moscow, Beijing, and Havana, now were increasingly being deployed to gather economic intelligence and to fight terrorism, international crime syndicates, proliferation of weapons of mass destruction—biological, chemical, and nuclear—and the international narcotics trade. Each of these areas was affected by the demise of the Soviet Union. If "the evil empire" was gone, so, too, was the restraint and stability with which it held sway over its client states in the long era of superpower rivalry. In its absence, age-old strains of nationalism and ethnic conflict erupted, drawing the CIA into them.

For Langley and for Freedman it was an unfamiliar world, one in which containing chaos, not Communism, often seemed to be centerstage. Both wondered how they would fit in and what their new role would be. Freedman did not have to wait long to find out. He was repeatedly dispatched to Africa, primarily in the north, returning again to Ethiopia. He also is said to have been sent to Poland. That mission, too, remains a mystery.

It had been almost more than Freedman could bear that he was not sent to the Gulf War in 1991, but had to sit by and watch as Desert Storm unfolded.

"Haven't you had enough?" his lifelong friend Paul Weinberg asked him.

"No," Freedman fired back. "One more war. I could go for a good war."

Years of Special Forces training had sharpened his skills but had also implanted in him a wariness and hair-trigger reaction that sometimes frightened those around him. And with reason. He could be the perfect killing machine and was now paying a price for his expertise. A hunter so long, he had come to know a little too much about what it was to be hunted.

He would not sit before windows or doors, aware that snipers like himself looked for just such opportunities to fell their prey. Always, he insisted on sitting with his back to the wall where he could survey everything and everyone around him. As his training increased, so, too, did the ferocity with which he reacted to perceived threats. In his profession deliberation meant death.

Late one evening in 1990, while on leave, he was staying with his sister, Sylvia. Sitting in a black leather chair, he was watching television. Even in Sylvia's suburban living room, he had strapped to his ankle his .357 Smith & Wesson with a two-and-a-half-inch barrel. It was loaded with special Teflon-pointed bullets. Sylvia entered the room a little too quietly, padding about in her slippers. She came upon him from behind and gently placed her hand upon his shoulder.

Before she knew it, Freedman had leaped over the back of the chair and was an instant away from delivering a potentially fatal strike. "I saw the look in his eyes and I learned never to do that again," Sylvia would say. After that she announced her entrances. Others of Freedman's friends had their own such encounters. They knew to approach him face-to-face and never to surprise him.

The Larry Freedman that Wynne Crocetto knew was a man who pulled the chair out for her, never cursed, and through the years remembered her on birthdays and Valentine's Day. But she, too, caught a terrifying glimpse of the other Larry Freedman, the master of close-quarters combat. "I'm really sorry," he told her. "I'll never do that again."

But it was not something he had control over. The skills that kept him alive in times of peril stalked him in times of peace. Even waking him could unleash the warrior's fury.

But there were by now other, more pressing problems in Freedman's life. His marriage to Teresa had worn hopelessly thin. Freedman wanted out. He may well have loved her but he could not live with her any longer. He took an apartment in Arlington, Virginia. Teresa remained in Fayetteville. He called it "a separation." It was headed inexorably toward divorce.

He still had a roving eye but little expectation of meeting someone special. He had had enough of marriage. But a year after he joined the CIA, in 1991, he found himself enamored with one of his female colleagues, a thin and athletic divorcée. She had even accompanied him on the back of his blackberry-colored Harley FXRT to Sturgis, South Dakota, where annually tens of thousands of bikers gather. It was the first time he had been with a woman who both understood and shared his passion for action and intrigue. At fifty Freedman had found a soulmate.

Freedman was even giving some thought to what life might be like in retirement. He and his buddy Larry Walz had spoken of buying Harleys in Anchorage, Alaska, and driving them for a year all the way to the tip of South America.

But he was also conscious that between now and retirement his life was fraught with risk. Late one afternoon Freedman was in his sister's backyard, rocking slowly in the hammock. Sylvia pulled up a lawn chair and they began to talk. He said that when he died he wanted to be buried in Arlington Cemetery and to have the complete military ceremony and even the small white government-issued tombstone. "I deserve that," he told her, "and I want to be among my peers."

By December 1992 Freedman's bona fides as one of the CIA's premier paramilitary operatives were well established. He had become one of the Agency's "go-to" players, someone who could be counted on to perform well even in the most hazardous of situations. One such situation was quickly taking shape in an area already familiar to Freedman—the horn of Africa.

. . .

The country of Somalia was virtually disintegrating before the eyes of the world. Warlords and factionalism had plunged it into a hellish chaos in which even the most dedicated relief workers could not get food and medicine to the country's 8 million people. At the White House President

Bush had determined that the United States would not sit by while count-less Somalis starved to death. A decision was made, on humanitarian grounds, that the U.S. would send a military force into the country to reestablish some semblance of order so that the "nongovernmental enti-ties," or NGOs, could go about their work of bringing relief to the coun-try. Already some 350,000 people had died from hunger or fighting.

As a preface to such military intervention, the National Security Council (NSC) decided it wanted the CIA to send operatives into Somalia to ensure that the airports would be open and secure. They did not want the NGOs to return only to become targets or to have their food looted or taken by militias. The CIA team could also provide U.S. troops with a clearer idea of what they might expect in country.

The Agency officers, operating under cover, were to arrive in ad-vance of the military. It would be a risky operation because CIA opera-tives would be inserted into a conflict in which there was no way to distinguish between good guys and bad guys. All sides were heavily armed.

The call for a CIA team went to Tom Twetten, then deputy director for operations, the man who oversaw the Agency's clandestine service. He understood only too well the risk of deploying people in areas where fac-tionalism was rife.

It was not that Twetten was squeamish about putting his officers into the field when it was necessary, but he was skeptical about the need for Agency people in Somalia. He had good reason to have his doubts.

Over the years, demands on the Agency increased while its budget remained the same or shrank. Cuts were made in personnel and opera-tions. Resources had to be husbanded. An internal CIA study was con-ducted to identify those countries in Africa in which the United States had little or no political, economic, or strategic interests. The idea was that in those countries the Agency could afford not to have a presence. The study was undertaken in the aftermath of the Cold War and was com-pleted in 1991.

It concluded that there were four countries in which the United States had no significant interests and that the Agency would therefore cease collecting intelligence on those nations. That list was forwarded to the State Department and the NSC.

"The Cold War was over and there was no more interest in those countries," recalls Twetten. "There was no U.S. presence there. They were essentially off our screen. We were trying to remold ourselves, so we were going to drop off what was least important and we listed those four countries in rank order and at the top of the list, that which was least important, in which there was no embassy, no American presence, and nobody had asked any question about for the last year—the name of that country was Somalia."

Now the Agency was being asked to put its officers at risk in a country it had determined was not even worthy of routine collection efforts. Twetten had a second reservation about Agency involvement. He viewed it as a request for military assistance, something the CIA tried to avoid unless there was a presidential finding. In Twetten's view it was the military who should fill the need.

Unspoken was yet a third reason. The Panama operation three years earlier had left some residual "bad blood" between Langley and the Pentagon. Twetten politely declined what he took to be an invitation for assistance and heard no more on the matter for a short time.

But a week later a second call came in. This time the NSC spoke to the Director Central Intelligence, Robert Gates. This time it was no longer a request, but a directive. The Agency was to field a team in Somalia. End of discussion.

"I was given the instruction 'You will do it,' " recalled Twetten. "The director of operations will organize an intelligence-gathering effort in several villages including Bardera and you will confirm that the airports are secure so that the NGOs can arrive. You will do that by working with the local authorities, whoever is in charge of the area. You have to go out on the ground and figure out who that is."

There was little discussion about who would be the right person to send. "Freedman was a character and really well known for his bravery and audacity," remembers Twetten. Besides, Freedman knew the landscape of the country, had the requisite skills, and was, as always, itching to go. A desk in Langley had never agreed with him. This was what he had joined the Agency to do. Twetten spoke with him personally as he readied himself for the assignment.

But Freedman was to be part of a second phase of the CIA operation. Even before he was to go into Somalia, the Agency had hired some bush pilots in Kenya to bring in pre-positioned Agency officers who had previous experience in Somalia. Once in country, the CIA case officers contacted Somali agents they had known from earlier operations and assigned them to collect intelligence on specific airports. Only then was Freedman to go in as part of a combined CIA and U.S. Army reconnaissance squadron.

A few days before Freedman was to leave he flew to Phoenix, Arizona, to visit a longtime friend, Gale McMillan. It was part business, part pleasure. McMillan was a specialty weapons maker who had outfitted elite Special Forces units. Freedman was there to pick up a ten-power sniper's scope to fit his .308 rifle.

But McMillan was much more than just a source of weapons. Freedman had known him since his days on Delta and had come to view him as a surrogate father. "He was kind of like a third son," said McMillan. One of the nights Freedman was in town McMillan put on a demonstration of his night scopes at the local police firing range and turned to Freedman to prove the accuracy of the rifle and scope. In the blackness of night Freedman set up his rifle, poised on a bipod that rested on a table. He sighted the target and squeezed off five shots at a target the distance of two football fields away. All five shots found their mark, dead center—all within three-tenths of an inch of each other. The police had never seen such a thing before.

The next morning Freedman was to fly back to Washington and then on to Somalia. McMillan met him for breakfast in the coffee shop of the local Sheraton. Freedman seemed ebullient. He was headed for action. He was also, he said, deeply in love with someone from the Agency. "I don't have to justify my work to her," he said. McMillan sensed that Freedman was thinking marriage.

McMillan just listened. He knew not to ask Freedman where he was headed or what he was going to do. Besides, Freedman would not have told him. Anyone he counted a friend understood that such questions would be unwelcomed. But McMillan had something he wanted to say to him, something he knew Freedman would not want to hear.

"Go in the rest room," McMillan told him, "and look at all the white in your hair. It means you better start slowing down and let the young guys take the risk."

Freedman shrugged it off.

"Mac," he said, "you know I'm doing what I love to do. If I have to go, what better way to go?"

When Freedman arrived in Somalia in December 1992, he was dressed in faded blue jeans and a khaki field jacket. He wore a tan Harley-Davidson hat that could not contain the cascades of long curly white locks that broke down his bull-like neck. His beard was nearly all white, and his eyes were hidden by a pair of dark aviator sunglasses.

A photo of him taken on December 18 captures him in a moment of impish delight, a black automatic weapon slung across his wide chest, a field radio pressed to his ear, and the broad grin of someone hamming it up, enjoying every moment. But for his age, he might easily have been mistaken for a kid at camp rather than a CIA operative in the vanguard of Operation Restore Hope.

Not long after he arrived, he and a team of three other combat-seasoned men set out to examine the situation around Bardera and its airport, some two hundred miles to the west of the capital, Mogadishu. It was of little strategic value but was squarely in what had become known as the famine belt. Feuding warlords and gun-toting thugs had completely disrupted the flow of relief. Some three hundred people a day were dying of hunger there.

The date was December 23, 1992. Freedman sat behind the wheel of a civilian vehicle as the four-member team took to the road. Along the way, Freedman stopped the vehicle and walked out to the edge of the bush to relieve himself. Someone snapped a picture of him from behind. Freedman laughed. He was in high spirits.

The journey resumed. But on a remote and dusty stretch of road outside Bardera at just about nine o'clock that Wednesday morning, the vehicle hit a land mine. In one hellacious nanosecond, fire and black smoke, red-hot shards of metal, and a deafening concussion filled the air.

And when it settled and the quiet returned, Larry Freedman lay dead.

He had suffered a massive head wound, his lower right leg had been blown off, and the right side of his chest was opened. Death had been instantaneous as surely as if one of Freedman's own sniper bullets had unerringly found its mark. The other men were wounded but alive.

Freedman's body and the three survivors were flown by chopper to the USS *Tripoli*, a helicopter carrier off Mogadishu. There Lieutenant Commander David A. Beatty, a U.S. Navy doctor, filled out the death certificate for Freedman. It listed Freedman as a civilian employee of the Department of Defense, a GS-12. His next of kin was listed as "unknown," as was his Social Security number.

So flamboyant a life was now masked in the cover language provided by the Agency. Those responsible for concealing Freedman's Agency identity and the identities of the other three men disseminated a mix of fact and falsehood. It was said the three survivors had been State Department security officers. Doubtful. Their names were never released. Nor was the nature of their mission. The mine was described as of Russian origin, an older model. How long it had been there was anyone's guess. Later it was whispered at the CIA and Delta that Freedman had been warned not to take that road, that it was not safe. And yet he chose to take it anyway. Maybe it was true, maybe not. It just seemed to fit into the myth that was already taking shape around Larry Freedman.

The day after Freedman was killed a battalion of marines entered Bardera and prepared to distribute food to the thousands of starving Somalis who gathered about. They would later spend Christmas Eve on the airstrip that Freedman had been assigned to.

Most of the marines had no inkling who Freedman was, but one senior officer did attempt to express his appreciation and debt to him. Lieutenant General R. B. Johnston of the Combined Task Force Somalia sat down and typed a letter addressed "To the Larry Freedman Family."

"There are many young Marines and Soldiers who can take credit for the early success of our operation in Somalia," he wrote. "But there are also a number of very special people like Larry who made the most significant contribution by performing missions that gave us the highest possible guarantee that our troops could enter the major relief centers safely. I cannot underscore how important was the performance of Larry and his fellow team members. They courageously put themselves in harm's way and took personal risks on behalf of our entire force . . . I know I speak for every man and woman in uniform here in Somalia in expressing to Larry's family our deepest sympathy."

The letter was dated December 24, 1992. That was the day Freedman's name was released to the press. At the CIA in Langley his colleagues were reeling from the loss. No one was more devastated than the woman Freedman had hoped to spend the rest of his life with.

But if December 24 was a day of mourning for some at Langley, it was a day of celebration for others. That very day, President George Bush, former head of the CIA, granted pardons to three Agency officials—Duane Clarridge, Alan Fiers, and Clare George—for their role in the Iran-Contra scandal. Bush had effectively put an end to further inquiries into the affair. That was just fine with the CIA.

. . .

On December 29, 1992, Freedman's funeral was held at the Fort Myer Chapel at Arlington National Cemetery. Even before the funeral got under way, Colonel Sanford Dresin, the officiating chaplain and a rabbi, assembled the family for a ritualistic rending of black cloth, a Jewish custom symbolic of grief and remembrance. But there was no black cloth to be found in the chapel and no pins with which to fasten it. So the rabbi had to make do with black construction paper which was torn into strips and attached to lapels with paper clips. Freedman, he observed, was an expert in resourcefulness and would have appreciated such field expediency.

Those who gathered in the chapel might just as well have come from a series of diverse Hollywood sets. Senior government officials arrived by limousine. From Langley came representatives of the Agency's clandestine service, men and women in black suits and silvered sunglasses. From Fort Bragg came beefy Special Forces types—Green Berets and Delta Force. Bikers from who knows where arrived on Harleys and Nortons. From Philadelphia came the old gang from the days at the Pit.

One of those was Petey Altman. He and his pals slowly walked behind the gleaming black caisson drawn by six white stallions as it made its way through the twisting paths of Arlington carrying Freedman's coffin. It came to a stop at the corner of Patton and Eisenhower where Freedman was to be buried. Four of the horses were mounted by soldiers, two were riderless, and one bore reversed boots in the stirrups, for the one who had brought them all together and was not here.

It was a cold Tuesday that threatened rain. Freedman's flag-draped coffin was protected by a plastic sheet. His family took their places in velvet-draped chairs as the rabbi, under shelter of a canopy, began the graveside service.

Freedman would have liked this. In a way, his final cover story—
that he was a "civilian employee of the Defense Department"—was
closer to the truth than even the Agency knew. Yes, he was CIA, but he
had never seen himself as an Agency man. He was a soldier and he was
going out that way.

Only the stone that Teresa had picked was, perhaps, at variance with
what he would have wanted. Instead of one of the simple white stones the
government provides and that dot the verdant hills in dizzying numbers,
she selected a block of jet-black granite. She had her reasons. When she
had gone to look at markers, she noticed that the men cutting the stones
were Harley bikers. She took this as a sign that they were meant to inscribe her husband's headstone. On it is a Star of David, a Green Beret,
and a paratrooper's wings. Inscribed are the words:

Lawrence N. Freedman
Sergeant Major
April 13, 1941—Dec. 23, 1992
"The Life of the Dead is Placed in the
Memory of the Living."

The day after the funeral, on the afternoon of December 30, 1992,
a memorial service for Freedman was held in the John F. Kennedy
Memorial Chapel at Fort Bragg. There Brigadier General Richard Potter
gave the eulogy to a chapel spilling over with Freedman's friends from
Delta and other Special Forces detachments, as well as those second-generation combatants he had trained. General Potter cited a passage from
Isaiah to explain what he called Freedman's "warrior ethic," his willingness
to serve wherever, whenever:

And I heard the voice of the Lord say "Who shall I
send and who will go for us?" and I answered,
"Here I am, send me."

Years later, in retirement, General Potter mused over the fuss shown
over Freedman's passing and the interest of an inquiring journalist. "I will
tell you that wherever Larry is in Valhalla up there with all the other war-

riors, he would probably be laughing that we are having this conversation."

. . .

Remembering Larry Freedman would take many forms:

In Buundo, Ethiopia, a bridge built by U.S. troops that supported tons of food for the starving bears his name. On a steel plate, in white paint, is stenciled "Lawrence R. Freedman Bridge." Never mind that his middle initial was "N" not "R."

In Keystone, South Dakota, just below Mount Rushmore, is a small wooden plaque that reads, "In Memory of Larry Freedman." It is affixed to a picnic shelter where Freedman often escaped the August heat on his annual pilgrimage to the Sturgis motorcycle rally.

In Fayetteville, North Carolina, in the Special Forces Memorial Plaza, his name appears on a plaque dedicated to those who died in the Somalia campaign, though here the CIA's cover story became entangled in yet another cover story. He is listed as an employee of the State Department, not the Pentagon.

And not far away, in the JFK Special Forces Museum, is a small stage named for him: the Larry "Superjew" Freedman Theater, a fitting tribute to a man with a keen sense of theater.

But it was the Agency's memorial service to Freedman the morning of January 5, 1993, that his family remembers best. The CIA assembled Freedman's colleagues and family in "the Bubble," the auditorium across from the headquarters building. Just inside the entrance was a life-sized portrait of Freedman set upon an easel. The room was filled with covert operatives and Agency brass. Even Colin Powell was there. Director Bob Gates spoke briefly, and then one of Freedman's colleagues offered a few remarks about the friend he missed:

"He was blessed with a sense of street savvy, which numbered Larry in that small handful whom, without hesitation, you can trust with covering your six o'clock when you walked into the woodline on a tactical mission . . . Pick a continent, pick a decade, Larry was there . . ."

Moments later the lights were lowered, Bette Midler's rendition of "The Wind Beneath My Wings" was played, and from floor to ceiling was projected a giant picture of Freedman against the left wall. It was a touch of drama Freedman could only have applauded.

Three days after the ceremony, on January 8, 1993, President George Bush, fresh from a trip to Somalia, visited Langley and addressed CIA employees. Langley was a special place for Bush and he could count on receiving a warm welcome there. It was not so with many of his successors. These were troubled times for the Agency.

"Last November," Bush told them, "when Bob [Gates] became director, I noted that the men and women of the intelligence community faced a new mission in a dramatically different world . . . I wish all of you could have been with me on this visit to Somalia. It was very moving. And we are doing the right thing." It was to be a pep talk designed to inspire the Agency personnel at a time when there was an increasing chorus of voices questioning the need for a CIA in a post–Cold War environment.

"The dangers that we face are real," Bush told them. "I still get emotionally convinced of that when I see the stars out in the hall of this building . . . So I came to say thank you." No reference was made to Freedman. Not long after, a nameless star was added to the wall and to the Book of Honor.

. . .

For some, Freedman's death remains a dark tragedy. In Fayetteville, North Carolina, his widow, Teresa, has created a kind of unseen shrine to him. She has kept his heavy black Harley-Davidson jacket with fringe sleeves as well as the dress uniform she had pressed in the belief that he could be buried in it. That was before she was told the coffin could not be opened. Behind the headboard of their king-sized bed are boxes and boxes of medals and memorabilia—Bronze Stars, a Purple Heart, pins and service ribbons, the otoscope of a medic, a piece of a gun, an old buck knife, dog tags from Vietnam, a Star of David, and a sterling-silver "Chi," Hebrew for "life." Here, too, hidden away, is the palm-sized gold medallion that reads, "Central Intelligence Agency For Valor: Lawrence N. Freedman 1992." It was awarded by CIA Director Robert Gates only eight days after Freedman's death. But it took three years before the Agency would consent to send the medal to Freedman's widow. It is an honor that even now she is not to put on display.

But if there are those who are still in mourning, there are others who find such solemnity ill-suited to one as lusty and vital as Larry Freedman.

It seemed somehow fitting when his sister, Sylvia, and his rowdy friends from Philadelphia decided to throw a party in Larry's memory. It was a raucous evening. As the video camera rolled, each friend outdid the other with outrageous stories of Freedman. In the background was a huge cake with the name Gus on it and a life-sized portrait in icing of Freedman, complete with his rakish smile and the desperado's mustache. No one dared cut a slice anywhere near his face. To this day, it remains in a Philadelphia freezer.

Sylvia still can't quite bring herself to believe that her brother is dead, only that he is not coming back. "My great fantasy," she says, "is that he went off to be James Bond and just didn't know how to leave us."

Epilogue

. . . the courage to bear great grief in silence . . .
DIRECTOR CENTRAL INTELLIGENCE GEORGE TENET

FROM AROUND the nation they came, arriving at CIA headquarters shortly before 11:00 A.M.—mostly widows, fatherless sons and daughters, mothers and fathers, dressed in the somber colors of grief and remembrance. Some cradled flowers, others photographs of long-departed loved ones. What they had in common was that their losses were now represented with a star on the Wall of Honor. It was May 14, 1998, a cloudless and sticky-hot Thursday. This was the Agency's twelfth annual memorial service to its own.

Family members had been told not to bring cameras or recording devices. There would be no reporters, no foreign dignitaries, no curious outsiders. Indeed, if the Agency had its way, no one beyond Langley's 258-acre compound would ever know such a convocation had taken place. No one was to speak of it afterward. A year later a warning was added to the program: "Due to cover considerations, we ask that no details of this ceremony be discussed outside of this building."

The invitations had gone out six weeks earlier in plain envelopes, sent by the CIA's Office of Protocol. Family members were met at the entrance and led to the rows of folding chairs that had been set up in front of the Wall of Honor inside the cavernous marble lobby. Already Agency staffers had begun to congregate in the upper lobby. They would have to stand—a token of honor due those assembled below.

Among the earliest to arrive was the family of John Merriman. His name appears in the Book of Honor beside the year 1964. It was Merriman whose plane was shot down in the Congo and whose injuries went untreated for days while he waited for the Agency to rescue him from a remote air base. To this day his death certificate records that he died in a car crash in Puerto Rico.

On this morning his widow, Val, carried an arrangement of pink lilies, white and lavender delphiniums, and three large mums. In her other hand she clutched a photo of her husband dressed smartly in a commercial pilot's uniform.

Sons Jon and Bruce, now adults, stopped in the men's room to wash up. A man with a trumpet wandered in and practiced playing "Taps," his instrument muted with a cap. When they left the bathroom, they noticed the clock on the wall said 3:45. They wondered if it was broken or perhaps it was the time in Moscow or Beijing. Then the Merriman brothers took their seats some eight rows back.

Soon after, Michael Maloney's widow, Adrienne, and sons Michael and Craig arrived and quietly took their places in the second row of the middle section. Michael Maloney had died in a chopper crash in Laos in October 1965. For thirty-two years his death was marked by an anonymous star. His widow had asked that his name be inscribed in the Book of Honor, but her requests always seemed to get lost in the bureaucracy. Now she had come from Connecticut to at last hear his name read aloud, a final tribute to Michael Maloney and a final act of emancipation from the secrecy that had smothered them all.

But the CIA's secrecy often defied explanation. There was no such lifting of the veil on the identity of the man who sat beside Michael Maloney on that fateful helicopter mission in Laos. For yet another year Mike Deuel's name was to remain in the limbo that befalls most nameless stars. Not until 1999 was it added to the book. Dick Holm, one of Deuel's closest friends and Agency colleagues, and the man who later married his widow, attended the ceremony in remembrance of Deuel. It was Holm who was himself disfigured in a fiery plane crash in the Congo but whose scars now seemed to melt away after a moment's conversation. He had gone on to a distinguished CIA career clouded at the last by a bungled covert operation in Paris.

Not far off sat Janet Weininger. She was seven when her father, Thomas "Pete" Ray, and three other Alabama Air National Guardsmen lost their lives in the fiasco known as the Bay of Pigs in 1961. For thirty-six years she had waited for the Agency to acknowledge that her father and the others had flown for the CIA and to publicly pay homage to their sacrifice. For decades the government lied and dismissed them as mercenaries. Now at last, the Agency was about to speak the truth, to recognize that he and the others had died in service to country and to the Agency in particular. She and her children had come from Miami just to hear her father's name read aloud.

Sitting close to the podium was Page Hart Boteler, sister-in-law of Bill Boteler, the handsome twenty-six-year-old covert operative killed by a pipe bomb in a café in Nicosia in 1956. Odd memories flooded her mind—the four wisdom teeth he had pulled, his jazzy little sports car, a last dinner together. Now he was one of the named stars, though like so many others, his name would mean nothing to those who daily passed by the wall.

Page Boteler introduced herself to a young woman who sat behind her. The woman said her last name was Bennett and that she was two years old when she lost her father. William E. Bennett had been a thirty-six-year-old covert operative working under cover as a political officer in Vietnam. He was reported killed on January 7, 1975, in an explosion at his home in Tuy Hoa on the central coast.

Many family members either could not make it to the ceremony or did not receive invitations. Sylvia Doner, sister of Larry Freedman, who was killed by a land mine in Somalia in 1992, spent that morning at her office desk. Antoinette Lewis, mother of James Lewis, who died in the 1983 bombing of the Beirut embassy, was at home in San Diego, having her morning coffee and toast. On son Jimmy's birthday and on the anniversary of his death, she has the priest read Mass for him and his wife,

Monique, who died with him in the blast. Nor was anyone at the ceremony to represent the family of Richard Spicer, a nameless star killed on October 19, 1984, in a plane crash in El Salvador while on a covert mission. It was said at the time that he died in a car crash in Florida. Few were fooled.

Buford Robbins, a Denver butcher, had hoped to live long enough to have daughter Barbara's name inscribed in the Book of Honor, replacing the nameless star that tormented him. The twenty-one-year-old CIA secretary had been killed in the 1965 bombing of the U.S. Embassy in Saigon. Three weeks before this memorial service, on April 22, 1998, he died of liver cancer. "I wish I had an answer," his widow, Ruth, would say. "It sounded like they were still trying to protect someone or something. I didn't know how to interpret it. If they have a good reason, I guess it's something we will never find out."

At precisely 11:30 the memorial service began. As Director Central Intelligence George Tenet took his seat, many in the audience sensed that the air-conditioning had finally come on. An African American woman, Keesha Gibbons, moved slowly to the front of the room and sang a gospel song, "Beams of Heaven." A soprano, she sang a cappella and the power of her voice brought all whispers to a halt. Then Jack G. Downing, deputy director for operations and overseer of the clandestine service, introduced Director Tenet.

This was not a day that Tenet looked forward to. An emotional man, he knew it would be hard to get through the service. Some of those in the Book of Honor behind him were much more than mere names to him. Four of the stars, two named and two nameless, had been lost on his watch.

"We stand together before this sacred wall of stars," he began, "united in fellowship as we remember our fallen colleagues. This silent constellation is the most eloquent testament we can give to CIA's half century of devoted service to the nation.

"We will never forget that each one of these stars also symbolizes a family's loss—the irreparable loss of a parent, a husband, a wife, a brother, a sister, a child, a grandparent.

"Each star, too, represents the loss of a friend, a colleague, a mentor."

While he spoke, an Agency camera mounted on a tripod was recording the event. It focused not on Tenet, but on a woman dressed in pink who was using her hands to capture Tenet's words in sign language for the deaf.

Then Tenet spoke of those singled out for honor this day. He mentioned a young man, an Arabist named Matt, who sported a roguish mustache, detested filling out travel vouchers, and was once arrested for driving the wrong way down a one-way street. There would be no last name offered. His identity was still cloaked in secrecy.

But the Matt of whom he spoke was no secret to the family of Matthew Gannon who sat arrayed before Tenet—eight brothers and sisters, his mother and father, his widow, Susan, and his daughter Julie. It was Matthew Gannon who had lost his life in the bombing of Pan Am 103. Tenet nearly choked on his prepared remarks as he read that Matt's young widow, Susan, had insisted that he open his Christmas presents before he left for Beirut.

With the Gannons sat Tom and Kay Twetten. It was hard for them to hear about Matt, the polite young case officer who had married their daughter. Tom had come from his quiet home in the far north of Vermont to be here in this place where, only a few years before, he had overseen all covert operations.

Among the Gannon brothers was Richard, who had himself survived the bombing of the Beirut embassy. He sat next to a small woman leaning on a cane. They introduced themselves to each other. "Hello," she said softly, "I'm Christina Welch and my husband was Richard Welch." Her husband, the CIA station chief in Athens, had been ambushed outside their home in 1975.

Tenet completed his remarks about "Matt," then spoke of the newest star on the wall. It belonged to a Japanese American named Chiyoki "Chick" Ikeda, killed in the explosion of Northwest Airlines flight 710 on March 17, 1960, over Indiana. A few hours after the plane took off, an anonymous caller claimed a bomb was on board. Ikeda, one of sixty-three fatalities, was listed simply as a civilian employee of the army. Tenet noted that Ikeda had been a veteran of the OSS, but he would say nothing of his work with the CIA, even thirty-eight years later.

"The work Chick did building strategic liaison relationships for the Agency," he said solemnly, "must still remain unspoken, for it continues to yield valuable dividends today."

What Tenet did not say was that on the day Ikeda was killed he was escorting a prominent Japanese visitor named Masami Nakamura, chief of the security division of Japan's national police, who was also on the Chicago to Miami flight. In the spring of 1960 the United States fretted deeply about Communist activity in Japan. Nakamura was in the United States for training, presumably in methods of crowd suppression and control, as well as intelligence-gathering techniques. At that very moment, Khrushchev's agents were believed to be busy in Tokyo preparing to disrupt a long-planned visit by President Eisenhower. In June 1960 the presidential trip was scuttled for fear of Communist demonstrations.

None of this was in Tenet's remarks. And none of it mattered to Ikeda's widow, Mildred, and two sons, John and George, who sat in the front row closest to the door. For Mildred Ikeda it was enough that her husband had finally been recognized.

Tenet was nearing the end of his remarks. His voice cracked with emotion.

"The families of our seventy-one heroes and heroines have to show courage in equal measure to that of the ones they lost—the courage to go on after a devastating personal loss, the courage of a single parent, the courage of a child growing up without a father or a mother, the courage to bear great grief in silence, and the courage to keep faith with our government for years, if necessary, until their loved ones' contributions can be acknowledged.

"In truth, we may never be able to reveal the name behind every star."

His remarks were then addressed to the Agency employees now clustered in the upper lobby.

"And so I say to the busy men and women of this Agency:

"Do not hurry past this Wall of Honor. Do not lower your eyes when you walk by. Slow your pace, pause for a moment, and gaze up at these shining stars.

"Take it from me, your worries will recede into perspective, you will feel even closer to your families and your colleagues, and you will return to work with a deepened sense of purpose. And before you continue on your way, linger just one moment more and say a silent prayer. Say to the men and women behind those stars:

" 'Thank you, friends. While I have the power to live and act, may I be worthy of your sacrifice.' "

With that, Tenet took his seat. His impassioned final words had been more than a rhetorical flourish. He was reaching out to the entire Agency community, much of which was laboring under a malaise of uncertainty and doubt. The Cold War had brought the Agency into existence in 1947 and now was relegated to history. Many believed the Agency might soon meet a similar end. What was to be its raison d'être in an era in which America was the sole superpower, in which Communism had not spread but imploded, and in which Moscow had been reduced to a wary but needy ally?

Against the backdrop of the Wall of Honor, Tenet's words were intended to counter a withering barrage of criticism. The Agency's mission, its competence, and its loyalties were all being questioned. The day before the memorial service, the headline in the *Washington Post* read, "CIA Missed Signs of India's Tests, U.S. Officials Say." Satellite imagery was said to show that a nuclear test was afoot, yet no one at the Agency issued a warning. The White House and Congress were flabbergasted.

Other intelligence failures followed. On August 20, 1998, the United States launched a cruise missile attack on the al-Shifa pharmaceutical plant in Sudan. The assault was based on CIA claims that soil samples gathered at the site offered incontrovertible evidence that the plant was used to manufacture deadly chemical agents. Within days of the deadly attack, doubts began to surface. Had the United States mistakenly obliterated a legitimate pharmaceutical plant? Agency analysts privately began to distance themselves from what increasingly appeared to be a questionable call.

The worst was yet to come. On May 7, 1999, at the height of NATO's assault on Yugoslavia, U.S. planes dropped laser-guided bombs on a Belgrade building said to be the Federal Directorate of Supply and Procurement. The decision was based on CIA maps and intelligence. It turned out that the building had for years been the Chinese Embassy. At least three people were killed. Twenty were wounded. Beijing was livid. It was a foreign policy disaster and an intelligence failure of the first magnitude. The CIA's George Tenet could speak only of "faulty information." This was paired with scandalous accounts of Chinese spying at U.S. nuclear weapons labs and the wholesale theft of America's most sensitive secrets.

A string of internal betrayals also shattered public confidence in the

Agency. CIA officer Aldrich Ames's treachery is believed to have led to the execution of at least a dozen foreign agents who had served the Agency. The CIA's Douglas F. Groat attempted to blackmail the Agency, demanding $1 million in exchange for not disclosing how the United States intercepted foreign communications. Senior CIA officer Harold James Nicholson also sold out to Moscow. For all its obsessive secrecy—indeed, perhaps because of it—the CIA could not protect its most sensitive secrets. "If we guard our toothbrushes and diamonds with equal zeal," once observed former national security adviser McGeorge Bundy, "we will lose fewer toothbrushes and more diamonds." As if to prove that very point, even a former director of Central Intelligence, John M. Deutch, had to be stripped of his security clearance in the summer of 1999 after it was discovered that he had placed sensitive national secrets on his unsecured home computer.

Public trust of the Agency remains at a low point. Allegations in the press, no matter how spurious, implicate the Agency in the introduction of crack cocaine to South-Central Los Angeles.

In the midst of such turmoil the Agency is attempting to rebuild itself. Since 1991 thousands of its most experienced officers, a quarter of its workforce, have retired or quit. New recruits were suspect. Many seemed as concerned with benefits and retirement plans as service. Old hands in the clandestine ranks mused that they never assumed they would live long enough to enjoy such rewards. The Agency seemed rudderless, losing four directors in six years.

That was why George Tenet urged Agency employees at the memorial service to linger at the Wall of Honor, hoping that they might draw strength from the collective memory of the Agency's past. A year earlier the CIA had put in a reflecting pool and garden dedicated to those killed in service. But its real purpose was to offer a place of refuge to an increasingly troubled cadre of employees.

Ironically the secrecy that had failed to protect the Agency from Soviet penetration had prevented Americans from coming to terms with their own past. In 1995 President Bill Clinton vowed to declassify vast amounts of Cold War documents, but three years later the CIA reneged on its promise to release accounts of major operations from that very period. The State Department, too, chastised the Agency for withholding materials vital to America's diplomatic history. The U.S. Archives has next to nothing from the Agency, which seems bent on controlling what little of its history it chooses to reveal.

In the Agency's own archives are an estimated 65 million classified documents more than twenty-five years old. That same compulsive secrecy enshrouds the Book of Honor. Douglas S. Mackiernan was killed on the Tibetan border in 1950. His star remains nameless. So, too, does that of Hugh Francis Redmond, who died in 1970 after nineteen years in a Chinese prison. In both instances the Chinese knew they were CIA spies. Only the American public did not.

In Washington the demand for Agency reform grows. Some call for its dismantlement. But though the Cold War is over, it is not a safer world. In lieu of the Soviet Union, the CIA continues to monitor foreign powers hostile to the United States but also targets the four "counters"—international narcotics, crime, proliferation of weapons of mass destruction, and terrorism. Its mandate is broader than ever; some would argue too broad to be effective.

But this was a day not for recriminations, but for remembering. Tenet completed his remarks and returned to his seat. "Would you please rise for the roll call?" asked Jack G. Downing, the CIA's spymaster. One by one, the names of those inscribed in the Book of Honor were read aloud:

Jerome P. Ginley, William P. Boteler, Howard Carey, Frank C. Grace, Wilburn S. Rose, Chiyoki Ikeda, Thomas "Pete" Ray, Riley Shamburger, Wade Gray, Leo Baker, John G. Merriman, Eugene Buster Edens, Edward Johnson, Mike Maloney, Louis A. O'Jibway, Walter Ray, Billy Jack Johnson, Jack Weeks, Paul C. Davis, David Konzelman, Wilbur Murray Greene, William E. Bennett, Richard Welch, James S. Rawlings, Robert C. Ames, Scott J. Van Lieshout, Curtis R. Wood, William F. Buckley, Richard Krobock, Lansing H. Bennett, Frank A. Darling, James Lewek, and John Celli.

They died in places far away and unnervingly close to home—the China Sea, Cyprus, Germany, Nevada, Indiana, Cuba, the Congo, Laos, Vietnam, China, Greece, Lebanon, El Salvador, Bosnia, Saudi Arabia. Lansing Bennett and Frank Darling had been cut down at the Agency's front gate in Langley, murdered on their morning commute by an AK-47-toting Pakistani named Aimil Kansi. The date was January 25, 1993.

Of the seventy-one stars, only thirty-three names were read aloud. The identities of the other thirty-eight remain classified.

Among those nameless stars is one representing Freddie Woodruff, who was shot to death in August 1993 in the former Soviet republic of Georgia. The forty-five-year-old son of a professor, he was an ordained minister who could read ancient Greek and speak Russian, German, Turkish, Armenian, and several other tongues. He had been in Georgia under cover as a political officer at the U.S. Embassy. His mission was to train the security force assigned to protect that nation's embattled leader, Eduard Shevardnadze.

Also unnamed was a young woman who died a violent and selfless death in 1996. An anonymous star in the Book of Honor, her name is withheld from this book. The Agency made a compelling case that to identify her would put others at risk.

After the reading of names, a wreath was set before the wall. Then came a moment of silence and, finally, the mournful sound of a trumpet playing "Taps." When the last note had faded, it seemed that no one knew what to do next. Families fidgeted nervously, awaiting some cue. At last, someone took to the podium and indecorously declared "It's over," and with that came an awkward laugh and a sigh of relief.

Afterward, some family members posed before the Wall of Honor as an Agency photographer took their pictures. Each person offered to give the photographer his or her name and address. But the photographer declined, smiling coyly. "We'll get them to you," he said. "We know who you are." In the past, some photographs arrived blurred or doctored so that individuals were not identifiable.

Following the ceremony, the families attended a brief reception on the upper lobby, sipping lemonade and nibbling on crackers and cubes of cheese, star fruits and grapes. Then the families went their separate ways.

Some went to the Agency museum and saw a tiny camera disguised as a matchbox, a walking cane that fired .22-caliber rounds, and an alarm clock once attached to a bomb that never went off. Its intended victims were CIA officers in the Mideast.

Others went to the employee store and bought souvenirs—a key chain, a shot glass, a paperweight, all bearing the Agency seal.

Many found time to walk along the gallery corridor pausing before the formal oil portraits of the Agency's past directors, each presented in a statesmanly pose. With pipe or spectacles in hand, these former directors looked almost infallible. These were the men in whom their loved ones had entrusted their lives. They were cordoned off by a velvet rope, their reputations only as secure as the secrets they kept.

Some family members planned to lunch together. They shared photographs and memories, exchanged addresses and phone numbers. On this day they could find some measure of relief, as if the silence to which they had been sentenced had been momentarily commuted.

Before leaving, most paused to take a final look at the Book of Honor, to press their finger against the glass, intone a silent prayer, or whisper a parting message to the star for which they had come so far.

Much of the story of the CIA is contained within these stars, but it is a story the Agency holds to itself. In the end the CIA and the families who gathered this day are both hostages to history. Whether the Agency will ever release its past and whether it will find for itself a meaningful future are both in some doubt. As from the beginning, the dilemmas it faces are not entirely of its own making. Those who daily enter the old headquarters lobby must still pass between the scriptural verse etched into the marble—"And ye shall know the truth, and the truth shall make you free"—and the cautionary Wall of Honor across from it. Between these two walls, between the values of an open society and the demands of a craft rooted in deception and betrayal, the CIA is asked to steer an uneasy, often irreconcilable course.

Afterword

Nine months have passed since *The Book of Honor* was published. In that time, much has happened, both to the families of the nameless stars and to the Agency itself. Publication provided a long-awaited lifting of the veil of secrecy, a chance for family members to revisit the events and, in some cases, to learn what really happened and to finally speak openly of both their grief and their pride. The book was the product of the families' collective courage in defying the CIA's edict of silence. It is only right, then, that they should finally be able to talk openly about their experiences.

Among those deeply affected was Losue Hagler. She is the sister of Bud Petty, who died in 1989 attempting to resupply Jonas Savimbi, Angola's rebel leader. The CIA, after a decade of ignoring her inquiries, invited her to attend the annual memorial service. It also promised to at last answer questions about her brother's death. But first she was required to pledge that she would not disclose whatever was revealed to her. This she reluctantly did. In the end, the Agency told her nothing new.

For the children of the nameless stars, the book provided the first credible account of what happened to their lost parents. Debbie Spessard's two sons, Jarad and Jason, were five and seven respectively when their father,

James, was killed in the same mission that claimed Bud Petty's life. Now they are teenagers. She called them into a room, sat them down, and had them read the chapter on their father. Then they talked about James Spessard's life and death, what they had learned, and what it meant to them.

I was also contacted by someone on behalf of Paul Weinberg, a lifelong friend of Larry Freedman, who was killed in Somalia in 1992. Weinberg had been of inestimable help in coming to understand Larry Freedman. I was asked to provide an advance copy of the book though the release date for publication was only a week away. Weinberg was dying of cancer. Unfortunately, he passed away only days later.

No meeting moved me more than that with Val Merriman. She was the widow of John Merriman, who was shot down over the Congo in 1964. For decades she had been lied to, told her husband died painlessly in a Puerto Rican hospital after receiving the best of medical attention. Nothing in the Agency's account was true. Val Merriman, together with her son Jon, met me at a book signing in Washington and presented me with a dozen long-stemmed red roses. "My family loves you," she said.

Nor will I forget what transpired in the minutes prior to the taping of ABC's *Good Morning America*, which did a segment on the book. The network had flown a dozen family members of the nameless stars to New York from around the country. Before taping, the families mingled outside a Manhattan restaurant. They were meeting for the first time. There were widows and sisters and brothers and nephews. Each had assumed that they alone had suffered the crushing effects of secrecy that had come to define their lives. Now they were no longer alone.

For others, the past months have not brought peace. The family of Matthew Gannon, together with the families of other victims of the bombing of Pan AM 103, endured a second kind of horror as two Libyan defendants were brought to trial in the Netherlands. The consensus of court observers was that the CIA had profoundly bungled the investigation, built its argument upon an informant of highly dubious character, and, in so doing, jeopardized the entire case. It was not only the CIA's witness whose credibility was shaken. So too was the Agency's. In the end, one of the Libyans was convicted of mass murder, the other walked.

In the weeks and months prior to and following publication of the book, the CIA inscribed into its own Book of Honor the names of several of those anonymous stars identified in my book. Among these were Mike

Deuel, Wayne McNulty, Ray Seaborg, and John W. Kearns. They had perished in Vietnam or Laos decades earlier.

But the CIA did not undergo any fundamental reexamination of its culture of secrecy. Nor did I expect it to. Officially, the CIA maintained its silence about my book. When reporters asked about it, Agency spokesmen replied with the usual mantra, "We will neither confirm nor deny . . ."

Though the book was on the *Washington Post* Bestseller List and was a frequent topic of conversation among Agency employees, it was not to be sold within the CIA's own store. There, the shelves are lined with books that have been vetted by the CIA or are deemed to promote its interests. It is as if by keeping my book from its shelves the Agency could ignore the truth of the stories contained therein and the tragedies it chronicled. That capacity to embrace fiction over fact, to adopt a kind of see-no-evil mentality, is not without precedent at the CIA.

Since publication, seven more stars have been added to the Agency's Book of Honor, four of them nameless. Two of the named stars belong to Norman A. Schwartz and Robert C. Snoddy. The two were killed on November 29, 1952, on a mission to snatch from Mainland China an operative named Li Chun-ying. The Chinese lay in wait ready to foil the attempt. Snoddy and Schwartz were killed as the plane came in. They were buried on the spot.

The families were told the plane went down in the Sea of Japan. Two decades passed before the incident was even acknowledged. In July 2000, three months after the CIA's memorial service, the city of Louisville, Kentucky, Schwartz's hometown, dedicated a simple limestone bench in a park as a place to meditate upon his loss and that of others. A brass plaque reads: IN COMMEMORATION OF PILOT NORMAN A. SCHWARTZ, WHO GAVE HIS LIFE FOR THE PRESERVATION OF PEACE, AND IN RECOGNITION OF ALL MEN AND WOMEN WHO SERVED IN THE COLD WAR (1945–1991). Relatives of Schwartz are pressing the Chinese to return the airman's remains. Also on board that same aircraft had been two young CIA operatives, John Downey and Richard Fecteau. They would spend two decades in a Chinese prison.

But even as the CIA's Book of Honor belatedly closes the chapter on the Cold War, it reflects the perils faced by today's clandestine operatives. Among the anonymous stars recently added to that tome are fresh victims of terrorism.

How long will they too remain faceless? Half a century later, the identity of the first star—the star that represents Douglas Seymour Mackiernan, gunned down in Tibet in 1950—remains a state secret. So too do the identities of Barbara Robbins, Hugh Redmond, John Peterson, Raymond Rayner, Ivan King, Dennis Gabriel, Matt Gannon, Larry Freedman, Fred Woodruff, the victims of the 1983 Beirut Bombing and the 1989 Angola operation. As of this writing, there are seventy-seven stars in the CIA's Book of Honor. Thirty-five have no name.

. . .

By the end of 2000, the CIA seemed largely immune to the sort of tough congressional scrutiny that alone may hold it accountable. It had survived a series of disturbing fiascoes—the bombing of the Chinese embassy in Yugoslavia, the targeting of a pharmaceutical plant in the Sudan, the bungling of the investigation of John Deutch's security violations, the failure to spot India's impending nuclear test, the mishandling of the Pan Am 103 probe. And still, Director CIA George Tenet and his agency appeared to enjoy the support of both the outgoing Clinton administration and the incoming Bush administration.

Tenet has been popular within the CIA and on Capitol Hill. He defends his Agency vigorously and is politically savvy. He has brought stability after years of turbulence and has overseen recruiting efforts designed to offset the hemorrhaging of experienced officers who have retired or resigned. Though he has steadfastly refused to speak with me, I know him to be a congenial figure and, by all accounts, a decent man. But his capacity to shield his Agency from the full brunt of operational and intelligence failures also reflects the vagaries of Washington's Old Boy Network. As the former senior staffer on the Senate Select Committee on Intelligence, Tenet's links to Capitol Hill, and the residual loyalties that go with them, have protected him from what might have been a more withering criticism from his former colleagues.

So too it has been with the House oversight committee. The House Permanent Select Committee on Intelligence is headed by Porter J. Goss, a conservative Florida congressman who seemingly cannot do enough to promote the interests and ambitions of Langley. Before becoming a congressman, Representative Goss was himself a CIA case officer. Such pervasive CIA influence also contributes to public cynicism and the perception that the Agency's tentacles of power render it answerable to no one.

Most ominous was a sweeping provision requested by the CIA and championed by Goss that Congress attached to the Intelligence Authorization Act for fiscal year 2001. That measure, passed behind closed doors and without a public hearing, would have made it a crime punishable by three years in prison for any official to disclose classified material. It was a thinly disguised antileak provision aimed at silencing those who talk to the press or who would challenge the near-absolute control that the U.S. national security apparatus exercises over what and when the public learns of its activities.

The bill was ultimately vetoed by President Clinton, but only after a concerted campaign by the nation's foremost news publications to sound the tocsin. Such a measure would have had dire consequences for the First Amendment and for the ability of reporters like myself to inform the public. Had such a provision been law at the time of my research for *The Book of Honor*, some four hundred current and retired covert operatives—all who spoke with me—might well have gone to prison. Of course, the more likely outcome would have been that the chilling effect of such a measure would have blunted my efforts to identify the anonymous stars.

In either case, there would have been no *The Book of Honor*. The measure would have created the perfect chokehold on the public's access to information concerning the conduct of foreign affairs and covert operations. It bears watching whether the new Bush administration will be emboldened to resurrect that measure.

Even as the bill made its way through Congress there was evidence aplenty that government secrecy had already gone too far rather than not far enough. The ordeal of Wen Ho Lee, the Chinese American scientist accused of security breaches at Los Alamos National Laboratory, finally came to an end, but not before his reputation and career were in ruins. Federal prosecutors never produced any evidence to support the allegation of espionage.

Then too there was the case of Mazen Al-Najjar, held in an American prison for three and a half years without being charged with a crime. He was seen as a security threat and held on "secret evidence" to which neither he nor his lawyers had access. His recent release would have been cause for celebration by civil libertarians were it not for the fact that so many others are still being held on "secret evidence."

We are forced to wonder whether it is not lax security but excessive secrecy that poses by far the greater threat to the interests of the American people.

A final word. In the wake of publication, the book was widely and favorably reviewed, but among the reviews were two recurrent observations with which I would take exception. First, that the men and women of whom I wrote understood that if they were killed their sacrifices would remain anonymous. Such is the nature of espionage, it is argued. Granted, these men and women accepted that if they were killed, security concerns would prohibit their roles and identities from being made public so long as security sensitivities remained. But it is equally true that in service to government they had every right to expect that when common sense dictated that such security concerns were no longer applicable, the strictures would be lifted and their surviving family members would no longer be made to suffer the cruelties of what would then be a blind and obsessive secrecy. In short, they could expect the government in whose service they gave their lives to behave humanely and not to use secrecy as a way to escape accountability.

The second criticism was that those whose deaths are recorded in this book died for naught, that their missions were failures and therefore their lives were wasted. It is true that in some cases these lives might have been saved and that in others the missions accomplished little. But I do not believe that it follows that their lives were wasted or devoid of meaning. Though I do not share many of the agendas in whose service they were deployed, I believe that in most instances these men and women were doing that which was most important to them. I am uncomfortable judging the value of another's life or sacrifice by outcome alone. I would not want my own life to be measured against such a standard. These men and women understood the risks attendant to their chosen careers. They acted out of love of country. If the wisdom of their missions was suspect— as often it was—then it casts a shadow not upon the individual but upon the institution that dispatched them.

What we, the living, can do, is honor them both by remembering them and by insisting that the very secrecy under which they died is not permitted to threaten the values for which they lived.

—Ted Gup
January 2001

Author's Note
and Acknowledgments

A decade ago, when I first stood before the CIA's Wall of Honor and contemplated a book that would attempt to identify the nameless stars, I knew that I would meet with stiff resistance from the Agency. In this the Agency did not disappoint me. What I could not have foreseen was the courage of those CIA families who chose to defy Agency pressures and who broke years of silence in the belief that the stories of their loved ones' lives and deaths could be told without jeopardizing national security. Many of these families came to believe, as I did, that the accounts of those who died on covert missions were not the sole property of the government, that they belonged to history. For allowing me to be the one to tell those stories I am deeply grateful and hope that in this work they will not find me unworthy of that trust.

I would also thank the more than four hundred current and former employees of the CIA who were willing to speak with me, even when the institution for which they worked forbade it. They had nothing to gain and much to lose. Deciphering the motives of those whose profession it is to deceive others is a fool's errand. But at the risk of sounding naive, I believe they shared a common interest in recognizing the sacrifices of former colleagues and in providing the public a more human, if not more vulnerable, side of America's clandestine service. Thanking them by name would be seen as a consummate act of ingratitude.

On a personal note I would thank several colleagues and friends without whom this book would in all likelihood have been stillborn. Len Downie, executive editor of the *Washington Post*, and Steve Coll, the paper's managing editor, are among these. I am also grateful to my former editor and colleague Bob Woodward, who taught me that there was nothing sacrosanct about secrecy, that often it was merely a way to avoid public scrutiny. Ben Bradlee, former editor of the *Post*, was the first to show me that there was nothing higher than being a reporter and nothing more humbling.

After spending three years with spies I came to think like a spy, demonstrating my own brand of obsessive secrecy. I compartmented my information and developed a kind of cover story for outsiders, telling them simply that I was writing a history of the CIA. The few with whom I felt comfortable sharing my true objectives and who did not unduly make fun of my paranoia deserve praise. First to mind comes Mike Riley, editor of the *Roanoke Times*, who gave me great support and sage advice along the lines of "get a life." Other friends to whom I am indebted include Ira Abrams, Barbara Feinman, Dick Thompson, and Tom Ewing.

I must also express my deep appreciation to the John D. and Catherine T. MacArthur Foundation. Their generosity in the form of a grant provided the seed money with which this research was undertaken. Their willingness to accept so unorthodox an investigative project when other foundations shied away will not be forgotten.

This was my first book and I was spoiled to have David Black as my agent and Bill Thomas of Doubleday as my editor. David understood what I was attempting to do long before I did. His devotion to words and story, not just making a sale, and his friendship in times of doubt will not go unpunished—I shall come to him as often as he will allow. Bill Thomas shared my passion for the subject and contributed both vision and discipline. He was the perfect editor, at times an ally, at times an adversary, and always at the right times for each. Never did he let me down.

Anya Richards, my researcher, proved to be an invaluable resource and friend.

As for my family, my wife, Peggy, and sons David and Matthew endured three years of intermittent absence and inattention. I am looking forward to making good on that debt.

Finally, I cannot take credit for the book's strengths, if any. That belongs to those whom I have cited above. Its shortcomings are mine alone.

—T.S.G.

Index

Abadie, Clarence, 244–45
Acheson, Dean, 9, 22–23, 39, 47
Achille Lauro, 302–3
Afghanistan, CIA operations in, 285, 351
Africa and CIA operations, 140, 337, 355–56. *See also* Congo (Zaire); Ethiopia; Libya; Somalia
Agency for International Development (AID), 163, 192–93, 195
Air America, 138, 184, 243–45, 255
Alabama Air National Guard and Cuban invasion, 112, 113, 117–23, 125, 367
Albania, 30
Allende, Salvador (Gossens), 199, 223
Al-Najjar, Mazen, 380
Alsop, Stewart, 14
Altman, Petey, 339, 350, 360
Ames, Aldrich, 372
Ames, Robert C., 261, 279, 280–81, 284
Ammundsen, Burton, 191
Anderson, Terry, 306

Angleton, James, 222
Angola: CIA operations in, 320, 324, 335, 337; Cuban troops in, 321; UNITA and Savimbi, 320–21, 324, 325, 335, 336–37
Arms race, 24, 33; Soviet A-Bomb, 24, 50; U.S. H-Bomb, 50–51, 97
Arnold, Dan, 184
Atkinson, Michael, 323–24, 325, 326
Averoff, Evanghelos, 93

Bailey, Mac, 112
Baird, Matt, 70
Baker, Leo, 118–19, 141
Baldwin, Larry, 274
Bane, Jack, 91, 92, 95
Bator, Wussman, 17, 25–26, 41
Beatty, David A., 358–59
Beckwith, Charles, 349
Bennett, Lansing, 373
Bennett, William E., 367
Bensch, George, 323, 325, 326
Bessac, Frank, 25, 34, 35–36, 39
Birch, John, 14

Bissell, Richard Mervin, 108–9, 111, 112, 140, 145, 170; Bay of Pigs and, 114–16, 116–23, 125–27, 140; death of, 127–28; visit from Janet Ray Weininger, 126–27

"Black" effort (disinformation), 176

Blaufarb, Philip, 195–96, 197

Bolivia, 140

Bonano, Joe, 116

Boteler, Charles, 69, 87

Boteler, Page Hart, 367

Boteler, William Pierce, 68–96; character and personality, 68–70, 78–79; cover, 71–72, 80–81; death of, 92, 367; funeral and memorial service, 94–95; in Germany, 70–71; in Nicosia, Cyrus, 79, 80, 84–92; Paffenberger, Anne, and, 81–84, 88–89, 92–93, 96; reactions to death of, 92–93; recruitment by CIA, 68, 69; secrecy and death of, 93; in Seoul, 71–73, 78; State Department honors, 95, 224

Book of Honor: Alabama Air National Guardsmen in, 129; in CIA headquarters, 2; convocation at Wall of Honor, 1998, 365–75; creation of, 223–29; decisions about who should be honored on, 225, 227; Laos secret war and, 205; Maloney, Michael's name revealed and inscription in, 204–5; named personnel in, 2, 161; named personnel, list of, 373; nameless stars, 2, 3, 129, 204, 205, 220, 229, 286, 315, 329, 335, 363, 367–75, 377, 379; questions raised by, 3; security and, 4

Brezhnev, Leonid, 235

Britain, in Cyprus, 79, 84–92

Bryan, Robert, 52

Buckley, William F., 2, 286, 306–7

Bundy, McGeorge, 158, 176, 372

Burke, Arleigh, 118

Bush, George: as CIA Director, 55, 240, 241; pardons issued, 360; as President, 328, 355, 363

Butterworth, Walton, 21–22

Cabell, Charles Pearre, 93–94

Camp Hale, 250

Camp Perry (the Farm), 76, 180, 250, 293

Canal Zone Jungle Warfare Training Center, 180–81

Carter, Jimmy, 347

Casey, William J., 283, 284, 287, 306, 307; CIA expansion under, 284–85

Casino Royale (Fleming), 51

Castro, Fidel, 127; American policy to overthrow, 112, 170–171; CIA assassination plans, 115–16

Central Intelligence Agency (CIA): Ad Hoc Committee on Prisoners, 65; Africa Division, 335; agents, defined, 50; Air America pilots and, 245; airlines of, proprietary, 53, 138, 239, 243–45, 321–23; Angola crash and security, 328–30; archives and classified documents, 373; assassinations and, 115–16, 145, 223; Bay of Pigs, *see* Cuba; Beirut embassy bombing and, 282–84, 291; betrayals, internal, 371–72; Bindery, 228; Book of Honor, *see* Book of Honor; budget, use of, 74, 314; career trainees (CTs), 76; case officers, 49–50; Casualty Affairs Branch, 54; "the Company," 10; compartmented information, 71, 76, 115, 226, 241; Congressional supervision and constraints, 207–8, 221–23, 292, 307, 320, 351; Contact Division, 56; contract workers, 142, 225; convocation at Wall of Honor, 1998, 365–75; Counterterrorist Center (CTC), 202, 291–92, 306, 309, 311; creation of agency, 1947, 15, 49; criticism of, external, and loss of credibility, 117, 120–21, 140, 177, 199, 207, 221–23, 351, 371; criticism of, internal, 101, 222, 241; Cuban pilots and, 142, 143–56, 161, 186–87; decision-making and accountability, 108, 120–21, 140, 223, 307; deniability and, 75, 110, 114, 121–22, 128, 150; Deputy Director of Intelligence (DDI),

72; Deputy Director of Plans (DDP), 72, 90, 109, 145, 157; Development Projects Staff, 109; directors, *see specific directors;* domestic activities, 1967, 207, 274–76; ethics and, 16, 74–75, 222, 292; expanded authority of, 1960, 111; expansion, 67–68, 73–74, 140–41, 284–85; as extended family and family company, 160, 187–88, 193–94, 230, 249, 296–97, 303–4, 323; Family Jewels or Skeletons, 222; FBI rivalry with, 15; Foreign Intelligence/ Requirements, 176; front companies, 142, 181, 230, 320; gold provided to agents, 25; headquarters, early, Tempo Buildings, 15, 56; headquarters, E Street, 67, 71; headquarters, Langley, Virginia, 1–2, 111, 121; Honors and Merits Board, 223–24; humint (human intelligence), 72, 240; intelligence failures, 1990s, 371, 379; intelligence failure, Soviet atomic bomb, 24, 50; junior-officers-in-training (JOTs), 76, 180–81, 296; KU CLUB, 90; Mafia and, 115–16, 170; memo on China, 1951, 49; mind control and LSD testing, 58, 241; misinformation released to the public, 3, 93, 119, 134, 192–93, 235, 338–39, 366, 367; mission, anti-Communist, 4, 16, 30, 51, 73–74, 76, 291, 370; mission, antiterrorist, 291–92 299; mission, redefining, 351–52, 363; mission statement, 74; morale low in, 199–200, 202, 222–23, 240; Near East Division, 305; nuclear war and, 78; "official cover" or "nonofficial cover" (NOC), 50, 71–72, 90, 163, 181, 224, 262, 309; Office of Communications, 230; Office of Security, 56; Office of Training, 167; Operations Directorate and DDO, 293, 298, 309, 314; OSS legacy seen in, 14, 140; personnel, father to son legacy of, 159–60, 163–206, 229; personnel, early,

military background, 14–15, 16, 48, 140, 165–70, 173, 372; personnel, 1950s, college, 68, 69–70; pseudonyms, use of, 72, 76, 113; public image of, 5, 6, 199, 223, 372; recruitment, 52–53, 68, 69, 76, 139; recruitment, IU Jewel program, 249, 267; recruitment, 1990s, 372; reduction of size and power, 141, 207, 240–41, 355; secrecy and security, 4, 5, 56, 57, 128–29, 134, 139, 157, 160, 163, 205, 224, 238–39, 249, 281–82, 287, 297, 298, 324, 326–30, 336, 359, 366, 372–73; Special Operations Group, 240, 245; Task Force W, 171; TDYs (temporary duties), 73; Technical Services (TS), 73, 228, 304, 319; training, 70, 76–78, 180–81, 293; use of scandal to discredit enemies, 110; War Plans Division, 167

Central Intelligence Group (CIG), 48–49

Chapell, Mack, 237–38

Chiang Kai-shek, 19, 100–101

Child, Julia, 14

Childs, Marquis W., 192

Chile, overthrow of Allende, 199, 223

China: Americans imprisoned in, 47, 51, 53, 58–59, 65–66, 98, 217, 218; anti-Communist resistance, Kazakh peoples, 17, 20, 25–26; CIA covert activities and, 9–11, 16–25, 44–46, 52–53, 61, 100, 141, 217, 230; Communist takeover, 9, 19–26; death of Hugh Redmond and release of James Walsh, 214–15; evacuation of U.S. personnel, 23–24; Nixon's improvement of ties with and release of Americans, 215, 216–18; Ping-Pong diplomacy, 216; Soviets in, 11; Tihwa, 9–10, 17–23; treatment of American prisoners, 52, 53, 58–60, 66, 98, 101, 105, 208–9, 211–12; U.S. support of Chiang Kai-shek, 100–101, 219

Chou En-lai, 217, 218

Church, Frank, 222

Civil Air Transport, 53, 138
Clinton, Bill, 372
Coastal Air Services, 239
Colby, William E., 196, 222
Cold War: China and, 11, 50; CIA in, 16, 75, 291, 320; declassifying documents, 372–73; end of, 351, 355; National Security Council Directive 68 and, 33; Redmond case as hallmark of, 99–100
Coleman, Jim, 91
Colombia, CIA operations in, 140
Communism: American hysteria, 1950s, 30–31, 50–51, 99; American opposition to expansion of, 33, 138; in China, 9, 19–26; CIA's mission to stop, 15–16, 30, 73–74; Domino Theory, 97; in Laos, 205–6; in Tibet, 38, 39; in Vietnam, 205. *See also* Cold War; Soviet Union
Company, the. *See* Central Intelligence Agency (CIA)
Computer Data Systems, 320
Congo (Zaire): assassination plans for Lumumba, 145; CIA in, 138, 144, 145, 158–59, 185–87, 318; Kamina Air Base, 146–47, 321, 323, 324; risk to pilots in and atrocities, 147; top secret mission in and crash of Merriman, 143–56
Courtney, Raymond F., 89
Cragin, Harold "Hal," 68, 70, 94
Crocetto, Wynne, 339, 353
Cuba: Angola and, 321; Bay of Pigs, 108, 113, 114, 116–23, 128–29, 141, 142; Castro assassination plot, 115–16, 170–71; CIA espionage and, 170–72; exiled pilots and CIA, 142, 143–56, 161, 186; missile crisis, 171, 211; U.S. policy and, 112
Cunningham, Hugh J., 94
Cyprus, 79–80, 84–92, 93, 95, 96; bombing of Little Soho restaurant, 89–92, 95, 367; CIA operatives in, 90–92

Dace, Jim, 91, 92, 95–96
Darling, Frank, 373
DeFelice, Ben, 54, 55, 64–65, 98, 104, 196, 197, 217, 224

Demetriou, Andreas, 84
Deuel, Mary, 197
Deuel, Mike, 163–65, 172; and Book of Honor, 378; character and fearlessness, 177–79, 196, 206; chopper crash and death, 190–91, 366–67; CIA training, 180–82, 296–97; cover, 181, 192–93; daughter Suzanne born, 197; Doherty, Judy, marriage to, 183–85; father, Wally, and, 184, 193, 195; funeral and burial, 194–95; Holm, Richard, and, 181–82, 182, 185, 187–89, 196, 367; in Laos, 182–85, 189–91; Marine Corps, 179; posthumous medal, 195–96
Deuel, Peter, 200
Deuel, Wallace "Wally," 172–77; character and intellect of, 172; chief of Foreign Intelligence/Requirements, 176; death of, 200; depression over declining CIA, 199–200; Helms friendship, 173, 176, 193, 196; Holm, Dick, and, 188, 197–98; joins CIA, 175; as newspaperman, 172–73, 174; retirement from CIA, 198; son's death and, 197–99; in OSS, 173–74; White House stint, 176
Deutch, John, 204
Devlin, Lawrence, 144, 159
Dillon, Robert S., 278, 280
Dodge, David, 278
Doherty, William, 94
Doner, Ivan, 342, 346
Doner, Sylvia, 339, 346, 353, 364, 367
Donovan, William "Wild Bill," 14, 173–74
Doolittle, James, 74
Downey, John T.: American China policy and, 100–101, 102; background, 52–53; confession to Chinese and CIA debriefing of, 219; crash and capture of, 53, 378; declared dead, 54, 55; discovery of imprisonment of, 63–64; imprisonment of, 66; mother's visit, 103–4; Nixon's China trip and release of, 218;

post-release legal career, 219;
salary paid and invested by
DeFelice, 64; U.S. denials
regarding, and continued
imprisonment, 99–100
Downey, Mary V., 65, 103
Downing, Jack G., 373
Draper, Theodore, 121
Dresin, Sanford, 360
Dulles, Allen Welsh: as CIA director,
55, 58, 73–74, 75, 94, 109, 120,
140, 145, 175, 221, 241, 298;
death of, 250; in OSS, 14, 173
Dulles, John Foster, 74, 75, 93

Edwards, Sheffield, 57
Eisenhower, Dwight D., 65, 74, 78,
97, 111, 112, 145, 169
El Salvador, CIA operative's death in,
367
Espionage (spycraft): black-bag jobs,
72, 76; caching, 77; courage and
tradecraft, 72, 76; demolition and
sabotage, 77; flaps and seals,
76–77; picks and locks, 76; spy
planes, 109; surveillance and
drops, 77–78; training, 76–78
Ethiopia: CIA operations in, 329,
346, 351; crash of Congressman
Leland and CIA officer, 328–29;
Freedman memorial, 362
Evergreen Airlines, 138

Families of CIA operatives: Book of
Honor and, 3, 161, 204–5,
365–75; clandestine culture of,
164–206, 230–31, 236, 303–4;
compensation to, 41, 64, 120,
156; convocation at Wall of
Honor, 1998, 365–75; DeFelice
and, 54, 55, 65; efforts to
uncover information about loved
ones' deaths, 123–29, 160–62,
203–4, 247–48, 326–27; fear,
threats, or surveillance after
relative's death, 118–20, 122,
247–48, 326–27, 333;
employment found for, 57;
generations joining CIA, 159–60,
163–206, 229; lack of
information provided to, 47; lies
told to, 135, 155, 333–34; medals

for deceased and secrecy, 55,
123, 195–96, 283, 331–32, 335,
363; in Marana Air Base, Arizona,
139–43; in Monrovia, Liberia,
232–36; notification of deaths,
54–55, 92, 119, 155, 190, 308–9,
324–25; secrecy maintained by,
55, 134, 155–56, 171–72, 195,
236, 270, 286, 326–27, 330, 334,
335, 366, 370
Faraci, Phyliss, 262, 279, 280–81
Farm, the. *See* Camp Perry
Fecteau, Jessie, 103–4
Fecteau, Richard G.: American China
policy and, 100–101, 102;
character of, 53, 64; children of,
53, 64, 217; crash and capture of,
53, 378; declared dead, 54, 55;
discovery of imprisonment of,
63–64; imprisonment of, 66;
mother's visit, 103–4;
readjustment to American
society, 217; release of, 216, 217;
salary paid and invested by
DeFelice, 64, 217; U.S. denials
regarding, and continued
imprisonment, 99–100
Federal Bureau of Investigation (FBI),
Hoover's resentment of CIA, 15,
56
FitzGerald, Desmond, 188, 196,
298–99
Flint, Lloyd "Red," 228–29
Folkins, David, 160
Folkins, Val Merriman, 134–35, 153,
154–62, 366
"For the Fallen" (Binyon), 256
Freedman, Lawrence N. "Gus,"
"Superjew," 338–64, 379, Army
Special Forces and Delta Force,
342, 344–49, 362; character and
personality, 338–40, 345–46,
353–54, 356; children, 343–44;
in CIA, 351–59; CIA girlfriend,
354, 357, 359; cover, 338, 359,
361; death of, 358, 377; early
years, 339–42; Ethiopia and, 346,
351; funeral and burial at
Arlington, 360–61; Harleys, love
of, 341, 354, 361; medals, 343;
memorials, honors, and eulogies,
359, 361–63; Operation Eagle

Claw, 347–49; posthumous medal, 363; in Somalia, 338, 354, 356–58; Teresa, second wife, 344, 354, 363; Thuy, first wife, 343–44; in Vietnam, 343; women, love of, 343, 346

Freeman, Fulton, 27

Friedman, Sol, 57, 213, 216

Gabriel, Dennis "Denny," 248–52, 379; background of, 248–49; cover, 252; medal, 250; Mideast missions, 251–52; personality, 249, 252; plane crash and death of, 237–39, 252; Renier, wife, 249; recruited by CIA, 249; Thailand and Air America, 250–51; Tibetan resistance, work with, 250; training, 250; in Vietnam, 250; watch from King Hussein, 251–52

Gabriel, Ron, 252, 257

Gadhafi, Muammar, 297, 298

Gambino, Robert, 157

Gannon, Matthew Kevin, 289–305, 309–14, 377, 379; as Arabist, 289, 293, 294–95, 304, 314; in Beirut, 306, 308; burial in Arlington and gravestone, 309; in Cairo, 293; character and personality, 292, 295–96; claims Klinghoffer's body, 303; cover, 309; daughters of, 290, 308; death and body recovery, 292, 308, 311; devotion to, rise in CIA, 300–302, 303–4, 305; early years, 292–93; eulogized, 1998, 369; joins CIA and Operations Directorate, 293; in Jordan, 296, 299–301; marriage to Susan Twetten, 290, 300–302; memorial service, 313–14; on Pan Am Flight 103, 289–91, 308, 311, 369; in Sanaa, Yemen, 294; in Syria, 302; TDY in Beirut, 289–90; and Twetten, Tom, 296, 299–300, 301, 303–4, 305, 315

Gannon, Richard: appearance and personality, 277; in Beirut, 302; brother Matthew and, 293, 294–95, 300–302, 310, 311, 313, 317, 369; Lockerbie pilgrimage, 311; in Moscow, 316–17; Pugh,

Robert, and, 310; RSO in Beirut embassy and bombing, 277–80, 287–88

Gannon, Susan Twetten, 290, 300–302, 304, 309, 314

Garber, Nick, 343

García, René, 146, 147–50, 153–54, 159

Garland, Myron S., 92

Garrison, Bud, 68, 69, 70–71, 94

Gates, Robert Michael, 285, 351–52, 362, 363

Gawchik, William, 65

Gearke, Don, 142–43, 155, 157

Genebra, Mario, 147

George, Lloyd, 196

Georgia, Republic of, CIA in, 374

Germany: Berlin discotheque bombing, 304; CIA in, 70–71, 101; fall of Berlin Wall, 320

Gilbert, Harry T., 70

Glerum, James, 239–40, 245

Godley, McMurtrie, 150, 151, 152–53

Gold, Kenny, 339

Goldberg, Arthur, 14

Goldwater, Barry, 139

Gómez, Fausto, 147

Goss, Porter J., 379

Gottlieb, Sidney, 144–45, 159

Gray, Wade, 118

Greenbrier, West Virginia, secret installation, 4

Gresinger, Susan, 192

Grivas, George, 80, 95

Groat, Douglas F., 372

Groff, Chuck, 91

Gup, Ted: Book of Honor project, 4–6; Greenbrier story broken by, 6; at Langley, 1–4; Maloney, Michael, revealed as nameless star, 204–5

Guatemala: CIA training base in, 113; toppling of government, 74, 109, 110

Guzmán, Jacobo Arbenz, 74

Haas, Kenneth Eugene, 262, 278, 280–81, 286

Halpern, Sam, 170

Harding, John, 85, 93

Healy, Colleen, 329

Helms, Richard "Dick": CIA career,

58, 176, 188; as CIA Director, 55, 139, 141, 196, 199, 202, 208, 241, 299; defense of agency, 223; firing of, 199; letters to Wally Deuel and Mal Maloney, 193; in OSS, 14, 173; Senate committee appearance and subsequent fine for lying, 223
Herter, Christian A., 95
Hibbard, Ed, 68, 69, 94
High Noon (film), 51
Hillenkoetter, Roscoe Henry, 19
Hiss, Alger, 30
Hixon, Deborah M., 262, 279, 280–81
Hlavacek, John, 40
Holm, Judy Doherty Deuel, 183–85, 187, 188, 367; cover, 183; death of husband Mike Deuel, 190, 191–92; daughter Suzanne born, 197; marriage to Dick Holm, 198
Holm, Richard "Dick": adopts Suzanne, 200; CIA career post-injuries, 201–2, 256; in Congo, 185; Deuel, Mike, and, 181–82, 192, 196, 367; in Hong Kong, 199, 201; in Laos, 182, 185; Maloney, Michael, and, 204; marries Judy Deuel, 198; medal, 202; in Paris, as Chief of Station, 202; plane crash and injury, 186–89, 202, 256; recovery, 197–98; resignation under cloud, 202
Holm, Suzanne, 197, 200, 205; search for information about biological father, 201; secrecy and real father, Mike Deuel, 200–201
Hong Kong, CIA in, 101, 199
Hoover, Herbert, 83
Hoover, J. Edgar, 15, 56
Houston, Lawrence, 40–41
Hudson, Bobbie, 239
Humelsine, Carlisle, 41

Ikeda, Chiyoki "Chick," 369–70
Indonesia: chaos in, 232; CIA failure in, 110–11
Intelligence Authorization Act, 380
Intermountain Aviation, 138, 155
Iran: American hostages in, 307,

347–49; -Contra, 307, 323, 360; downing of Airbus 300, 306; ouster of premier, 74, 110
"Irish Airman Foresees His Death, An" (Yeats), 133

Jacobsen, David, 306
Johnson, Lyndon, 145, 157–58, 193, 199, 205, 207
Johnson, Miles and Shep, 142
Johnston, Frank J., 262, 279, 280
Johnston, R. B., 359
Jonson, Ben, elegy by, 163

Karaolis, Michael, 84
Kearns, John "Lone Star," 205; and Book of Honor, 378
Kennedy, John F., 108, 112–13, 116, 117, 120, 121, 123, 145, 170, 176, 182
Kennedy, Robert, 110, 170
Khrushchev, Nikita, 111
Kiba, Steven, 218
King, Clarence, 243, 244, 247–48
King, Ivan Berl, 241–48; Air America and, 243–45; background of, 241–43; character and personality, 241, 243; CIA hiring of, 245; death of brother, David, 244, 247; eulogy delivered by Rhyne, 245, 246; as pilot, 243, 246; plane crash and death, 237–39, 241; secrecy and, 244, 247, 379
King, Mabel, 242, 246
King, Velma, 244, 247–48
King, William Isiah, 242, 246–47
Kissinger, Henry, 217
Klinghoffer, Leon, 302–3
Knowland, William, 47
Korea, CIA in Seoul, 71–73
Korean War, 36, 50, 58, 67, 74
Kreinheder, Dorothy "Dot," 134, 155
Krychkov, Vladimir, 285
Kuwait, 286; Iraqi invasion of, 351

Lacy, George Vincent, 323, 325, 326, 335–37
Lacy, Mildred, 336
Landry, Pat, 184
Laos: CIA paramilitary efforts in, 138, 182–85, 189–93, 196, 205, 243,

244–45, 267–68; nameless stars in Book of Honor and, 205; as "the secret war," 182, 205, 250

Laubinger, Frank, 72–73, 83, 94

Lebartarde, Luis, 239

Lebanon: American hostages in, 286, 306, 308; CIA operations in, 261–62, 278, 289–90, 306; Deuel, Wally, in, 176; Israeli conflict with, 277–78; kidnapping of David Dodge, 278; murder of Buckley, 2, 286, 306–7; U.S. embassy in Beirut, 262, 278–79, 291; U.S. embassy bombing, 261–62, 277, 279–82, 291; U.S. Marines barracks bombing, 286

Lee, Wen Ho, 380

LeGallo, Andre, 181, 182, 197

Lehman, Herbert, 51

Leland, Mickey, 328–29

Lewis, Antoinette Pittman, 263, 265, 270, 287, 367–68

Lewis, Donald, 287

Lewis, George, 265

Lewis, James Foley, 261–77; appearance and personality, 262–65; army, Mike Force unit and Vietnam, 265–67; in Beirut, Lebanon, 261–62, 276–77; bombing of embassy and death of, with wife Monique, 279–82, 287, 367; Chicago operations by, 274–76; CIA memorial ceremony, posthumous medals, and condolence letters, 282–83, 367–68; CIA recruitment of, under Jewel program, 267; code name, 267; cover, 262; father's abandonment and, 263; in Laos, 267–68; letter to father, 271–73; prisoner in Vietnam, Sontay prison, 268–70; reentry into society after imprisonment and CIA debriefing, 273–74; release from prison, 270; training for Mideast, 276; wife, Monique, 261, 262, 274, 275, 276–77

Lewis, Susan, 264, 271, 275, 287

Liberia, 232; Monrovia, CIA posting in, 231–36; WAWA (West Africa Wins Again), 233, 235

Libya: Benghazi embassy attack, 297–98; CIA and Gadhafi, 298–99, 316; Gadhafi takeover of, 298; Pan Am 103 bombing and, 312–13; U.S. strikes on, 304–5

Lockerbie, Scotland, Pan Am 103 bombing, 289, 291, 308, 369; Libya responsible for, 311–13; remains and recovered possessions, 311, 313

Lodge, Henry Cabot, 64

Long, Dick, 137

LSD, CIA experimentation with, 58

Luce, Clare Booth, 22, 56

Lumumba, Patrice, 145, 176

Macbeth (Shakespeare), 318

Mackiernan, Angus, 12

Mackiernan, Darrell Brown, 11, 13–14, 18, 36–37, 41

Mackiernan, Douglas Seymour, Jr., 9–42, 49; anti-Communist resistance, Kazakh peoples, and, 17, 20, 25–26; Brown, Darrell (first wife), and, 11, 13, 18, 36–37; character and personality, 11; childhood, 12; CIA mission of, 49–50; cover as Vice-Consul, 9–10; daughter, Gail, and, 11, 13–14, 36–37; death of, 35; education, 13; escape from Tihwa, 24–35; estate, settlement of, 39, 41; Lyons, Pegge (second wife), and, 17–23, 27; memorialized by State Department, 224; posthumous medal, 39; secrecy regarding death of, 36, 38, 39, 379; State Department commendation, 14; Tihwa, Cryptographic Cryptoanalysis Section, Army Air Force (in World War II) , 13; Tihwa, life in, 17–23; twins, Michael and Mary, 18; White Russian friends, 16

Mackiernan, Douglas S., Sr., 12, 28–30

Mackiernan, Duncan, 12

Mackiernan, Gail, 11, 13–14, 36–37, 41

Mackiernan, Malcolm, 12

Mackiernan, Mary, 18, 37, 67
Mackiernan, Michael, 18, 37, 67
Mackiernan, Pegge Lyons, 17–23, 27, 37–38, 39, 40, 67
Mackiernan, Stuart, 12
MacLendon, Joe, 325–26
MacPherson, Alex: background, 255
    in Beirut, 281; covert career of, ultimate paramilitary officer, 253–56; Holm and, 256; medals and awards, 254; North Carolina plane crash, 237–40, 252–53; prayer before missions, 256; secrecy maintained by, 254, 255, 257
Maloney, Adrienne La Marsh, 189, 191–92, 203, 204–5, 366
Maloney, Arthur "Mal," 165–70; Cuba and, 170–72; family's harrowing flight to Hawaii, 167–68; joins CIA, 167; medals, 166, 169; retirement from CIA, 202; son's death and, 190, 193–94, 203; war injuries, 166–67, 168, 169
Maloney, Craig Michael, 203, 204, 366
Maloney, Mary Evangeline Arens, 165, 167–68
Maloney, Michael Arthur "Mike," 163–66; Adrienne, wife, 189, 191–92, 203, 366; children of, 189, 203, 366; chopper crash and death, 190–91, 366; CIA and military heritage of, 166; cover, 192; in Laos, 189–90; name revealed as one of the Book of Honor's nameless stars, 204–5, 366
Maloney, Michael, Jr., 189, 203, 204, 366
Manning, Robert, 181, 197
Mansfield, Mike, 327
Mao Zedong, 9, 19, 26, 49, 218
Marana Air Base, Arizona, 139–43, 250
Marcuse, Herbert, 14
Martin, Edwin W., 65
McCann, Murray J., 262, 281, 287
McCarthy, Joseph, 30–31, 50–51, 56, 97
McCleskey, Walter S., 239
McCone, John, 157

McCord, James W., 56
McInenly, Bill, 43, 44, 220
McLean, Ralph, 181, 182
McMillan, Gale, 357
McNulty, Wayne, 205; and Book of Honor, 378
Merchant, L. T., 39–40
Merriman, John Gaither, 133–62; Alaskan rescue by, 136–37; background of and piloting skill, 135–38, 139, 142–43; character of, 135, 139, 146; Cuban pilots' friendship and efforts to obtain care for John, 142–54; funeral, 133–35, 155–56; hired by CIA proprietary airline, 138–39; lies about death, 134, 135, 155; at Marana Air Base, 139–43; medals, 137, 157; neglect of and death, 150–55, 161; recruitment by CIA, 139; secrecy and, 136; sons of, 134, 154, 159–60, 366; top secret Congo mission and crash, 143–56, 366; Val, wife, 134–35, 153, 154–62, 366, 377
Miller, Bill, 249
MKULTRA, 58
Mobuto, Joseph, 143, 158–59, 321
Monroe, Timmy, 238
Mulvey, Donald P., 91
Mussadegh, Muhammad, 74

Nassar, Gamal, 297
National Security Act of 1947, 15
National Security Council: Directive 68, 33; Directive 10/2, 75
NATO, 80, 85
Nicaragua: American operations base in (Happy Valley), 117, 141; CIA support of Contras, 285, 307
Nicholson, Harold James, 372
Nixon, Richard M., 199, 215, 216, 217–18, 222
Noriega, Manuel, 332
North, Oliver, 314
North Pole expedition, 1903, 28–30
Nosenko, Yuri Ivanovich, 241

Office of Strategic Services (OSS), 14; disbanding of, 14; personnel,

former, 14, 101. *See also*
Donovan, William "Wild Bill"
Olson, Frank, 58
Operation Ajax, 74
Operation Alert, 78
Operation Eagle Claw, 347–49
Operation Mongoose, 170–71
Operation Restore Hope, 358
Operation Success, 74
Orwell, George, ix

Paffenberger, Anne, 81–84, 88–89,
92–93, 96
Palacios, Alberto, 59, 60
Palestine Liberation Front, 303, 312
Palmer, Joe, 298
Panama, toppling of Noriega, 332,
351, 356
Parmly, Eleazar, 267
Paxton, John Hall, 23
Peron, Juan, 186–87
Peru, CIA operations in, 140
Peterson, John, 205, 379
Petty, Alton, 334
Petty, Joyce, 323, 333
Petty, Losue, 323
Petty, Pharies "Bud": background, 322;
body, questions regarding, 326,
333–34; as CIA contract
personnel, 322–23; death of, 325,
376, 377; Doris, first wife, 333;
Hagler, Losue, sister, 376; medals,
322, 335; memorials to, 335;
saying of, 334; widow, Gracie,
333–34, 335
Petty, Teresa, 333–34
Pewitt, Harrym, 239
Pittman, James Forrest, 263, 271–73
Plausible deniability, 75, 110, 114,
121–22, 128, 150
Ponzoa, Gus, 142, 143, 146, 147–50,
152, 159
Pope, Allen, 110
Popovich, Eli, 180–81
Potter, Richard, 345, 361
Powell, Colin, 363
Powers, Gary, 111
Pudlo, Fran, 125
Pugh, Robert: and Beirut embassy
bombing, 279, 281, 287; death of
wife, Bonnie, in UTA flight 772
bombing, 310, 312; letter to

Dick Gannon, 310; in retirement,
87; on terrorism, 284

Quemoy and Matsu, 230

Radio Free Europe, 30
Ramparts, 207
Raven Rock, 78
Ray, Margaret, 112, 113, 118–20,
122, 125
Ray, Thomas Willard "Pete," 108, 109,
111; Bay of Pigs and, 115,
116–23, 141; daughter Janet and,
114, 120, 122–29, 367; death of,
118–19, 124, 367; death of and
secrecy, 119, 123–29;
posthumous medal, 123; remains
returned from Cuba, 124; son
Tom and, 113–14, 120, 124;
training for Cuban assignment,
113–14; volunteer for Cuban
assignment, 112–13; wife
Margaret and, 112, 113, 118–20,
122, 125
Rayner, Barbara Ann, 230, 231
Rayner, Margaret Mary "Peggy,"
230–36
Rayner, Raymond Carlin, 229–36,
379; attack on and death of,
234–35; character and
personality, 229–30, 231;
children of, 231, 236; CIA job
obtained through brother, 230;
cover, 232; marriage to Peggy,
230–35; in Monrovia, Liberia,
231; posts, various, 231; on
Quemoy and Matsu, 230; secrecy
about position, 230–31, 236
Rayner, William "Bill," 230, 231
Reagan, Ronald, 305; support for
CIA, 284–85, 321
Redmond, Hugh Francis, 43–66;
American China policy and,
100–101, 102; arrest and early
imprisonment of, 45, 47–66, 67;
ashes sent home, 214; character
and morale of, 60, 63, 101–2,
104–5, 106–7; CIA mission of,
49–50; condition of, in prison,
58–59, 66, 98, 101, 105, 208–9,
211–12; cover, 45; Cultural
Revolution and, 208; death

reported, 214; first letter
received from, 66; imprisonment
and fading efforts for release,
97–107, 209–13; lawyer,
Friedman, hired for, 57; letter,
July 4, 1967, 208; Lydia (wife)
and, 45, 57, 103, 209–11;
memorials to, 215–16; mother's
visit, 103–6; park named for, 219;
ransom plan for release, failure
of, 213; secrecy maintained in
case of, 219–20, 379; in
Shanghai, China, 44–46, 49; trial
and conviction of, 60–61;
Westrell and Redmond case,
55–57, 58; in WWII, 44; Yonkers
Citizens Committee for his
release, 61–62, 65, 97, 98, 213
Redmond, Lydia "Lily," 45, 57, 103,
209–11, 219
Redmond, Ruth, 43, 45, 46, 47–48,
51, 57, 59, 60, 61, 63, 65–66, 98,
106–7; deteriorating health of,
212, 215; final efforts on behalf
of son, 213; first China visit,
103–6; and Lydia, 209–11;
second China visit, 211–12
Rhyne, Jim, 244, 245–46
Rieger, Gerhard Hermann, 323, 325,
326, 334
Robbins, Barbara, 286–87, 367, 379
Robbins, Buford, 286–87, 367
Roberts, Dave, 277, 280
Robin Sage (mission), 239
Rostow, Walt, 14
Rusk, Dean, 47, 116, 150, 174–75

St. Lucia Airways, 323, 324
Savimbi, Jonas, 320–21, 325, 335
Schindler, Robert, 234–35
Schlesinger, Arthur, 14
Schoomaker, Peter J., 346
Schwartz, Norman, 53; and Book of
Honor, 378
Seaborg, Ray, 378
Seigrest, Connie, 142
Shackley, Theodore, 196
Shamburger, Riley, 118
Shanghai, China, 44–46, 49
Sheil, William Richard, 262, 279,
280–81, 282
Shirer, William L., 172

Shutov, Leonid, 25, 26, 31, 34–35
Sichel, Peter, 101
Smith, Margaret Chase, 41
Smith, Paul F., 167
Smith, Walter Bedell, 50
Snepp, Frank, 199
Snoddy, Robert, 53; and Book of
Honor, 378
Somalia: CIA in, 338, 354, 355;
famine and upheaval, 354–55;
Freedman death in, 338, 354,
356–58
"Sources and methods," 4
Soviet Union: in Afghanistan, 351;
atomic bomb and, 24, 50; in
China, 11; détente and, 222, 235;
downing of Korean airliner, KAL
007, 285; fall of, 320, 351; fear of
U.S. preemptive nuclear strike,
1983, 285; influence, expansion
of, 74, 140; unwritten agreement
not to kill U.S. CIA operatives
and vice versa, 285–86
Spessard, Debra, 318–19, 324–25,
327, 330–32, 335, 376–77
Spessard, James "Jimmy," 318–33; in
Angola, 320, 321–22; body
return and funeral, 325–27,
330–31; CIA concealing of links
to, 330–32; in CIA S&T, 319,
320; cover, 318; early years, 319;
memorials to, 335; posthumous
medal, 331–32; sons Jared and
Jason, 319, 335, 376–77; wife,
Debra, and, 318–19; in Zaire,
318, 320
Spicer, Richard, 367
SR-71 Blackbird, 109, 125
Steere, Peter, 68–69
Stembridge, Syd, 135, 154–55, 157,
160
Stevenson, Adlai, 117, 174, 175
Stolz, Dick, 309
Strategic Services Unit (SSU), 48
Sukarno, President of Indonesia, 110
Sutherland, Thomas, 306
Syria, CIA operations in, 302

Teasley, Barbara, 235
Teller, Edward, ix
Templesman, Maurice, 159
Tempo Buildings, 15

Tenet, George, 367–71, 372, 379
Tepper Aviation, 322, 325, 333
Terrorism, 290; *Achille Lauro*, 302–3;
  Berlin discotheque bombing,
  304; Buckley killing and, 286,
  306–7; CIA's post–Cold War
  priority, 285–86, 299; Cyprus
  (EOKA), 84–92, 95; embassy
  bombings, 261–62, 277, 284,
  286, 297; hostages taken in
  Beirut, 286, 306, 308; hostages
  taken in Iran, 307; Lockerbie,
  Scotland, Pan Am 103 bombing,
  289, 291, 308, 311–13; murders
  in front of Langley, 373; U.S.
  military barracks bombing, 286;
  UTA 772 bombing, 310, 312
Thailand: Air America in, 250; CIA
  office in Bangkok, 183
Thorsrude, Gar, 141, 143, 155, 159
Thurmer, Angus, 40
Tibet: Chinese takeover, 38–39; Dalai
  Lama and, 33; Mackiernan's
  escape to and death in, 26–35;
  resistance aided by CIA, 141,
  250
Tihwa (Urumchi), Xinjiang
  (Sinkiang), China, 9–11, 17–23
Time magazine, 1
Truman, Harry, 15, 24, 30, 33, 93
Tunon, Juan, 186
Turner, Stansfield, 240–41
Twetten, Tom, 296; Benghazi embassy
  attack and, 297–98; chief of TS,
  304; deputy chief Near East
  Division, 305; deputy director for
  operations, 314–15, 355; death of
  Matthew Gannon and, 308–9,
  369; early years, 296; Gadhafi
  and, 297, 298; joins CIA, 1961,
  296; Lockerbie bombing and,
  312; on MacPherson, Alexander,
  254; nepotism, avoidance of, 301,
  305, 306, 309; retirement,
  315–16; Somalia operations and,
  355, 356; wife, Kay, and, 309,
  314, 369

U-2 spy plane, 109, 111
United Fruit Company, 181
United States State Department: CIA

agents cover and memorials, 39,
  95, 224, 287, 329; on Congo,
  176; Cuban invasion and, 116;
  memorial, 224
UNITA, 320–21, 324
UTA 772 bombing, 310, 312

Vandervoort, Ben, 169
Varela, Jack, 146, 147–48, 159
Vetch Book Shop, Beijing, 25
Vietnam: American prisoners, Sontay
  prison, 268–70; CIA covert
  operations in, 138, 199, 243,
  250, 265–67, 286; Dien Bien
  Phu, 97; fall of, 205, 221,
  268; Phoenix Program, 199,
  223
Vogel, Harold, 225–28

Waiting for Godot (Beckett), 97
Wall, Jack, 142
Wallace, George, 125
Walsh, James Edward, 214–15
Walz, Larry, 354
Washington Post, 4, 204, 378
Watergate, 56, 199, 221–22
Webster, William H., 307, 328, 330,
  331, 332, 351
Weeks, Sinclair, 137
Weinberg, Paul, 339, 352, 377
Weininger, Janet Ray, 114, 120,
  123–29, 161, 367
Welch, Richard, 2, 369
Western Enterprises, 142
Westrell, Harlan, 55–57, 58
White, Lawrence K. "Red," 169
Williams, Pete, 327
Wisner, Frank, 298
Woodruff, Freddie, 374, 379
Woods, Robert William, 329

Yale University, CIA recruitment at,
  52–53, 219
Yanuishkin, Stephani, 25, 26, 31,
  34–35
Yemen, CIA operations in, 294

Zaire. *See* Congo (Zaire)
Ziegler, William, 28, 30
Zvonzov, Vassily, 16–17, 24, 25, 26,
  28, 31, 32, 34–36